THE MAN FROM ALEXANDRIA

BY
JOHN CHAPMAN

ISBN: 978-1-961677-18-0 (Paperback)

Library of Congress Control Number: 2023915117

Printed in the United States of America

Published by

info@thequippyquill.com
(302) 295-2278

CONTENTS

The book is divided into parts/chapters and sections. The list below shows thetopics within each entry.

4

APPENDICES

Preface

There are three concepts which always seem to get inextricably mixed up - they are faith, religion and culture. They are usually also overlaid by politics, but for the momentI will discount that.

Faith is a belief in something that one feels instinctively to be true but which cannever be proven or disproven by scientific or historical analysis. To my mind when onesees a human being just before and just after death you cannot escape the conclusion that something has left the body. This I call the soul. This raises all sorts of different questions - where has it gone? Where was it before birth? Is there an afterlife? Then one can consider the question of God. Is there a God who is monitoring one's every thought and action? Does he need placating or worshipping? Will he judge my life? There are no answers to such questions. one comes to a conclusion oneself and that becomes part of one's faith.

Religion on the other hand tries to impose faith on an individual by defining rituals and indoctrination. Most religions start in the same way. A person emerges who sets out ideas and concepts, usually about man's relationship with the gods or a God but then goes on to suggest rules of behavior and conduct which, it is stated, will appease or appeal to the deity. Occasionally this person will write this down but more usuallyit is one of the followers who does the documentation in an attempt to perpetuate the teachings. A religion also often tries to offer an exclusivity to its adherents -' *if you conform you will go to heaven and everyone else will go to hell*' is the threat or promise which binds the group together.

The third element, culture, is a set of conventions which bind a particular group together. Usually there are strong family or racial connections between the members of the group and leaders often try to enforce religious practice and faith on all the other members of the group to establish a pecking order or social hierarchy.

I grew up accepting what may be described as an English culture with Christianity as my religion. My faith tells me that there is a God, who created everything and is omnipotent and that every human being has a soul which has a 'state' after death. It also tells me that there is no such thing as exclusivity and that all human souls will achieve this state.

What exactly will determine one's state is a matter I know nothing of, but rely on the love of God to determine.

Over the years as I encountered more and more denominations of Christianity and more and more religions, I grew more and more convinced that there can be no exclusivity for Christians, let alone of any particular denomination. It was inconceivable that a God of love could dismiss or exclude the many people I met or read about simply on the grounds that they had signed up to the wrong religion.

As a boy I heard many bible stories read to me and read many myself. It became apparent however that there were many contradictions and that the bible could not be an infallible source of truth. At an early age I was very much influenced by Freeman Wills-Croft who attempted to weave the gospel stories together to form one story. However, he also brought out the point that there are many conflicting stories.

In later life my interests took me into politics and history. Seeing the way politics worked from the inside and reading about how different cultures and religions fought against each other over the centuries and produced propaganda to support their several causes, I began to try to repeat Will-Croft's exercise, but using the whole of the New Testament and the many other texts which have emerged from holes in the desert to secret places in archives.

What I am trying to do in this work is to piece many different texts together to tell what I believe to be a more accurate historical account of Jesus' life and the history of the early church. I had almost finished when I came across a book entitled 'A History of Christianity' by Paul Johnson, written back in 1976.

He covers the whole of the period to date but does not include the actual texts, although he provides a long list of other sources. What he brings out however is the way the church emerges through a plethora of politics, argument and treachery, as the competing factions in Jewish, Roman and Greek society vied for supremacy.

Let me set out up front what I believe the outline of the story is. This does not agree with any of the established histories although it echoes thoughts which have occurred and been documented and dismissed as fanciful or heretical over the years.

First of all, I do not believe that Jesus was born in Bethlehem or that his family were paupers. It is my view that he was born in Alexandria of a wealthy merchant named Joseph of Arimathea and was given full access to the education that was possible only there at the time. It is not therefore very far-fetched to imagine that on a least one occasion Jesus travelled on one of his father's trading ships to Britain so that the legends of Glastonbury are not as farfetched as is often made out.

The second strand revolves around Jesus' early manhood. Alexandria was a major Centre of the early Jewish diaspora and was predominantly Essene in character. The normal course of event for an educated Essene young man would be to go to the 'headquarters' at Qumran and further his education in the Essene culture.

A tiny minority of such youth would become initiates to the Essene monastery which was obsessed with ritual cleanliness and a somewhat larger proportion would stay around Qumran to act as farmers and craftsmen to support the community, but the majority would move on to marry and develop Essene communities elsewhere, particularly in the Galilee region which was developing as the second largest Centre of Essene culture.

This brings us to Jesus' married status. We have to remember that in Jewish culture 'Jewishness' is passed on through the female line. The idea that Jesus remained unmarried and childless would go against everything that Judaism sought to uphold. He would never have been allowed to speak in a synagogue or participate in Jewish society if he remained unwed.

So, I believe he married Mary of Magdala and that they had at least one child, John Mark. Her family came from Bethany where Jesus visited on many occasions.

The third strand concerns the events that followed Jesus' death. During his life he had stirred up considerable controversy between the numerous Jewish factions and when he was crucified the Romans said that he had claimed to be 'King of the Jews' at the time Herod Antipas was King of Palestine and when sages came from the east enquiring about the 'star' (i.e. Jesus), Herod saw the Jesus movement as a threat to his throne and set about making sure that there were no follow on claimants. It is this that stimulated the persecutions and the flight to Egypt by Mary Magdalene with her family and subsequent move to safety in southern France.

The final alternative strand sees the controversies between the several emerging Christian factions, torn between Roman, Greek and Jewish cultures. The Gentile (Roman and Greek) sides were promoted by Paul and Luke whilst the Jewish side was led by James. In both cases the message of Jesus was forgotten as issues such as circumcision and sin were hotly debated and the ferment in the Jewish community ignited into open rebellion against the Romans who effectively expelled the Jews from Palestine.

For the next two hundred years the church expanded, wrote down what could be remembered of Jesus' life and invented stories to prove that ancient prophesies had been fulfilled. It was the church in Rome that eventually triumphed and they who weeded out all the inconvenient texts which contradicted their version of events. In this work I have tried to incorporate all the 'historical' text of the New Testament as well as several other ancient texts which have emerged in recent years. I have tried to point out which contained the seeds of real history and which were mere products of a fanciful imagination. They do not appear in the same chronological sequence as in the Gospels, as I also believe that those writers who were aware of the 'truth' were often at pains to record it, but set it into a context which did not compromise security.

In recounting the story, I have tried to piece all the relevant texts to a particular incident together so that the reader can see the different takes that different writer took on the same incident, so that, together with an abbreviated commentary, one can follow the story almost like a novel. In many cases the authors of the New Testament are either wrong historically or deliberately distorted for security reasons; but they still reflect the key message that God is Love.

I must say a big word of thanks to all those who have put copies of texts onto the internet which has saved me the trouble of retyping; but especially to Peter Kirby who has assembled a staggering collection of early Christian and Jewish texts and made them available via CD.

Just as this book was ready to go to press the issue of copyright emerged so that rather than use modern versions of text, I had to revert all the biblical references to the King James version.

Chapter 1 – Introduction

1.1 Aims

This book is an attempt to reconstruct the events that led to the formation of the Christian church and its development to the time of Constantine when Christianity became the official religion of the Roman Empire. It looks principally at the first century AD and draws its information mainly from the New Testament. It is fairly obvious to anyone who studies the New Testament that there are often different, contradictory versions of the same events, that some of the events described are not easily credible and that the main purpose of writing down the events was not to tell a historical story, but rather to reveal God's messages to mankind.

As a general rule I have tried to use contemporary texts to tell the story, but one has to be aware of the conditions at the time and the ways in which these texts have survived. For most of the period that we are considering, Christians were a persecuted minority sect and when matters were set down in writing, great care had to be exercised that the security of the small groups of Christians was not compromised. This meant that often stories were placed in an alternative setting and details disguised, but as most of the contemporary writers were intent on communicating a message rather than writing history, they did not see this as being of great significance. Secondarily one must recognize that most of these texts were later edited and selected to fit current thinking and personal interpretations.

The big question however revolves around who actually wrote the first version and when. One must assume that most of the followers of Jesus were actually illiterate and would not have been able to put down their memories on paper (or papyrus!). They would have passed on their memories in an oral tradition, telling the story and answering questions. It would have been a later scribe who wrote down what had been folk memory and ascribed it to someone of significance.

This seems to have happened in the early second century, probably at least seventy years after the time of the Passion.

The key texts that have survived were of course those of the New Testament; but many of the texts that circulated in these early centuries were not included in what became the canon of the New Testament.

It is only in recent years that fragments of these texts have emerged. Many throw a very different light upon the traditionally accepted history of Jesus' lifetime and the development of the Christian church.

1.2 My Perspective

One cannot attempt a book of this sort unless one has a specific view of that history, on what is the essential truth and what events may or may not be true without it seriously affecting the message. Personally, I have never held the view that the Bible was the literal word of God, dictated to human scribes in some mysterious way and to be taken word for word as absolute truth. Thus, I believe the fundamentalist position to be quite untenable. But religion without belief or conviction is also untenable. So, I need to start by trying to make clear my own position, for it is from that perspective that I shall try to recreate the story.

That there is a God I have no doubts whatsoever. He is a product of human experience and almost every society known to history has among its beliefs a sense of a being and a presence beyond human knowledge. Equally I cannot hold an exclusive view of God. There cannot be a God whom Christian's worship, a God whom the Hindus worship and a God whom African animists worship. There is one God and only one God, we know Him in different ways.

The heart of the Christian faith is that God came down to earth in human form, lived amongst us for a number of years, suffered a humiliating execution and demonstrated as clearly as possible that there was life after death and that we could experience God in our own lives. This has the implication that Jesus was fully human but held the soul of God.

That faith has been preserved by a body which we refer to as the Church. This word Church has two distinct meanings, The first being a building in which worship takes place. It also has a collective meaning as the set of people who have accepted the Christian faith and the specific meaning of an organisation embracing ministry and authority.

It is this latter meaning that I take when I talk about the history of the early Church, because I have a specific interest in how that body came to be formed and how it received its authority.

Over the subsequent centuries the Church has developed dogmas and theology, it has split and quarreled within itself, but whatever else one may believe about it, it remains as a visible and tangible body.

1.3 Fundamental Splits

It was in the first 100-200 years that the crucial splits occurred. There were three main tensions; the Jewish church under James which saw Jesus' teachings as an extension of traditional rabbinic teaching; the Pauline church which saw Christianity as a distinctive faith for all men and the Gnostic traditions which saw Jesus's message as a path to personal enlightenment. In the end it was the Pauline church which triumphed and it was that Church which compiled the writings which we now know as the New Testament and dismissed as heresy any writings that disagreed with their core beliefs.

In the early days there was no 'church' as we understand it today. Rather there were numerous groups of Christians who worshipped together, had their own leaders and developed their own practices and theology. Most of these groups within the Roman sphere of influence gradually came together to form what we know as the Catholic church centered on Rome; but many other communities formed local groupings and today we see remnants of these in, for instance, the Coptic and Armenian churches. The greater splits between Catholic and Orthodox and the rise of Protestantism did not occur until centuries later.

1.4 The Bible

It is a plain fact of history that members of the Church wrote all the books of the New Testament and that the Church existed perfectly happily for many years without a formal Bible, using a wide variety of writings to record, teach and inspire. Each congregation used its own selection which often included works which are no longer in the modern canon. It is equally true that in no case do we have an 'original version' of the text. All versions we have today are copies of earlier versions, and when copies were made there were often significant errors in transcription, often huge chunks were omitted and other text inserted.

We have copies of text from a variety of sources and ages, but it is not sensible to assume that an older version is truer to the original than a later version.

The later version may be based upon a copying sequence which was much truer to the original than the earlier work.

One further point needs to be made. Many modern versions have attempted to present the text in language which is familiar to and understandable by, the present generation. The Good News Bible for instance tries to translate all weights and measures and currency into modern metric values. In many cases this completely loses the point that the author is trying to make, and anyway there is not a lot of agreement as to what the conversion factors really are. There is therefore a very strong argument for sticking to a version which is a good translation of whatever text it is based upon and which retains a majesty of phraseology which can inspire. My own personal preference is for the New English Bible. One also must recognise that typing in the whole text of the New Testament would be a formidable task, so I am most grateful to those who have done the job for me and made their text available via the Internet.

I have used the King James version for all the quotations from the New Testament and the Qur'an Project version for extracts from the Qur'an. For the Works of Josephus, I have used William Whiston's 1905 version and those from Eusebius from W J Ferrar's translation of 1920.

But as I have been at this work for more than fifteen years, I am afraid I cannot recall where I got the rest from, and hope I have not infringed anyone's copyright.

There are three types of text in the New Testament. There is history, there is poetry and there are stories. It is often difficult to tell the difference between them. Of the life of Jesus, we have four books to choose from. But of these only John seems to be reliable as history, and he was not primarily concerned with writing history. Luke who on the surface is writing a history is perhaps the most unreliable. What he seems to be doing is filling in the gaps. He was writing for an audience that wanted to know how it happened. By the time he came to write it, there would have been no one alive who was a firsthand witness.

Luke does appear to have used some long-forgotten book as a basis for his own account. But much of Luke is of the nature of Kipling's 'Just-so Stories'. This was a very popular medium at the time. A truth was known and the author set out to spin a yarn to explain how the truth came about. Jesus and John, the Baptist were real live historical figures.

Jesus particularly was recognised as someone very special. Not just special, in the eyes of Christians he was the Son of God, the Messiah.

The first thing therefore to explain was how he came to be born. There had to be something very special about his birth, what better than to look in the scriptures to see what the prophets had written about the coming of the Messiah and to weave a story around their prophecies. It was little wonder therefore that Matthew and Luke told different stories and that they were inconsistent, not just between themselves; but with the known facts of the Roman world. Mark and John ignored the matter.

In the three synoptic Gospels it would appear that Jesus began his ministry in Galilee and then moved to Jerusalem where almost all the action took place just before the Passion.

John on the other hand has Jesus going to and from all over Palestine - a much more realistic scenario considering His ministry lasted about three years.

When we come to the account of the Passion again, only John, seems to have any understanding of Roman laws and procedures. He also displays a first-rate knowledge of the geography of Jerusalem and an understanding of life in Judea, sadly lacking in the three synoptic Gospels which describe events and places in Judea from a purely Galilean perspective. It is very much as a present day English person might describe events in South Africa, compared with the version of a native South African. The point is therefore that John's account is much better founded on fact, much more credible and is the version I shall use as the basis of the rest of this book.

What I am trying to do in this book is to tell the story of the early church using mainly the material that is in the Bible. The majority will of course come from the four Gospels and the Acts of the Apostles.

The arrangement is generally chronological, starting from just before Jesus' birth to about the end of the second century when the church was well established. This means picking and choosing sections and putting them in a different sequence than appears in the Bible. Where one book tells essentially the same story, sometimes only one version will be provided in full. On the whole the teachings and stories that Jesus told will not be included.

A major problem with the four gospels is that, to many people, the events described do not fit together or appear to tell a credible story. For many the story of the three wise men fits this description; but there are alternative ways of weaving the stories together. Throughout the book I have tried to follow traditional teachings and note the discrepancies.

I also try to construct a somewhat different story which makes more sense of the historic background and tends to support a number of alternative traditions which the Church has often condemned as heresy. But was the twisting of sequences done deliberately by the writers and editors of the gospels in order to protect the early church?

That is a question that I am unable to answer; but it does seem to me that, at the end of the day, Constantine was using the church and the Christian messages for his personal political objectives and would have had few qualms about exercising his own brand of censorship.

1.5 Religions

It may be useful to step back for a moment and consider religions in general. They all seem to have both a starting point and an outline history in common. Essentially religion emanates from a sense of the 'other world'. This seems to be embedded in humankind as far back as one can ascertain. The sense that there are forces around which are beyond human control, the concept of a life after death and a general sense of awe at the natural world around one.

We cannot know the sequence of events for pre-historic religions but where we have history, they all seem to follow the same general sequence of events. We start with a remarkable person who seems to have an insight into this other-world; we shall call him the 'Guru'.

He travels around preaching and teaching and soon acquires a small band of dedicated followers who we shall term 'apostles' and a wider circle of followers who believe him and who we shall term 'disciples'.

Occasionally the Guru writes down his thoughts; but more usually it is one or other of the apostles who do the writing. This we shall term 'the scripture'.

Then the Guru dies and this is usually the signal for the apostles to get writing from their own personal recollection of the preaching and teaching. Then they find there are things they should have known about; but didn't, so, to complete the story, they add what they thought should have happened.

This is where the myths begin. The apostles are convinced that the Guru has superhuman talents and start searching for 'prophets' who forecast these momentous events.

With a little bit of imagination, a story is conceived which mixes facts which people can still remember with the proof that the Guru was what they believe.

Then the apostles die off and it is the disciples who need to keep the movement going. They need to get organised, so a hierarchy develops with a team leader who is thought of as a new apostle with assistants who are commissioned to perform the rituals that bind the disciples into a coherent group. This evolves into rules of behaviour to demonstrate to the outside world the unity of the group. Before long, these rules begin to also apply to dress, diet and relationships and it becomes difficult to differentiate between the religion and the culture. However different assistants have different ideas about what these rules should be and so sects begin to appear. Around this point in time someone conceives the idea of collecting together all the writings of the guru, the apostles and the myths that have developed. This becomes their 'bible' and acquires a sacred status.

Failure to follow the rules becomes a punishable offence but adherence becomes the guarantee of success in the afterlife. Mankind is then seen as being made up of three groups:

— Adherents who are guaranteed the benefits of the afterlife

— Potential converts who could be persuaded to join the fold

— The Damned

As time goes by further divisions occur, due mainly to either new philosophical thought or particular local circumstances and result in the rejection of the previous authority. Their reaction is usually to denounce the new ideas and practices as heresy and whether or not a compromise can be reached depends very much on personalities; but where a compromise is not reached the two contenders are much more inclined to make war on each other than with some other religion.

1.6 Early Christianity

One can see these processes developing in early Christianity but they have echoes in all religions and sects ranging from Buddhism to Jehovah's Witnesses.

Over the centuries we see new sects developing, all claiming to be true to the original Guru and reading into their 'bible' the justifications for their deviations. Often this develops into violent suppression of those who disagree and we can see this very clearly in Christianity with the suppression of the Albigensians, the Inquisition and the religious wars of the sixteenth and seventeenth centuries. Islam is going through similar turmoil today with battles between Sunni and Shias with Wahabis standing in the wings watching how things develop but generally preferring not to get too involved.

Another problem that religions face is that often secular society moves well ahead of the current religious orthodoxy. The Catholic church's attitudes towards contraception and personal relationships are a case in point and it takes a very strong leader to make even the most minor changes.

However - back to the first century and let us see what we can make of the history of Christianity. The key piece of information we are missing is the early life of Jesus. I think we can dismiss the Luke account as pure myth and speculation as Jesus was clearly a learned and well-educated man so that I believe he was born and brought up in Alexandria to relatively wealthy parents and within the Essene community which thrived there at the time. The idea that Jesus was celibate is also something that I have to reject. As a Jew he would never have been allowed to preach in a synagogue were he a single man and the numerous references to a Mary who was not his mother clearly indicate a relationship which was a lot deeper than merely that of a disciple. This gives a much more credible sense to the flight into Egypt and the visit of the Magi as we shall see as I arrange the story into what I believe to be much closer to the historical truth than the traditional sequence of events.

1.7 Reproduction and Marriage

One of the huge problems with Christianity today is the conflict between those who see marriage as an agreement for life between a man and a woman and those that are prepared to accept divorce and remarriage.

To those on the 'liberal' side of the argument the reluctance of those on the 'conservative' side is seen as just bigotry and a toleration of gross inequality which extends to gender issues as well as marriage. It is worth reconsidering how people in the biblical age saw the questions that seem so obvious to today's minds.

The first thing to note is that it was not until the early nineteenth century that there was any real understanding of how babies came about. The ancients did not understand basic biology, let alone genetics. The birth of a baby was seen as a gift to a woman from God, the father was defined as the man she had married or in whose harem she was. If she had never married or been in a harem, then the baby was the work of the devil. Marriage was therefore seen as the gateway to the gift of children.

This meant that the definition of a virgin was quite different to what we understand today. A virgin was simply a woman who had not laid with a man. Lying with a man other than one's husband was a serious offence against society but sexual intercourse had little to do with reproduction. For men sexual pleasure was just one of the benefits of marriage or, if you were wealthy, to have taken a woman into your harem. It was bad enough doing it with another woman; but doing it with another man was considered far worse.

When a baby was born to a Jewish woman then the baby was considered Jewish and its father was the man in whose house she was. Thus, there is no confusion between two of the gospellers reciting Jesus' heredity and the concept of Jesus being born of a virgin. (See section 2.9)

We also have to deal with St Paul's views. He was so convinced that Jesus would be back in a very short period of time to bring the world to an end that questions of marriage and sexual gratification were quite irrelevant. So, he is seen as a misogynist who saw very little role for women and, to a large extent, his views coloured the Roman Church's attitude to women for the next two millennia.

1.8 Roles and Gifts

Another area where we need to look back at differing views is the whole question of governance and certification. Forgetting for a moment the many different views as to the meaning of the Eucharist, what was clear was that it was meaningful only if the consecration had been done by someone qualified so to do. This person was identified as a priest. So, who could ordain priests?

This brought up the question of the Apostolic Succession. Jesus is understood to give his Apostles (i.e., the twelve) the power to ordain priests and for them to consecrate others in the Apostolic tradition. We thus have a hierarchy of bishops, priests and laymen within the Church all of whom have to be men.

Then one had communities of Christians springing up all around the ancient world. They too had a hierarchy: a patron who provided space for worship and protection, a governor who acted as the 'manager' of the community's resources and people who participated in the worship and constituted the community.

The big problem which bedeviled Western Christianity especially in the tenth to sixteenth centuries was how one held land. It was recognised that as land had been created by God it belonged to God; but its fruits could be enjoyed by the holder. But did the king hold it from God or did he hold it from God's representative, i.e., the Pope? The compromise was that the king held civil land directly but church land was held by the Pope. But as Henry VIII found that when laymen left their holdings to the church in exchange for prayers for the soul, there was not much in the way of fruits left for the king.

Particularly in mediaeval times many of these communities were well endowed and governed by a woman (Abbess or Prioress) who had both the capability and the contacts to fulfil the role. Many were excess daughters of kings and noblemen who could not easily be married off. Even when the governor was a man (Abbot, Prior etc.) they did not have to be consecrated or even ordained, what was required was the ability to do the job.

Thus, in order to maintain an ability to serve a wider community by providing priests they had to have access to a bishop.

Before the emergence of dioceses as we understand them today a man would be chosen as a bishop and sent off to Rome for consecration on the basis of his learning and godliness. It was only when the civil powers got into the act and kings insisted on selecting bishops who would do their bidding (aka Henry II and Thomas á Becket) that the role of bishop and governor became united. The kings often rued their choices; but the trend had been set and we saw the emergence of powerful bishops running dioceses with parishes governed by priests.

Now that many churches have accepted the concept of women priests and even women bishops and many others have not, we are faced with situations where many Christians find it hard to accept the status quo. Perhaps a better understanding of the history of how we got into this mess may help resolve some of the issues so we can see the Church as Jesus envisaged.

1.9 Herod

The name Herod occurs many times in the New Testament and as there were at least five Herod's in the period it is often difficult to know which was which. The background to all of this is in Roman politics and we need some simplification.

We can consider Palestine in the period as made up of three territories: Judea in the south; Galilee in the north and Samaria in the middle. There were several other territories involved but they play little or no part in our story.

We start with Herod the Great who was Governor of Galilee from 47 to 37 BC. In 37 BC he was made King of the Jews and governed all three territories until his death in 4 BC.

Then Palestine was divided between two of his sons: Herod Antipas ruling Galilee and Samaria with a third brother Phillip and Herod Archaelus governing Judea. In 6 AD Archaelus was ruled incompetent and it all came under Herod Antipas who held the title Tetrarch rather than king which was a very sore point with him. However, in 37 AD the title king was granted.

After Caligula became Emperor in 39 AD, Herod Antipas was exiled to France and Herod Agrippa I took over. He was a grandson of Herod the Great but lasted only until his early death in 44 AD when his son Herod Agrippa II took over.

1.10 The Arrangement

This book is in 6 parts covering the period from Mary's birth to the Council of Nicea. Each part is divided into Chapters and then into Sections. It is not in strict Chronological order as one of the aims is to contrast the stories as told by the several authors to bring out the inconsistencies which tend to be glossed over when one reads one passage from one book.

PART 1
SON OF GOD

We begin the story by setting the scene and looking at Jesus' life before he began his Mission.

We can tell something of the Roman world around the time of Jesus' birth and we can deduce that Jesus was well educated. The idea that God imparted Jesus with all knowledge from birth is a bit far-fetched as undoubtedly, if he had, then Jesus would have spoken of the power of technology in the twenty first century. He did not and his thoughts and sentiments tallied very closely with those of the Egyptians and reflect a good education in Alexandria.

By the time the proto-gospel, which was the basis for Matthew, Mark and Luke, was written, there would have been no one around to recall details of his birth. But there were still many who saw Jesus as the Messiah, so it is evident the writer turned to Isaiah and other prophets to reconstruct a story which we know as the Christmas story. He gave the game away by referring to something that happened 'So that the scripture shall be fulfilled'

The one story which is really believable is the one that most Christians are most likely not to believe and that is the story of the three Wise Men but it belongs in Chapter 21 not here.

We also deal with Jesus' early manhood and note that an unmarried Jesus would never have been allowed to preach in a synagogue and that the numerous references to a Mary who was not his mother indicates quite clearly who his wife was.

Finally, we look at the Essene communities in Alexandria, Qumran and Galilee and the emergence of John the Baptist.

Chapter 2 – Mary and the Nativity

2.1 Palestine 6 BC

In 6 BC Palestine was made up of three territories; Galilee in the north, Samaria in the middle and Judea in the south. Politically it was a remote part of the Roman Empire having become so in 63 BC when Pompey had conquered the Seleucids. Parthian troops had occupied Palestine in 40 BC but they were expelled by Roman troops in the following year. Herod the Great had been appointed as King of Judea in 37 BC and remained as a Roman protege until his death in 4 BC during which time Palestine had prospered. In 6 BC Cyrenius had just been appointed governor of Syria and Judea was added to the Province of Syria. The emperor was keen to know what additional taxable resources were available as Josephus recounts.

Josephus Antiquities book XVIII p1

Now Cyrenius, a Roman senator, and one who had gone through other magistracies and had passed through them until he had been consul and one who on other accounts was of great dignity came at this time into Syria with a few others being sent by Caesar to be a judge of that nation and to take an account of their substance. Coponius also, a man of the equestrian order was sent together with him to have the supreme power over the Jews. Moreover, Cyrenius came himself into Judea which was now added to the province of Syria to take an account of their substance and to dispose of Archelaeus's money; but the Jews although at the beginning they took the report of taxation heinously, yet did they leave off any further opposition to it, by the persuasion of Joazar who was the son of Boethus and high priest. So, they, being over-persuaded by Joazar's words gave an account of their estates without any dispute about it.

What this all means is not entirely clear, but it appears that the rulers of Palestine did not raise any serious objections to the Roman system of tax collection. It was not like a kind of income tax raised upon individuals which was passed to some central authority but rather a requirement which was placed on a ruler of a particular territory to send a certain sum to the Emperor as a sort of tribute. The ruler in turn placed an onus on his underlings to come up with designated sums which generally greatly exceeded in total the sum demanded by the Emperor.

The process repeated itself down the hierarchy with each person in the sequence making a tidy profit for himself. Whether it was taxation or extortion at the bottom of the chain is a matter for speculation. But as was pointed out about Matthew, tax collectors were not popular.

2.2 The Birth of Mary

The Qur'an gives some information about the birth of Mary and names her father as Imran who was expecting a son. Who Imran was is not clear but he seems to have been a person of considerable importance with several wives and a harem. Some traditions have him as a prophet with a wife named Hannah.

When Hannah was expecting a child, she informed Imran.

Qur'an Sura 3 35 – 36

[35] When the wife of Imran said "My Lord, indeed I have pledged to you what is in my womb [for your service] so accept this from me. Indeed, you are the Hearing, the Knowing"
[36] But when she delivered her, she said "My Lord, I have delivered a female" And God was most knowing of what she delivered, and the male is not like the female. "And I have named her Mary, and I seek refuge for her in You and for her descendants from Satan, the expelled [from the mercy of God]"

2.3 The Role of Zachariah

Zechariah seems to have been one of Imran's servants and a priest in the temple. When the baby was born there was a ballot to decide who should look after her, Zechariah won and was reminded of the event much later when Mary herself was about to have a child and the angel came tell him of his forthcoming fatherhood.

Qur'an Sura 3 44

[44] That is from the news of the unseen which we reveal to you [O Muhammad], And you were not with them when they cast their pens as to which of them should be responsible for Mary. Nor were you with them when they disputed.

So, Zechariah cared for her despite her being a girl and not the son Imran had hoped for.

Qur'an Sura 3 37

[37] So her Lord accepted her with good acceptance and caused her to grow in a good manner and put her in the care of Zechariah. Every time Zechariah entered upon her in the prayer chamber, he found her with her provision. He said "O Mary, from where is this [coming] to you?" She said "It is from God. Indeed, God provides for whom he wills without account.

2.4 The Annunciation

An angel comes to Mary to tell her that the child she is bearing will be the Messiah. The conversation is repeated to Zechariah for him to keep in mind when he is dumb before his son, John, is born.

Qur'an Sura 3 42 – 43

[42] And [mention] when the angels said "O Mary, indeed God has chosen you and purified you and chosen you above the women of the worlds.
[43] O Mary, be devoutly obedient to your Lord and prostrate and bow with those who bow [in prayer]"

The Qur'an then reveals that the details were revealed to Muhammed long after all the ancient writers had been forgotten.

Qur'an Sura 3 45 - 49.

[45] [And mention] when the angels said "O Mary, indeed God gives you good tidings of a word from Him, whose name will be the Messiah, Jesus, the son of Mary - distinguished in this world and the Hereafter and among those brought near [to God].
[46] He will speak to the people in the cradle and in maturity and will be of the righteous".
[47] She said, "My Lord, how will I have a child when no man has touched me?" [The angel] said, "Such is God; He creates what He wills.
When He decrees a matter, He only says to it "Be," and it is.
[48] And he will teach him writing and wisdom and the Torah and the Gospel.
[49] And [make him] a messenger to the Children of Israel, [who will say] "Indeed I have come to you with a sign from your Lord in that I design for you from clay [that which is] like the form of a bird, then I breathe into it and it becomes a bird by permission of God. And I cure the blind [from birth] and the leper, and I give life to the dead - by permission of God. And I inform you of what you eat and what you store in your houses. Indeed, in that is a sign for you, if you are believers.

The Qur'an then goes to make the point that Jesus was made by God, but was not God.

Qur'an Sura 3 59

[59] Indeed the example of Jesus to God is like that of Adam. He created him from dust then he said to him, "Be," and he was.

About the only 'facts' that Luke had to go on were that he was born, that his mother was Mary and that to be the Son of God there had to be something very special about the manner of his birth. And what a wonderful story Luke told.

He begins by describing how Mary knew she was to have a baby.

Luke 1 26 - 56

[26] And in the sixth month the angel Gabriel was sent from God unto a city of Galilee, named Nazareth,

[27] To a virgin espoused to a man whose name was Joseph, of the house of David; and the virgin's name was Mary.

[28] And the angel came in unto her, and said, Hail, thou that art highly favoured, the Lord is with thee: blessed art thou among women.

[29] And when she saw him, she was troubled at his saying, and cast in her mind what manner of salutation this should be.

[30] And the angel said unto her, Fear not, Mary: for thou hast found favour with God.

[31] And, behold, thou shalt conceive in thy womb, and bring forth a son, and shalt call his name JESUS.

[32] He shall be great, and shall be called the Son of the Highest: and the Lord God shall give unto him the throne of his father David:

[33] And he shall reign over the house of Jacob forever; and of his kingdom there shall be no end.

[34] Then said Mary unto the angel, how shall this be, seeing I know not a man?

[35] And the angel answered and said unto her, The Holy Ghost shall come upon thee, and the power of the Highest shall overshadow thee: therefore, also that holy thing which shall be born of thee shall be called the Son of God.

[36] And, behold, thy cousin Elisabeth, she hath also conceived a son in her old age: and this is the sixth month with her, who was called barren.

[37] For with God nothing shall be impossible.

[38] And Mary said, Behold the handmaid of the Lord; be it unto me according to thy word. And the angel departed from her.

[39] And Mary arose in those days, and went into the hill country with haste, into a city of Juda;

[40] And entered into the house of Zacharias, and saluted Elisabeth.

[41] And it came to pass, that, when Elisabeth heard the salutation of Mary, the babe leaped in her womb; and Elisabeth was filled with the Holy Ghost:

[42] And she spake out with a loud voice, and said, Blessed art thou among women, and blessed is the fruit of thy womb.

[43] And whence is this to me, that the mother of my Lord should come to me?

[44] For, lo, as soon as the voice of thy salutation sounded in mine ears, the babe leaped in my womb for joy.

[45] And blessed is she that believed: for there shall be a performance of those things which were told her from the Lord.

[46] And Mary said, My soul doth magnify the Lord,

[47] And my spirit hath rejoiced in God my Saviour.

[48] For he hath regarded the low estate of his handmaiden: for, behold, from henceforth all generations shall call me blessed.

[49] For he that is mighty hath done to me great things; and holy is his name.

[50] And his mercy is on them that fear him from generation to generation.

[51] He hath shewed strength with his arm; he hath scattered the proud in the imagination of their hearts.

[52] He hath put down the mighty from their seats, and exalted them of low degree.

[53] He hath filled the hungry with good things; and the rich he hath sent empty away.

[54] He hath holpen his servant Israel, in remembrance of his mercy;

[55] As he spake to our fathers, to Abraham, and to his seed forever.

[56] And Mary abode with her about three months, and returned to her own house.

Matthew tells the story from Joseph's point of view.

Matthew 1 18 - 25

[18] Now the birth of Jesus Christ was on this wise: When as his mother Mary was espoused to Joseph, before they came together, she was found with child of the Holy Ghost.

[19] Then Joseph her husband, being a just man, and not willing to make her a public example, was minded to put her away privily.

[20] But while he thought on these things, behold, the angel of the Lord appeared unto him in a dream, saying, Joseph, thou son of David, fear not to take unto thee Mary thy wife: for that which is conceived in her is of the Holy Ghost.

[21] And she shall bring forth a son, and thou shalt call his name JESUS: for he shall save his people from their sins.

[22] Now all this was done, that it might be fulfilled which was spoken of the Lord by the prophet, saying,

[23] Behold, a virgin shall be with child, and shall bring forth a son, and they shall call his name Emmanuel, which being interpreted is, God with us.

[24] Then Joseph being raised from sleep did as the angel of the Lord had bidden him, and took unto him his wife:

[25] And knew her not till she had brought forth her firstborn son: and he called his name JESUS.

2.5 The Birth of Jesus

Luke builds the story of the shepherds and the birth at Bethlehem, the latter seemingly only because the prophets had said the Messiah would come from the house of David and as Mary came from Galilee. He had to make up a story as to why they would be in Bethlehem for the birth. He hit upon the idea of a census, but unfortunately, in trying to be convincing, got his dates muddled. Quirinius became Governor of Syria in 6 BC, Herod the Great had died by around 4 BC and the idea of a 'world' tax which involved non-Roman citizens was a bit preposterous. In any case a woman did not count in those days and there would have been no need for her to have gone along. Josephus was perhaps more correct when he suggested that it was Cyrenius who was more interested in knowing what taxable resources he had acquired when Judea was added to his Syrian Province in 6 BC.

Luke 2 1 - 7

[1] And it came to pass in those days, that there went out a decree from Caesar Augustus, that all the world should be taxed.

[2] (And this taxing was first made when Cyrenius was governor of Syria.)

[3] And all went to be taxed, every one into his own city.

[4] And Joseph also went up from Galilee, out of the city of Nazareth, into Judaea, unto the city of David, which is called Bethlehem; (because he was of the house and lineage of David:)

[5] To be taxed with Mary his espoused wife, being great with child.

[6] And so it was, that, while they were there, the days were accomplished that she should be delivered.

[7] And she brought forth her firstborn son, and wrapped him in swaddling clothes, and laid him in a manger; because there was no room for them in the inn.

2.6 The coming of the Shepherds

Luke also is the only one telling of the coming of the Shepherds.

Luke 2 8 - 20

[15] And it came to pass, as the angels were gone away from them into heaven, the shepherds said one to another, let us now go even unto Bethlehem, and see this thing which is come to pass, which the Lord hath made known unto us.

[16] And they came with haste, and found Mary, and Joseph, and the babe lying in a manger.

[17] And when they had seen it, they made known abroad the saying which was told them concerning this child.

[18] And all they that heard it wondered at those things which were told them by the shepherds.

[19] But Mary kept all these things, and pondered them in her heart.

[20] And the shepherds returned, glorifying and praising God for all the things that they had heard and seen, as it was told unto them.

2.7 The Circumcision

In accordance with Jewish custom Mary had to go to the Temple to be purified and for Jesus to be circumcised and given his name.

Luke 2 21 - 24

[21] And when eight days were accomplished for the circumcising of the child, his name was called JESUS, which was so named of the angel before he was conceived in the womb.

[22] And when the days of her purification according to the law of Moses were accomplished, they brought him to Jerusalem, to present him to the Lord;

[23] (As it is written in the law of the Lord, every male that opened the womb shall be called holy to the Lord;)

[24] And to offer a sacrifice according to that which is said in the law of the Lord, A pair of turtledoves, or two young pigeons.

Luke also tells the story of Simeon and gives us the Nunc Dimittis.

Luke 2 25 - 38

[25] And, behold, there was a man in Jerusalem, whose name was Simeon; and the same man was just and devout, waiting for the consolation of Israel: and the Holy Ghost was upon him.

[26] And it was revealed unto him by the Holy Ghost, that he should not see death, before he had seen the Lord's Christ.

[27] And he came by the Spirit into the temple: and when the parents brought in the child Jesus, to do for him after the custom of the law,

[28] Then took he him up in his arms, and blessed God, and said,

[29] Lord, now let test thou thy servant depart in peace, according to thy word:

[30] For mine eyes have seen thy salvation,

[31] Which thou hast prepared before the face of all people;

[32]A light to lighten the Gentiles, and the glory of thy people Israel.

[33] And Joseph and his mother marveled at those things which were spoken of him.

[34] And Simeon blessed them, and said unto Mary his mother, Behold, this child is set for the fall and rising again of many in Israel; and for a sign which shall be spoken against;

[35] (Yea, a sword shall pierce through thy own soul also,) that the thoughts of many hearts may be revealed.

[36] And there was one Anna, a prophetess, the daughter of Phanuel, of the tribe of Aser: she was of a great age, and had lived with a husband seven years from her virginity;

[37] And she was a widow of about fourscore and four years, which departed not from the temple, but served God with fasting's and prayers night and day.

[38] And she coming in that instant gave thanks likewise unto the Lord, and spake of him to all them that looked for redemption in Jerusalem.

2.8 The Magi

Matthew tells a very different tale and he too places the birth in Bethlehem for the same reason. We tell here the Bible version but in Section 21.13 we will tell what we believe to be closer to the real story and which is much more believable.

Matthew 2 1 - 18

[1] Now when Jesus was born in Bethlehem of Judaea in the days of Herod the king, behold, there came wise men from the east to Jerusalem,

[2] Saying, where is he that is born King of the Jews? for we have seen his star in the east, and are come to worship him.

[3] When Herod the king had heard these things, he was troubled, and all Jerusalem with him.

[4] And when he had gathered all the chief priests and scribes of the people together, he demanded of them where Christ should be born.

[5] And they said unto him, In Bethlehem of Judaea: for thus it is written by the prophet,

[6] And thou Bethlehem, in the land of Juda, art not the least among the princes of Juda: for out of thee shall come a Governor, that shall rule my people, Israel.

[7] Then Herod, when he had privily called the wise men, inquired of them diligently what time the star appeared.

[8] And he sent them to Bethlehem, and said, Go and search diligently for the young child; and when ye have found him, bring me word again, that I may come and worship him also.

[9] When they had heard the king, they departed; and, lo, the star, which they saw in the east, went before them, till it came and stood over where the young child was.

[10] When they saw the star, they rejoiced with exceeding great joy.

[11] And when they were come into the house, they saw the young child with Mary his mother, and fell down, and worshipped him: and when they had opened their treasures, they presented unto him gifts; gold, and frankincense, and myrrh.

[12] And being warned of God in a dream that they should not return to Herod, they departed into their own country another way.

[13] And when they were departed, behold, the angel of the Lord appeareth to Joseph in a dream, saying, Arise, and take the young child and his mother, and flee into Egypt, and be thou there until I bring thee word: for Herod will seek the young child to destroy him.

[14] When he arose, he took the young child and his mother by night, and departed into Egypt:

[15] And was there until the death of Herod: that it might be fulfilled which was spoken of the Lord by the prophet, saying, Out of Egypt have I called my son.

[16] Then Herod, when he saw that he was mocked of the wise men, was exceeding wroth, and sent forth, and slew all the children that were in Bethlehem, and in all the coasts thereof, from two years old and under, according to the time which he had diligently inquired of the wise men.

[17] Then was fulfilled that which was spoken by Jeremy the prophet, saying,

[18] In Rama was there a voice heard, lamentation, and weeping, and great mourning, Rachel weeping for her children, and would not be comforted, because they are not.

King Herod the Great died in the year 4 BC. After his death the realm was divided between his sons: Herod Archelus became king of Judea and Samaria with Galilee, the northern part of the kingdom, jointly ruled by his two sons Herod Antipas and Philip the Tetrarch.

Matthew 2 19 - 23

[19] But when Herod was dead, behold, an angel of the Lord appeareth in a dream to Joseph in Egypt,

[20] Saying, Arise, and take the young child and his mother, and go into the land of Israel: for they are dead which sought the young child's life.

[21] And he arose, and took the young child and his mother, and came into the land of Israel.

[22] But when he heard that Archelaus did reign in Judaea in the room of his father Herod, he was afraid to go thither: notwithstanding, being warned of God in a dream, he turned aside into the parts of Galilee:

[23] And he came and dwelt in a city called Nazareth: that it might be fulfilled which was spoken by the prophets, He shall be called a Nazarene.

The story of the Magi does not seem to really fit with the story of the Nativity although it does provide an explanation as to why Joseph and Mary relocated to Nazareth after the birth.

It is St Luke who placed the Annunciation in Nazareth but other evidence points to Mary as coming from Jerusalem. Perhaps a better explanation of the story of the Magi will be found after Jesus' death and resurrection. (See Section 21.13)

2.9 Genealogy

Matthew attempts to provide a 'family tree' of Jesus, tracing him back through threecycles of 14 generations to Abraham

Matthew 1 1-17

[1] The book of the generation of Jesus Christ, the son of David, the son of Abraham.

[2] Abraham begat Isaac; and Isaac begat Jacob; and Jacob begat Judas and his brethren;

[3] And Judas begat Phares and Zara of Thamar; and Phares begat Esrom; and Esrom begat Aram;

[4] And Aram begat Aminadab; and Aminadab begat Naasson; and Naasson begat Salmon;

[5] And Salmon begat Booz of Rachab; and Booz begat Obed of Ruth; and Obed begat Jesse;

[6] And Jesse begat David the king; and David the king begat Solomon of her that had been the wife of Urias;

[7] And Solomon begat Roboam; and Roboam begat Abia; and Abia begat Asa;

[8] And Asa begat Josaphat; and Josaphat begat Joram; and Joram begat Ozias;

[9] And Ozias begat Joatham; and Joatham begat Achaz; and Achaz begat Ezekias;

[10] And Ezekias begat Manasses; and Manasses begat Amon; and Amon begat Josias;

[11] And Josias begat Jechonias and his brethren, about the time they were carried away to Babylon:

[12] And after they were brought to Babylon, Jechonias
begat Salathiel; and Salathiel begat Zorobabel;

[13] And Zorobabel begat Abiud; and Abiud begat Eliakim; and Eliakim begat Azor;

[14] And Azor begat Sadoc; and Sadoc begat Achim; and Achim begat Eliud;

[15] And Eliud begat Eleazar; and Eleazar begat Matthan; and Matthan begat Jacob;

[16] And Jacob begat Joseph the husband of Mary, of whom was born Jesus, who is called Christ.

[17] So all the generations from Abraham to David are fourteen generations; and from David until the carrying away into Babylon are fourteen generations; and from the carrying away into Babylon unto Christ are fourteen generations.

Mark ignores the birth and family entirely and Luke provides a table similar to that of Matthew but leading back to Adam. He mentions Mary and Joseph but however he makes it plain that Joseph was not Jesus' natural father and hence the genealogies are somewhat pointless. He also destroys his explanation that Jesus was the son of God because having traced him, through Joseph back to Adam, he defines Adam as the son of God.

Luke 3 23-38

[23] And Jesus himself began to be about thirty years of age, being (as was supposed) the son of Joseph, which was the son of Heli,

[24] Which was the son of Matthat, which was the son of Levi, which was the son of Melchi, which was the son of Janna, which was the son of Joseph,

[25] Which was the son of Mattathias, which was the son of Amos, which was the son of Naum, which was the son of Esli, which was the son of Nagge,

[26] Which was the son of Maath, which was the son of Mattathias, which was the son of Semei, which was the son of Joseph, which was the son of Juda,

[27] Which was the son of Joanna, which was the son of Rhesa, which was the son of Zorobabel, which was the son of Salathiel, which was the son of Neri,

[28] Which was the son of Melchi, which was the son of Addi, which was the son of Cosam, which was the son of Elmodam, which was the son of Er,

[29] Which was the son of Jose, which was the son of Eliezer, which was the son of Jorim, which was the son of Matthat, which was the son of Levi,

[30] Which was the son of Simeon, which was the son of Juda, which was the son of Joseph, which was the son of Jonan, which was the son of Eliakim,

[31] Which was the son of Melea, which was the son of Menan, which was the son of Mattatha, which was the son of Nathan, which was the son of David,

[32] Which was the son of Jesse, which was the son of Obed, which was the son of Booz, which was the son of Salmon, which was the son of Naasson,

[33] Which was the son of Aminadab, which was the son of Aram, which was the son of Esrom, which was the son of Phares, which was the son of Juda,

[34] Which was the son of Jacob, which was the son of Isaac, which was the son of Abraham, which was the son of Thara, which was the son of Nachor,

[35] Which was the son of Saruch, which was the son of Ragau, which was the son of Phalec, which was the son of Heber, which was the son of Sala,

[36] Which was the son of Cainan, which was the son of Arphaxad, which was the son of Sem, which was the son of Noe, which was the son of Lamech,

[37] Which was the son of Mathusala, which was the son of Enoch, which was the son of Jared, which was the son of Maleleel, which was the son of Cainan,

[38] Which was the son of Enos, which was the son of Seth, which was the son of Adam, which was the son of God.

John on the other hand places Jesus in a mystical context

John 1 1-5
[1] In the beginning was the Word, and the Word was with God, and the Word was God.

[2] The same was in the beginning with God.

[3] All things were made by him; and without him was not anything made that was made.

[4] In him was life; and the life was the light of men.

[5] And the light shineth in darkness; and the darkness comprehended it not

Chapter 3 – John the Baptist

It is convenient to group all the material about John the Baptist together in one chapter. This will entail some of the material being repeated in other chapters as we tell the story of Jesus.

3.1 The Role of Zachariah

It was around 6 BC that two babies were born. They were vaguely related. The first was to an elderly couple named Zechariah and Elizabeth. She had been thought of as well past child bearing age.

Zechariah had been put in charge of Mary since her birth He had no children of his own and while he longed for a son his chances seemed remote. After he had been told of Mary's impending confinement he appealed to God.

Qur'an Sura 3 38-41
[38] At that, Zechariah called upon his Lord saying "My Lord, grant me from Yourself a good offspring. Indeed, you are the Hearer of supplication".
[39] So the angels called him while he was standing in prayer in the chamber, "Indeed, God gives you good tidings of John, confirming a word from God and who will be honorable, abstaining from a woman and a prophet from among the righteous.
[40] He said "My Lord, how will I have a boy when I have reached old age and my wife is barren? He [the angel] said, "Such is God; He does what he wills.
[41] He said "My Lord, make for me a sign" He said "Your sign is that you will not [be able to] speak to the people for three days except by gesture. And remember Your Lord much and exalt [Him with praise] in the evening and in the morning.

Luke tells a very similar story to that of the Qur'an although he omits Zechariah's guardianship of Mary and elaborates the rest.

Luke 1 5 - 25

[5] There was in the days of Herod, the king of Judaea, a certain priest named Zacharias, of the course of Abia: and his wife was of the daughters of Aaron, and her name was Elisabeth.

[6] And they were both righteous before God, walking in all the commandments and ordinances of the Lord blameless.

[7] And they had no child, because that Elisabeth was barren, and they both were now well stricken in years.

[8] And it came to pass, that while he executed the priest's office before God in the order of his course,

[9] According to the custom of the priest's office, his lot was to burn incense when he went into the temple of the Lord.

[10] And the whole multitude of the people were praying without at the time of incense.

[11] And there appeared unto him an angel of the Lord standing on the right side of the altar of incense.

[12] And when Zacharias saw him, he was troubled, and fear fell upon him.

[13] But the angel said unto him, Fear not, Zacharias: for thy prayer is heard; and thy wife Elisabeth shall bear thee a son, and thou shalt call his name John.

[14] And thou shalt have joy and gladness; and many shall rejoice at his birth.

[15] For he shall be great in the sight of the Lord, and shall drink neither wine nor strong drink; and he shall be filled with the Holy Ghost, even from his mother's womb.

[16] And many of the children of Israel shall he turn to the Lord their God.

[17] And he shall go before him in the spirit and power of Elias, to turn the hearts of the fathers to the children, and the disobedient to the wisdom of the just; to make ready a people prepared for the Lord.

[18] And Zacharias said unto the angel, whereby shall I know this? for I am an old man, and my wife well stricken in years.

[19] And the angel answering said unto him, I am Gabriel, that stand in the presence of God; and am sent to speak unto thee, and to shew thee these glad tidings.

[20] And, behold, thou shalt be dumb, and not able to speak, until the day that these things shall be performed, because thou believest not my words, which shall be fulfilled in their season.

[21] And the people waited for Zacharias, and marveled that he tarried so long in the temple.

Luke picks up the tale again reporting the birth of John. Zachariah remembers God's name for the child.

Luke 1 57 - 80

[57] Now Elisabeth's full time came that she should be delivered; and she brought forth a son.

[58] And her neighbours and her cousins heard how the Lord had shewed great mercy upon her; and they rejoiced with her.

[59] And it came to pass, that on the eighth day they came to circumcise the child; and they called him Zacharias, after the name of his father.

[60] And his mother answered and said, Not so; but he shall be called John.

[61] And they said unto her, There is none of thy kindred that is called by this name.

[62] And they made signs to his father, how he would have him called.

[63] And he asked for a writing table, and wrote, saying, His name is John. And they marvelled all.

[64] And his mouth was opened immediately, and his tongue loosed, and he spake, and praised God.

[65] And fear came on all that dwelt round about them: and all these sayings were noised abroad throughout all the hill country of Judaea.

[66] And all they that heard them laid them up in their hearts, saying, What manner of child shall this be! And the hand of the Lord was with him.

[67] And his father Zacharias was filled with the Holy Ghost, and prophesied, saying,

[68] Blessed be the Lord God of Israel; for he hath visited and redeemed his people,

[69] And hath raised up a horn of salvation for us in the house of his servant David;

[70] As he spake by the mouth of his holy prophets, which have been since the world began:

[71] That we should be saved from our enemies, and from the hand of all that hate us;

[72] To perform the mercy promised to our fathers, and to remember his holy covenant;

[73] The oath which he sware to our father Abraham,

[74] That he would grant unto us, that we being delivered out of the hand of our enemies might serve him without fear,

[75] In holiness and righteousness before him, all the days of our life.

[76] And thou, child, shalt be called the prophet of the Highest: for thou shalt go before the face of the Lord to prepare his ways;

[77] To give knowledge of salvation unto his people by the remission of their sins,

[78] Through the tender mercy of our God; whereby the dayspring from on high hath visited us,

[79] To give light to them that sit in darkness and in the shadow of death, to guide our feet into the way of peace.
[80] And the child grew, and waxed strong in spirit, and was in the deserts till the day of his shewing unto Israel.

3.2 John the Baptist

We hear nothing more of John until he reaches early manhood, so we begin from the premise that both John and Jesus were associate members of the Essene community at Qumran. First Jesus left to live in Galilee and then John left the community with a mission to preach and teach.

Mark starts his gospel with John the Baptist:

Mark 1 1 - 8
[1] The beginning of the gospel of Jesus Christ, the Son of God;
[2] As it is written in the prophets, Behold, I send my messenger before thy face, which shall prepare thy way before thee.
[3] The voice of one crying in the wilderness, Prepare ye the way of the Lord, make his paths straight.
[4] John did baptize in the wilderness, and preach the baptism of repentance for the remission of sins.
[5] And there went out unto him all the land of Judaea, and they of Jerusalem, and were all baptized of him in the river of Jordan, confessing their sins.
[6] And John was clothed with camel's hair, and with a girdle of a skin about his loins; and he did eat locusts and wild honey;
[7] And preached, saying, There cometh one mightier than I after me, the latchet of whose shoes I am not worthy to stoop down and unloose.
[8] I indeed have baptized you with water: but he shall baptize you with the Holy Ghost.

Matthew picks up the story and elaborates.

Luke 3 1 - 20
[1] Now in the fifteenth year of the reign of Tiberius Caesar, Pontius Pilate being governor of Judaea, and Herod being tetrarch of Galilee, and his brother Philip tetrarch of Ituraea and of the region of Trachonitis, and Lysanias the tetrarch of Abilene,
[2] Annas and Caiaphas being the high priests, the word of God came unto John the son of Zacharias in the wilderness.

[3] And he came into all the country about Jordan, preaching the baptism of repentance for the remission of sins;

[4] As it is written in the book of the words of Esaias the prophet, saying, The voice of one crying in the wilderness, Prepare ye the way of the Lord, make his paths straight.

[5] Every valley shall be filled, and every mountain and hill shall be brought low; and the crooked shall be made straight, and the rough ways shall be made smooth;

[6] And all flesh shall see the salvation of God.

[7] Then said he to the multitude that came forth to be baptized of him, O generation of vipers, who hath warned you to flee from the wrath to come?

[8] Bring forth therefore fruits worthy of repentance, and begin not to say within yourselves, We have Abraham to our father: for I say unto you, That God is able of these stones to raise up children unto Abraham.

[9] And now also the axe is laid unto the root of the trees: every tree therefore which bringeth not forth good fruit is hewn down, and cast into the fire.

[10] And the people asked him, saying, What shall we do then?

[11] He answereth and saith unto them, He that hath two coats, let him impart to him that hath none; and he that hath meat, let him do likewise.

[12] Then came also publicans to be baptized, and said unto him, Master, what shall we do?

[13] And he said unto them, Exact no more than that which is appointed you.

[14] And the soldiers likewise demanded of him, saying, And what shall we do? And he said unto them, Do violence to no man, neither accuse any falsely; and be content with your wages.

[15] And as the people were in expectation, and all men mused in their hearts of John, whether he were the Christ, or not;

[16] John answered, saying unto them all, I indeed baptize you with water; but one mightier than I cometh, the latchet of whose shoes I am not worthy to unloose: he shall baptize you with the Holy Ghost and with fire:

[17] Whose fan is in his hand, and he will throughly purge his floor, and will gather the wheat into his garner; but the chaff he will burn with fire unquenchable.

[18] And many other things in his exhortation preached he unto the people.

[19] But Herod the tetrarch, being reproved by him for Herodias his brother Philip's wife, and for all the evils which Herod had done,

[20] Added yet this above all, that he shut up John in prison.

3.3 The Baptism of Jesus

John had been preaching and baptising for some time, continually on the lookout for the person who would be recognised as the Messiah. Matthew tells us how Jesus came to be baptised and John tries to dissuade him: -

Matthew 3 13 - 17

[13] Then cometh Jesus from Galilee to Jordan unto John, to be baptized of him.

[14] But John forbad him, saying, I have need to be baptized of thee, and comest thou to me?

[15] And Jesus answering said unto him, Suffer it to be so now: for thus it becometh us to fulfil all righteousness. Then he suffered him.

[16] And Jesus, when he was baptized, went up straightway out of the water: and, lo, the heavens were opened unto him, and he saw the Spirit of God descending like a dove, and lighting upon him:

[17] And lo a voice from heaven, saying, This is my beloved Son, in whom I am well pleased.

Luke tells his version of the story: -

Luke 3 21 - 22

[21] Now when all the people were baptized, it came to pass, that Jesus also being baptized, and praying, the heaven was opened,

[22] And the Holy Ghost descended in a bodily shape like a dove upon him, and a voice came from heaven, which said, Thou art my beloved Son; in thee I am well pleased.

Mark's version is similar.

Mark 1 9 - 11

[9] And it came to pass in those days, that Jesus came from Nazareth of Galilee, and was baptized of John in Jordan.

[10] And straightway coming up out of the water, he saw the heavens opened, and the Spirit like a dove descending upon him:

[11] And there came a voice from heaven, saying, Thou art my beloved Son, in whom I am well pleased.

Now we can turn to John's gospel and see a very different style. John is not concerned with how things happened; he is trying to draw out the good news. His version is much more dramatic and memorable. His facts are much more believable and he does not bother to embellish them with background.

He starts by identifying John the Baptist and making clear that he was not the Messiah foretold in the scriptures:

John 1 6 - 9
[6] There was a man sent from God, whose name was John.
[7] The same came for a witness, to bear witness of the Light, that all men through him might believe.
[8] He was not that Light, but was sent to bear witness of that Light.
[9] That was the true Light, which lighteth every man that cometh into the world.

He quotes John's own words to confirm this:

John 1.15
[15] John bare witness of him, and cried, saying, This was he of whom I spake, He that cometh after me is preferred before me: for he was before me.

John recalls later what happened.

John 1 32 - 34
[32] And John bare record, saying, I saw the Spirit descending from heaven like a dove, and it abode upon him.
[33] And I knew him not: but he that sent me to baptize with water, the same said unto me, Upon whom thou shalt see the Spirit descending, and remaining on him, the same is he which baptizeth with the Holy Ghost.
[34] And I saw, and bare record that this is the Son of God.

3.4 Looking for the Messiah

Sections of the Jewish hierarchy were constantly on the lookout for the Messiah who they believed would rid them of Roman domination. When they heard of John the Baptist's activities, they sent a deputation of the Jewish Clergy down to the Bethany in Galilee to see what John the Baptist was up to:

John 1 19 - 28

[19] And this is the record of John, when the Jews sent priests and Levites from Jerusalem to ask him, Who art thou?

[20] And he confessed, and denied not; but confessed, I am not the Christ.

[21] And they asked him, What then? Art thou Elias? And he saith, I am not. Art thou that prophet? And he answered, No.

[22] Then said they unto him, Who art thou? that we may give an answer to them that sent us. What sayest thou of thyself?

[23] He said, I am the voice of one crying in the wilderness, Make straight the way of the Lord, as said the prophet Esaias.

[24] And they which were sent were of the Pharisees.

[25] And they asked him, and said unto him, Why baptizest thou then, if thou be not that Christ, nor Elias, neither that prophet?

[26] John answered them, saying, I baptize with water: but there standeth one among you, whom ye know not;

[27] He it is, who coming after me is preferred before me, whose shoe's latchet I am not worthy to unloose.

[28] These things were done in Bethabara beyond Jordan, where John was baptizing.

Next day he spotted Jesus coming towards him and pointed him out:

John 1 29 - 31

[29] The next day John seeth Jesus coming unto him, and saith, Behold the Lamb of God, which taketh away the sin of the world.

[30] This is he of whom I said, After me cometh a man which is preferred before me: for he was before me.

[31] And I knew him not: but that he should be made manifest to Israel, therefore am I come baptizing with water.

On the following day when John was standing with two of his disciples, Jesus passed again. This time John sent the two after him:

John 1 35 - 39

[35] Again the next day after John stood, and two of his disciples;

[36] And looking upon Jesus as he walked, he saith, Behold the Lamb of God!

[37] And the two disciples heard him speak, and they followed Jesus.

[38] Then Jesus turned, and saw them following, and saith unto them, What seek ye? They said unto him, Rabbi, (which is to say, being interpreted, Master,) where dwellest thou?

[39] He saith unto them, Come and see. They came and saw where he dwelt, and abode with him that day: for it was about the tenth hour.

As will be seen the outcome was not as John had anticipated. Instead of Jesus joining his movement Andrew joins Jesus.

3.5 Competition with Jesus

For a short while both Jesus and John the Baptist were preaching and baptising people in Judea.

John 3 22 - 24

[22] After these things came Jesus and his disciples into the land of Judaea; and there he tarried with them, and baptized.
[23] And John also was baptizing in Aenon near to Salim, because there was much water there: and they came, and were baptized.
[24] For John was not yet cast into prison.

This was obviously causing some confusion

John 3 25 - 36

[25] Then there arose a question between some of John's disciples and the Jews about purifying.
[26] And they came unto John, and said unto him, Rabbi, he that was with thee beyond Jordan, to whom thou barest witness, behold, the same baptizeth, and all men come to him.
[27] John answered and said, A man can receive nothing, except it be given him from heaven.
[28] Ye yourselves bear me witness, that I said, I am not the Christ, but that I am sent before him.
[29] He that hath the bride is the bridegroom: but the friend of the bridegroom, which standeth and heareth him, rejoiceth greatly because of the bridegroom's voice: this my joy therefore is fulfilled.
[30] He must increase, but I must decrease.
[31] He that cometh from above is above all: he that is of the earth is earthly, and speaketh of the earth: he that cometh from heaven is above all.
[32] And what he hath seen and heard, that he testifieth; and no man receiveth his testimony.
[33] He that hath received his testimony hath set to his seal that God is true.

The dispute reached the ears of the Pharisees and when Jesus heard of their interest, he set off back north to Galilee.

John 4 1 - 4

[1] When therefore the Lord knew how the Pharisees had heard that Jesus made and baptized more disciples than John,

[2] (Though Jesus himself baptized not, but his disciples,)

[3] He left Judaea, and departed again into Galilee.

[4] And he must needs go through Samaria.

3.6 John's Arrest

John's preaching was stirring up the Jewish religious elements and he was perceived to be a considerable threat to Herod Antipas. As a result Herod placed him under arrest.

Matthew gives Jesus' reaction to the news.

Matthew 4 12 - 17

[12] Now when Jesus had heard that John was cast into prison, he departed into Galilee;

[13] And leaving Nazareth, he came and dwelt in Capernaum, which is upon the sea coast, in the borders of Zabulon and Nephthalim:

[14] That it might be fulfilled which was spoken by Esaias the prophet, saying,

[15] The land of Zabulon, and the land of Nephthalim, by the way of the sea, beyond Jordan, Galilee of the Gentiles;

[16] The people which sat in darkness saw great light; and to them which sat in the region and shadow of death light is sprung up.

[17] From that time Jesus began to preach, and to say, Repent: for the kingdom of heaven is at hand.

While under arrest John enquires after Jesus.

Matthew 11 2 - 6

[2] Now when John had heard in the prison the works of Christ, he sent two of his disciples,

[3] And said unto him, Art thou he that should come, or do we look for another?

[4] Jesus answered and said unto them, Go and shew John again those things which ye do hear and see:

[5] The blind receives their sight, and the lame walk, the lepers are cleansed, and the deaf hear, the dead are raised up, and the poor have the gospel preached to them.

[6] And blessed is he, whosoever shall not be offended in me.

Then he praises John and his work.

Matthew 11 7 - 19

[7] And as they departed, Jesus began to say unto the multitudes concerning John, What went ye out into the wilderness to see? A reed shaken with the wind?

[8] But what went ye out for to see? A man clothed in soft raiment? behold, they that wear soft clothing are in kings' houses.

[9] But what went ye out for to see? A prophet? yea, I say unto you, and more than a prophet.

[10] For this is he, of whom it is written, Behold, I send my messenger before thy face, which shall prepare thy way before thee.

[11] Verily I say unto you, Among them that are born of women there hath not risen a greater than John the Baptist: notwithstanding he that is least in the kingdom of heaven is greater than he.

[12] And from the days of John the Baptist until now the kingdom of heaven suffered violence, and the violent take it by force.

[13] For all the prophets and the law prophesied until John.

[14] And if ye will receive it, this is Elias, which was for to come.

[15] He that hath ears to hear, let him hear.

[16] But whereunto shall I liken this generation? It is like unto children sitting in the markets, and calling unto their fellows,

[17] And saying, We have piped unto you, and ye have not danced; we have mourned unto you, and ye have not lamented.

[18] For John came neither eating nor drinking, and they say, He hath a devil.

[19] The Son of man came eating and drinking, and they say, Behold a man gluttonous, and a winebibber, a friend of publicans and sinners. But wisdom is justified of her children

3.7 Execution of John the Baptist

We hear nothing more of John until much later when his death is recalled. John had been kept in prison to keep the peace and Herod had been quite impressed by what he had to say. However, his wife, who had previously been married to his brother Phillip had a grudge against him. John had been preaching that to take a brother's widow was immoral, although it had been the traditional practice of the Jews for centuries.

Mark 6 17 – 29

[17] For Herod himself had sent forth and laid hold upon John, and bound him in prison for Herodias' sake, his brother Philip's wife: for he had married her.

[18] For John had said unto Herod, It is not lawful for thee to have thy brother's wife.

[19] Therefore Herodias had a quarrel against him, and would have killed him; but she could not:

[20] For Herod feared John, knowing that he was a just man and an holy, and observed him; and when he heard him, he did many things, and heard him gladly.

[21] And when a convenient day was come, that Herod on his birthday made a supper to his lords, high captains, and chief estates of Galilee;

[22] And when the daughter of the said Herodias came in, and danced, and pleased Herod and them that sat with him, the king said unto the damsel, Ask of me whatsoever thou wilt, and I will give it thee.

[23] And he sware unto her, Whatsoever thou shalt ask of me, I will give it thee, unto the half of my kingdom.

[24] And she went forth, and said unto her mother, What shall I ask? And she said, The head of John the Baptist.

[25] And she came in straightway with haste unto the king, and asked, saying, I will that thou give me by and by in a charger the head of John the Baptist.

[26] And the king was exceeding sorry; yet for his oath's sake, and for their sakes which sat with him, he would not reject her.

[27] And immediately the king sent an executioner, and commanded his head to be brought: and he went and beheaded him in the prison,

[28] And brought his head in a charger, and gave it to the damsel: and the damsel gave it to her mother.

[29] And when his disciples heard of it, they came and took up his corpse, and laid it in a tomb.

Matthew tells essentially the same story and gives Jesus' reaction to the news of John's death.

Matthew 14 1 - 13

[1] At that time Herod the tetrarch heard of the fame of Jesus,

[2] And said unto his servants, This is John the Baptist; he is risen from the dead; and therefore mighty works do shew forth themselves in him.

[3] For Herod had laid hold on John, and bound him, and put him in prison for Herodias' sake, his brother Philip's wife.

[4] For John said unto him, It is not lawful for thee to have her.

[5] And when he would have put him to death, he feared the multitude, because they counted him as a prophet.

[6] But when Herod's birthday was kept, the daughter of Herodias danced before them, and pleased Herod.

[7] Whereupon he promised with an oath to give her whatsoever she would ask.

[8] And she, being before instructed of her mother, said, Give me here John Baptist's head in a charger.

[9] And the king was sorry: nevertheless for the oath's sake, and them which sat with him at meat, he commanded it to be given her.

[10] And he sent, and beheaded John in the prison.

[11] And his head was brought in a charger, and given to the damsel: and she brought it to her mother.

[12] And his disciples came, and took up the body, and buried it, and went and told Jesus.

[13] When Jesus heard of it, he departed thence by ship into a desert place apart: and when the people had heard thereof, they followed him on foot out of the cities.

This raises all sorts of interesting questions. A monarch such as Herod seems most unlikely to have allowed the whims of a dancing girl to have influenced him in the life-or-death decisions of John. Thus, one can only draw the conclusion that Herod saw the death of John as a means of getting rid of a trouble maker - or was he got at? In either event the story of Salome can be nothing more than a very lame excuse.

Chapter 4 Jesus' Early Life

4.1 Jesus' Boyhood

Of Jesus' early life we know very little. One thing however was very clear. Jesus was very well read in the scriptures. He must therefore have spent a considerable time in study, learning to read and working with the rabbis. Luke inserts a vignette which points this out.

Luke 2 41 - 52

[41] Now his parents went to Jerusalem every year at the feast of the Passover.

[42] And when he was twelve years old, they went up to Jerusalem after the custom of the feast.

[43] And when they had fulfilled the days, as they returned, the child Jesus tarried behind in Jerusalem; and Joseph and his mother knew not of it.

[44] But they, supposing him to have been in the company, went a day's journey; and they sought him among their kinsfolk and acquaintance.

[45] And when they found him not, they turned back again to Jerusalem, seeking him.

[46] And it came to pass, that after three days they found him in the temple, sitting in the midst of the doctors, both hearing them, and asking them questions.

[47] And all that heard him were astonished at his understanding and answers.

[48] And when they saw him, they were amazed: and his mother said unto him, Son, why hast thou thus dealt with us? behold, thy father and I have sought thee sorrowing.

[49] And he said unto them, How is it that ye sought me? wist ye not that I must be about my Father's business?

[50] And they understood not the saying which he spake unto them.

[51] And he went down with them, and came to Nazareth, and was subject unto them: but his mother kept all these sayings in her heart.

[52] And Jesus increased in wisdom and stature, and in favour with God and man.

Of his later childhood and early manhood, we know nothing except a brief reference in Mark to his having been a carpenter.

Mark 6 2 - 3

[2] And when the sabbath day was come, he began to teach in the synagogue: and many hearing him were astonished, saying, From whence hath this man these things? and what wisdom is this which is given unto him, that even such mighty works are wrought by his hands?

[3] Is not this the carpenter, the son of Mary, the brother of James, and Joses, and of Juda, and Simon? and are not his sisters here with us? And they were offended at him.

4.2 Jesus' Family

To many Christians a great deal of weight is placed on two tenets of faith: first that Mary was and remained a virgin: second that Jesus remained celibate. However, neither the gospels nor science support these and, in fact, directly contradict them.

The virgin birth was promulgated to defend the concept of original sin. St Paul was a noted misogynist and saw sex as evil and sinful. Thus if Jesus was perfect he could not have been tainted with original sin and hence sex could have had nothing to do with his birth. From a scientific point of view, a birth without sex is possible, but extremely rare. What can happen is that when the woman produces an egg it begins to clone and can develop into a child. However, if this happens there can be no Y chromosome present and the child has to be a female. Some feminists have tried to claim that Jesus was in fact female but this would be difficult enough to conceal today and virtually impossible in biblical times.

As we shall see when we come to consider the Essenes, (see section 4.5) celibacy in Jewish circles would have excluded a man from society and confined him to a monastery. He would never have been allowed to preach in a synagogue. If we follow the logic of perpetual virginity then Jesus could not have had brothers or sisters unless they too had been touched by God.

The matter of Mary's virginity seems to have become an issue when the church was trying to counter the Albigensian heresies in the twelfth century which arose from the legend that Mary Magdalene escaped to the south of France with Jesus' son. (see section 21.13)

Matthew names his family:

Matthew 13 53-56

[53] And it came to pass, that when Jesus had finished these parables, he departed thence.

[54] And when he was come into his own country, he taught them in their synagogue, insomuch that they were astonished, and said, Whence hath this man this wisdom, and these mighty works?

[55] Is not this the carpenter's son? is not his mother called Mary? and his brethren, James, and Joses, and Simon, and Judas?

[56] And his sisters, are they not all with us? Whence then hath this man all these things?

4.3 The Glastonbury Legend

Numerous legends have arisen. Perhaps the one most appealing to British Christians is the one linking Jesus to Glastonbury in Somerset.

The legend gives Joseph of Arimathea as Jesus' uncle and a wealthy trader. The story goes that the young Jesus would accompany Joseph on some of his voyages, one which took him to tin mines of Cornwall and on to Somerset levels. In those times there would be many trade goods as well as the tin which would fetch a good price back in Palestine.

Certainly, Phoenician boats regularly traded with Britain. While they were there Jesus and Joseph visited Glastonbury which was on an island in the marshes and which had been a holy site for centuries. Joseph is reputed to have planted his staff at Glastonbury which took root and which flowered every Christmas thereafter.

4.4 The Essene Connection

What actually seems very much more likely is that Jesus was actually brought up in Alexandria in Egypt. Alexandria had a very large Jewish quarter which had a strong Essene flavour. The other major Essene stronghold was of course Galilee. Alexandria was also the Roman world's seat of learning with its fabulous library and tradition of scholarship going back centuries. Much of what Jesus was to preach has echoes in Alexandrine philosophy and it would have indeed provided him with the opportunity to bring that knowledge back to Palestine and amaze the teachers at the Temple.

What seems most likely however is that Jesus was born and brought up into an Essene community in Alexandria and, when he was in his early manhood, moved to Qumran, the Essene spiritual home, to get his final education. Instead of going into the inner monastery at Qumran he was sent to live in the other major Essene community in Galilee where he married and took on the role of a carpenter to make his living.

A view of all of this is that Joseph, the husband of Mary and Joseph of Arimathea were actually one and the same person. Later we will see Joseph still around at the time of the crucifixion and providing Jesus with his tomb.

The scenario that we shall follow therefore is that Jesus was truly human in the physical sense; but that His soul was the soul of God. His coming to earth was the means whereby God experienced the full pleasures and terrors of the world he had created.

4.5 The Essenes

In recent years considerable evidence has emerged that Jesus was involved with a particular sect known as the Essenes. Whether he was an actual member of the community whose documents have become known as the Dead Sea Scrolls is still a matter for speculation; but what is clear is that many of the thoughts and precepts which Jesus expounded and taught were drawn from material developed well before his birth. It seems highly likely therefore that he did indeed spend some time with the Essenes, studied the scriptures with them and absorbed much of their philosophy and outlook. It could well be that this was what he was doing mainly in his early manhood and that the phrase 'forty days and forty nights' was figurative speaking for several years and when Jesus retreated into the desert, he was in fact visiting the Essene community on the shores of the Dead Sea at Qumran.

Equally it seems likely that John the Baptist too was a member of the Essenes. Could his baptism by John have occurred much earlier than we are often led to believe, certainly the evidence of John the Gospel writer seems to indicate this and it was considerably later that the encounter in Bethany triggered a period of intense study and prayer with the Essenes and that he emerged to replace John when John was arrested?

The Essenes were a Jewish sect who had been established about 150 BC. They were described by several early writers including Pliny who refers to a single community based between Jericho and Engedi which is reasonably identified as Qumran near the Dead Sea.

Pliny Natural History Chapter V 17.4

To the west (of the Dead Sea) the Essenes have put the necessary distance between themselves and the insalubrious shore Below the Essenes was the town of Engada (Engedi).

He goes on

They are a people unique and admirable beyond all others in the whole world, without women and renouncing love entirely, without money.

Philo of Alexandria is quoted by Eusebius and refers to several communities scattered throughout Judea and other lands.

Eusebius 17:13 ff

The community is to be found in many parts of the world, for it is right that what is perfectly good should be shared by Greek and foreign lands. It is very strong in Egypt in each of the nomes and especially in the Alexandrian area. The best men in each region set out as colonists for a highly suitable spot, regarding it as the homeland of the Theraputae ......The whole period from dawn to dusk is given up to spiritual discipline. They read the sacred scriptures and study their ancestral wisdom philosphically.... Thus, they not only practice contemplation but also compose songs and hymns to God in all kinds of metres and melodies Philo does not specify these communities as Essene and Eusebius tends to interpret them as early Christian foundations. In a later section Eusebius lists the Essenes as one of the Jewish sects:

Eusebius 22.5

Hegesippus also names the sects that once existed among the Jews There were various groups in the Circumcision among the Children of Israel, all hostile to the tribe of Judah and the Christ. They were these – Essenes, Galileans, Homeopathists, Masbotheans, Samaritans, Sadducees and Pharisees.

Flavius Josephus describes the sect as comprising of 4000 members in Palestine.

Josephus from his "Antiquities of the Jews" 18, 18-22:

The Essenes like to teach that in all things one should rely on God. They also declare that souls are immortal They put their property in a common stock, and the rich man enjoys no more of his fortune than does the man with absolutely nothing. And there are more than 4000 men who behave in this way. In addition, they take no wives and acquire no slaves; in fact, they consider slavery an injustice.

He goes on to list them as one of the sects

Josephus from "The Jewish War" Book 2, Chapter 8

For there are three philosophic sects among the Jews. The followers of the first of whom are the Pharisees; of the second Saducees and the third sect, who pretends to severer disciplines are called Essenes. These last are Jews by birth and seem to have a greater affection for one another than the other sects have. These Essenes reject pleasures as an evil, but esteem continence and the conquest over our passions to be virtue They neglect wedlock, but choose out other person's children, while they are pliable and fit for learning and esteem them to be of their kindred and form them according to their own manners. They do not absolutely deny the fitness of marriage and the succession of mankind thereby continued; but they guard against the lascivious behaviour of women and are persuaded that none of them preserve their fidelity to one man.

There appears to have been two quite distinct groups; the monks who lived at Qumran who were celibate and who followed a very strict rule; and the 'associates' who lived with their families under the tutelage of a superior. They were concerned almost exclusively with religion and maintained themselves by following normal occupations but any money they earned and other possessions went to the superior and they received food and other things as they needed it.

The monks themselves did not marry, and indeed seem to have a disdain of women, however they were very keen to 'adopt' other people's children and mould them in their own image:

But let us return to what the Bible tells us.

4.6 The Temptations

Sometime after he has been baptised, Jesus retreats into the desert to contemplate his future ministry. He must have been sore tempted to not go ahead with his mission. Mark makes a passing reference to this.

Mark 1 12 - 13
[12] And immediately the Spirit driveth him into the wilderness.
[13] And he was there in the wilderness forty days, tempted of Satan; and was with the wild beasts; and the angels ministered unto him.

Matthew elaborates. The high mountain referred to is reputedly the Mount of Temptation just to the west of Jericho.:

Matthew 4 1 - 17
[1] Then was Jesus led up of the Spirit into the wilderness to be tempted of the devil.
[2] And when he had fasted forty days and forty nights, he was afterward an hungred.
[3] And when the tempter came to him, he said, If thou be the Son of God, command that these stones be made bread.
[4] But he answered and said, It is written, Man shall not live by bread alone, but by every word that proceedeth out of the mouth of God.
[5] Then the devil taketh him up into the holy city, and setteth him on a pinnacle of the temple,
[6] And saith unto him, If thou be the Son of God, cast thyself down: for it is written, He shall give his angels charge concerning thee: and in their hands they shall bear thee up, lest at any time thou dash thy foot against a stone.
[7] Jesus said unto him, It is written again, Thou shalt not tempt the Lord thy God.
[8] Again, the devil taketh him up into an exceeding high mountain, and sheweth him all the kingdoms of the world, and the glory of them;
[9] And saith unto him, All these things will I give thee, if thou wilt fall down and worship me.
[10] Then saith Jesus unto him, Get thee hence, Satan: for it is written, Thou shalt worship the Lord thy God, and him only shalt thou serve.
[11] Then the devil leaveth him, and, behold, angels came and ministered unto him.
[12] Now when Jesus had heard that John was cast into prison, he departed into Galilee;
[13] And leaving Nazareth, he came and dwelt in Capernaum, which is upon the sea coast, in the borders of Zabulon and Nephthalim:

[14] That it might be fulfilled which was spoken by Esaias the prophet, saying,

[15] The land of Zabulon, and the land of Nephthalim, by the way of the sea, beyond Jordan, Galilee of the Gentiles;

[16] The people which sat in darkness saw great light; and to them which sat in the region and shadow of death light is sprung up.

[17] From that time Jesus began to preach, and to say, Repent: for the kingdom of heaven is at hand.

Again, Luke tells a very similar account indicating a common source.

Luke 4 1 - 13

[1] And Jesus being full of the Holy Ghost returned from Jordan, and was led by the Spirit into the wilderness,

[2] Being forty days tempted of the devil. And in those days, he did eat nothing: and when they were ended, he afterward hungered.

[3] And the devil said unto him, If thou be the Son of God, command this stone that it be made bread.

[4] And Jesus answered him, saying, It is written, That man shall not live by bread alone, but by every word of God.

[5] And the devil, taking him up into an high mountain, shewed unto him all the kingdoms of the world in a moment of time.

[6] And the devil said unto him, All this power will I give thee, and the glory of them: for that is delivered unto me; and to whomsoever I will I give it.

[7] If thou therefore wilt worship me, all shall be thine.

[8] And Jesus answered and said unto him, Get thee behind me, Satan: for it is written, Thou shalt worship the Lord thy God, and him only shalt thou serve.

[9] And he brought him to Jerusalem, and set him on a pinnacle of the temple, and said unto him, If thou be the Son of God, cast thyself down from hence:

[10] For it is written, He shall give his angels charge over thee, to keep thee:

[11] And in their hands they shall bear thee up, lest at any time thou dash thy foot against a stone.

[12] And Jesus answering said unto him, It is said, Thou shalt not tempt the Lord thy God.

[13] And when the devil had ended all the temptation, he departed from him for a season.

One can interpret these temptations as being related to Jesus accepting the discipline of the Essene sect. He knows his mission but until these 'devils' have been conquered he knows he will not be up to it. However, he succeeds and at last Jesus is ready. His ministry is about to begin

Chapter 5 Mary of Magdala

5.1 Which Mary?

One of the great controversies of the early twenty first century revolves around the personality of Mary Magdalene. There are several Marys appearing in the New Testament, Mary of Magdala, Mary of Bethany, Mary the mother of James and John, Mary the wife of Cleopas, Mary the mother of John Mark and of course Mary the mother of Jesus. There are also several women who appear very close to Jesus and perform duties that only a wife might perform in Jewish society.

If Jesus were brought up in Jewish society, in the normal course of events he could expect to be married in his late teens or early twenties, long before his ministry begins. He is frequently referred to as a rabbi and was evidently well versed in the scriptures. In contemporary Jewish society he could not have been a rabbi unless married.

On the other hand, he is often associated with the Essene community at Qumran. This community is generally regarded as celibate but it had a very strict hierarchy with well defined criteria to advance from novice to full member. To reach the higher ranks they would have to have been at least thirty years of age. However, there were associate members who were married although women were not allowed into the heart of the community.

However, what seems much more likely is that Jesus was brought up in Alexandria, moved to Qumran in his late teens and then married and settled in Galilee where he worked as a carpenter.

5.2 Jesus' Marital Status

Jewish society set a very high value on family life. It was the means whereby the Jewish race perpetuated and protected itself. For a young man not to marry would be regarded as very odd behaviour indeed. But there is no mention of Jesus' marital state anywhere in the New Testament.

Either he was married, in which case some reference to his wife would certainly have been made, or he was not, in which case some explanation for this extraordinary state of affairs would have been offered.

The explanation may be that he was indeed married, and had a son who was seen as essential to the continuing authority of the church and therefore whose identity and even existence needed to be protected at all costs.

Jesus was very well versed in the scriptures. He had had a sound rabbinical training and was recruited by John the Baptist into a desert based movement which we may speculate was that of the Essenes at Qumran, near the Dead Sea. Excavations there have shown this to be a family settlement, not just a community of celibate monks. It is very significant that it is only in John's accounts (John 1.35 to 1.41) that we read of the recruitment and of the wedding (John 2.1 to 2.12). The other gospel writers ignore these matters.

5.3 Who was Jesus' Wife

There seems to be only one obvious candidate, Mary of Magdala, the sister of Martha. Sometimes she is identified in one way and sometimes in the other, but they never appear together. The closest link is at the anointing of Jesus with oil of Spikenard just before the Passion. John clearly identifies the woman as Mary the sister of Martha, Mark and Matthew refer to her only as a woman; but forecast she will become famous.

At the crucifixion it is Mary his mother and Mary of Magdala who are present according to John. Matthew has two Marys also, Mary of Magdala and Mary the mother of James and Joseph, plus a third woman whom Mark identifies as Salome. Luke refers simply to 'the women who had accompanied him from Galilee'.

Magdala is a town in Galilee near Tiberius. If he was indeed married surely his wife and mother would be there together with him at the end.

At the empty tomb it is Mary of Magdala who is first on the scene and to whom Jesus appears first and at the end Luke reports on Jesus' last walk with his disciples to Bethany where he promptly vanishes.

Time and time again during his ministry Jesus returns to Bethany and one gains the distinct impression that he regards it as the closest thing he has to a home.

We can speculate that Jesus was married almost immediately after he left Qumran for Galilee and that, as was the norm, the marriage was arranged between Joseph of Arimathea and Simon the Pharisee. Then they went to live in Magdala where Jesus earned his living as a carpenter and Mary acquired the soubriquet Mary of Magdala, a small village on the shores of the Sea of Galilee between Tiberius and Capernaum.

Luke introduces her as a woman whom Jesus had cured of infirmities.

Luke 8 1 - 3
[1] And it came to pass afterward, that he went throughout every city and village, preaching and shewing the glad tidings of the kingdom of God: and the twelve were with him,
[2] And certain women, which had been healed of evil spirits and infirmities, Mary called Magdalene, out of whom went seven devils,
[3] And Joanna the wife of Chuza Herod's steward, and Susanna, and many others, which ministered unto him of their substance.

Jesus is often referred to as 'Jesus of Nazareth' which people take to mean he lived in Nazareth; however, it is much more likely that we have a misinterpretation and the original read 'Jesus the Nazarene'

5.4 The Wedding at Cana
While he was in Galilee Jesus attended a wedding. It was obviously of someone very close because his mother seemed to be in charge. One might speculate that it was Jesus' own wedding and that several of his friends who later became disciples were also there.

John 2 1 - 11

[1] And the third day there was a marriage in Cana of Galilee; and the mother of Jesus was there:

[2] And both Jesus was called, and his disciples, to the marriage.

[3] And when they wanted wine, the mother of Jesus saith unto him, They have no wine.

[4] Jesus saith unto her, Woman, what have I to do with thee? mine hour is not yet come.

[5] His mother saith unto the servants, Whatsoever he saith unto you, do it.

[6] And there were set there six waterpots of stone, after the manner of the purifying of the Jews, containing two or three firkins apiece.

[7] Jesus saith unto them, Fill the waterpots with water. And they filled them up to the brim.

[8] And he saith unto them, Draw out now, and bear unto the governor of the feast. And they bare it.

[9] When the ruler of the feast had tasted the water that was made wine, and knew not whence it was: (but the servants which drew the water knew;) the governor of the feast called the bridegroom,

[10] And saith unto him, Every man at the beginning doth set forth good wine; and when men have well drunk, then that which is worse: but thou hast kept the good wine until now.

[11] This beginning of miracles did Jesus in Cana of Galilee, and manifested forth his glory; and his disciples believed on him.

5.5 Mary's Family

We will find out more about Mary's family as the story unfolds but in summary is seems that her father was Simon the leper sometimes referred to as Simon the Pharisee. Her sister was named Martha and her brothers were Judas and Lazarus.

Throughout the Gospels there are references to women who perform acts which it would be normal for a wife to perform. Luke tells of Mary ignoring the chores to be with Jesus

Luke 10 38 - 42

[38] Now it came to pass, as they went, that he entered into a certain village: and a certain woman named Martha received him into her house.

[39] And she had a sister called Mary, which also sat at Jesus' feet, and heard his word.

[40] But Martha was cumbered about much serving, and came to him, and said, Lord, dost thou not care that my sister hath left me to serve alone? bid her therefore that she help me.

[41] And Jesus answered and said unto her, Martha, Martha, thou art careful and troubled about many things:

[42] But one thing is needful: and Mary hath chosen that good part, which shall not be taken away from her.

There are other stories of women anointing Jesus with oil. Luke starts with a dinner given by one of the Pharisees. One can interpret this as Simon interviewing his potential son-in-law and Jesus' meeting Mary, his wife to be, for the first time.

Luke 7 36 - 50

[36] And one of the Pharisees desired him that he would eat with him. And he went into the Pharisee's house, and sat down to meat.

[37] And, behold, a woman in the city, which was a sinner, when she knew that Jesus sat at meat in the Pharisee's house, brought an alabaster box of ointment,

[38] And stood at his feet behind him weeping, and began to wash his feet with tears, and did wipe them with the hairs of her head, and kissed his feet, and anointed them with the ointment.

[39] Now when the Pharisee which had bidden him saw it, he spake within himself, saying, This man, if he were a prophet, would have known who and what manner of woman this is that toucheth him: for she is a sinner.

[40] And Jesus answering said unto him, Simon, I have somewhat to say unto thee. And he saith, Master, say on.

[41] There was a certain creditor which had two debtors: the one owed five hundred pence, and the other fifty.

[42] And when they had nothing to pay, he frankly forgave them both. Tell me therefore, which of them will love him most?

[43] Simon answered and said, I suppose that he, to whom he forgave most. And he said unto him, Thou hast rightly judged.

[44] And he turned to the woman, and said unto Simon, Seest thou this woman? I entered into thine house, thou gavest me no water for my feet: but she hath washed my feet with tears, and wiped them with the hairs of her head.

[45] Thou gavest me no kiss: but this woman since the time I came in hath not ceased to kiss my feet.

[46] My head with oil thou didst not anoint: but this woman hath anointed my feet with ointment.

[47] Wherefore I say unto thee, Her sins, which are many, are forgiven; for she loved much: but to whom little is forgiven, the same loveth little.

[48] And he said unto her, Thy sins are forgiven.

[49] And they that sat at meat with him began to say within themselves, Who is this that forgiveth sins also?

[50] And he said to the woman, Thy faith hath saved thee; go in peace.

Mark tells a slightly different version. He places it in Bethany and also refers to Simon, but as a leper not a Pharisee.

Mark 14 3 - 9

[3] And being in Bethany in the house of Simon the leper, as he sat at meat, there came a woman having an alabaster box of ointment of spikenard very precious; and she brake the box, and poured it on his head.

[4] And there were some that had indignation within themselves, and said, Why was this waste of the ointment made?

[5] For it might have been sold for more than three hundred pence, and have been given to the poor. And they murmured against her.

[6] And Jesus said, Let her alone; why trouble ye her? she hath wrought a good work on me.

[7] For ye have the poor with you always, and whensoever ye will ye may do them good: but me ye have not always.

[8] She hath done what she could: she is come aforehand to anoint my body to the burying.

[9] Verily I say unto you, Wheresoever this gospel shall be preached throughout the whole world, this also that she hath done shall be spoken of for a memorial of her.

John goes further and identifies the woman as Mary and Simon as the father of Judas Iscariot.

John 12 1 - 8

[1] Then Jesus six days before the passover came to Bethany, where Lazarus was which had been dead, whom he raised from the dead.

[2] There they made him a supper; and Martha served: but Lazarus was one of them that sat at the table with him.

[3] Then took Mary a pound of ointment of spikenard, very costly, and anointed the feet of Jesus, and wiped his feet with her hair: and the house was filled with the odour of the ointment.

[4] Then saith one of his disciples, Judas Iscariot, Simon's son, which should betray him,

[5] Why was not this ointment sold for three hundred pence, and given to the poor?

[6] This he said, not that he cared for the poor; but because he was a thief, and had the bag, and bare what was put therein.

[7] Then said Jesus, Let her alone: against the day of my burying hath she kept this.

[8] For the poor always ye have with you; but me ye have not always.

There are many other references to Jesus visiting Bethany whilst in Judea. It would seem that this was his home. (see section 9.7)

5.6 John Mark

The final part of the jigsaw is found in Acts. Herod is persecuting Christians and had already beheaded James the brother of John. Peter had been arrested but makes a miraculous escape from prison and goes immediately to the house of Mary, mother of John Mark.

Acts 12 11 - 17

[11] And when Peter was come to himself, he said, Now I know of a surety, that the Lord hath sent his angel, and hath delivered me out of the hand of Herod, and from all the expectation of the people of the Jews.

[12] And when he had considered the thing, he came to the house of Mary the mother of John, whose surname was Mark; where many were gathered together praying.

[13] And as Peter knocked at the door of the gate, a damsel came to hearken, named Rhoda.

[14] And when she knew Peter's voice, she opened not the gate for gladness, but ran in, and told how Peter stood before the gate.

[15] And they said unto her, Thou art mad. But she constantly affirmed that it was even so. Then said they, It is his angel.

[16] But Peter continued knocking: and when they had opened the door, and saw him, they were astonished.

[17] But he, beckoning unto them with the hand to hold their peace, declared unto them how the Lord had brought him out of the prison. And he said, Go shew these things unto James, and to the brethren. And he departed, and went into another place.

Who was John Mark? - His story and an alternative interpretation of the story of the Magi can be found in Chapter 21.

5.7 The Cult of Mary

In the first millennium, references to Mary were almost always about Mary Magdalene and were especially prevalent in the south of France, whither she is reputed to have fled. The first historian of the church, Eusebius, writing around 315 AD makes no references to the Magdalene and but four fleeting references to the other Mary, the mother of Jesus

Her special role as a virgin and 'Mother of God' was enshrined at the Council of Chalcedon in 451 AD after having been incorporated into the creeds at earlier Councils. But these were theological inferences. If Jesus were indeed God then his birth must have been something special and the woman who played the central role must also be special. It was not based upon any knowledge.

The secret of the lineage was kept and although many hints were dropped and the kings of the Merovingian line in France claimed a special place among the crowned heads of Europe nothing was said overtly. However the cult of the Magdalene was gathering force and threatening to usurp the power of Rome and the papacy.

The official church launched a massive campaign around 1100 to counter this, focusing on the person of Mary the mother of God. All over Christendom churches were re-dedicated to the Virgin Mary, especially in England which became known as Mary's dowry.

To me this came close to home as my own parish church was so rededicated after rebuilding in 1150 following destruction during the Anarchy.

At the same time a counter force was coming into vogue, the cult of the Holy Grail. The quest for the Holy Grail was supposedly linked with Arthur in 6th century England, but most of the romances actually surfaced around 1100 in France. It is but a slight corruption to read 'Sainte Graal' as it was called in French rather as 'Sang Real' or royal blood, thus making the search for the holy grail, not for a chalice, but for a legitimacy of kingship. The intriguing questions posed by research into the Templars and the Priory of Zion have yet to be answered sensibly, but the theory makes a lot more sense of the New Testament stories than a merely literal reading does.

PART 2
THE PREACHER

In Part 2 we look at Jesus' Mission and see what the gospellers say about his extraordinary career as a preacher, healer and miracle worker.

In general, we can take it for granted that most of what was recorded did indeed reflect what Jesus said and did prior to the great events of the Passion. However, there is considerable discrepancy in that the proto-gospeller records it as all happening in Galilee, whereas John notes Jesus as a considerable traveller who also visited Samaria and Judea over the three years of his ministry.

Chapter 6 – Jesus' Mission

6.1 Dilemmas

If we accept the core Christian doctrine that Jesus was 'The Son of God', but also that he was truly human, we have a dilemma to resolve. At some point in his life Jesus must have come to the realisation that he was someone special and that he had a mission to accomplish. If however he was aware of this from birth and acquired all knowledge as a birthright, then he could not have been truly human, experiencing the full gamut of human emotions and frustrations. We will therefore take the view that Jesus acquired his knowledge from a process of education and that his sense of mission developed from around the age of twelve. It would be another eighteen years or so before he felt ready to embark on this mission and begin his ministry.

The Gospellers present quite different views of Jesus' Ministry. From the Synoptics (Matthew, Mark and Luke) one gets the impression that almost all of the Ministry took place in Galilee and that he went to Jerusalem only for the last eight days. John on the other hand starts the ministry in Jerusalem and has Jesus going to and from between Judea and Galilee on several occasions.

> During his ministry Jesus seems to be playing three quite different roles:
>
> A teacher trying to communicate who God was and what he expected of mankind.
>
> A healer curing a variety of ailments and apparent miracle worker. Someone challenging the accepted order.

While many non-Jews became his Disciples he was dealing mostly with the Jews in Palestine. This was a matter that was to be the subject of intense dispute in the early years. Did one have to be, or become a Jew to be a Christian?

6.2 The Palestinian Cauldron

We have to remember that Palestine at this time was not a bucolic rural society with simple farmers and fishermen following their vocations and small towns with their synagogues and priestly groups engaged in peaceful theological discussions. Rather it was a land occupied by a brutal alien regime for whom Palestine was merely one more province in a huge empire based upon trade and wealth. It was seething with discontent with numerous factions and parties each with their own particular issue and each plotting the overthrow of the Romans with little or no idea as to how this was to be accomplished. The country was split down the middle between those whose main aim was to get along with the Romans and make the best of a bad job for a quiet life and those who supported these factions.

The issue was principally one of land ownership. The Romans saw land as merely another commodity which could be owned and bought and sold. The Jewish zealots on the other hand saw Palestine as a land given to the people as a whole by God and for the use of the Jews only. This was the issue that was at the heart of the return from Babylon some 500 years previously and which would re-emerge as the crucial issue between Israelis and Palestinians in the late twentieth Century. It became a crucial issue in feudal times in England as the prevailing view was that land was created and 'owned' by God and could only be 'held' by men. The King held all his realm for God; but did the church hold land from the King or from the Pope? And who therefore could appoint bishops to hold the church's land within England.

The Zealots were looking for their Messiah, foretold in the scriptures and particularly in Isaiah. The word Messiah simply means 'the annointed one' translated into 'Christ' in Greek and 'king' in modern English. They were looking for a king who would be quite different from the Herods who were content to get along with the Romans. Their Messiah would be a war leader who would drive the Romans out of Palestine for good. This was what John the Baptist was foretelling.

The Gospels give a somewhat misleading view of Jewish religious observances. For example, there are several hints that Jesus' family went up to Jerusalem every year for the Passover and other festivals and the impression is given that this was a general Jewish practice but the idea that the whole Jewish population travelled up to Jerusalem each year is clearly absurd. It could have been the case that it was expected that everyone makes at least one visit in a lifetime, similar to the Moslem Hajj. This is what seems to be happening when Jesus was brought to the Temple around the age of twelve when he was celebrating his Bar-Mitzva.

However, what seems much more likely is that it was the population of Jerusalem and around that went up to the Temple for the major festivals and that Jesus had friends and family in the area.

Onto this stage strode Jesus.

6.3 The Order of Events

There are three distinct phases to Jesus' preparation for his ministry. There was his baptism and identification by John, his time in the desert and the gathering of his band of disciples. It would seem most likely that Jesus became involved with the Essenes at a very early age and that John was probably also a member of the same group.

We will take the order of events as follows:

Jesus leaves Alexandria to join the Essene community in the desert at Qumran as a young man aged around sixteen.
Jesus leaves the Qumran community and moves to Galilee
Jesus marries at age eighteen or thereabouts and earns his living as a carpenter in Nazareth
John leaves the Essene community and begins to preach of the coming Messiah
Jesus aged around thirty meets with John who identifies and baptizes him.
Jesus begins collecting together his disciples in readiness for his mission.
Jesus returns to Galilee to settle his family business.
Jesus goes back to the desert to do his final preparations.
Jesus emerges as a preacher in Galilee.

6.4 Apostles and Disciples

It would seem that many of the disciples were friends and acquaintances of Jesus from his boyhood and early manhood. Thus, it is not surprising that they were noted as being among the guests at the wedding in Cana and had realised from way back that Jesus was something special.

We need to make a distinction between Disciple and Apostle. A Disciple is essentially a follower of a teacher or religious leader whereas an Apostle is someone who is especially commissioned by the leader to act as his substitute.

Jesus had many Disciples, many of them women, but he commissioned twelve to be his Apostles although it could be argued that at one time, he had no less than seventy-two Apostles.

Jesus continued recruiting his disciples but selected twelve particular ones to be his Apostles. To these he gave some limited powers to 'cast out devils'. The number twelve seems to relate to the twelve tribes of Israel.

6.5 The Twelve Apostles

The Apostles are named in each of the three synoptic Gospels: -

Matthew 10 1 - 4
[1] And when he had called unto him his twelve disciples, he gave them power against unclean spirits, to cast them out, and to heal all manner of sickness and all manner of disease.
[2] Now the names of the twelve apostles are these; The first, Simon, who is called Peter, and Andrew his brother; James the son of Zebedee, and John his brother;
[3] Philip, and Bartholomew; Thomas, and Matthew the publican; James the son of Alphaeus, and Lebbaeus, whose surname was Thaddaeus;
[4] Simon the Canaanite, and Judas Iscariot, who also betrayed him.

Mark 3 14 - 21
[14] And he ordained twelve, that they should be with him, and that he might send them forth to preach,
[15] And to have power to heal sicknesses, and to cast out devils:
[16] And Simon he surnamed Peter;
[17] And James the son of Zebedee, and John the brother of James; and he surnamed them Boanerges, which is, The sons of thunder:
[18] And Andrew, and Philip, and Bartholomew, and Matthew, and Thomas, and James the son of Alphaeus, and Thaddaeus, and Simon the Canaanite,
[19] And Judas Iscariot, which also betrayed him: and they went into an house.
[20] And the multitude cometh together again, so that they could not so much as eat bread.

[21] And when his friends heard of it, they went out to lay hold on him: for they said, He is beside himself.

Luke 6 13 – 16

[13] And when it was day, he called unto him his disciples: and of them he chose twelve, whom also he named apostles;

[14] Simon, (whom he also named Peter,) and Andrew his brother, James and John, Philip and Bartholomew,

[15] Matthew and Thomas, James the son of Alphaeus, and Simon called Zelotes,

[16] And Judas the brother of James, and Judas Iscariot, which also was the traitor.

Simon Peter

After Jesus' baptism John the Baptist and Jesus' paths did not cross for some time. But on two successive days, John spots Jesus and sends two of his disciples to persuade him to join his (John's) sect. What happened however was the reverse of what John had expected. Jesus decided to form his own group and Andrew was persuaded to become his first disciple and switch allegiance from John

John 1 40 - 42

[40] One of the two which heard John speak, and followed him, was Andrew, Simon Peter's brother.

[41] He first findeth his own brother Simon, and saith unto him, we have found the Messias, which is, being interpreted, the Christ.

[42] And he brought him to Jesus. And when Jesus beheld him, he said, thou art Simon the son of Jona: thou shalt be called Cephas, which is by interpretation, A stone.

Matthew records the meeting with Simon and Andrew in a very different light but John's version is much more convincing. We may treat Matthew's version therefore as simply trying to explain how Jesus came to acquire disciples without being actually aware of the real facts.

Matthew 4 18 - 19

[18] And Jesus, walking by the sea of Galilee, saw two brethren, Simon called Peter, and Andrew his brother, casting a net into the sea: for they were fishers.

[19] And he saith unto them, follow me, and I will make you fishers of men.

Mark's version is similar to Matthew's.

Mark 1 14 - 18

[14] Now after that John was put in prison, Jesus came into Galilee, preaching the gospel of the kingdom of God,

[15] And saying, The time is fulfilled, and the kingdom of God is at hand: repent ye, and believe the gospel.

[16] Now as he walked by the sea of Galilee, he saw Simon and Andrew his brother casting a net into the sea: for they were fishers.

[17] And Jesus said unto them, Come ye after me, and I will make you to become fishers of men.

[18] And straightway they forsook their nets, and followed him.

Andrew

Andrew had originally been a disciple of John the Baptist but not only moved his allegiance to Jesus but brought his brother Simon along too. See above.

James the Great and John

James and his brother John were also fishermen and sons of Zebedee.

Matthew 4 20 - 22

[20] And they straightway left their nets, and followed him.

[21] And going on from thence, he saw other two brethren, James the son of Zebedee, and John his brother, in a ship with Zebedee their father, mending their nets; and he called them.

[22] And they immediately left the ship and their father, and followed him.

Mark 1 19 - 20

19: And when he had gone a little further thence, he saw James the son of Zebedee, and John his brother, who also were in the ship mending their nets.

20: And straightway he called them: and they left their father Zebedee in the ship with the hired servants, and went after him.

Philip

Before he could embark on the period of study required to join the movement, Jesus had family matters to attend to, but before he set off for home he called upon Philip to go with him:

John 1 43 - 44

[43] The day following Jesus would go forth into Galilee, and findeth Philip, and saith unto him, Follow me.

[44] Now Philip was of Bethsaida, the city of Andrew and Peter.

Nathanael

Nathanael is also named as Bartholomew.

John 1 45 - 51

[45] Philip findeth Nathanael, and saith unto him, We have found him, of whom Moses in the law, and the prophets, did write, Jesus of Nazareth, the son of Joseph.

[46] And Nathanael said unto him, Can there any good thing come out of Nazareth? Philip saith unto him, Come and see.

[47] Jesus saw Nathanael coming to him, and saith of him, Behold an Israelite indeed, in whom is no guile!

[48] Nathanael saith unto him, Whence knowest thou me? Jesus answered and said unto him, Before that Philip called thee, when thou wast under the fig tree, I saw thee.

[49] Nathanael answered and saith unto him, Rabbi, thou art the Son of God; thou art the King of Israel.

[50] Jesus answered and said unto him, Because I said unto thee, I saw thee under the fig tree, believest thou? thou shalt see greater things than these.

[51] And he saith unto him, Verily, verily, I say unto you, Hereafter ye shall see heaven open, and the angels of God ascending and descending upon the Son of man.

Thomas

Thomas was also known as Didymus implying he was a twin, He comes into prominence later when he doubts the Resurrection and acquires the soubriquet 'Doubting'.

Matthew

Mark reports the recruiting of Matthew to his followers.

Mark 2 13 - 14

[13] And he went forth again by the sea side; and all the multitude resorted unto him, and he taught them.

[14] And as he passed by, he saw Levi the son of Alphaeus sitting at the receipt of custom, and said unto him, Follow me. And he arose and followed him.

Tax collectors were generally hated as being agents of Rome and again Jesus had to rebuff the criticisms. *See Matthew's version in section 7.15.*

Mark 2 15 - 17

[15] And it came to pass, that, as Jesus sat at meat in his house, many publicans and sinners sat also together with Jesus and his disciples: for there were many, and they followed him.

[16] And when the scribes and Pharisees saw him eat with publicans and sinners, they said unto his disciples, How is it that he eateth and drinketh with publicans and sinners?

[17] When Jesus heard it, he saith unto them, They that are whole have no need of the physician, but they that are sick: I came not to call the righteous, but sinners to repentance.

James the Less

The other James was the son of Alphaeus.

Thaddeus

Thaddeus is alternatively known as Judas or just Jude

Simon the Zealot

Simon was a Canaanite

Judas Iscariot

The term 'Judas' has come to mean someone who betrays his friends and this is how Judas Iscariot is portrayed in the Gospels. But as we shall see later in Chapter 15 Judas seems to have been Jesus' brother-in-law and did what Jesus had asked him to do.

We have recorded what the gospellers said about the recruitment of apostles but as we shall see later it was not always accurate. It also seems that most of them were not strangers to Jesus but men with whom he had been friends with in the past.

6.6 The Apostles' Mission

Jesus had returned to Galilee from Jerusalem and had been preaching at Capernaum. He needed to cover much more ground than he could by himself so he sent out his apostles as his deputies.

Mark 6 1 - 13

[1] And he went out from thence, and came into his own country; and his disciples follow him.

[2] And when the sabbath day was come, he began to teach in the synagogue: and many hearing him were astonished, saying, From whence hath this man these things? and what wisdom is this which is given unto him, that even such mighty works are wrought by his hands?

[3] Is not this the carpenter, the son of Mary, the brother of James, and Joses, and of Juda, and Simon? and are not his sisters here with us? And they were offended at him.

[4] But Jesus said unto them, A prophet is not without honour, but in his own country, and among his own kin, and in his own house.

[5] And he could there do no mighty work, save that he laid his hands upon a few sick folk, and healed them.

[6] And he marvelled because of their unbelief. And he went round about the villages, teaching.

[7] And he called unto him the twelve, and began to send them forth by two and two; and gave them power over unclean spirits;

[8] And commanded them that they should take nothing for their journey, save a staff only; no scrip, no bread, no money in their purse:

[9] But be shod with sandals; and not put on two coats.

[10] And he said unto them, In what place soever ye enter into an house, there abide till ye depart from that place.

[11] And whosoever shall not receive you, nor hear you, when ye depart thence, shake off the dust under your feet for a testimony against them. Verily I say unto you, It shall be more tolerable for Sodom and Gomorrha in the day of judgment, than for that city.

[12] And they went out, and preached that men should repent.

[13] And they cast out many devils, and anointed with oil many that were sick, and healed them.

6.7 Going to Jerusalem

Jesus has recruited his Apostles and set them on their first mission, travelling, probably in ones and twos, around the country but; following St John' version, Jesus is about to start his mission in Jerusalem.

Jesus' mission was to bring a new understanding of the relationship between mankind and God. He rejected the concept that people had to live by a strict code of laws enforced by a priesthood in favour of a very simple precept 'Love God and your neighbour as yourself'.

He pointed out that if you followed Him and obeyed these very simple rules then you would do good works and receive your rewards in heaven. Regrettably religious leaders are still inclined to tell people what to do in order to go to heaven or gain some benefit or other.

The Prophets had been forecasting a Messiah who was going to lead the Jewish people out of domination by Romans or any other alien power. He was envisaged as a war leader who would become a king. Jesus had other ideas however and his revolutionary view of life would bring him into conflict with both the Roman occupiers and the established priesthood.

Chapter 7 Jesus' Ministry

Jesus' ministry lasted about three years during which time he travelled all over Palestine engaged mainly in four activities:

> Preaching and Teaching Healing
>
> Doing Miracles
>
> Disputing with Pharisees and Saducees

We will follow the story as told by John but we will not include the text of all the parables and the texts relating to healing, miracles and disputation which will be dealt with in the next three chapters.

We pick up the story after Jesus has selected his twelve Apostles and sent them on their first mission and will take it to just before the final journey to Jerusalem which presaged the Passion and Crucifixion. Where the other Gospellers have their version of the same events, we will include it and also add some of the events covered by them which do not appear in John. It is also difficult to reconcile the idea that the Apostles were operating independently and with Jesus all the time. Perhaps they met up just from time to time.

What is also puzzling is that in his account of Jesus' ministry, John recounts detailed conversations between Jesus and third parties when there was no-one around to record these conversations.

In this chapter we will deal with the occasional visits to Jerusalem which seem unconnected to others. In chapter 12 we see Jesus making a major visit to Jerusalem getting into disputes around the Feast of Tabernacles This occurs around late September to mid-October and cannot be the same time as Passover which takes place in Spring. Then chapter 13 picks up the story just before Passover and the start of the final debates followed by Palm Sunday in Chapter 14.

The four intermediate chapters will deal with Jesus' ministry. First as a healer (chapter 8) then a miracle worker (chapter 9), then debating issues in Galilee (chapter 10) and finally communicating his message through parables (chapter 11).

7.1 Business in Galilee

Before he went up to Jerusalem to begin his ministry he had some business in Galilee to attend to.

John 2 11 - 12
[11] This beginning of miracles did Jesus in Cana of Galilee, and manifested forth his glory; and his disciples believed on him.
[12] After this he went down to Capernaum, he, and his mother, and his brethren, and his disciples: and they continued there not many days.

7.2 The Merchants and Money Lenders

His first encounter in Jerusalem was with the money lenders: John puts this as his first visit whereas the other gospellers have it at the start of Holy Week.

John 2 13 - 16
[13] And the Jews' passover was at hand, and Jesus went up to Jerusalem,
[14] And found in the temple those that sold oxen and sheep and doves, and the changers of money sitting:
[15] And when he had made a scourge of small cords, he drove them all out of the temple, and the sheep, and the oxen; and poured out the changers' money, and overthrew the tables;
[16] And said unto them that sold doves, Take these things hence; make not my Father's house an house of merchandise.

Mark included this within the run up to Holy Week.

Mark 11 15 - 19
[15] And they come to Jerusalem: and Jesus went into the temple, and began to cast out them that sold and bought in the temple, and overthrew the tables of the moneychangers, and the seats of them that sold doves;
[16] And would not suffer that any man should carry any vessel through the temple.

[17] And he taught, saying unto them, Is it not written, My house shall be called of all nations the house of prayer? but ye have made it a den of thieves.

[18] And the scribes and chief priests heard it, and sought how they might destroy him: for they feared him, because all the people was astonished at his doctrine.

[19] And when even was come, he went out of the city.

Matthew also gives it a mention

Matthew 21 12 - 13

[12] And Jesus went into the temple of God, and cast out all them that sold and bought in the temple, and overthrew the tables of the moneychangers, and the seats of them that sold doves,

[13] And said unto them, It is written, My house shall be called the house of prayer; but ye have made it a den of thieves.

As does Luke

Luke 19 45 - 46

[45] And he went into the temple, and began to cast out them that sold therein, and them that bought;

[46] Saying unto them, It is written, My house is the house of prayer: but ye have made it a den of thieves.

7.3 Rasing the Temple

Jesus justified his actions but it was not until after his death that the Apostles realised the significance.

John 2 17 - 25

[11] This beginning of miracles did Jesus in Cana of Galilee, and manifested forth his glory; and his disciples believed on him.

[12] After this he went down to Capernaum, he, and his mother, and his brethren, and his disciples: and they continued there not many days.

[13] And the Jews' passover was at hand, and Jesus went up to Jerusalem,

[14] And found in the temple those that sold oxen and sheep and doves, and the changers of money sitting:

[15] And when he had made a scourge of small cords, he drove them all out of the temple, and the sheep, and the oxen; and poured out the changers' money, and overthrew the tables;

[16] And said unto them that sold doves, Take these things hence; make not my Father's house an house of merchandise.

[17] And his disciples remembered that it was written, The zeal of thine house hath eaten me up.

[18] Then answered the Jews and said unto him, What sign shewest thou unto us, seeing that thou doest these things?

[19] Jesus answered and said unto them, Destroy this temple, and in three days I will raise it up.

[20] Then said the Jews, Forty and six years was this temple in building, and wilt thou rear it up in three days?

[21] But he spake of the temple of his body.

[22] When therefore he was risen from the dead, his disciples remembered that he had said this unto them; and they believed the scripture, and the word which Jesus had said.

[23] Now when he was in Jerusalem at the passover, in the feast day, many believed in his name, when they saw the miracles which he did.

[24] But Jesus did not commit himself unto them, because he knew all men,

[25] And needed not that any should testify of man: for he knew what was in man.

7.4 Nicodemus

He immediately aroused the interest of the Jewish Council and one of them, a Pharisee called Nicodemus, came to see him.

John 3 1 - 21

[1] There was a man of the Pharisees, named Nicodemus, a ruler of the Jews:

[2] The same came to Jesus by night, and said unto him, Rabbi, we know that thou art a teacher come from God: for no man can do these miracles that thou does, except God be with him.

[3] Jesus answered and said unto him, Verily, verily, I say unto thee, Except a man be born again, he cannot see the kingdom of God.

[4] Nicodemus saith unto him, How can a man be born when he is old? can he enter the second time into his mother's womb, and be born?

[5] Jesus answered, Verily, verily, I say unto thee, Except a man be born of water and of the Spirit, he cannot enter into the kingdom of God.

[6] That which is born of the flesh is flesh; and that which is born of the Spirit is spirit.

[7] Marvel not that I said unto thee, Ye must be born again.

[8] The wind bloweth where it listeth, and thou hearest the sound thereof, but canst not tell whence it cometh, and whither it goeth: so is every one that is born of the Spirit.

[9] Nicodemus answered and said unto him, How can these things be?

[10] Jesus answered and said unto him, Art thou a master of Israel, and knowest not these things?

[11] Verily, verily, I say unto thee, We speak that we do know, and testify that we have seen; and ye receive not our witness.

[12] If I have told you earthly things, and ye believe not, how shall ye believe, if I tell you of heavenly things?

[13] And no man hath ascended up to heaven, but he that came down from heaven, even the Son of man which is in heaven.

[14] And as Moses lifted up the serpent in the wilderness, even so must the Son of man be lifted up:

[15] That whosoever believeth in him should not perish, but have eternal life.

[16] For God so loved the world, that he gave his only begotten Son, that whosoever believeth in him should not perish, but have everlasting life.

[17] For God sent not his Son into the world to condemn the world; but that the world through him might be saved.

[18] He that believeth on him is not condemned: but he that believeth not is condemned already, because he hath not believed in the name of the only begotten Son of God.

[19] And this is the condemnation, that light is come into the world, and men loved darkness rather than light, because their deeds were evil.

[20] For every one that doeth evil hateth the light, neither cometh to the light, lest his deeds should be reproved.

[21] But he that doeth truth cometh to the light, that his deeds may be made manifest, that they are wrought in God.

7.5 John the Baptist

After his encounter with Nicodemus Jesus and his disciples move out of Jerusalem into the Judean countryside. Here for a while he seems to be in competition with John the Baptist for converts. (see section 3.4) Jesus learns that the Pharisees are concerned about his successes, although it is his disciples who are doing the baptising, not Jesus. However Jesus senses that Judea is not yet ready for his message so decides to return to Galilee.

John 3.22 - to 4.3

[22] After these things came Jesus and his disciples into the land of Judaea; and there he tarried with them, and baptized.

[23] And John also was baptizing in Aenon near to Salim, because there was much water there: and they came, and were baptized.

[24] For John was not yet cast into prison.

[25] Then there arose a question between some of John's disciples and the Jews about purifying.

[26] And they came unto John, and said unto him, Rabbi, he that was with thee beyond Jordan, to whom thou barest witness, behold, the same baptizeth, and all men come to him.

[27] John answered and said, A man can receive nothing, except it be given him from heaven.

[28] Ye yourselves bear me witness, that I said, I am not the Christ, but that I am sent before him.

[29] He that hath the bride is the bridegroom: but the friend of the bridegroom, which standeth and heareth him, rejoiceth greatly because of the bridegroom's voice: this my joy therefore is fulfilled.

[30] He must increase, but I must decrease.

[31] He that cometh from above is above all: he that is of the earth is earthly, and speaketh of the earth: he that cometh from heaven is above all.

[32] And what he hath seen and heard, that he testifieth; and no man receiveth his testimony.

[33] He that hath received his testimony hath set to his seal that God is true.

[34] For he whom God hath sent speaketh the words of God: for God giveth not the Spirit by measure unto him.

[35] The Father loveth the Son, and hath given all things into his hand.

[36] He that believeth on the Son hath everlasting life: and he that believeth not the Son shall not see life; but the wrath of God abideth on him.

[1] When therefore the Lord knew how the Pharisees had heard that Jesus made and baptized more disciples than John,

[2] (Though Jesus himself baptized not, but his disciples,)

[3] He left Judaea, and departed again into Galilee.

7.6 Samaria

En route back to Galilee Jesus pauses at Sychar in Samaria and talks to a woman at a well.

John 4 4 - 26

[4] And he must needs go through Samaria.

[5] Then cometh he to a city of Samaria, which is called Sychar, near to the parcel of ground that Jacob gave to his son Joseph.

[6] Now Jacob's well was there. Jesus therefore, being wearied with his journey, sat thus on the well: and it was about the sixth hour.

[7] There cometh a woman of Samaria to draw water: Jesus saith unto her, Give me to drink.

[8] (For his disciples were gone away unto the city to buy meat.)

[9] Then saith the woman of Samaria unto him, How is it that thou, being a Jew, askest drink of me, which am a woman of Samaria? for the Jews have no dealings with the Samaritans.

[10] Jesus answered and said unto her, If thou knewest the gift of God, and who it is that saith to thee, Give me to drink; thou wouldest have asked of him, and he would have given thee living water.

[11] The woman saith unto him, Sir, thou hast nothing to draw with, and the well is deep: from whence then hast thou that living water?

[12] Art thou greater than our father Jacob, which gave us the well, and drank thereof himself, and his children, and his cattle?

[13] Jesus answered and said unto her, whosoever drinketh of this water shall thirst again:

[14] But whosoever drinketh of the water that I shall give him shall never thirst; but the water that I shall give him shall be in him a well of water springing up into everlasting life.

[15] The woman saith unto him, Sir, give me this water, that I thirst not, neither come hither to draw.

[16] Jesus saith unto her, Go, call thy husband, and come hither.

[17] The woman answered and said, I have no husband. Jesus said unto her, Thou hast well said, I have no husband:

[18] For thou hast had five husbands; and he whom thou now hast is not thy husband: in that saidst thou truly.

[19] The woman saith unto him, Sir, I perceive that thou art a prophet.

[20] Our fathers worshipped in this mountain; and ye say, that in Jerusalem is the place where men ought to worship.

[21] Jesus saith unto her, Woman, believe me, the hour cometh, when ye shall neither in this mountain, nor yet at Jerusalem, worship the Father.

[22] Ye worship ye know not what: we know what we worship: for salvation is of the Jews.

[23] But the hour cometh, and now is, when the true worshippers shall worship the Father in spirit and in truth: for the Father seeketh such to worship him.

[24] God is a Spirit: and they that worship him must worship him in spirit and in truth.

[25] The woman saith unto him, I know that Messias cometh, which is called Christ: when he is come, he will tell us all things.

[26] Jesus saith unto her, I that speak unto thee am he.

The disciples returned at this point and wondered what he was up to.

John 4 27 - 38

[27] And upon this came his disciples, and marvelled that he talked with the woman: yet no man said, What seekest thou? or, Why talkest thou with her?
[28] The woman then left her waterpot, and went her way into the city, and saith to the men,
[29] Come, see a man, which told me all things that ever I did: is not this the Christ?
[30] Then they went out of the city, and came unto him.
[31] In the mean while his disciples prayed him, saying, Master, eat.
[32] But he said unto them, I have meat to eat that ye know not of.
[33] Therefore said the disciples one to another, Hath any man brought him ought to eat?
[34] Jesus saith unto them, My meat is to do the will of him that sent me, and to finish his work.
[35] Say not ye, There are yet four months, and then cometh harvest? behold, I say unto you, Lift up your eyes, and look on the fields; for they are white already to harvest.
[36] And he that reapeth receiveth wages, and gathereth fruit unto life eternal: that both he that soweth and he that reapeth may rejoice together.
[37] And herein is that saying true, One soweth, and another reapeth.
[38] I sent you to reap that whereon ye bestowed no labour: other men laboured, and ye are entered into their labours.

The Samaritans would have liked Jesus to stay longer

John 4 39 - 44

[39] And many of the Samaritans of that city believed on him for the saying of the woman, which testified, He told me all that ever I did.
[40] So when the Samaritans were come unto him, they besought him that he would tarry with them: and he abode there two days.
[41] And many more believed because of his own word;
[42] And said unto the woman, Now we believe, not because of thy saying: for we have heard him ourselves, and know that this is indeed the Christ, the Saviour of the world.
[43] Now after two days he departed thence, and went into Galilee.
[44] For Jesus himself testified, that a prophet hath no honour in his own country.

7.7 Galilee - Nobleman's Son

Jesus gets back to Galilee and heals the nobleman's son. *For the healing story see section 8.3*

John 4 45 - 46
[45] Then when he was come into Galilee, the Galilaeans received him, having seen all the things that he did at Jerusalem at the feast: for they also went unto the feast.
[46] So Jesus came again into Cana of Galilee, where he made the water wine. And there was a certain nobleman, whose son was sick at Capernaum.

Then he tours Galilee and is pursued by huge crowds who come from all parts of the Roman Province of Syria.

7.8 Jerusalem - Pool at Bethesda

Jesus goes back to Jerusalem and heals a man at the Pool of Bethesda. This raises another problem because he told the man to take up his bed and walk and it was the Sabbath so the authorities got upset.

See section 8.4 for the miracle and section 10.5 for the dispute about working on Sabbath

7.9 The Sermon on the Mount

On his return from Jerusalem the crowds are still there waiting for him and so he climbs a hill and delivers his Sermon on the Mount (see Matthew 5.1 to 7.29). All the time he is emphasising his message, seeking to change people's hearts and minds rather than control their behaviour.

Matthew records further incidents of healing (see chapter 8): cleansing a leper; another version of the healing of the centurion's son and Peter's Mother-in-law.

7.10 Galilee - Feeding the Five thousand

After the Sermon Jesus performs another miracle and feeds the crowd with bread and fish. (See chapter 9)

The crowds were so taken with Jesus that they wanted to make him a king.

John 6 14 - 15

[14] Then those men, when they had seen the miracle that Jesus
did, said, This is of a truth that prophet that should come into the world.
[15] When Jesus therefore perceived that they would come and take him by
force, to make him a king, he departed again into a mountain himself alone.

According to John Jesus has retired to a mountain to pray alone, but
Matthew has Jesus boarding the boat with the disciples and rebuking the
winds rather than walking on water: -

7.11 Stilling the Storm

Jesus was on the Tiberius side of the lake and the crowds were getting too
big for him so he decides to cross over to the other side:

Matthew 8 18 - 27

[18] Now when Jesus saw great multitudes about him, he gave
commandment to depart unto the other side.
[19] And a certain scribe came, and said unto him, Master, I will follow thee
whithersoever thou goest.
[20] And Jesus saith unto him, The foxes have holes, and the birds of the
air have nests; but the Son of man hath not where to lay his head.
[21] And another of his disciples said unto him, Lord, suffer me first to go
and bury my father.
[22] But Jesus said unto him, Follow me; and let the dead bury their dead.
[23] And when he was entered into a ship, his disciples followed him.
[24] And, behold, there arose a great tempest in the sea, insomuch that the
ship was covered with the waves: but he was asleep.
[25] And his disciples came to him, and awoke him, saying, Lord, save us:
we perish.
[26] And he saith unto them, Why are ye fearful, O ye of little faith? Then he
arose, and rebuked the winds and the sea; and there was a great calm.
[27] But the men marvelled, saying, What manner of man is this, that even
the winds and the sea obey him!

7.12 The Gadarene Swine

Here he was confronted by two mad men and Jesus transfers their demons
to a herd of pigs. This alarms the Gadarenes and he is asked to leave and
returns to Capurnaum.

Matthew 8 28 – 9 1

[28] And when he was come to the other side into the country of the Gergesenes, there met him two possessed with devils, coming out of the tombs, exceeding fierce, so that no man might pass by that way.

[29] And, behold, they cried out, saying, What have we to do with thee, Jesus, thou Son of God? art thou come hither to torment us before the time?

[30] And there was a good way off from them an herd of many swine feeding.

[31] So the devils besought him, saying, If thou cast us out, suffer us to go away into the herd of swine.

[32] And he said unto them, Go. And when they were come out, they went into the herd of swine: and, behold, the whole herd of swine ran violently down a steep place into the sea, and perished in the waters.

[33] And they that kept them fled, and went their ways into the city, and told every thing, and what was befallen to the possessed of the devils.

[34] And, behold, the whole city came out to meet Jesus: and when they saw him, they besought him that he would depart out of their coasts.

[1] And he entered into a ship, and passed over, and came into his own city.

7.13 Walking on Water

According to John Jesus misses the boat and walks on water to join the other disciples. (*See section 9.3*)

The next day when the crowds realised Jesus was no longer with them, they too crossed over.

John 6 22 - 26

[22] The day following, when the people which stood on the other side of the sea saw that there was none other boat there, save that one whereinto his disciples were entered, and that Jesus went not with his disciples into the boat, but that his disciples were gone away alone;

[23] (Howbeit there came other boats from Tiberias nigh unto the place where they did eat bread, after that the Lord had given thanks:)

[24] When the people therefore saw that Jesus was not there, neither his disciples, they also took shipping, and came to Capernaum, seeking for Jesus.

[25] And when they had found him on the other side of the sea, they said unto him, Rabbi, when calmest thou hither?

[26] Jesus answered them and said, Verily, verily, I say unto you, Ye seek me, not because ye saw the miracles, but because ye did eat of the loaves, and were filled.

7.14 Bread of Life

Jesus explains about the bread of life

John 6 27 - 40

[27] Labour not for the meat which perisheth, but for that meat which endureth unto everlasting life, which the Son of man shall give unto you: for him hath God the Father sealed.

[28] Then said they unto him, What shall we do, that we might work the works of God?

[29] Jesus answered and said unto them, This is the work of God, that ye believe on him whom he hath sent.

[30] They said therefore unto him, What sign shewest thou then, that we may see, and believe thee? what dost thou work?

[31] Our fathers did eat manna in the desert; as it is written, He gave them bread from heaven to eat.

[32] Then Jesus said unto them, Verily, verily, I say unto you, Moses gave you not that bread from heaven; but my Father giveth you the true bread from heaven.

[33] For the bread of God is he which cometh down from heaven, and giveth life unto the world.

[34] Then said they unto him, Lord, evermore give us this bread.

[35] And Jesus said unto them, I am the bread of life: he that cometh to me shall never hunger; and he that believeth on me shall never thirst.

[36] But I said unto you, That ye also have seen me, and believe not.

[37] All that the Father giveth me shall come to me; and him that cometh to me I will in no wise cast out.

[38] For I came down from heaven, not to do mine own will, but the will of him that sent me.

[39] And this is the Father's will which hath sent me, that of all which he hath given me I should lose nothing, but should raise it up again at the last day.

[40] And this is the will of him that sent me, that every one which seeth the Son, and believeth on him, may have everlasting life: and I will raise him up at the last day.

The people could not understand how he could have come down from heaven when they knew his parents. He had some explaining to do in the synagogue. What he said has become the basis for the celebration of the Eucharist.

John 6 41 - 59

[41] The Jews then murmured at him, because he said, I am the bread which came down from heaven.

[42] And they said, Is not this Jesus, the son of Joseph, whose father and mother we know? how is it then that he saith, I came down from heaven?

[43] Jesus therefore answered and said unto them, Murmur not among yourselves.

[44] No man can come to me, except the Father which hath sent me draw him: and I will raise him up at the last day.

[45] It is written in the prophets, And they shall be all taught of God. Every man therefore that hath heard, and hath learned of the Father, cometh unto me.

[46] Not that any man hath seen the Father, save he which is of God, he hath seen the Father.

[47] Verily, verily, I say unto you, He that believeth on me hath everlasting life.

[48] I am that bread of life.

[49] Your fathers did eat manna in the wilderness, and are dead.

[50] This is the bread which cometh down from heaven, that a man may eat thereof, and not die.

[51] I am the living bread which came down from heaven: if any man eat of this bread, he shall live for ever: and the bread that I will give is my flesh, which I will give for the life of the world.

[52] The Jews therefore strove among themselves, saying, How can this man give us his flesh to eat?

[53] Then Jesus said unto them, Verily, verily, I say unto you, Except ye eat the flesh of the Son of man, and drink his blood, ye have no life in you.

[54] Whoso eateth my flesh, and drinketh my blood, hath eternal life; and I will raise him up at the last day.

[55] For my flesh is meat indeed, and my blood is drink indeed.

[56] He that eateth my flesh, and drinketh my blood, dwelleth in me, and I in him.

[57] As the living Father hath sent me, and I live by the Father: so he that eateth me, even he shall live by me.

[58] This is that bread which came down from heaven: not as your fathers did eat manna, and are dead: he that eateth of this bread shall live for ever.

[59] These things said he in the synagogue, as he taught in Capernaum.

He had to emphasise the point to his disciples and hints at his ascension but he disillusioned several of his disciples.

John 6 60 - 66

[60] Many therefore of his disciples, when they had heard this, said, This is an hard saying; who can hear it?

[61] When Jesus knew in himself that his disciples murmured at it, he said unto them, Doth this offend you?

[62] What and if ye shall see the Son of man ascend up where he was before?

[63] It is the spirit that quickeneth; the flesh profiteth nothing: the words that I speak unto you, they are spirit, and they are life.

[64] But there are some of you that believe not. For Jesus knew from the beginning who they were that believed not, and who should betray him.

[65] And he said, Therefore said I unto you, that no man can come unto me, except it were given unto him of my Father.

[66] From that time many of his disciples went back, and walked no more with him.

But the twelve apostles stuck with him.

John 6 67 - 71

[67] Then said Jesus unto the twelve, Will ye also go away?

[68] Then Simon Peter answered him, Lord, to whom shall we go? thou hast the words of eternal life.

[69] And we believe and are sure that thou art that Christ, the Son of the living God.

[70] Jesus answered them, Have not I chosen you twelve, and one of you is a devil?

[71] He spake of Judas Iscariot the son of Simon: for he it was that should betray him, being one of the twelve.

Insofar as John is concerned this is the end of the first part of Jesus' ministry and he is now set to enter the maelstrom of Jewish politics in Jerusalem. However, the other gospellers recalled other events.

7.15 Back to Capurnaum

The Gospellers frequently refer to Capurnaum as Jesus' home town and Nazareth seems forgotten. Matthew picks up the story when Jesus returns after dealing with the Gardarene Swine on the opposite side of the lake. Then a paralysed man is brought to him and is cured. Then Matthew recounts his first meeting with Jesus and recruitment as a disciple.

Matthew 9 2 - 13

[2] And, behold, they brought to him a man sick of the palsy, lying on a bed: and Jesus seeing their faith said unto the sick of the palsy; Son, be of good cheer; thy sins be forgiven thee.

[3] And, behold, certain of the scribes said within themselves, This man blasphemeth.

[4] And Jesus knowing their thoughts said, Wherefore think ye evil in your hearts?

[5] For whether is easier, to say, Thy sins be forgiven thee; or to say, Arise, and walk?

[6] But that ye may know that the Son of man hath power on earth to forgive sins, (then saith he to the sick of the palsy,) Arise, take up thy bed, and go unto thine house.

[7] And he arose, and departed to his house.

[8] But when the multitudes saw it, they marvelled, and glorified God, which had given such power unto men.

[9] And as Jesus passed forth from thence, he saw a man, named Matthew, sitting at the receipt of custom: and he saith unto him, Follow me. And he arose, and followed him.

[10] And it came to pass, as Jesus sat at meat in the house, behold, many publicans and sinners came and sat down with him and his disciples.

[11] And when the Pharisees saw it, they said unto his disciples, Why eateth your Master with publicans and sinners?

[12] But when Jesus heard that, he said unto them, They that be whole need not a physician, but they that are sick.

[13] But go ye and learn what that meaneth, I will have mercy, and not sacrifice: for I am not come to call the righteous, but sinners to repentance.

See Mark's version in section 6.5

Chapter 8 The Healing Ministry

8.1 The Ability to Heal

Jesus' great attraction to the crowds was his ability to heal all sorts of diseases and conditions. However, despite his many successes as a healer his messages were not finding fruit and so he decided to return to Galilee. It is convenient however to bring together all the reports of healing before we look at the two quite different campaigns in Galilee and Judea.

Healing was one of the key features of the Essenes. The Dead Sea Scrolls contain numerous documents referring to the diagnosis and cure of diseases and the process whereby a cure could be certified. For instance in Scroll 4Q266 we are told about what to do when someone has suffered a serious blow and how to watch the wound healing.

8.2 Touring Galilee

Jesus continued to tour Galilee and preach and heal. It is not clear however from Matthew whether the people came in large numbers from the regions listed or that there were large crowds wherever Jesus went.

Matthew 4 23 - 25

[23] And Jesus went about all Galilee, teaching in their synagogues, and preaching the gospel of the kingdom, and healing all manner of sickness and all manner of disease among the people.

[24] And his fame went throughout all Syria: and they brought unto him all sick people that were taken with divers diseases and torments, and those which were possessed with devils, and those which were lunatick, and those that had the palsy; and he healed them.

[25] And there followed him great multitudes of people from Galilee, and from Decapolis, and from Jerusalem, and from Judaea, and from beyond Jordan.

Mark makes a similar comment

Mark 1 32 - 39

[32] And at even, when the sun did set, they brought unto him all that were diseased, and them that were possessed with devils.

[33] And all the city was gathered together at the door.

[34] And he healed many that were sick of divers diseases, and cast out many devils; and suffered not the devils to speak, because they knew him.

[35] And in the morning, rising up a great while before day, he went out, and departed into a solitary place, and there prayed.

[36] And Simon and they that were with him followed after him.

[37] And when they had found him, they said unto him, All men seek for thee.

[38] And he said unto them, Let us go into the next towns, that I may preach there also: for therefore came I forth.

[39] And he preached in their synagogues throughout all Galilee, and cast out devils.

Matthew tells a similar story

Matthew 9 32 - 35

[32] As they went out, behold, they brought to him a dumb man possessed with a devil.

[33] And when the devil was cast out, the dumb spake: and the multitudes marvelled, saying, It was never so seen in Israel.

[34] But the Pharisees said, He casteth out devils through the prince of the devils.

[35] And Jesus went about all the cities and villages, teaching in their synagogues, and preaching the gospel of the kingdom, and healing every sickness and every disease among the people.

8.3 Jesus heals the Officer's son

On his way back from Jerusalem to Galilee Jesus was persuaded to spend two days in Sychar and afterwards he set out once again for Galilee. When he arrived he was greeted with rapture by the Galileans.

John 4 46 - 54

[46] So Jesus came again into Cana of Galilee, where he made the water wine. And there was a certain nobleman, whose son was sick at Capernaum.

[47] When he heard that Jesus was come out of Judaea into Galilee, he went unto him, and besought him that he would come down, and heal his son: for he was at the point of death.

[48] Then said Jesus unto him, Except ye see signs and wonders, ye will not believe.

[49] The nobleman saith unto him, Sir, come down ere my child die.

[50] Jesus saith unto him, Go thy way; thy son liveth. And the man believed the word that Jesus had spoken unto him, and he went his way.

[51] And as he was now going down, his servants met him, and told him, saying, Thy son liveth.

[52] Then inquired he of them the hour when he began to amend. And they said unto him, Yesterday at the seventh hour the fever left him.

[53] So the father knew that it was at the same hour, in the which Jesus said unto him, Thy son liveth: and himself believed, and his whole house.

[54] This is again the second miracle that Jesus did, when he was come out of Judaea into Galilee.

Matthew's version involves the healing of a servant of the officer rather than his son and identifies him as a centurion.

Matthew 8 5 - 13

[5] And when Jesus was entered into Capernaum, there came unto him a centurion, beseeching him,

[6] And saying, Lord, my servant lieth at home sick of the palsy, grievously tormented.

[7] And Jesus saith unto him, I will come and heal him.

[8] The centurion answered and said, Lord, I am not worthy that thou shouldest come under my roof: but speak the word only, and my servant shall be healed.

[9] For I am a man under authority, having soldiers under me: and I say to this man, Go, and he goeth; and to another, Come, and he cometh; and to my servant, Do this, and he doeth it.

[10] When Jesus heard it, he marvelled, and said to them that followed, Verily I say unto you, I have not found so great faith, no, not in Israel.

[11] And I say unto you, That many shall come from the east and west, and shall sit down with Abraham, and Isaac, and Jacob, in the kingdom of heaven.

[12] But the children of the kingdom shall be cast out into outer darkness: there shall be weeping and gnashing of teeth.

[13] And Jesus said unto the centurion, Go thy way; and as thou hast believed, so be it done unto thee. And his servant was healed in the selfsame hour.

Mark's version is similar to that of John

Mark 1 21 - 28

[21] And they went into Capernaum; and straightway on the sabbath day he entered into the synagogue, and taught.

[22] And they were astonished at his doctrine: for he taught them as one that had authority, and not as the scribes.

[23] And there was in their synagogue a man with an unclean spirit; and he cried out,

[24] Saying, Let us alone; what have we to do with thee, thou Jesus of Nazareth? art thou come to destroy us? I know thee who thou art, the Holy One of God.

[25] And Jesus rebuked him, saying, Hold thy peace, and come out of him.

[26] And when the unclean spirit had torn him, and cried with a loud voice, he came out of him.

[27] And they were all amazed, insomuch that they questioned among themselves, saying, What thing is this? what new doctrine is this? for with authority commandeth he even the unclean spirits, and they do obey him.

[28] And immediately his fame spread abroad throughout all the region round about Galilee

8.4 The Pool at Bethesda

John 5 1 - 15

[1] After this there was a feast of the Jews; and Jesus went up to Jerusalem.

[2] Now there is at Jerusalem by the sheep market a pool, which is called in the Hebrew tongue Bethesda, having five porches.

[3] In these lay a great multitude of impotent folk, of blind, halt, withered, waiting for the moving of the water.

[4] For an angel went down at a certain season into the pool, and troubled the water: whosoever then first after the troubling of the water stepped in was made whole of whatsoever disease he had.

[5] And a certain man was there, which had an infirmity thirty and eight years.

[6] When Jesus saw him lie, and knew that he had been now a long time in that case, he saith unto him, Wilt thou be made whole?

[7] The impotent man answered him, Sir, I have no man, when the water is troubled, to put me into the pool: but while I am coming, another steppeth down before me.

[8] Jesus saith unto him, Rise, take up thy bed, and walk.

[9] And immediately the man was made whole, and took up his bed, and walked: and on the same day was the sabbath.

[10] The Jews therefore said unto him that was cured, It is the sabbath day: it is not lawful for thee to carry thy bed.

[11] He answered them, He that made me whole, the same said unto me, Take up thy bed, and walk.

[12] Then asked they him, What man is that which said unto thee, Take up thy bed, and walk?

[13] And he that was healed wist not who it was: for Jesus had conveyed himself away, a multitude being in that place.

[14] Afterward Jesus findeth him in the temple, and said unto him, Behold, thou art made whole: sin no more, lest a worse thing come unto thee.

[15] The man departed, and told the Jews that it was Jesus, which had made him whole..

The story is continued in Chapter 10.

8.5 Simon's Mother-in-Law

Jesus' fame as a healer has begun. Next, he heals Simon's mother-in-law.

Mark 1 29 - 31

[29] And forthwith, when they were come out of the synagogue, they entered into the house of Simon and Andrew, with James and John.

[30] But Simon's wife's mother lay sick of a fever, and anon they tell him of her.

[31] And he came and took her by the hand, and lifted her up; and immediately the fever left her, and she ministered unto them.

Matthew's version.

Matthew 8 14 - 17

[14] And when Jesus was come into Peter's house, he saw his wife's mother laid, and sick of a fever.

[15] And he touched her hand, and the fever left her: and she arose, and ministered unto them.

[16] When the even was come, they brought unto him many that were possessed with devils: and he cast out the spirits with his word, and healed all that were sick:

[17] That it might be fulfilled which was spoken by Esaias the prophet, saying, Himself took our infirmities, and bare our sicknesses.

8.6 Lepers

He goes on to heal some lepers. Mark reports only one who was eager to tell everyone about it.

Mark 1 40 - 45

[40] And there came a leper to him, beseeching him, and kneeling down to him, and saying unto him, If thou wilt, thou canst make me clean.

[41] And Jesus, moved with compassion, put forth his hand, and touched him, and saith unto him, I will; be thou clean.

[42] And as soon as he had spoken, immediately the leprosy departed from him, and he was cleansed.

[43] And he straitly charged him, and forthwith sent him away;

[44] And saith unto him, See thou say nothing to any man: but go thy way, shew thyself to the priest, and offer for thy cleansing those things which Moses commanded, for a testimony unto them.

[45] But he went out, and began to publish it much, and to blaze abroad the matter, insomuch that Jesus could no more openly enter into the city, but was without in desert places: and they came to him from every quarter..

Matthew's version is similar

Matthew 8 2 - 4

[2] And, behold, there came a leper and worshipped him, saying, Lord, if thou wilt, thou canst make me clean.

[3] And Jesus put forth his hand, and touched him, saying, I will; be thou clean. And immediately his leprosy was cleansed.

[4] And Jesus saith unto him, See thou tell no man; but go thy way, shew thyself to the priest, and offer the gift that Moses commanded, for a testimony unto them.

8.7 The Gadarene Swine

Jesus had to cross the Sea of Galilee to reach the country of the Gadarenes beneath the Golan Heights. One needs to remember that Jews would have nothing whatever to do with pigs and so the story relates to men of Greek culture. (See 7.12)

8.8 Jairus' Daughter

Jesus is approached and begged to bring Jairus' daughter back to life.

Matthew 9 18 - 19

[18] While he spake these things unto them, behold, there came a certain ruler, and worshipped him, saying, My daughter is even now dead: but come and lay thy hand upon her, and she shall live.

[19] And Jesus arose, and followed him, and so did his disciples.

The story continues after the incident of the bleeding woman.

Matthew 9 23 - 26

[23] And when Jesus came into the ruler's house, and saw the minstrels and the people making a noise,

[24] He said unto them, Give place: for the maid is not dead, but sleepeth. And they laughed him to scorn.

[25] But when the people were put forth, he went in, and took her by the hand, and the maid arose.

[26] And the fame hereof went abroad into all that land.

8.9 A Bleeding Woman

When Jesus was walking from Capernaum to the house of the synagogue leader he encountered a woman who had been hemorrhaging badly.

Matthew 9 20 - 22

[20] And, behold, a woman, which was diseased with an issue of blood twelve years, came behind him, and touched the hem of his garment:

[21] For she said within herself, If I may but touch his garment, I shall be whole.

[22] But Jesus turned him about, and when he saw her, he said, Daughter, be of good comfort; thy faith hath made thee whole. And the woman was made whole from that hour.

8.10 The Blind

We have some quite different stories of Jesus healing blind men. Matthew has two men whose eyes Jesus touched.

Matthew 9 27 - 31

[27] And when Jesus departed thence, two blind men followed him, crying, and saying, Thou Son of David, have mercy on us.

[28] And when he was come into the house, the blind men came to him: and Jesus saith unto them, Believe ye that I am able to do this? They said unto him, Yea, Lord.

[29] Then touched he their eyes, saying, According to your faith be it unto you.

[30] And their eyes were opened; and Jesus straitly charged them, saying, See that no man know it.

[31] But they, when they were departed, spread abroad his fame in all that country

John tells of a man blind from birth; but related blindness to sin. Jesus cures the blindness with spittle and clay.

John 9 1 - 7

[1] And as Jesus passed by, he saw a man which was blind from his birth.

[2] And his disciples asked him, saying, Master, who did sin, this man, or his parents, that he was born blind?

[3] Jesus answered, Neither hath this man sinned, nor his parents: but that the works of God should be made manifest in him.

[4] I must work the works of him that sent me, while it is day: the night cometh, when no man can work.

[5] As long as I am in the world, I am the light of the world.

[6] When he had thus spoken, he spat on the ground, and made clay of the spittle, and he anointed the eyes of the blind man with the clay,

[7] And said unto him, Go, wash in the pool of Siloam, (which is by interpretation, Sent.) He went his way therefore, and washed, and came seeing.

His friends and neighbors could not believe it was the same man and brought him to the Pharisees who raised the question of healing on the Sabbath and doubted that the man was who he was said to be.

John 9 8 - 17

[8] The neighbours therefore, and they which before had seen him that he was blind, said, Is not this he that sat and begged?

[9] Some said, This is he: others said, He is like him: but he said, I am he.

[10] Therefore said they unto him, How were thine eyes opened?

[11] He answered and said, A man that is called Jesus made clay, and anointed mine eyes, and said unto me, Go to the pool of Siloam, and wash: and I went and washed, and I received sight.

[12] Then said they unto him, Where is he? He said, I know not.

[13] They brought to the Pharisees him that aforetime was blind.

[14] And it was the sabbath day when Jesus made the clay, and opened his eyes.

[15] Then again the Pharisees also asked him how he had received his sight. He said unto them, He put clay upon mine eyes, and I washed, and do see.
[16] Therefore said some of the Pharisees, This man is not of God, because he keepeth not the sabbath day. Others said, How can a man that is a sinner do such miracles? And there was a division among them.
[17] They say unto the blind man again, What sayest thou of him, that he hath opened thine eyes? He said, He is a prophet.

But the Jews did not believe concerning him, that he had been blind, and received his sight, until they called the parents of him that had received his sight...

John 9 18 - 23

[18] But the Jews did not believe concerning him, that he had been blind, and received his sight, until they called the parents of him that had received his sight.
[19] And they asked them, saying, Is this your son, who ye say was born blind? how then doth he now see?
[20] His parents answered them and said, We know that this is our son, and that he was born blind:
[21] But by what means he now seeth, we know not; or who hath opened his eyes, we know not: he is of age; ask him: he shall speak for himself.
[22] These words spake his parents, because they feared the Jews: for the Jews had agreed already, that if any man did confess that he was Christ, he should be put out of the synagogue.
[23] Therefore said his parents, He is of age; ask him.

So, the Pharisees went back to the man who confirmed his story but rejected their assertion that Jesus was not a godly man. The formerly blind man prefers to judge by results rather than the opinions of the Pharisees.

John 9 24 - 34

[24] Then again called they the man that was blind, and said unto him, Give God the praise: we know that this man is a sinner.
[25] He answered and said, Whether he be a sinner or no, I know not: one thing I know, that, whereas I was blind, now I see.
[26] Then said they to him again, What did he to thee? how opened he thine eyes?
[27] He answered them, I have told you already, and ye did not hear: wherefore would ye hear it again? will ye also be his disciples?

[28] Then they reviled him, and said, Thou art his disciple; but we are Moses' disciples.

[29] We know that God spake unto Moses: as for this fellow, we know not from whence he is.

[30] The man answered and said unto them, Why herein is a marvellous thing, that ye know not from whence he is, and yet he hath opened mine eyes.

[31] Now we know that God heareth not sinners: but if any man be a worshipper of God, and doeth his will, him he heareth.

[32] Since the world began was it not heard that any man opened the eyes of one that was born blind.

[33] If this man were not of God, he could do nothing.

[34] They answered and said unto him, Thou wast altogether born in sins, and dost thou teach us? And they cast him out.

Jesus gets to hear that the Pharisees have cast the man out and has the last word.

John 9 35 - 41

[35] Jesus heard that they had cast him out; and when he had found him, he said unto him, Dost thou believe on the Son of God?

[36] He answered and said, Who is he, Lord, that I might believe on him?

[37] And Jesus said unto him, Thou hast both seen him, and it is he that talketh with thee.

[38] And he said, Lord, I believe. And he worshipped him.

[39] And Jesus said, For judgment I am come into this world, that they which see not might see; and that they which see
might be made blind.

[40] And some of the Pharisees which were with him heard these words, and said unto him, Are we blind also?

[41] Jesus said unto them, If ye were blind, ye should have no sin: but now ye say, We see; therefore your sin remaineth.

Mark's story is set in Bethsaida and Jesus healed him by spitting in his eyes.

Mark 8 22 - 26

[22] And he cometh to Bethsaida; and they bring a blind man unto him, and besought him to touch him.

[23] And he took the blind man by the hand, and led him out of the town; and when he had spit on his eyes, and put his hands upon him, he asked him if he saw ought.

[24] And he looked up, and said, I see men as trees, walking.

106

[25] After that he put his hands again upon his eyes, and made him look up: and he was restored, and saw every man clearly.

[26] And he sent him away to his house, saying, Neither go into the town, nor tell it to any in the town.

Finally, Luke's version is set in Jericho and Jesus heals just by speaking.

Luke 18 35 - 43

[35] And it came to pass, that as he was come nigh unto Jericho, a certain blind man sat by the way side begging:

[36] And hearing the multitude pass by, he asked what it meant.

[37] And they told him, that Jesus of Nazareth passeth by.

[38] And he cried, saying, Jesus, thou Son of David, have mercy on me.

[39] And they which went before rebuked him, that he should hold his peace: but he cried so much the more, Thou Son of David, have mercy on me.

[40] And Jesus stood, and commanded him to be brought unto him: and when he was come near, he asked him,

[41] Saying, What wilt thou that I shall do unto thee? And he said, Lord, that I may receive my sight.

[42] And Jesus said unto him, Receive thy sight: thy faith hath saved thee.

[43] And immediately he received his sight, and followed him, glorifying God: and all the people, when they saw it, gave praise unto God.

8.11 A paralysed man

Matthew tells the story of a paralysed man

Matthew 9 1 - 8

[1] And he entered into a ship, and passed over, and came into his own city.

[2] And, behold, they brought to him a man sick of the palsy, lying on a bed: and Jesus seeing their faith said unto the sick of the palsy; Son, be of good cheer; thy sins be forgiven thee.

[3] And, behold, certain of the scribes said within themselves, This man blasphemeth.

[4] And Jesus knowing their thoughts said, Wherefore think ye evil in your hearts?

[5] For whether is easier, to say, Thy sins be forgiven thee; or to say, Arise, and walk?

[6] But that ye may know that the Son of man hath power on earth to forgive sins, (then saith he to the sick of the palsy,) Arise, take up thy bed, and go unto thine house.

[7] And he arose, and departed to his house.

[8] But when the multitudes saw it, they marvelled, and glorified God, which had given such power unto men.

So, does Mark

Mark 2 1 - 5

[1] And again he entered into Capernaum, after some days; and it was noised that he was in the house.

[2] And straightway many were gathered together, insomuch that there was no room to receive them, no, not so much as about the door: and he preached the word unto them.

[3] And they come unto him, bringing one sick of the palsy, which was borne of four.

[4] And when they could not come nigh unto him for the press, they uncovered the roof where he was: and when they had broken it up, they let down the bed wherein the sick of the palsy lay.

[5] When Jesus saw their faith, he said unto the sick of the palsy, Son, thy sins be forgiven thee

What Jesus was doing did not sit well with the Jewish religious leaders some of whom were sitting listening to him

Mark 2 6 - 12

[6] But there were certain of the scribes sitting there, and reasoning in their hearts,

[7] Why doth this man thus speak blasphemies? who can forgive sins but God only?

[8] And immediately when Jesus perceived in his spirit that they so reasoned within themselves, he said unto them, Why reason ye these things in your hearts?

[9] Whether is it easier to say to the sick of the palsy, Thy sins be forgiven thee; or to say, Arise, and take up thy bed, and walk?

[10] But that ye may know that the Son of man hath power on earth to forgive sins, (he saith to the sick of the palsy,)

[11] I say unto thee, Arise, and take up thy bed, and go thy way into thine house.

[12] And immediately he arose, took up the bed, and went forth before them all; insomuch that they were all amazed, and glorified God, saying, We never saw it on this fashion.

8.12 Retrospect

There are more stories of healing in the lead up to the Passion.

The success of Jesus as a healer was a gift he handed on to the Apostles. Although we can guess at some of the conditions described and a few such as leprosy are readily recognisable today, on the whole society had a very different view of disease. There had to be a cause and the obvious cause was that the sufferer had sinned.

Jesus' view of sin was again very different from that of the eighteenth and nineteenth century hell fire raisers who preached from their pulpits that unless people mended their ways they would face torment and brimstone in hell after they died. It was also a very profitable theme for much of the mediaeval church as the sale of indulgences to excuse the living and the payments for prayers for the dead either from a will or from relatives. Jesus' view of sin was that it was a 'state' of society. The popular view was that anyone obviously suffering from a medical condition was to be shunned and so far as Jesus was concerned this was quite the wrong way of treating them. He recognised that they had not committed any offences, no blame should be attributed to them and society should heal the separation and care for them.

The Pharisees view of course was that they and they alone had the power to pronounce that a person had recovered and they did this by forgiving them of their sins so Jesus' actions in both healing the sick and forgiving the sin that had caused the sickness was utterly abhorrent to them. Jesus, of course went much further and 'forgave' the sins of anyone who was being shunned by society from tax collectors to prostitutes. When one compares the several versions of what are evidently the same incident it becomes even more obvious that the Gospels are not an accurate historical record. We are left bemused by Jesus' ability to heal, was it by magic? Or did Jesus have knowledge of medical cures that even we are not aware of yet?

Chapter 9 Miracles

9.1 What are Miracles?

A dictionary definition of a miracle is something wonderful, beyond human power and deviating from the common action of nature. However, one might say that a miracle is something in the eye of the beholder and what might appear miraculous to one person seems quite normal to another. Many of the phenomena we take for granted today would appear miraculous to someone in Jesus' time.

The miracles that Jesus performed have pretty well stood the test of time. We have excluded the healing miracles (see Chapter 8) so in this chapter will focus on those other reports which even today have no rational explanation.

The first miracle attributed to Jesus was the turning of water into wine at the wedding in Cana for which see section 5.4.

The next is how a small amount of food can feed a large number of people and still leave lots over. It is worth comparing the popular five thousand version with an alternative four thousand version in section 9.5.

9.2 Feeding the Five Thousand

When Jesus hears of John the Baptist's execution he crosses over Lake Tiberius to be alone but is followed by a huge crowd.

Matthew 14 13 - 21

[13] When Jesus heard of it, he departed thence by ship into a desert place apart: and when the people had heard thereof, they followed him on foot out of the cities.

[14] And Jesus went forth, and saw a great multitude, and was moved with compassion toward them, and he healed their sick.

[15] And when it was evening, his disciples came to him, saying, This is a desert place, and the time is now past; send the multitude away, that they may go into the villages, and buy themselves victuals.

[16] But Jesus said unto them, They need not depart; give ye them to eat.

[17] And they say unto him, We have here but five loaves, and two fishes.

[18] He said, Bring them hither to me.

[19] And he commanded the multitude to sit down on the grass, and took the five loaves, and the two fishes, and looking up to heaven, he blessed, and brake, and gave the loaves to his disciples, and the disciples to the multitude.

[20] And they did all eat, and were filled: and they took up of the fragments that remained twelve baskets full.

[21] And they that had eaten were about five thousand men, beside women and children.

John tells roughly the same story.

John 6 1 - 15

[1] After these things Jesus went over the sea of Galilee, which is the sea of Tiberias.

[2] And a great multitude followed him, because they saw his miracles which he did on them that were diseased.

[3] And Jesus went up into a mountain, and there he sat with his disciples.

[4] And the passover, a feast of the Jews, was nigh.

[5] When Jesus then lifted up his eyes, and saw a great company come unto him, he saith unto Philip, Whence shall we buy bread, that these may eat?

[6] And this he said to prove him: for he himself knew what he would do.

[7] Philip answered him, Two hundred pennyworth of bread is not sufficient for them, that every one of them may take a little.

[8] One of his disciples, Andrew, Simon Peter's brother, saith unto him,

[9] There is a lad here, which hath five barley loaves, and two small fishes: but what are they among so many?

[10] And Jesus said, Make the men sit down. Now there was much grass in the place. So the men sat down, in number about five thousand.

[11] And Jesus took the loaves; and when he had given thanks, he distributed to the disciples, and the disciples to them that were set down; and likewise of the fishes as much as they would.

[12] When they were filled, he said unto his disciples, Gather up the fragments that remain, that nothing be lost.

[13] Therefore they gathered them together, and filled twelve baskets with the fragments of the five barley loaves, which remained over and above unto them that had eaten.

[14] Then those men, when they had seen the miracle that Jesus did, said, This is of a truth that prophet that should come into the world.

[15] When Jesus therefore perceived that they would come and take him by force, to make him a king, he departed again into a mountain himself alone.

Mark links the feeding with the return of the Apostles from their mission.

Mark 6 30 - 44

[30] And the apostles gathered themselves together unto Jesus, and told him all things, both what they had done, and what they had taught.

[31] And he said unto them, Come ye yourselves apart into a desert place, and rest a while: for there were many coming and going, and they had no leisure so much as to eat.

[32] And they departed into a desert place by ship privately.

[33] And the people saw them departing, and many knew him, and ran afoot thither out of all cities, and outwent them, and came together unto him.

[34] And Jesus, when he came out, saw much people, and was moved with compassion toward them, because they were as sheep not having a shepherd: and he began to teach them many things.

[35] And when the day was now far spent, his disciples came unto him, and said, This is a desert place, and now the time is far passed:

[36] Send them away, that they may go into the country round about, and into the villages, and buy themselves bread: for they have nothing to eat.

37: He answered and said unto them, Give ye them to eat. And they say unto him, Shall we go and buy two hundred pennyworth of bread, and give them to eat?

38: He saith unto them, How many loaves have ye? go and see. And when they knew, they say, Five, and two fishes.

39: And he commanded them to make all sit down by companies upon the green grass.

40: And they sat down in ranks, by hundreds, and by fifties.

41: And when he had taken the five loaves and the two fishes, he looked up to heaven, and blessed, and brake the loaves, and gave them to his disciples to set before them; and the two fishes divided he among them all.

42: And they did all eat, and were filled.

43: And they took up twelve baskets full of the fragments, and of the fishes.

44: And they that did eat of the loaves were about five thousand men.

Luke's version is similar.

Luke 9 10 - 17

[10] And the apostles, when they were returned, told him all that they had done. And he took them, and went aside privately into a desert place belonging to the city called Bethsaida.

[11] And the people, when they knew it, followed him: and he received them, and spake unto them of the kingdom of God, and healed them that had need of healing.

[12] And when the day began to wear away, then came the twelve, and said unto him, Send the multitude away, that they may go into the towns and country round about, and lodge, and get victuals: for we are here in a desert place.

[13] But he said unto them, Give ye them to eat. And they said, We have no more but five loaves and two fishes; except we should go and buy meat for all this people.

[14] For they were about five thousand men. And he said to his disciples, Make them sit down by fifties in a company.

[15] And they did so, and made them all sit down.

[16] Then he took the five loaves and the two fishes, and looking up to heaven, he blessed them, and brake, and gave to the disciples to set before the multitude.

[17] And they did eat, and were all filled: and there was taken up of fragments that remained to them twelve baskets.

9.3 Walking on Water

After the feeding of the five thousand Jesus reportedly crosses lake Tiberius to return to Capurnaum. This is somewhat odd as the traditional site for the feeding was on a hill overlooking Capernaum and he would have had no need to take a boat. It must therefore have been a crossing from Capernaum to a site on the eastern shore of the Lake.

John 6 16 - 24

[16] And when even was now come, his disciples went down unto the sea,

[17] And entered into a ship, and went over the sea toward Capernaum. And it was now dark, and Jesus was not come to them.

[18] And the sea arose by reason of a great wind that blew.

[19] So when they had rowed about five and twenty or thirty furlongs, they see Jesus walking on the sea, and drawing nigh unto the ship: and they were afraid.

[20] But he saith unto them, It is I; be not afraid.

[21] Then they willingly received him into the ship: and immediately the ship was at the land whither they went.

[22] The day following, when the people which stood on the other side of the sea saw that there was none other boat there, save that one whereinto his disciples were entered, and that Jesus went not with his disciples into the boat, but that his disciples were gone away alone;

[23] (Howbeit there came other boats from Tiberias nigh unto the place where they did eat bread, after that the Lord had given thanks:)

[24] When the people therefore saw that Jesus was not there, neither his disciples, they also took shipping, and came to Capernaum, seeking for Jesus.

Matthew has the disciples crossing to get away from the crowds leaving Jesus in Capurnaum. Jesus goes alone to a mountain to pray - possibly Mount Tavor where the Church of the Beatitudes now stands.

Matthew 14 22 - 33
[22] And straightway Jesus constrained his disciples to get into a ship, and to go before him unto the other side, while he sent the multitudes away.
[23] And when he had sent the multitudes away, he went up into a mountain apart to pray: and when the evening was come, he was there alone.
[24] But the ship was now in the midst of the sea, tossed with waves: for the wind was contrary.
[25] And in the fourth watch of the night Jesus went unto them, walking on the sea.
[26] And when the disciples saw him walking on the sea, they were troubled, saying, It is a spirit; and they cried out for fear.
[27] But straightway Jesus spake unto them, saying, Be of good cheer; it is I; be not afraid.
[28] And Peter answered him and said, Lord, if it be thou, bid me come unto thee on the water.
[29] And he said, Come. And when Peter was come down out of the ship, he walked on the water, to go to Jesus.
[30] But when he saw the wind boisterous, he was afraid; and beginning to sink, he cried, saying, Lord, save me.
[31] And immediately Jesus stretched forth his hand, and caught him, and said unto him, O thou of little faith, wherefore didst thou doubt?
[32] And when they were come into the ship, the wind ceased.
[33] Then they that were in the ship came and worshipped him, saying, Of a truth thou art the Son of God.

Mark identifies the place where the disciples went as Bethsaida

Mark 6 45 - 55
[45] And straightway he constrained his disciples to get into the ship, and to go to the other side before unto Bethsaida, while he sent away the people.
[46] And when he had sent them away, he departed into a mountain to pray.
[47] And when even was come, the ship was in the midst of the sea, and he alone on the land.

[48] And he saw them toiling in rowing; for the wind was contrary unto them: and about the fourth watch of the night he cometh unto them, walking upon the sea, and would have passed by them.

[49] But when they saw him walking upon the sea, they supposed it had been a spirit, and cried out:

[50] For they all saw him, and were troubled. And immediately he talked with them, and saith unto them, Be of good cheer: it is I; be not afraid.

[51] And he went up unto them into the ship; and the wind ceased: and they were sore amazed in themselves beyond measure, and wondered.

[52] For they considered not the miracle of the loaves: for their heart was hardened.

[53] And when they had passed over, they came into the land of Gennesaret, and drew to the shore.

[54] And when they were come out of the ship, straightway they knew him,

[55] And ran through that whole region round about, and began to carry about in beds those that were sick, where they heard he was...

John records the events of the following morning. The crowds were on the 'opposite shore' ie 'in the land of Gennesaret' beneath the Golan Heights on the east bank of the lake where Jesus had dealt with the Gadarene swine. There was only the one boat there and the people from Capernaum knew that Jesus had not embarked with the rest of the disciples and the boats from Tiberius were bringing more people to Capernaum

John 6 22 - 23

[22] The day following, when the people which stood on the other side of the sea saw that there was none other boat there, save that one whereinto his disciples were entered, and that Jesus went not with his disciples into the boat, but that his disciples were gone away alone;

[23] (Howbeit there came other boats from Tiberias nigh unto the place where they did eat bread, after that the Lord had given thanks.

The question was 'Where was Jesus? 'They found him in the synagogue in Capernaum and Jesus began to explain to them the difference between ordinary bread and the Bread of Life. (see John 6.26 to 6.58) Many of the Jews who heard him did not approve much of what he said. Even the Disciples were affected.

116

John 6 59 - 71

[59] These things said he in the synagogue, as he taught in Capernaum.

[60] Many therefore of his disciples, when they had heard this, said, This is an hard saying; who can hear it?

[61] When Jesus knew in himself that his disciples murmured at it, he said unto them, Doth this offend you?

[62] What and if ye shall see the Son of man ascend up where he was before?

[63] It is the spirit that quickeneth; the flesh profiteth nothing: the words that I speak unto you, they are spirit, and they are life.

[64] But there are some of you that believe not. For Jesus knew from the beginning who they were that believed not, and who should betray him.

[65] And he said, Therefore said I unto you, that no man can come unto me, except it were given unto him of my Father.

[66] From that time many of his disciples went back, and walked no more with him.

[67] Then said Jesus unto the twelve, Will ye also go away?

[68] Then Simon Peter answered him, Lord, to whom shall we go? thou hast the words of eternal life.

[69] And we believe and are sure that thou art that Christ, the Son of the living God.

[70] Jesus answered them, Have not I chosen you twelve, and one of you is a devil?

[71] He spake of Judas Iscariot the son of Simon: for he it was that should betray him, being one of the twelve.

9.4 Quelling the Elements

After the feeding Jesus crosses the lake to deal with the Gadarene swine (see section 8.7) but a storm comes up.

Luke 8 22 - 25

[22] Now it came to pass on a certain day, that he went into a ship with his disciples: and he said unto them, Let us go over unto the other side of the lake. And they launched forth.

[23] But as they sailed he fell asleep: and there came down a storm of wind on the lake; and they were filled with water, and were in jeopardy.

[24] And they came to him, and awoke him, saying, Master, master, we perish. Then he arose, and rebuked the wind and the raging of the water: and they ceased, and there was a calm.

[25] And he said unto them, Where is your faith? And they being afraid wondered, saying one to another, What manner of man is this! for he commandeth even the winds and water, and they obey him.

Matthew 8 23 - 27

[23] And when he was entered into a ship, his disciples followed him.

[24] And, behold, there arose a great tempest in the sea, insomuch that the ship was covered with the waves: but he was asleep.

[25] And his disciples came to him, and awoke him, saying, Lord, save us: we perish.

[26] And he saith unto them, Why are ye fearful, O ye of little faith? Then he arose, and rebuked the winds and the sea; and there was a great calm.

[27] But the men marvelled, saying, What manner of man is this, that even the winds and the sea obey him!

9.5 Feeding the Four Thousand

Matthew and Mark also recount the feeding of the four thousand. This is described as being in a desert setting - hardly the same as on a hill overlooking Capurnaum which is the traditional setting for the feeding of the five thousand.

Mark 8 1 - 10

[1] In those days the multitude being very great, and having nothing to eat, Jesus called his disciples unto him, and saith unto them,

[2] I have compassion on the multitude, because they have now been with me three days, and have nothing to eat:

[3] And if I send them away fasting to their own houses, they will faint by the way: for divers of them came from far.

[4] And his disciples answered him, From whence can a man satisfy these men with bread here in the wilderness?

[5] And he asked them, How many loaves have ye? And they said, Seven.

[6] And he commanded the people to sit down on the ground: and he took the seven loaves, and gave thanks, and brake, and gave to his disciples to set before them; and they did set them before the people.

[7] And they had a few small fishes: and he blessed, and commanded to set them also before them.

[8] So they did eat, and were filled: and they took up of the broken meat that was left seven baskets.

[9] And they that had eaten were about four thousand: and he sent them away.

[10] And straightway he entered into a ship with his disciples, and came into the parts of Dalmanutha.

Matthew on the other hand places it firmly in Galilee although probably more likely in the Golan Heights than above Capurnaum.

Matthew 15.29 to 16.4

[29] And Jesus departed from thence, and came nigh unto the sea of Galilee; and went up into a mountain, and sat down there.

[30] And great multitudes came unto him, having with them those that were lame, blind, dumb, maimed, and many others, and cast them down at Jesus' feet; and he healed them:

[31] Insomuch that the multitude wondered, when they saw the dumb to speak, the maimed to be whole, the lame to walk, and the blind to see: and they glorified the God of Israel.

[32] Then Jesus called his disciples unto him, and said, I have compassion on the multitude, because they continue with me now three days, and have nothing to eat: and I will not send them away fasting, lest they faint in the way.

[33] And his disciples say unto him, Whence should we have so much bread in the wilderness, as to fill so great a multitude?

[34] And Jesus saith unto them, How many loaves have ye? And they said, Seven, and a few little fishes.

[35] And he commanded the multitude to sit down on the ground.

[36] And he took the seven loaves and the fishes, and gave thanks, and brake them, and gave to his disciples, and the disciples to the multitude.

[37] And they did all eat, and were filled: and they took up of the broken meat that was left seven baskets full.

[38] And they that did eat were four thousand men, beside women and children.

[39] And he sent away the multitude, and took ship, and came into the coasts of Magdala,

[1] The Pharisees also with the Sadducees came, and tempting desired him that he would shew them a sign from heaven.

[2] He answered and said unto them, When it is evening, ye say, It will be fair weather: for the sky is red.

[3] And in the morning, It will be foul weather to day: for the sky is red and lowring. O ye hypocrites, ye can discern the face of the sky; but can ye not discern the signs of the times?

[4] A wicked and adulterous generation seeketh after a sign; and there shall no sign be given unto it, but the sign of the prophet Jonas. And he left them, and departed.

Matthew goes on to use the story to make points relating to the disputes between the several sects of Judaism in Palestine at the time. The Pharisees and Saducees were in hot dispute as to whether the feast of unleavened bread should always fall on a Sabbath, as the Pharisees argued, or whether it could fall on any day of the week as the Saducees argued. Eventually it was the Pharisees view which prevailed but it was typical of the seemingly trivial issues which were tearing Jewish society apart.

Matthew 16.5 to 16.10

[5] And when his disciples were come to the other side, they had forgotten to take bread.

[6] Then Jesus said unto them, Take heed and beware of the leaven of the Pharisees and of the Saducees.

[7] And they reasoned among themselves, saying, It is because we have taken no bread.

[8] Which when Jesus perceived, he said unto them, O ye of little faith, why reason ye among yourselves, because ye have brought no bread?

[9] Do ye not yet understand, neither remember the five loaves of the five thousand, and how many baskets ye took up?

[10] Neither the seven loaves of the four thousand, and how many baskets ye took up?

9.6 The Voice of God

Jesus goes up into a mountain to pray and the three disciples with him dozed off and was it in their dreams they saw Jesus talking to Moses and Elijah?

Luke 9 28 - 36

[28] And it came to pass about an eight days after these sayings, he took Peter and John and James, and went up into a mountain to pray.

[29] And as he prayed, the fashion of his countenance was altered, and his raiment was white and glistering.

[30] And, behold, there talked with him two men, which were Moses and Elias:

[31] Who appeared in glory, and spake of his decease which he should accomplish at Jerusalem.

[32] But Peter and they that were with him were heavy with sleep: and when they were awake, they saw his glory, and the two men that stood with him.

[33] And it came to pass, as they departed from him, Peter said unto Jesus, Master, it is good for us to be here: and let us make three tabernacles; one for thee, and one for Moses, and one for Elias: not knowing what he said.

[34] While he thus spake, there came a cloud, and overshadowed them: and they feared as they entered into the cloud.

[35] And there came a voice out of the cloud, saying, This is my beloved Son: hear him.

[36] And when the voice was past, Jesus was found alone. And they kept it close, and told no man in those days any of those things which they had seen.

9.7 Raising Lazarus

Lazarus was the brother of Mary and Martha so had a family connection to Jesus. This must have been one of the occasions when he visited Bethany. According to John it was sometime after the Feast of the Dedication which occurs in winter time. And sometime before the events of the Passion. Jesus was not in Judea when he heard the news of Lazarus' sickness.

John 11 1 - 5

[1] Now a certain man was sick, named Lazarus, of Bethany, the town of Mary and her sister Martha.

[2] (It was that Mary which anointed the Lord with ointment, and wiped his feet with her hair, whose brother Lazarus was sick.)

[3] Therefore his sisters sent unto him, saying, Lord, behold, he whom thou lovest is sick.

[4] When Jesus heard that, he said, This sickness is not unto death, but for the glory of God, that the Son of God might be glorified thereby.

[5] Now Jesus loved Martha, and her sister, and Lazarus.

[6] When he had heard therefore that he was sick, he abode two days still in the same place where he was.

Jesus decided to go to Bethany to visit but his disciples urged him to keep away. However, when Lazarus had died. They agreed to go with him.

John 11 6 - 16

[6] When he had heard therefore that he was sick, he abode two days still in the same place where he was.

[7] Then after that saith he to his disciples, Let us go into Judaea again.

[8] His disciples say unto him, Master, the Jews of late sought to stone thee; and goest thou thither again?

[9] Jesus answered, Are there not twelve hours in the day? If any man walk in the day, he stumbleth not, because he seeth the light of this world.

[10] But if a man walk in the night, he stumbleth, because there is no light in him.

[11] These things said he: and after that he saith unto them, Our friend Lazarus sleepeth; but I go, that I may awake him out of sleep.

[12] Then said his disciples, Lord, if he sleep, he shall do well.

[13] Howbeit Jesus spake of his death: but they thought that he had spoken of taking of rest in sleep.

[14] Then said Jesus unto them plainly, Lazarus is dead.

[15] And I am glad for your sakes that I was not there, to the intent ye may believe; nevertheless let us go unto him.

[16] Then said Thomas, which is called Didymus, unto his fellow disciples, Let us also go, that we may die with him.

When they arrived in Bethany, Lazarus had been dead and buried for four days. Martha heard of his imminent arrival and came out to meet him.

John 11 17 - 28

[17] Then when Jesus came, he found that he had lain in the grave four days already.

[18] Now Bethany was nigh unto Jerusalem, about fifteen furlongs off:

[19] And many of the Jews came to Martha and Mary, to comfort them concerning their brother.

[20] Then Martha, as soon as she heard that Jesus was coming, went and met him: but Mary sat still in the house.

[21] Then said Martha unto Jesus, Lord, if thou hadst been here, my brother had not died.

[22] But I know, that even now, whatsoever thou wilt ask of God, God will give it thee.

[23] Jesus saith unto her, Thy brother shall rise again.

[24] Martha saith unto him, I know that he shall rise again in the resurrection at the last day.

[25] Jesus said unto her, I am the resurrection, and the life: he that believeth in me, though he were dead, yet shall he live:

[26] And whosoever liveth and believeth in me shall never die. Believest thou this?

[27] She saith unto him, Yea, Lord: I believe that thou art the Christ, the Son of God, which should come into the world.

[28] And when she had so said, she went her way, and called Mary her sister secretly, saying, The Master is come, and calleth for thee.

At last Mary is told of Jesus' arrival and went out to meet him and take him to Lazarus' tomb.

John 11 29 - 37

[29] As soon as she heard that, she arose quickly, and came unto him.

[30] Now Jesus was not yet come into the town, but was in that place where Martha met him.

[31] The Jews then which were with her in the house, and comforted her, when they saw Mary, that she rose up hastily and went out, followed her, saying, She goeth unto the grave to weep there.

[32] Then when Mary was come where Jesus was, and saw him, she fell down at his feet, saying unto him, Lord, if thou hadst been here, my brother had not died.

[33] When Jesus therefore saw her weeping, and the Jews also weeping which came with her, he groaned in the spirit, and was troubled,

[34] And said, Where have ye laid him? They said unto him, Lord, come and see.

[35] Jesus wept.

[36] Then said the Jews, Behold how he loved him!

[37] And some of them said, Could not this man, which opened the eyes of the blind, have caused that even this man should not have died?

All his friends and relatives had been castigating Jesus for not coming sooner and preventing Lazarus' death. So when he arrived he ordered the stone taken away and Lazarus to come out.

John 11 38 - 44

[38] Jesus therefore again groaning in himself cometh to the grave. It was a cave, and a stone lay upon it.

[39] Jesus said, Take ye away the stone. Martha, the sister of him that was dead, saith unto him, Lord, by this time he stinketh: for he hath been dead four days.

[40] Jesus saith unto her, Said I not unto thee, that, if thou wouldest believe, thou shouldest see the glory of God?

[41] Then they took away the stone from the place where the dead was laid. And Jesus lifted up his eyes, and said, Father, I thank thee that thou hast heard me.

[42] And I knew that thou hearest me always: but because of the people which stand by I said it, that they may believe that thou hast sent me.

[43] And when he thus had spoken, he cried with a loud voice, Lazarus, come forth.

[44] And he that was dead came forth, bound hand and foot with graveclothes: and his face was bound about with a napkin. Jesus saith unto them, Loose him, and let him go.

This all-rouses considerable suspicion on the part of the Pharisees and becomes part of the great debate.

Chapter 10 - Sects and Disputes

The Jews always were and still are a very argumentative people. But at the time of Jesus they reached perhaps their zenith of disputation. There were numerous sects and splinter groups arguing about almost every aspect of Judaism and into this cauldron stepped Jesus bringing completely new insights, although the ideas behind much of what he preached had been well developed by the Essenes and by the Egyptians over many years.

The several sects developed almost into separate tribes as they generally forbade marriage outside of their sect and often preferred to live in communities made up exclusively of their own kind. However they all looked towards Jerusalem and it was there that the great clashes of ideas occurred.

10.1 The Sects

Eusebius lists seven such sects and Josephus identifies three of these. It is worth pausing awhile to take stock of the principal contenders as several of them appear regularly in the Gospels as disputing with Jesus.

Essenes - have already been dealt with in section 4.5

Galileans - The Galileans were the most religious Jews in the world during Jesus' time and had close relations with the Essenes. They revered and knew the Scriptures well. They were passionately committed to living out their faith and passing their faith, knowledge, and lifestyle to their children. This led to the establishment of vibrant religious communities; a strong commitment to families and country; and active participation in the local synagogues - the community centres of that day. In fact, more famous Jewish teachers came from Galilee more than anywhere else. The Galileans resisted the pagan influences of Hellenism far longer than their Judean counterparts, and when the great revolt against the Romans and their collaborators finally occurred (66-74 AD), it began among the Galileans.

Hemerobaptists - An ancient Jewish sect probably related to the Essenes and the Saducees. They were distinguished by their fetish for regular ablutions and denial of the resurrection of the dead.

Samaritans - The Samaritans lived in the lands between Judea and Galilee. The Jews did not accept them as Jewish although they claimed to be descended from two of the lost tribes of Israel. They were sent from Assyria to Palestine in the eighth century BC and regarded the Judeans and Galilleans as upstarts, not recognising any of the Talmud beyond Joshua. In their turn the Jews despised the Samaritans

Saducees - They are sometimes referred to as the Zadokites and arose from a political party founded in the second century BC. They claimed to be followers of the teachings of the High Priest Zadok but indications are that they were actually followers of a later Zadok who had rebelled against the rabbinate. Most of what we know about them comes from Josephus as itwas their bitter rivals the Pharisees who eventually triumphed and the Saducees disappear at the end of the 1first Century AD.

Pharisees - They arose as a movement against the Hellenisation of their world in the second century BC. In terms of religious belief they were almost indistinguishable from the traditional rabbinism of their time and by the second century AD had seen off most of their rivals and reverted to being the mainstream of traditional rabbinical Judaism.

In addition, there are several references to 'Lawyers' whom we may take as the mainstream Jewish rabbinate.

The several sects all had powerful followings but none had a majority and it is doubtful whether the average Jew cared one way or the other about them. They were simply a fact of life.

10.2 The Disputes

When reading the gospels it is useful to be aware of the positions of the several sects on a number of matters. In many cases when representatives of these sects came to dispute with Jesus the questions they ask relate to the positions they have taken and about the issues over which they are most passionate.

The areas of dispute that will be dealt with in subsequent sections are (in no particular order):

2 The question of the resurrection of the dead
Ritual cleansing
Work on the Sabbath
The immortality of the soul
The existence of spirits and angels
Interpretation of the Torah
Authority of the scriptures

Observance of the law
How to live in a Roman world

10.3 The Resurrection of the Dead

The Saduccees did not believe in the resurrection of the dead. They posed an interesting problem to Jesus: -

Matthew 22 23 - 28

[23] The same day came to him the Sadducees, which say that there is no resurrection, and asked him,

[24] Saying, Master, Moses said, If a man die, having no children, his brother shall marry his wife, and raise up seed unto his brother.

[25] Now there were with us seven brethren: and the first, when he had married a wife, deceased, and, having no issue, left his wife unto his brother:

[26] Likewise the second also, and the third, unto the seventh.

[27] And last of all the woman died also.

[28] Therefore in the resurrection whose wife shall she be of the seven? for they all had her.

The answer Jesus gave silenced them. He pointed out that their basic premise was wrong and that resurrection did not bring one back to the present world

Matthew 22 29 - 33

[29] Jesus answered and said unto them, Ye do err, not knowing the scriptures, nor the power of God.

[30] For in the resurrection they neither marry, nor are given in marriage, but are as the angels of God in heaven.

[31] But as touching the resurrection of the dead, have ye not read that which was spoken unto you by God, saying,

[32] I am the God of Abraham, and the God of Isaac, and the God of Jacob? God is not the God of the dead, but of the living.

[33] And when the multitude heard this, they were astonished at his doctrine.

10.4 Ritual cleansing

Ritual cleansing took three quite different forms. First there was the cleansing after touching something 'unclean'. This could range from a corpse to taking off ones shoes or cutting ones toenails. Leviticus Chapters 14 and 15 lists a great number of possible contaminations. Second the cleansing before one undertook certain tasks. Such tasks included priests performing their priestly duties or the immersion of men about to go on a pilgrimage or before they took on an office. The third cleansing was symbolic where saying a prayer or receiving a blessing was sufficient.

There are two basic reasons for all this. One is the practical reason of hygiene; not catching or passing on a disease. The Jews knew nothing about viruses or bacteria but they were well aware that is you touched a person suffering from a disease, particularly if he had discharges, then the chance was that you could catch the same disease. The second reason revolved around the idea of sin. To a Jew at the time, especially one from a zealous sect, sin was a disease just like any other. It could relate to either a past or future act and was caused by the person being possessed by Satan. Once when Jesus was by the lakeside in Galilee he was accused by the lawyers of casting out devils because he himself was possessed.

Mark 3 22 - 26
[22] And the scribes which came down from Jerusalem said, He hath Beelzebub, and by the prince of the devils casteth he out devils.
[23] And he called them unto him, and said unto them in parables, How can Satan cast out Satan?
[24] And if a kingdom be divided against itself, that kingdom cannot stand.
[25] And if a house be divided against itself, that house cannot stand.
[26] And if Satan rise up against himself, and be divided, he cannot stand, but hath an end.

Jesus' view of sin was that it was the cause of a separation between the 'sinner' and his fellow men and could always be forgiven by the parties refusing to acknowledge the separation:

Mark 3 v28
[28]: Verily I say unto you, All sins shall be forgiven unto the sons of men, and blasphemies wherewith soever they shall blaspheme:

He did not elaborate on how this forgiveness could come about although it seems pretty clear that some sort of formal process was involved which fitted in well with the traditional Jewish cleansing rituals.

10.5 Work on the Sabbath

This is probably the dispute which is most often mentioned in the Gospels. Jesus was rebuked on several occasions by one or other of the sects. Traditional Judaism required a very strict observance of the Sabbath and down the years the scholars had interpreted the law to define precisely what did and what did not constitute work, for example walking. It was obvious that sitting absolutely still for twenty four hours was not an option so the limit was defined as 500 paces. Similarly with food - one could eat and drink; but only from food prepared the day before - cooking was not allowed.

Bethesda

Jesus' main problem was his propensity to heal on the Sabbath. When he cured the cripple at the pool of Bethesda that was bad enough; but when the man who was cured told everyone that Jesus had told him to pick up his bed and carry it, the crowd were outraged. The story has been told in section 8.4. John continues the account as it changes tenor: -

John 5 15 - 47
[15] The man departed, and told the Jews that it was Jesus, which had made him whole.
[16] And therefore did the Jews persecute Jesus, and sought to slay him, because he had done these things on the sabbath day.
[17] But Jesus answered them, My Father worketh hitherto, and I work.
[18] Therefore the Jews sought the more to kill him, because he not only had broken the sabbath, but said also that God was his Father, making himself equal with God.
[19] Then answered Jesus and said unto them, Verily, verily, I say unto you, The Son can do nothing of himself, but what he seeth the Father do: for what things soever he doeth, these also doeth the Son likewise.
[20] For the Father loveth the Son, and sheweth him all things that himself doeth: and he will shew him greater works than these, that ye may marvel.
[21] For as the Father raiseth up the dead, and quickeneth them; even so the Son quickeneth whom he will.
[22] For the Father judgeth no man, but hath committed all judgment unto the Son:

[23] That all men should honour the Son, even as they honour the Father. He that honoureth not the Son honoureth not the Father which hath sent him.

[24] Verily, verily, I say unto you, He that heareth my word, and believeth on him that sent me, hath everlasting life, and shall not come into condemnation; but is passed from death unto life.

[25] Verily, verily, I say unto you, The hour is coming, and now is, when the dead shall hear the voice of the Son of God: and they that hear shall live.

[26] For as the Father hath life in himself; so hath he given to the Son to have life in himself;

[27] And hath given him authority to execute judgment also, because he is the Son of man.

[28] Marvel not at this: for the hour is coming, in the which all that are in the graves shall hear his voice,

[29] And shall come forth; they that have done good, unto the resurrection of life; and they that have done evil, unto the resurrection of damnation.

[30] I can of mine own self do nothing: as I hear, I judge: and my judgment is just; because I seek not mine own will, but the will of the Father which hath sent me.

[31] If I bear witness of myself, my witness is not true.

[32] There is another that beareth witness of me; and I know that the witness which he witnesseth of me is true.

[33] Ye sent unto John, and he bare witness unto the truth.

[34] But I receive not testimony from man: but these things I say, that ye might be saved.

[35] He was a burning and a shining light: and ye were willing for a season to rejoice in his light.

[36] But I have greater witness than that of John: for the works which the Father hath given me to finish, the same works that I do, bear witness of me, that the Father hath sent me.

[37] And the Father himself, which hath sent me, hath borne witness of me. Ye have neither heard his voice at any time, nor seen his shape.

[38] And ye have not his word abiding in you: for whom he hath sent, him ye believe not.

[39] Search the scriptures; for in them ye think ye have eternal life: and they are they which testify of me.

[40] And ye will not come to me, that ye might have life.

[41] I receive not honour from men.

[42] But I know you, that ye have not the love of God in you.

[43] I am come in my Father's name, and ye receive me not: if another shall come in his own name, him ye will receive.

[44] How can ye believe, which receive honour one of another, and seek not the honour that cometh from God only?

[45] Do not think that I will accuse you to the Father: there is one that accuseth you, even Moses, in whom ye trust.

[46] For had ye believed Moses, ye would have believed me: for he wrote of me.

[47] But if ye believe not his writings, how shall ye believe my words?

Wheatfields

Matthew sets the Wheatfields scene in Galilee. His disciples pick grain to eat.

Matthew 12 1 - 8

[1] At that time Jesus went on the sabbath day through the corn; and his disciples were an hungred, and began to pluck the ears of corn, and to eat.

[2] But when the Pharisees saw it, they said unto him, Behold, thy disciples do that which is not lawful to do upon the sabbath day.

[3] But he said unto them, Have ye not read what David did, when he was an hungred, and they that were with him;

[4] How he entered into the house of God, and did eat the shewbread, which was not lawful for him to eat, neither for them which were with him, but only for the priests?

[5] Or have ye not read in the law, how that on the sabbath days the priests in the temple profane the sabbath, and are blameless?

[6] But I say unto you, That in this place is one greater than the temple.

[7] But if ye had known what this meaneth, I will have mercy, and not sacrifice, ye would not have condemned the guiltless.

[8] For the Son of man is Lord even of the sabbath day.

Mark's version is very similar

Mark 2 23 - 28

[23] And it came to pass, that he went through the corn fields on the sabbath day; and his disciples began, as they went, to pluck the ears of corn.

[24] And the Pharisees said unto him, Behold, why do they on the sabbath day that which is not lawful?

[25] And he said unto them, Have ye never read what David did, when he had need, and was an hungred, he, and they that were with him?

[26] How he went into the house of God in the days of Abiathar the high priest, and did eat the shewbread, which is not lawful to eat but for the priests, and gave also to them which were with him?

[27] And he said unto them, The sabbath was made for man, and not man for the sabbath:

[28] Therefore the Son of man is Lord also of the sabbath.

As is Luke's

Luke 6 1 - 5
[1] And it came to pass on the second sabbath after the first, that he went through the corn fields; and his disciples plucked the ears of corn, and did eat, rubbing them in their hands.
[2] And certain of the Pharisees said unto them, Why do ye that which is not lawful to do on the sabbath days?
[3] And Jesus answering them said, Have ye not read so much as this, what David did, when himself was an hungered, and they which were with him;
[4] How he went into the house of God, and did take and eat the shewbread, and gave also to them that were with him; which it is not lawful to eat but for the priests alone?
[5] And he said unto them, That the Son of man is Lord also of the sabbath.

A shrivelled hand
Jesus goes on to heal a man with a shrivelled hand and this gave the Pharisees a chance to test him.

Matthew 12 9 - 14
[9] And when he was departed thence, he went into their synagogue:
[10] And, behold, there was a man which had his hand withered. And they asked him, saying, Is it lawful to heal on the sabbath days? that they might accuse him.
[11] And he said unto them, What man shall there be among you, that shall have one sheep, and if it fall into a pit on the sabbath day, will he not lay hold on it, and lift it out?
[12] How much then is a man better than a sheep? Wherefore it is lawful to do well on the sabbath days.
[13] Then saith he to the man, Stretch forth thine hand. And he stretched it forth; and it was restored whole, like as the other.
[14] Then the Pharisees went out, and held a council against him, how they might destroy him. .

Again, Mark tells essentially the same story

Mark 3 1 - 6
[1]: And he entered again into the synagogue; and there was a man there which had a withered hand.

[2]: And they watched him, whether he would heal him on the sabbath day; that they might accuse him.

[3]: And he saith unto the man which had the withered hand, Stand forth.

[4]: And he saith unto them, Is it lawful to do good on the sabbath days, or to do evil? to save life, or to kill? But they held their peace.

[5]: And when he had looked round about on them with anger, being grieved for the hardness of their hearts, he saith unto the man, Stretch forth thine hand. And he stretched it out: and his hand was restored whole as the other.

[6]: And the Pharisees went forth, and straightway took counsel with the Herodians against him, how they might destroy him.

Luke's version is again very similar but he makes it a completely different occasion.

Luke 6 6 - 11

[6] And it came to pass also on another sabbath, that he entered into the synagogue and taught: and there was a man whose right hand was withered.

[7] And the scribes and Pharisees watched him, whether he would heal on the sabbath day; that they might find an accusation against him.

[8] But he knew their thoughts, and said to the man which had the withered hand, Rise up, and stand forth in the midst. And he arose and stood forth.

[9] Then said Jesus unto them, I will ask you one thing; Is it lawful on the sabbath days to do good, or to do evil? to save life, or to destroy it?

[10] And looking round about upon them all, he said unto the man, Stretch forth thy hand. And he did so: and his hand was restored whole as the other.

[11] And they were filled with madness; and communed one with another what they might do to Jesus.

Unabashed Jesus continued to heal; but the argument moved from working on the Sabbath to a dispute about the nature of demons and evil spirits.

10.6 Angels and Demons

One of the key areas of dispute, particularly between the Pharisees and Saduccees was the question of spirits. So far as the Saducees were concerned there was no life after death; but the Pharisees thought differently - to them demons were a reality.

After challenging Jesus about the Sabbath they turned their attention to the matter of demons that possessed some people: -

Matthew 12 15 - 24

[15] But when Jesus knew it, he withdrew himself from thence: and great multitudes followed him, and he healed them all;

[16] And charged them that they should not make him known:

[17] That it might be fulfilled which was spoken by Esaias the prophet, saying,

[18] Behold my servant, whom I have chosen; my beloved, in whom my soul is well pleased: I will put my spirit upon him, and he shall shew judgment to the Gentiles.

[19] He shall not strive, nor cry; neither shall any man hear his voice in the streets.

[20] A bruised reed shall he not break, and smoking flax shall he not quench, till he send forth judgment unto victory.

[21] And in his name shall the Gentiles trust.

[22] Then was brought unto him one possessed with a devil, blind, and dumb: and he healed him, insomuch that the blind and dumb both spake and saw.

[23] And all the people were amazed, and said, Is not this the son of David?

[24] But when the Pharisees heard it, they said, This fellow doth not cast out devils, but by Beelzebub the prince of the devils.

Mark puts a somewhat different twist to the story. He tells how Jesus forbids the evil spirits that he has driven out to tell anyone who he really was.

Mark 3 7 - 12

[7] But Jesus withdrew himself with his disciples to the sea: and a great multitude from Galilee followed him, and from Judaea,

[8] And from Jerusalem, and from Idumaea, and from beyond Jordan; and they about Tyre and Sidon, a great multitude, when they had heard what great things he did, came unto him.

[9] And he spake to his disciples, that a small ship should wait on him because of the multitude, lest they should throng him.

[10] For he had healed many; insomuch that they pressed upon him for to touch him, as many as had plagues.

[11] And unclean spirits, when they saw him, fell down before him, and cried, saying, Thou art the Son of God.

[12] And he straitly charged them that they should not make him known.

10.7 What about the Pharisees?

Jesus had already justified himself to the crowds and he made himself very clear as to what he thought of the Pharisees

Matthew 12 25 - 37
[25] And Jesus knew their thoughts, and said unto them, Every kingdom divided against itself is brought to desolation; and every city or house divided against itself shall not stand:

[26] And if Satan cast out Satan, he is divided against himself; how shall then his kingdom stand?

[27] And if I by Beelzebub cast out devils, by whom do your children cast them out? therefore they shall be your judges.

[28] But if I cast out devils by the Spirit of God, then the kingdom of God is come unto you.

[29] Or else how can one enter into a strong man's house, and spoil his goods, except he first bind the strong man? and then he will spoil his house.

[30] He that is not with me is against me; and he that gathereth not with me scattereth abroad.

[31] Wherefore I say unto you, All manner of sin and blasphemy shall be forgiven unto men: but the blasphemy against the Holy Ghost shall not be forgiven unto men.

[32] And whosoever speaketh a word against the Son of man, it shall be forgiven him: but whosoever speaketh against the Holy Ghost, it shall not be forgiven him, neither in this world, neither in the world to come.

[33] Either make the tree good, and his fruit good; or else make the tree corrupt, and his fruit corrupt: for the tree is known by his fruit.

[34] O generation of vipers, how can ye, being evil, speak good things? for out of the abundance of the heart the mouth speaketh.

[35] A good man out of the good treasure of the heart bringeth forth good things: and an evil man out of the evil treasure bringeth forth evil things.

[36] But I say unto you, That every idle word that men shall speak, they shall give account thereof in the day of judgment.

[37] For by thy words thou shalt be justified, and by thy words thou shalt be condemned.

The Pharisees wanted to see for themselves how Jesus performed his miracles, but as usual Jesus was not prepared to perform on demand.

Matthew 12 38 - 45
[38] Then certain of the scribes and of the Pharisees answered, saying, Master, we would see a sign from thee.

[39] But he answered and said unto them, An evil and adulterous generation seeketh after a sign; and there shall no sign be given to it, but the sign of the prophet Jonas:

[40] For as Jonas was three days and three nights in the whale's belly; so shall the Son of man be three days and three nights in the heart of the earth.

[41] The men of Nineveh shall rise in judgment with this generation, and shall condemn it: because they repented at the preaching of Jonas; and, behold, a greater than Jonas is here.

[42] The queen of the south shall rise up in the judgment with this generation, and shall condemn it: for she came from the uttermost parts of the earth to hear the wisdom of Solomon; and, behold, a greater than Solomon is here.

[43] When the unclean spirit is gone out of a man, he walketh through dry places, seeking rest, and findeth none.

[44] Then he saith, I will return into my house from whence I came out; and when he is come, he findeth it empty, swept, and garnished.

[45] Then goeth he, and taketh with himself seven other spirits more wicked than himself, and they enter in and dwell there: and the last state of that man is worse than the first. Even so shall it be also unto this wicked generation.

10.8 The Immortality of the soul

Life after death had been an obsession of the Egyptians, particularly, for many centuries. Different Jewish sects had quite differing views on the matter; the Hemerobaptists saw this life as the one and only and the Saducees had a similar view. Both these sects saw the illogicalities that would arise from someone pursuing his life after simply moving to another world. Whether they had any appreciation of the infinity of time and how bored anyone would be living their life over and over again is a matter for conjecture; but they obviously saw it as something not really to be desired.

Jesus drew a very clear distinction between the resurrection of the body, either at a later date or in another world and the existence of a soul as what epitomises a human being. Although he doesn't spell it out in any detail he hints that merely to be with God is more than enough.

In a way John sees the presence of Jesus on earth as a reversal of the process; God's soul has come down to earth:-

John 1 1 - 4

[1] In the beginning was the Word, and the Word was with God, and the Word was God.
[2] The same was in the beginning with God.
[3] All things were made by him; and without him was not any thing made that was made.
[4] In him was life; and the life was the light of men.

John also records the point where Jesus is praying alone, recognising the soul would return to God

John 17 1 - 3

[1] These words spake Jesus, and lifted up his eyes to heaven, and said, Father, the hour is come; glorify thy Son, that thy Son also may glorify thee:
[2] As thou hast given him power over all flesh, that he should give eternal life to as many as thou hast given him.
[3] And this is life eternal, that they might know thee the only true God, and Jesus Christ, whom thou hast sent.

10.9 Interpretation of the Scriptures

One of the great problems with religions generally is the question of who has the right to interpret the scriptures. This was at the heart of Luther's insistence that the bible should be made available in the vernacular so that everyone could read it and interpret is as they wished. For the previous millennium it had been the church who did the interpreting and passed on that knowledge hedged around with its own doctrines. We see the same thing happening today with the Qur'an where cultural and religious practices are seen to be inseparable.

But what was Jesus' take on this issue? When dealing with the Pharisees he was very critical of their interpretations:

John 5 39 - 47

[39] Search the scriptures; for in them ye think ye have eternal life: and they are they which testify of me.
[40] And ye will not come to me, that ye might have life.
[41] I receive not honour from men.
[42] But I know you, that ye have not the love of God in you.
[43] I am come in my Father's name, and ye receive me not: if another shall come in his own name, him ye will receive.

[44] How can ye believe, which receive honour one of another, and seek not the honour that cometh from God only?

[45] Do not think that I will accuse you to the Father: there is one that accuseth you, even Moses, in whom ye trust.

[46] For had ye believed Moses, ye would have believed me: for he wrote of me.

[47] But if ye believe not his writings, how shall ye believe my words?

10.10 Authority of the Scriptures

A quite separate question is what is the authority of the scriptures? This is the essential question which started the process of writing this book as so many people love to pick on one or two key passages and follow their instruction to the letter, often ignoring opposite instruction elsewhere. This is where the majority of breakaway Christian sects find themselves, upholding a view of the Bible that it was dictated personally by God and any inconsistencies are merely the product of our own flawed interpretation.

For the Jews a large part of the Torah can be seen as a title deed to the land of Israel written subsequent to 500 BC after the return from exile. For many Muslims the Qur'an was similarly dictated by God to Mohammed and even the slightest deviation is punishable by death.

10.11 Observance of the law

The question of authority having been settled in some people's mind the next question is where do we stand when civil society passes laws which we believe contradicts the authority of the scriptures? We see this again to today on questions of Gay rights and marriage. It was a serious question to people in England after it was ordained by law that everyone must attend the Anglican church every Sunday on pain of a shilling fine increasing as time went by. Some Catholics and Non-conformists acquiesced and attended keeping their eyes and ears closed but many suffered serious punishments for non observance.

For many Jews of the time it was very difficult for them to share their land with other people, but as Israel was at the crossing of so many trade routes the influence of Greek and Eqyptian cultures was firmly seated and those from even farther away such as from India and China emerged from time to time. How could you frame laws which applied only to the Jews and consequently left many other citizens to do as they wished with impunity. The simple answer was they couldn't and when the law was dictated by the Romans .....!

10.12 Living with the Romans

It had been bad enough for both the Pharisees and the Sadducees to see the influence of the Hellenistic world on Jewish society; but to have Roman domination imposed as well was just too much. The Pharisees wanted to see where Jesus stood on the issue: -

Matthew 22 15 - 22

[15] Then went the Pharisees, and took counsel how they might entangle him in his talk.

[16] And they sent out unto him their disciples with the Herodians, saying, Master, we know that thou art true, and teachest the way of God in truth, neither carest thou for any man: for thou regardest not the person of men.

[17] Tell us therefore, What thinkest thou? Is it lawful to give tribute unto Caesar, or not?

[18] But Jesus perceived their wickedness, and said, Why tempt ye me, ye hypocrites?

[19] Shew me the tribute money. And they brought unto him a penny.\

[20] And he saith unto them, Whose is this image and superscription?

[21] They say unto him, Caesar's. Then saith he unto them, Render therefore unto Caesar the things which are Caesar's; and unto God the things that are God's.

[22] When they had heard these words, they marvelled, and left him, and went their way.

10.13 Unleavened Bread

The significance of unleavened bread arises from the Exodus when the escaping Jews did not have enough time to allow the bread they were taking for the journey to rise. Thereafter only unleavened bread was to be eaten during Passover and the custom was passed on to the Roman Church as the only form for the Eucharist. When the break with the Orthodox church occurred, they went the opposite way and forbad the use of unleavened bread in the Eucharist as symbolizing the Old Testament rather than the new life promised by Jesus.

10.14 Fasting

Strict Orthodox Jews will fast six days a year. It is seen as an act of repentance with Yom Kippur the most significant. Originally it meant going without any food or drink for a day but as observance lapsed, water was allowed.

Matthew 9 14 - 17

[14] Then came to him the disciples of John, saying, Why do we and the Pharisees fast oft, but thy disciples fast not?

[15] And Jesus said unto them, Can the children of the bridechamber mourn, as long as the bridegroom is with them? but the days will come, when the bridegroom shall be taken from them, and then shall they fast.

[16] No man putted a piece of new cloth unto an old garment, for that which is put in to fill it up taketh from the garment, and the rent is made worse.

[17] Neither do men put new wine into old bottles: else the bottles break, and the wine runneth out, and the bottles perish: but they put new wine into new bottles, and both are preserved.

Chapter 11 Parables

One of Jesus' methods of conveying a message was using parables. We have collected the majority of those that appear in the Gospels here, in no particular order.

11.1 The Vineyard

Mark 12 1 - 12

[1] And he began to speak unto them by parables. A certain man planted a vineyard, and set an hedge about it, and digged a place for the wine fat, and built a tower, and let it out to husbandmen, and went into a far country.
[2] And at the season he sent to the husbandmen a servant, that he might receive from the husbandmen of the fruit of the vineyard.
[3] And they caught him, and beat him, and sent him away empty.
[4] And again he sent unto them another servant; and at him they cast stones, and wounded him in the head, and sent him away shamefully handled.
[5] And again he sent another; and him they killed, and many others; beating some, and killing some.
[6] Having yet therefore one son, his well-beloved, he sent him also last unto them, saying, they will reverence my son.
[7] But those husbandmen said among themselves, This is the heir; come, let us kill him, and the inheritance shall be ours.
[8] And they took him, and killed him, and cast him out of the vineyard.
[9] What shall therefore the lord of the vineyard do? he will come and destroy the husbandmen, and will give the vineyard unto others.
[10] And have ye not read this scripture; The stone which the builders rejected is become the head of the corner:
[11] This was the Lord's doing, and it is marvelous in our eyes?
[12] And they sought to lay hold on him, but feared the people: for they knew that he had spoken the parable against them: and they left him, and went their way.

Luke 20 9 - 18

[9] Then began he to speak to the people this parable; A certain man planted a vineyard, and let it forth to husbandmen, and went into a far country for a long time.

[10] And at the season he sent a servant to the husbandmen, that they should give him of the fruit of the vineyard: but the husbandmen beat him, and sent him away empty.

[11] And again he sent another servant: and they beat him also, and entreated him shamefully, and sent him away empty.

[12] And again he sent a third: and they wounded him also, and cast him out.

[13] Then said the lord of the vineyard, What shall I do? I will send my beloved son: it may be they will reverence him when they see him.

[14] But when the husbandmen saw him, they reasoned among themselves, saying, This is the heir: come, let us kill him, that the inheritance may be ours.

[15] So they cast him out of the vineyard, and killed him. What therefore shall the lord of the vineyard do unto them?

[16] He shall come and destroy these husbandmen, and shall give the vineyard to others. And when they heard it, they said, God forbid.

[17] And he beheld them, and said, What is this then that is written, The stone which the builders rejected, the same is become the head of the corner?

[18] Whosoever shall fall upon that stone shall be broken; but on whomsoever it shall fall, it will grind him to powder.

Matthew 21 28 - 43

[28] But what think ye? A certain man had two sons; and he came to the first, and said, Son, go work to day in my vineyard.

[29] He answered and said, I will not: but afterward he repented, and went.

[30] And he came to the second, and said likewise. And he answered and said, I go, sir: and went not.

[31] Whether of them twain did the will of his father? They say unto him, The first. Jesus saith unto them, Verily I say unto you, That the publicans and the harlots go into the kingdom of God before you.

[32] For John came unto you in the way of righteousness, and ye believed him not: but the publicans and the harlots believed him: and ye, when ye had seen it, repented not afterward, that ye might believe him.

[33] Hear another parable: There was a certain householder, which planted a vineyard, and hedged it round about, and digged a winepress in it, and built a tower, and let it out to husbandmen, and went into a far country:

[34] And when the time of the fruit drew near, he sent his servants to the husbandmen, that they might receive the fruits of it.

[35] And the husbandmen took his servants, and beat one, and killed another, and stoned another.

[36] Again, he sent other servants more than the first: and they did unto them likewise.

[37] But last of all he sent unto them his son, saying, They will reverence my son.

[38] But when the husbandmen saw the son, they said among themselves, This is the heir; come, let us kill him, and let us seize on his inheritance.

[39] And they caught him, and cast him out of the vineyard, and slew him.

[40] When the lord therefore of the vineyard cometh, what will he do unto those husbandmen?

[41] They say unto him, He will miserably destroy those wicked men, and will let out his vineyard unto other husbandmen, which shall render him the fruits in their seasons.

[42] Jesus saith unto them, Did ye never read in the scriptures, The stone which the builders rejected, the same is become the head of the corner: this is the Lord's doing, and it is marvelous in our eyes?

[43] Therefore say I unto you, The kingdom of God shall be taken from you, and given to a nation bringing forth the fruits thereof.

11.2 The Wedding Banquet

Matthew 22 1 - 14

[1] And Jesus answered and spake unto them again by parables, and said,

[2] The kingdom of heaven is like unto a certain king, which made a marriage for his son,

[3] And sent forth his servants to call them that were bidden to the wedding: and they would not come.

[4] Again, he sent forth other servants, saying, Tell them which are bidden, Behold, I have prepared my dinner: my oxen and my fatlings are killed, and all things are ready: come unto the marriage.

[5] But they made light of it, and went their ways, one to his farm, another to his merchandise:

[6] And the remnant took his servants, and entreated them spitefully, and slew them.

[7] But when the king heard thereof, he was wroth: and he sent forth his armies, and destroyed those murderers, and burned up their city.

[8] Then saith he to his servants, The wedding is ready, but they which were bidden were not worthy.

[9] Go ye therefore into the highways, and as many as ye shall find, bid to the marriage.

[10] So those servants went out into the highways, and gathered together all as many as they found, both bad and good: and the wedding was furnished with guests.

[11] And when the king came in to see the guests, he saw there a man which had not on a wedding garment:

[12] And he saith unto him, Friend, how camest thou in hither not having a wedding garment? And he was speechless.

[13] Then said the king to the servants, Bind him hand and foot, and take him away, and cast him into outer darkness; there shall be weeping and gnashing of teeth.

[14] For many are called, but few are chosen.

11.3 The Widow's Mite

Then he used the example of the widow giving her mite.

Mark 12 41 - 44

[41] And Jesus sat over against the treasury, and beheld how the people cast money into the treasury: and many that were rich cast in much.

[42] And there came a certain poor widow, and she threw in two mites, which make a farthing.

[43] And he called unto him his disciples, and saith unto them, Verily I say unto you, That this poor widow hath cast more in, than all they which have cast into the treasury:

[44] For all they did cast in of their abundance; but she of her want did cast in all that she had, even all her living. .

Luke 21 1 - 4

[1] And he looked up, and saw the rich men casting their gifts into the treasury.

[2] And he saw also a certain poor widow casting in thither two mites.

[3] And he said, Of a truth I say unto you, that this poor widow hath cast in more than they all:

[4] For all these have of their abundance cast in unto the offerings of God: but she of her penury hath cast in all the living that she had.

11.4 The Talents

This was told on the Mount of Olives according to Matthew.

Matthew 25 14 - 30

[14] For the kingdom of heaven is as a man travelling into a far country, who called his own servants, and delivered unto them his goods.

[15] And unto one he gave five talents, to another two, and to another one; to every man according to his several ability; and straightway took his journey.

[16] Then he that had received the five talents went and traded with the same, and made them other five talents.

[17] And likewise he that had received two, he also gained other two.

[18] But he that had received one went and digged in the earth, and hid his lord's money.

[19] After a long time the lord of those servants cometh, and reckoneth with them.

[20] And so he that had received five talents came and brought other five talents, saying, Lord, thou deliveredst unto me five talents: behold, I have gained beside them five talents more.

[21] His lord said unto him, Well done, thou good and faithful servant: thou hast been faithful over a few things, I will make thee ruler over many things: enter thou into the joy of thy lord.

[22] He also that had received two talents came and said, Lord, thou deliveredst unto me two talents: behold, I have gained two other talents beside them.

[23] His lord said unto him, Well done, good and faithful servant; thou hast been faithful over a few things, I will make thee ruler over many things: enter thou into the joy of thy lord.

[24] Then he which had received the one talent came and said, Lord, I knew thee that thou art an hard man, reaping where thou hast not sown, and gathering where thou hast not strawed:

[25] And I was afraid, and went and hid thy talent in the earth: lo, there thou hast that is thine.

[26] His lord answered and said unto him, Thou wicked and slothful servant, thou knewest that I reap where I sowed not, and gather where I have not strawed:

[27] Thou oughtest therefore to have put my money to the exchangers, and then at my coming I should have received mine own with usury.

[28] Take therefore the talent from him, and give it unto him which hath ten talents.

[29] For unto every one that hath shall be given, and he shall have abundance: but from him that hath not shall be taken away even that which he hath.

[30] And cast ye the unprofitable servant into outer darkness: there shall be weeping and gnashing of teeth.

11.5 The Thief in the Night

Matthew 24 43 - 51

[43] But know this, that if the goodman of the house had known in what watch the thief would come, he would have watched, and would not have suffered his house to be broken up.

[44] Therefore be ye also ready: for in such an hour as ye think not the Son of man cometh.

[45] Who then is a faithful and wise servant, whom his lord hath made ruler over his household, to give them meat in due season?

[46] Blessed is that servant, whom his lord when he cometh shall find so doing.

[47] Verily I say unto you, That he shall make him ruler over all his goods.

[48] But and if that evil servant shall say in his heart, My lord delayeth his coming;

[49] And shall begin to smite his fellowservants, and to eat and drink with the drunken;

[50] The lord of that servant shall come in a day when he looketh not for him, and in an hour that he is not aware of,

[51] And shall cut him asunder, and appoint him his portion with the hypocrites: there shall be weeping and gnashing of teeth.

11.6 The Foolish Virgins

Matthew 25 1 - 13

[1] Then shall the kingdom of heaven be likened unto ten virgins, which took their lamps, and went forth to meet the bridegroom.

[2] And five of them were wise, and five were foolish.

[3] They that were foolish took their lamps, and took no oil with them:

[4] But the wise took oil in their vessels with their lamps.

[5] While the bridegroom tarried, they all slumbered and slept.

[6] And at midnight there was a cry made, Behold, the bridegroom cometh; go ye out to meet him.

[7] Then all those virgins arose, and trimmed their lamps.

[8] And the foolish said unto the wise, Give us of your oil; for our lamps are gone out.

[9] But the wise answered, saying, Not so; lest there be not enough for us and you: but go ye rather to them that sell, and buy for yourselves.

[10] And while they went to buy, the bridegroom came; and they that were ready went in with him to the marriage: and the door was shut.

[11] Afterward came also the other virgins, saying, Lord, Lord, open to us.

[12] But he answered and said, Verily I say unto you, I know you not.

[13] Watch therefore, for ye know neither the day nor the hour wherein the Son of man cometh.

11.7 The Sheep and the Goats

Matthew 25 31 - 46

[31] When the Son of man shall come in his glory, and all the holy angels with him, then shall he sit upon the throne of his glory:

[32] And before him shall be gathered all nations: and he shall separate them one from another, as a shepherd divideth his sheep from the goats:

[33] And he shall set the sheep on his right hand, but the goats on the left.

[34] Then shall the King say unto them on his right hand, Come, ye blessed of my Father, inherit the kingdom prepared for you from the foundation of the world:

[35] For I was an hungred, and ye gave me meat: I was thirsty, and ye gave me drink: I was a stranger, and ye took me in:

[36] Naked, and ye clothed me: I was sick, and ye visited me: I was in prison, and ye came unto me.

[37] Then shall the righteous answer him, saying, Lord, when saw we thee an hungred, and fed thee? or thirsty, and gave thee drink?

[38] When saw we thee a stranger, and took thee in? or naked, and clothed thee?

[39] Or when saw we thee sick, or in prison, and came unto thee?

[40] And the King shall answer and say unto them, Verily I say unto you, In as much as ye have done it unto one of the least of these my brethren, ye have done it unto me.

[41] Then shall he say also unto them on the left hand, Depart from me, ye cursed, into everlasting fire, prepared for the devil and his angels:

[42] For I was an hungred, and ye gave me no meat: I was thirsty, and ye gave me no drink:

[43] I was a stranger, and ye took me not in: naked, and ye clothed me not: sick, and in prison, and ye visited me not.

[44] Then shall they also answer him, saying, Lord, when saw we thee an hungred, or athirst, or a stranger, or naked, or sick, or in prison, and did not minister unto thee?

[45] Then shall he answer them, saying, Verily I say unto you, In as much as ye did it not to one of the least of these, ye did it not to me.

[46] And these shall go away into everlasting punishment: but the righteous into life eternal.

11.8 The Good Shepherd

John 10 1 - 18

[1] Verily, verily, I say unto you, He that entereth not by the door into the sheepfold, but climbeth up some other way, the same is a thief and a robber.

[2] But he that entereth in by the door is the shepherd of the sheep.

[3] To him the porter openeth; and the sheep hear his voice: and he calleth his own sheep by name, and leadeth them out.

[4] And when he putteth forth his own sheep, he goeth before them, and the sheep follow him: for they know his voice.

[5] And a stranger will they not follow, but will flee from him: for they know not the voice of strangers.

[6] This parable spake Jesus unto them: but they understood not what things they were which he spake unto them.

[7] Then said Jesus unto them again, Verily, verily, I say unto you, I am the door of the sheep.

[8] All that ever came before me are thieves and robbers: but the sheep did not hear them.

[9] I am the door: by me if any man enter in, he shall be saved, and shall go in and out, and find pasture.

[10] The thief cometh not, but for to steal, and to kill, and to destroy: I am come that they might have life, and that they might have it more abundantly.

[11] I am the good shepherd: the good shepherd giveth his life for the sheep.

[12] But he that is an hireling, and not the shepherd, whose own the sheep are not, seeth the wolf coming, and leaveth the sheep, and fleeth: and the wolf catcheth them, and scattereth the sheep.

[13] The hireling fleeth, because he is an hireling, and careth not for the sheep.

[14] I am the good shepherd, and know my sheep, and am known of mine.

[15] As the Father knoweth me, even so know I the Father: and I lay down my life for the sheep.

[16] And other sheep I have, which are not of this fold: them also I must bring, and they shall hear my voice; and there shall be one fold, and one shepherd.

PART 3
THE DEBATE

Jewish society was very argumentative and the Jewish Authorities would argue among themselves about almost anything. Most of all they were seeking to hold their position and influence in the face of Roman occupation and indifference to much that they held dear.

Jesus' final foray into Jerusalem drew huge crowds who perceived him as the Messiah, come to liberate them from the Romans. He was in public dispute with representatives of the Jewish Authorities and it became clear that, far from being the Messiah, Jesus was challenging them on matters they held as fundamental to Jewish society.

The four gospellers tell very different stories about this period and it is not clear when many of the events described actually took place. John has Jesus coming and going all across Palestine and visiting Jerusalem several times, whereas Matthew, Mark and Luke have Jesus coming to Jerusalem only for the final events of his life and give us all his disputing as taking place within a few days.

So, we will reserve chapter 13 for the great debates and give the different versions of the arguments together rather than in any particular chronological order using the other chapter to recount the chronology of the events which led to the Passion.

Chapter 12 Into the Maelstrom

According to John, Jesus made several visits to Jerusalem whilst he was conducting his Mission, in fact John asserts that he began his Ministry there when he confronted the money lenders - see section 7.2. In this chapter we are concerned with the two final visits. On many occasions Jesus moves to the Mount of Olives to be alone with his Disciples and, where it is clear that sayings attributed to him are located there, we include them in Chapter 17.

Jesus had been making a name for himself in the previous three years and the Jewish authorities were getting very suspicious of his intentions. What seemed to have started as the advent of the long expected Messiah was beginning to appear more like an attempt to subvert the authority of the Jewish priesthood, which they had been carefully preserving amid the occupation by Romans who were quite happy to let them get on with it so long as they kept the peace. The Romans were well used to dealing with what they saw as oddball religions.

As we have seen, the Jewish religious scene was a maelstrom of conflicting dogma, practice and custom with many different sects vying for supremacy. This was the setting for Jesus' visits to Jerusalem.

12.1 The Feast of Tabernacles

The feast of Tabernacles was coming up and the Disciples tried to persuade Jesus to go to Jerusalem for the feast. At first Jesus refused to go as he was aware of the opposition of the clergy and that the expectations of the crowds for a Messiah to rid them of the Romans was one he could not meet. However, he was also aware of the dangers in Galilee as their Tetrach, Herod was getting very suspicious of his motives.

John 7 1 - 9

[1] After these things Jesus walked in Galilee: for he would not walk in Jewry, because the Jews sought to kill him.

[2] Now the Jews' feast of tabernacles was at hand.

[3] His brethren therefore said unto him, Depart hence, and go into Judaea, that thy disciples also may see the works that thou doest.

[4] For there is no man that doeth any thing in secret, and he himself seeketh to be known openly. If thou do these things, shew thyself to the world.

[5] For neither did his brethren believe in him.

[6] Then Jesus said unto them, My time is not yet come: but your time is alway ready.

[7] The world cannot hate you; but me it hateth, because I testify of it, that the works thereof are evil.

[8] Go ye up unto this feast: I go not up yet unto this feast; for my time is not yet full come.

[9] When he had said these words unto them, he abode still in Galilee.

However, after they had gone he changed his mind and went up to Jerusalem and began to preach in the Temple.

John 7 10 - 31

[10] But when his brethren were gone up, then went he also up unto the feast, not openly, but as it were in secret.

[11] Then the Jews sought him at the feast, and said, Where is he?

[12] And there was much murmuring among the people concerning him: for some said, He is a good man: others said, Nay; but he deceiveth the people.

[13] Howbeit no man spake openly of him for fear of the Jews.

[14] Now about the midst of the feast Jesus went up into the temple, and taught.

[15] And the Jews marvelled, saying, How knoweth this man letters, having never learned?

[16] Jesus answered them, and said, My doctrine is not mine, but his that sent me.

[17] If any man will do his will, he shall know of the doctrine, whether it be of God, or whether I speak of myself.

[18] He that speaketh of himself seeketh his own glory: but he that seeketh his glory that sent him, the same is true, and no unrighteousness is in him.

[19] Did not Moses give you the law, and yet none of you keepeth the law? Why go ye about to kill me?

[20] The people answered and said, Thou hast a devil: who goeth about to kill thee?

[21] Jesus answered and said unto them, I have done one work, and ye all marvel.

[22] Moses therefore gave unto you circumcision; (not because it is of Moses, but of the fathers;) and ye on the sabbath day circumcise a man.

[23] If a man on the sabbath day receive circumcision, that the law of Moses should not be broken; are ye angry at me, because I have made a man every whit whole on the sabbath day?

[24] Judge not according to the appearance, but judge righteous judgment.

[25] Then said some of them of Jerusalem, Is not this he, whom they seek to kill?

[26] But, lo, he speaketh boldly, and they say nothing unto him. Do the rulers know indeed that this is the very Christ?

[27] Howbeit we know this man whence he is: but when Christ cometh, no man knoweth whence he is.

[28] Then cried Jesus in the temple as he taught, saying, Ye both know me, and ye know whence I am: and I am not come of myself, but he that sent me is true, whom ye know not.

[29] But I know him: for I am from him, and he hath sent me.

[30] Then they sought to take him: but no man laid hands on him, because his hour was not yet come.

[31] And many of the people believed on him, and said, When Christ cometh, will he do more miracles than these which this man hath done?

The Jewish hierarchy were none too pleased about his preaching and sent police to arrest him, but his words so impressed the police that they backed off.

John 7 32 - 36

[32] The Pharisees heard that the people murmured such things concerning him; and the Pharisees and the chief priests sent officers to take him.

[33] Then said Jesus unto them, Yet a little while am I with you, and then I go unto him that sent me.

[34] Ye shall seek me, and shall not find me: and where I am, thither ye cannot come.

[35] Then said the Jews among themselves, Whither will he go, that we shall not find him? will he go unto the dispersed among the Gentiles, and teach the Gentiles?

[36] What manner of saying is this that he said, Ye shall seek me, and shall not find me: and where I am, thither ye cannot come?

On the last day of the Festival of Tabernacles Jesus was still preaching and members of the crowd started debating whether or not Jesus was the promised Messiah.

John 7 37 - 39

[37] In the last day, that great day of the feast, Jesus stood and cried, saying, If any man thirst, let him come unto me, and drink.

[38] He that believeth on me, as the scripture hath said, out of his belly shall flow rivers of living water.

[39] (But this spake he of the Spirit, which they that believe on him should receive: for the Holy Ghost was not yet given; because that Jesus was not yet glorified.)

Many in the crowd were now convinced he was the Messiah

John 7 40 - 44

[40] Many of the people therefore, when they heard this saying, said, Of a truth this is the Prophet.

[41] Others said, This is the Christ. But some said, Shall Christ come out of Galilee?

[42] Hath not the scripture said, That Christ cometh of the seed of David, and out of the town of Bethlehem, where David was?

[43] So there was a division among the people because of him.

[44] And some of them would have taken him; but no man laid hands on him.

The Pharisees were very put out that Jesus had not been arrested as they had ordered.

John 7 45 - 52

[45] Then came the officers to the chief priests and Pharisees; and they said unto them, Why have ye not brought him?

[46] The officers answered, Never man spake like this man.

[47] Then answered them the Pharisees, Are ye also deceived?

[48] Have any of the rulers or of the Pharisees believed on him?

[49] But this people who knoweth not the law are cursed.

[50] Nicodemus saith unto them, (he that came to Jesus by night, being one of them,)

[51] Doth our law judge any man, before it hear him, and know what he doeth?

[52] They answered and said unto him, Art thou also of Galilee? Search, and look: for out of Galilee ariseth no prophet.

12.2 The Woman Caught in Adultery

Jesus left to spend time in the Mount of Olives but next day he was back in the Temple and was confronted by a woman caught in adultery. There is considerable dispute about this passage. The Jerusalem Bible includes it, the New English Bible prints it as a footnote to John's Gospel.

John 7 53 - 8 11

[53] And every man went unto his own house.

[1] Jesus went unto the mount of Olives.

[2] And early in the morning he came again into the temple, and all the people came unto him; and he sat down, and taught them.

[3] And the scribes and Pharisees brought unto him a woman taken in adultery; and when they had set her in the midst,

[4] They say unto him, Master, this woman was taken in adultery, in the very act.

[5] Now Moses in the law commanded us, that such should be stoned: but what sayest thou?

[6] This they said, tempting him, that they might have to accuse him. But Jesus stooped down, and with his finger wrote on the ground, as though he heard them not.

[7] So when they continued asking him, he lifted up himself, and said unto them, He that is without sin among you, let him first cast a stone at her.

[8] And again he stooped down, and wrote on the ground.

[9] And they which heard it, being convicted by their own conscience, went out one by one, beginning at the eldest, even unto the last: and Jesus was left alone, and the woman standing in the midst.

[10] When Jesus had lifted up himself, and saw none but the woman, he said unto her, Woman, where are those thine accusers? hath no man condemned thee?

[11] She said, No man, Lord. And Jesus said unto her, Neither do I condemn thee: go, and sin no more.

12.3 Further Argument

Jesus moved to the Treasury and resumed his preaching.

John 8 12 - 30

[12] Then spake Jesus again unto them, saying, I am the light of the world: he that followeth me shall not walk in darkness, but shall have the light of life.

[13] The Pharisees therefore said unto him, Thou bearest record of thyself; thy record is not true.

[14] Jesus answered and said unto them, Though I bear record of myself, yet my record is true: for I know whence I came, and whither I go; but ye cannot tell whence I come, and whither I go.

[15] Ye judge after the flesh; I judge no man.

[16] And yet if I judge, my judgment is true: for I am not alone, but I and the Father that sent me.

[17] It is also written in your law, that the testimony of two men is true.

[18] I am one that bear witness of myself, and the Father that sent me beareth witness of me.

[19] Then said they unto him, Where is thy Father? Jesus answered, Ye neither know me, nor my Father: if ye had known me, ye should have known my Father also.

[20] These words spake Jesus in the treasury, as he taught in the temple: and no man laid hands on him; for his hour was not yet come.

[21] Then said Jesus again unto them, I go my way, and ye shall seek me, and shall die in your sins: whither I go, ye cannot come.

[22] Then said the Jews, Will he kill himself? because he saith, Whither I go, ye cannot come.

[23] And he said unto them, Ye are from beneath; I am from above: ye are of this world; I am not of this world.

[24] I said therefore unto you, that ye shall die in your sins: for if ye believe not that I am he, ye shall die in your sins.

[25] Then said they unto him, Who art thou? And Jesus saith unto them, Even the same that I said unto you from the beginning.

[26] I have many things to say and to judge of you: but he that sent me is true; and I speak to the world those things which I have heard of him.

[27] They understood not that he spake to them of the Father.

[28] Then said Jesus unto them, When ye have lifted up the Son of man, then shall ye know that I am he, and that I do nothing of myself; but as my Father hath taught me, I speak these things.

[29] And he that sent me is with me: the Father hath not left me alone; for I do always those things that please him.

[30] As he spake these words, many believed on him.

Jesus then turned to his followers and spoke to them as descendants of Abraham.

John 8 31 - 47

[31] Then said Jesus to those Jews which believed on him, If ye continue in my word, then are ye my disciples indeed;

[32] And ye shall know the truth, and the truth shall make you free.

[33] They answered him, We be Abraham's seed, and were never in bondage to any man: how sayest thou, Ye shall be made free?
[34] Jesus answered them, Verily, verily, I say unto you, Whosoever committeth sin is the servant of sin.
[35] And the servant abideth not in the house for ever: but the Son abideth ever.
[36] If the Son therefore shall make you free, ye shall be free indeed.
[37] I know that ye are Abraham's seed; but ye seek to kill me, because my word hath no place in you.
[38] I speak that which I have seen with my Father: and ye do that which ye have seen with your father.
[39] They answered and said unto him, Abraham is our father. Jesus saith unto them, If ye were Abraham's children, ye would do the works of Abraham.
[40] But now ye seek to kill me, a man that hath told you the truth, which I have heard of God: this did not Abraham.
[41] Ye do the deeds of your father. Then said they to him, We be not born of fornication; we have one Father, even God.
[42] Jesus said unto them, If God were your Father, ye would love me: for I proceeded forth and came from God; neither came I of myself, but he sent me.
[43] Why do ye not understand my speech? even because ye cannot hear my word.
[44] Ye are of your father the devil, and the lusts of your father ye will do. He was a murderer from the beginning, and abode not in the truth, because there is no truth in him. When he speaketh a lie, he speaketh of his own: for he is a liar, and the father of it.
[45] And because I tell you the truth, ye believe me not.
[46] Which of you convinceth me of sin? And if I say the truth, why do ye not believe me?
[47] He that is of God heareth God's words: ye therefore hear them not, because ye are not of God.

Jesus is now accused of being a Samaritan and being possessed. He ended up getting stoned.

John 8 48 - 59
[48] Then answered the Jews, and said unto him, Say we not well that thou art a Samaritan, and hast a devil?
[49] Jesus answered, I have not a devil; but I honour my Father, and ye do dishonour me.
[50] And I seek not mine own glory: there is one that seeketh and judgeth.

[51] Verily, verily, I say unto you, If a man keep my saying, he shall never see death.

[52] Then said the Jews unto him, Now we know that thou hast a devil. Abraham is dead, and the prophets; and thou sayest, If a man keep my saying, he shall never taste of death.

[53] Art thou greater than our father Abraham, which is dead? and the prophets are dead: whom makest thou thyself?

[54] Jesus answered, If I honour myself, my honour is nothing: it is my Father that honoureth me; of whom ye say, that he is your God:

[55] Yet ye have not known him; but I know him: and if I should say, I know him not, I shall be a liar like unto you: but I know him, and keep his saying.

[56] Your father Abraham rejoiced to see my day: and he saw it, and was glad.

[57] Then said the Jews unto him, Thou art not yet fifty years old, and hast thou seen Abraham?

[58] Jesus said unto them, Verily, verily, I say unto you, Before Abraham was, I am.

[59] Then took they up stones to cast at him: but Jesus hid himself, and went out of the temple, going through the midst of them, and so passed by

His next encounter is with a man who has been blind since birth. This is dealt with in Section 8.10 and he goes on to tell the parable of the Good Shepherd. (See Section 11.8) This causes more splits in the crowds.

John 10 19 - 21

[19] There was a division therefore again among the Jews for these sayings.

[20] And many of them said, He hath a devil, and is mad; why hear ye him?

[21] Others said, These are not the words of him that hath a devil. Can a devil open the eyes of the blind?

12.4 Feast of the Dedication

One time when winter was upon them, Jesus was walking around the Temple on the Feast of the Dedication when he was confronted by more crowds and more stoning.

John 10 22 - 39

[22] And it was at Jerusalem the feast of the dedication, and it was winter.

[23] And Jesus walked in the temple in Solomon's porch.

[24] Then came the Jews round about him, and said unto him, How long dost thou make us to doubt? If thou be the Christ, tell us plainly.

[25] Jesus answered them, I told you, and ye believed not: the works that I do in my Father's name, they bear witness of me.

[26] But ye believe not, because ye are not of my sheep, as I said unto you.

[27] My sheep hear my voice, and I know them, and they follow me:

[28] And I give unto them eternal life; and they shall never perish, neither shall any man pluck them out of my hand.

[29] My Father, which gave them me, is greater than all; and no man is able to pluck them out of my Father's hand.

[30] I and my Father are one.

[31] Then the Jews took up stones again to stone him.

[32] Jesus answered them, Many good works have I shewed you from my Father; for which of those works do ye stone me?

[33] The Jews answered him, saying, For a good work we stone thee not; but for blasphemy; and because that thou, being a man, makest thyself God.

[34] Jesus answered them, Is it not written in your law, I said, Ye are gods?

[35] If he called them gods, unto whom the word of God came, and the scripture cannot be broken;

[36] Say ye of him, whom the Father hath sanctified, and sent into the world, Thou blasphemest; because I said, I am the Son of God?

[37] If I do not the works of my Father, believe me not.

[38] But if I do, though ye believe not me, believe the works: that ye may know, and believe, that the Father is in me, and I in him.

[39] Therefore they sought again to take him: but he escaped out of their hand,

12.5 Backing off from Controversy

Jesus' foray to Jerusalem had not been a great success. His reputation in Galilee was not sufficient to protect him from the mob, who, egged on by the Authorities, had stoned him and made him feel quite unwelcome. He withdrew back across the Jordan to consolidate his position.

John 10 40 - 42

[40] And went away again beyond Jordan into the place where John at first baptized; and there he abode.

[41] And many resorted unto him, and said, John did no miracle: but all things that John spake of this man were true.

[42] And many believed on him there.

While he was there he heard that his brother in law Lazarus had fallen ill and he returned to Bethany to find he had died. There followed the miracle of raising Lazarus from the dead which is dealt with in section 9.7

12.6 The Authorities Sense Danger

Jesus' appearance at Bethany, only a few miles from Jerusalem, soon came to the ears of the Council. Caiaphas, the High Priest campaigned to have him done away with and Jesus took the hint and retired to Ephraim.

> **John 11 45 - 54**
> [45] Then many of the Jews which came to Mary, and had seen the things which Jesus did, believed on him.
> [46] But some of them went their ways to the Pharisees, and told them what things Jesus had done.
> [47] Then gathered the chief priests and the Pharisees a council, and said, What do we? for this man doeth many miracles.
> [48] If we let him thus alone, all men will believe on him: and the Romans shall come and take away both our place and nation.
> [49] And one of them, named Caiaphas, being the high priest that same year, said unto them, Ye know nothing at all,
> [50] Nor consider that it is expedient for us, that one man should die for the people, and that the whole nation perish not.
> [51] And this spake he not of himself: but being high priest that year, he prophesied that Jesus should die for that nation;
> [52] And not for that nation only, but that also he should gather together in one the children of God that were scattered abroad.
> [53] Then from that day forth they took counsel together for to put him to death.
> [54] Jesus therefore walked no more openly among the Jews; but went thence unto a country near to the wilderness, into a city called Ephraim, and there continued with his disciples.

12.7 Is He Coming?

Jesus' work was almost complete. He had spent several years preaching and teaching. He had made at least two well publicised visits to Jerusalem, but his support there had never been strong enough and he had backed off a confrontation with the Authorities. Passover was coming and people began to speculate as to whether Jesus would try again.

John 11 55 - 57

[55] And the Jews' passover was nigh at hand: and many went out of the country up to Jerusalem before the passover, to purify themselves.

[56] Then sought they for Jesus, and spake among themselves, as they stood in the temple, What think ye, that he will not come to the feast?

[57] Now both the chief priests and the Pharisees had given a commandment, that, if any man knew where he were, he should shew it, that they might take him.

Chapter 13 Holy Week

We refer to the eight days leading to the Resurrection as Holy Week and beginning with Palm Sunday. Jesus is going to use his wife Mary's family home as his base. The events related in chapters 14 to 19 were all sandwiched into a mere 8 days. It is instructive to consider the timetable of events as there is considerable discrepancy between the four Gospel writers.

We start with the Jewish Passover. This festival lasted seven days and ends on the 14th day after the new moon, but very conveniently the date of the new moon is regulated so that Passover cannot fall on a Monday, Wednesday or Friday. We must also remember that a Jewish day began at sundown on the previous day. There is a reasonable agreement that in the year of these events Passover fell on the Saturday and thus began at around 6 pm on the Friday.

It is John's timetable we will follow as it is much more realistic. The other gospellers see Jesus as making only the one visit to Jerusalem at the end of his ministry and therefore have to cram in events which clearly took place months if not years before.

13.1 The Timetable

For convenience in keeping track we will designate the key periods of time by letters, starting on Saturday evening and treating evening and daytime as two separate periods If we work backwards and forwards from the crucifixion, the calendar of events reads like this:-

A **Saturday Evening** - Passover Festival starts (Anointing with oil)
B **Sunday** - Entry into Jerusalem
C **Sunday evening** - Bethany
D **Monday** - Fig Tree, Meeting the Greeks, Debates
E **Monday evening** - Bethany?
F **Tuesday** - Debates
G **Tuesday evening** - Judas does a deal
H **Wednesday** - Preparations for last supper
J **Wednesday Evening** - Last Supper, Jesus arrested

K **Thursday** - Trial by Council - seen by Herod
L **Thursday Evening** in Roman Hands - flogged
M **Friday** - Formal trial and Crucifixion
N **Friday Evening** - Burial P Saturday - In the tomb
Q **Sunday** - The empty tomb - the resurrection

A Passover meal would be held on the Friday evening - hence the Jewish reluctance to be contaminated by being present at the formal trial (see chapter 18). This tends to confirm that the Last Supper was a farewell meal rather than a Passover meal (Seder) whether it was held on the Wednesday Evening as John implies or Thursday.

A - SATURDAY EVENING

13.2 Seeing Lazarus

Six days before the Passover (ie Saturday Evening) Jesus went to Bethany to visit Mary to have supper with her and her family. One of the family members was Lazarus whom Jesus had raised from the dead.

The news that Jesus was as close as Bethany soon spread and people came out to see him and also to marvel at Lazarus, living proof of Jesus' ability to overcome death.

John 12.1
[1] Then Jesus six days before the passover came to Bethany, where Lazarus was which had been dead, whom he raised from the dead. .

Caiaphas and his cronies realised that they had to deal with Lazarus as well as Jesus.

John 12 9 - 11
[9] Much people of the Jews therefore knew that he was there: and they came not for Jesus' sake only, but that they might see Lazarus also, whom he had raised from the dead.
[10] But the chief priests consulted that they might put Lazarus also to death;
[11] Because that by reason of him many of the Jews went away, and believed on Jesus.

13.3 Supper at Bethany

At the supper Mary annointed Jesus with oil of spikenard. This is very much in the Jewish tradition of welcoming a visitor after a long journey, hence John's version seems much more accurate, rather than it being a random act later in the week when he had been staying in Bethany for several nights or earlier in a Pharisees house.

John 12 2 - 8

[2] There they made him a supper; and Martha served: but Lazarus was one of them that sat at the table with him.

[3] Then took Mary a pound of ointment of spikenard, very costly, and anointed the feet of Jesus, and wiped his feet with her hair: and the house was filled with the odour of the ointment.

[4] Then saith one of his disciples, Judas Iscariot, Simon's son, which should betray him,

[5] Why was not this ointment sold for three hundred pence, and given to the poor?

[6] This he said, not that he cared for the poor; but because he was a thief, and had the bag, and bare what was put therein.

[7] Then said Jesus, Let her alone: against the day of my burying hath she kept this.

[8] For the poor always ye have with you; but me ye have not always.

The other gospellers place the supper later in the week and identify the venue as the house of Simon the leper, who was Mary's father.

Mark does not name the woman but hints that the ointment should have been used to anoint his body after his death.

Mark 14 3 - 9

[3] And being in Bethany in the house of Simon the leper, as he sat at meat, there came a woman having an alabaster box of ointment of spikenard very precious; and she brake the box, and poured it on his head.

[4] And there were some that had indignation within themselves, and said, Why was this waste of the ointment made?

[5] For it might have been sold for more than three hundred pence, and have been given to the poor. And they murmured against her.

[6] And Jesus said, Let her alone; why trouble ye her? she hath wrought a good work on me.

[7] For ye have the poor with you always, and whensoever ye will ye may do them good: but me ye have not always.

[8] She hath done what she could: she is come aforehand to anoint my body to the burying.

[9] Verily I say unto you, Wheresoever this gospel shall be preached throughout the whole world, this also that she hath done shall be spoken of for a memorial of her.

Matthew too does not name the woman and hints at the burial.

Matthew 26 6 - 13

[6] Now when Jesus was in Bethany, in the house of Simon the leper,

[7] There came unto him a woman having an alabaster box of very precious ointment, and poured it on his head, as he sat at meat.

[8] But when his disciples saw it, they had indignation, saying, To what purpose is this waste?

[9] For this ointment might have been sold for much, and given to the poor.

[10] When Jesus understood it, he said unto them, Why trouble ye the woman? for she hath wrought a good work upon me.

[11] For ye have the poor always with you; but me ye have not always.

[12] For in that she hath poured this ointment on my body, she did it for my burial.

[13] Verily I say unto you, wheresoever this gospel shall be preached in the whole world, there shall also this, that this woman hath done, be told for a memorial of her.

Luke's version seems totally different - He has Jesus dining at a Pharisee's house some time earlier. But Simon is a Pharisee.

Luke 7 35 - 38

[36] And one of the Pharisees desired him that he would eat with him. And he went into the Pharisee's house, and sat down to meat.

[37] And, behold, a woman in the city, which was a sinner, when she knew that Jesus sat at meat in the Pharisee's house, brought an alabaster box of ointment,

[38] And stood at his feet behind him weeping, and began to wash his feet with tears, and did wipe them with the hairs of her head, and kissed his feet, and anointed them with the ointment.

Then Luke actually identifies the Pharisee as Simon and refers to the woman as a sinner, which is usually a metaphor for Mary Magdalene.

Luke 7 39 - 50

[39] Now when the Pharisee which had bidden him saw it, he spake within himself, saying, This man, if he were a prophet, would have known who and what manner of woman this is that toucheth him: for she is a sinner.

[40] And Jesus answering said unto him, Simon, I have somewhat to say unto thee. And he saith, Master, say on.

[41] There was a certain creditor which had two debtors: the one owed five hundred pence, and the other fifty.

[42] And when they had nothing to pay, he frankly forgave them both. Tell me therefore, which of them will love him most?

[43] Simon answered and said, I suppose that he, to whom he forgave most. And he said unto him, Thou hast rightly judged.

[44] And he turned to the woman, and said unto Simon, Seest thou this woman? I entered into thine house, thou gavest me no water for my feet: but she hath washed my feet with tears, and wiped them with the hairs of her head.

[45] Thou gavest me no kiss: but this woman since the time I came in hath not ceased to kiss my feet.

[46] My head with oil thou didst not anoint: but this woman hath anointed my feet with ointment.

[47] Wherefore I say unto thee, Her sins, which are many, are forgiven; for she loved much: but to whom little is forgiven, the same loveth little.

[48] And he said unto her, Thy sins are forgiven.

[49] And they that sat at meat with him began to say within themselves, Who is this that forgiveth sins also?

[50] And he said to the woman, Thy faith hath saved thee; go in peace.

When one puts all of this together it seems fairly clear that one can identify Mary of Bethany with Mary of Magdala. We may possibly make other identifications for example, John refers to Judas as the son of Simon and Simon was a leper who had been cleansed by Jesus. The meal was at Simon's house but also at Mary's House - Was Simon, Mary's father and thus Judas, who is Mary's brother is Jesus' brother-in-law?

Whatever one's conclusions on these matters Jesus was about to set out on his final week, but first, in Chapter 14 we will cover the Great Debate which took place mainly on the Monday and Tuesday of Holy Week. Throughout Jesus' ministry he had been questioned by various representatives of the Jewish Authority; but largely he had had the people on his side and receptive to his ideas. When he got to Jerusalem however the situation was very different. At first the people thought he was the Messiah; but soon realised he was not that sort of leader at all.

The questions came from all sides and here we look at a selection of questions and how Jesus' response was reported by the different go spellers.

Chapter 14 Entry to Jerusalem

B – SUNDAY

We start Holy Week with the events of Palm Sunday.

14.1 Getting the Donkey

Jesus is ready for the final events of his life. He begins by a triumphal entry to Jerusalem; but not in the style one would usually associate with such an event - He sent two of his disciples to collect a donkey.

Mark 11 1 - 7

[1] And when they came nigh to Jerusalem, unto Bethphage and Bethany, at the mount of Olives, he sendeth forth two of his disciples,

[2] And saith unto them, Go your way into the village over against you: and as soon as ye be entered into it, ye shall find a colt tied, whereon never man sat; loose him, and bring him.

[3] And if any man say unto you, Why do ye this? say ye that the Lord hath need of him; and straightway he will send him hither.

[4] And they went their way, and found the colt tied by the door without in a place where two ways met; and they loose him.

[5] And certain of them that stood there said unto them, What do ye, loosing the colt?

[6] And they said unto them even as Jesus had commanded: and they let them go.

[7] And they brought the colt to Jesus, and cast their garments on him; and he sat upon him.

Luke and Matthew's stories are essentially similar

Luke 19 28 - 35

[28] And when he had thus spoken, he went before, ascending up to Jerusalem.

[29] And it came to pass, when he was come nigh to Bethphage and Bethany, at the mount called the mount of Olives, he sent two of his disciples,

[30] Saying, Go ye into the village over against you; in the which at your entering ye shall find a colt tied, whereon yet never man sat: loose him, and bring him hither.

[31] And if any man ask you, Why do ye loose him? thus shall ye say unto him, Because the Lord hath need of him.

[32] And they that were sent went their way, and found even as he had said unto them.

[33] And as they were loosing the colt, the owners thereof said unto them, Why loose ye the colt?

[34] And they said, The Lord hath need of him.

[35] And they brought him to Jesus: and they cast their garments upon the colt, and they set Jesus thereon.

Matthew 21 1 - 5

[1] And when they drew nigh unto Jerusalem, and were come to Bethphage, unto the mount of Olives, then sent Jesus two disciples,

[2] Saying unto them, Go into the village over against you, and straightway ye shall find an ass tied, and a colt with her: loose them, and bring them unto me.

[3] And if any man say ought unto you, ye shall say, The Lord hath need of them; and straightway he will send them.

[4] All this was done, that it might be fulfilled which was spoken by the prophet, saying,

[5] Tell ye the daughter of Sion, Behold, thy King cometh unto thee, meek, and sitting upon an ass, and a colt the foal of an ass

14.2 Procession of Palms

Jesus sets off for Jerusalem mounted on the donkey. He was greeted with rapture by the other pilgrims.

John 12 12 - 15

[12] On the next day much people that were come to the feast, when they heard that Jesus was coming to Jerusalem,

[13] Took branches of palm trees, and went forth to meet him, and cried, Hosanna: Blessed is the King of Israel that cometh in the name of the Lord.

[14] And Jesus, when he had found a young ass, sat thereon; as it is written,

[15] Fear not, daughter of Sion: behold, thy King cometh, sitting on an ass's colt.

Matthew 21 6 - 11

[6] And the disciples went, and did as Jesus commanded them,

[7] And brought the ass, and the colt, and put on them their clothes, and they set him thereon.

[8] And a very great multitude spread their garments in the way; others cut down branches from the trees, and strawed them in the way.

[9] And the multitudes that went before, and that followed, cried, saying, Hosanna to the Son of David: Blessed is he that cometh in the name of the Lord; Hosanna in the highest.

[10] And when he was come into Jerusalem, all the city was moved, saying, Who is this?

[11] And the multitude said, This is Jesus the prophet of Nazareth of Galilee.

Luke also notes that some of the Pharisees tried to persuade Jesus to call off his followers.

Luke 19 36 - 44

[36] And as he went, they spread their clothes in the way.

[37] And when he was come nigh, even now at the descent of the mount of Olives, the whole multitude of the disciples began to rejoice and praise God with a loud voice for all the mighty works that they had seen;

[38] Saying, Blessed be the King that cometh in the name of the Lord: peace in heaven, and glory in the highest.

[39] And some of the Pharisees from among the multitude said unto him, Master, rebuke thy disciples.

[40] And he answered and said unto them, I tell you that, if these should hold their peace, the stones would immediately cry out.

[41] And when he was come near, he beheld the city, and wept over it,

[42] Saying, If thou hadst known, even thou, at least in this thy day, the things which belong unto thy peace! but now they are hid from thine eyes.

[43] For the days shall come upon thee, that thine enemies shall cast a trench about thee, and compass thee round, and keep thee in on every side,

[44] And shall lay thee even with the ground, and thy children within thee; and they shall not leave in thee one stone upon another; because thou knewest not the time of thy visitation.

Mark gives a similar picture.

Mark 11 8 - 10

[8] And many spread their garments in the way: and others cut down branches off the trees, and strawed them in the way.

[9] And they that went before, and they that followed, cried, saying, Hosanna; Blessed is he that cometh in the name of the Lord:

[10] Blessed be the kingdom of our father David, that cometh in the name of the Lord: Hosanna in the highest.

C - SUNDAY EVENING

14.3Return to Bethany

By now it was getting late so he had to return to Bethany.

Mark 11.11

11: And Jesus entered into Jerusalem, and into the temple:

and when he had looked round about upon all things, and now the eventide was come, he went out unto Bethany with the twelve.

D – MONDAY

Monday and Tuesday are going to be taken up mainly with debating with a variety of people. As the gospellers relate matters in different orders it is difficult to form a coherent chronology, so we will treat all the debates as occurring on Monday although many would have taken place on Tuesday. Jesus returns from Bethany and goes to the Temple. Later he moves to the Treasury.

14.4 The Fig Tree

On his way back to Jerusalem the next morning Jesus noted a fig tree which he would use for one of his parables. Mark also notes this on the Mount of Olives.

Mark 11 12 - 14

12: And on the morrow, when they were come from Bethany, he was hungry:

13: And seeing a fig tree afar off having leaves, he came, if haply he might find anything thereon: and when he came to it, he found nothing but leaves; for the time of figs was not yet.

14: And Jesus answered and said unto it, No man eat fruit of thee hereafter for ever. And his disciples heard it.

Matthew 21 18 - 22

[18] Now in the morning as he returned into the city, he hungered.

[19] And when he saw a fig tree in the way, he came to it, and found nothing thereon, but leaves only, and said unto it, Let no fruit grow on thee henceforward for ever. And presently the fig tree withered away.

[20] And when the disciples saw it, they marvelled, saying, How soon is the fig tree withered away!

[21] Jesus answered and said unto them, Verily I say unto you, If ye have faith, and doubt not, ye shall not only do this which is done to the fig tree, but also if ye shall say unto this mountain, Be thou removed, and be thou cast into the sea; it shall be done.

[22] And all things, whatsoever ye shall ask in prayer, believing, ye shall receive.

14.5 Meeting the Greeks

Among the visitors were some people from Greece. It would seem that they were Jews as they had come to worship at the Passover festival. They would have been used to intellectual dispute and were curious to learn what all the fuss was about. Jesus sensing that time was running out made it clear that he was looking for followers with real commitment.

John 12 20 - 36

[20] And there were certain Greeks among them that came up to worship at the feast:

[21] The same came therefore to Philip, which was of Bethsaida of Galilee, and desired him, saying, Sir, we would see Jesus.

[22] Philip cometh and telleth Andrew: and again Andrew and Philip tell Jesus.

[23] And Jesus answered them, saying, The hour is come, that the Son of man should be glorified.

[24] Verily, verily, I say unto you, Except a corn of wheat fall into the ground and die, it abideth alone: but if it die, it bringeth forth much fruit.

[25] He that loveth his life shall lose it; and he that hateth his life in this world shall keep it unto life eternal.

[26] If any man serve me, let him follow me; and where I am, there shall also my servant be: if any man serve me, him will my Father honour.

[27] Now is my soul troubled; and what shall I say? Father, save me from this hour: but for this cause came I unto this hour.

[28] Father, glorify thy name. Then came there a voice from heaven, saying, I have both glorified it, and will glorify it again.

[29] The people therefore, that stood by, and heard it, said that it thundered: others said, An angel spake to him.

[30] Jesus answered and said, This voice came not because of me, but for your sakes.

[31] Now is the judgment of this world: now shall the prince of this world be cast out.

[32] And I, if I be lifted up from the earth, will draw all men unto me.

[33] This he said, signifying what death he should die.

[34] The people answered him, We have heard out of the law that Christ abideth for ever: and how sayest thou, The Son of man must be lifted up? who is this Son of man?

[35] Then Jesus said unto them, Yet a little while is the light with you. Walk while ye have the light, lest darkness come upon you: for he that walketh in darkness knoweth not whither he goeth.

[36] While ye have light, believe in the light, that ye may be the children of light. These things spake Jesus, and departed, and did hide himself from them.

14.6 By Whose Authority?

By now the Temple hierarchy were prepared to challenge Jesus and started by asking what his authority was. Jesus had moved to the Treasury and resumed his preaching.

John 8 12 - 20

[12] Then spake Jesus again unto them, saying, I am the light of the world: he that followeth me shall not walk in darkness, but shall have the light of life.

[13] The Pharisees therefore said unto him, Thou bearest record of thyself; thy record is not true.

[14] Jesus answered and said unto them, Though I bear record of myself, yet my record is true: for I know whence I came, and whither I go; but ye cannot tell whence I come, and whither I go.

[15] Ye judge after the flesh; I judge no man.

[16] And yet if I judge, my judgment is true: for I am not alone, but I and the Father that sent me.

[17] It is also written in your law, that the testimony of two men is true.

[18] I am one that bear witness of myself, and the Father that sent me beareth witness of me.

[19] Then said they unto him, Where is thy Father? Jesus answered, Ye neither know me, nor my Father: if ye had known me, ye should have known my Father also.

[20] These words spake Jesus in the treasury, as he taught in the temple: and no man laid hands on him; for his hour was not yet come. .

Mark 11 27 - 33

27: And they come again to Jerusalem: and as he was walking in the temple, there come to him the chief priests, and the scribes, and the elders,

28: And say unto him, By what authority doest thou these things? and who gave thee this authority to do these things?

29: And Jesus answered and said unto them, I will also ask of you one question, and answer me, and I will tell you by what authority I do these things.

30: The baptism of John, was it from heaven, or of men? answer me.

31: And they reasoned with themselves, saying, If we shall say, From heaven; he will say, Why then did ye not believe him?

32: But if we shall say, Of men; they feared the people: for all men counted John, that he was a prophet indeed.

33: And they answered and said unto Jesus, We cannot tell. And Jesus answering saith unto them, Neither do I tell you by what authority I do these things.

Matthew 21 23 - 27

[23] And when he was come into the temple, the chief priests and the elders of the people came unto him as he was teaching, and said, By what authority doest thou these things? and who gave thee this authority?

[24] And Jesus answered and said unto them, I also will ask you one thing, which if ye tell me, I in like wise will tell you by what authority I do these things.

[25] The baptism of John, whence was it? from heaven, or of men? And they reasoned with themselves, saying, If we shall say, From heaven; he will say unto us, Why did ye not then believe him?

[26] But if we shall say, Of men; we fear the people; for all hold John as a prophet.

[27] And they answered Jesus, and said, We cannot tell. And he said unto them, Neither tell I you by what authority I do these things.

Luke notes that this reply started them arguing amongst themselves.

Luke 20 1 - 8

[1] And it came to pass, that on one of those days, as he taught the people in the temple, and preached the gospel, the chief priests and the scribes came upon him with the elders,

[2] And spake unto him, saying, Tell us, by what authority doest thou these things? or who is he that gave thee this authority?

[3] And he answered and said unto them, I will also ask you one thing; and answer me:

[4] The baptism of John, was it from heaven, or of men?

[5] And they reasoned with themselves, saying, If we shall say, From heaven; he will say, Why then believed ye him not?

[6] But and if we say, Of men; all the people will stone us: for they be persuaded that John was a prophet.

[7] And they answered, that they could not tell whence it was.

[8] And Jesus said unto them, Neither tell I you by what authority I do these things.

14.7 Caesar's Money

The Temple officials now tried him out with some trick questions - First the Pharisees tried to get him into a dispute with the Roman authorities.

Mark 12 13 - 17

13: And they send unto him certain of the Pharisees and of the Herodians, to catch him in his words.

14: And when they were come, they say unto him, Master, we know that thou art true, and carest for no man: for thou regardest not the person of men, but teachest the way of God in truth: Is it lawful to give tribute to Caesar, or not?

15: Shall we give, or shall we not give? But he, knowing their hypocrisy, said unto them, Why tempt ye me? bring me a penny, that I may see it.

16: And they brought it. And he saith unto them, Whose is this image and superscription? And they said unto him, Caesar's.

17: And Jesus answering said unto them, Render to Caesar the things that are Caesar's, and to God the things that are God's. And they marvelled at him.

Luke 20 21 - 26

[21] And they asked him, saying, Master, we know that thou sayest and teachest rightly, neither acceptest thou the person of any, but teachest the way of God truly:

[22] Is it lawful for us to give tribute unto Caesar, or no?

[23] But he perceived their craftiness, and said unto them, Why tempt ye me?

[24] Shew me a penny. Whose image and superscription hath it? They answered and said, Caesar's.

[25] And he said unto them, Render therefore unto Caesar the things which be Caesar's, and unto God the things which be God's.

[26] And they could not take hold of his words before the people: and they marvelled at his answer, and held their peace.

Matthew 22 15 - 22

[15] Then went the Pharisees, and took counsel how they might entangle him in his talk.

[16] And they sent out unto him their disciples with the Herodians, saying, Master, we know that thou art true, and teachest the way of God in truth, neither carest thou for any man: for thou regardest not the person of men.

[17] Tell us therefore, What thinkest thou? Is it lawful to give tribute unto Caesar, or not?

[18] But Jesus perceived their wickedness, and said, Why tempt ye me, ye hypocrites?

[19] Shew me the tribute money. And they brought unto him a penny.

[20] And he saith unto them, Whose is this image and superscription?

[21] They say unto him, Caesar's. Then saith he unto them, Render therefore unto Caesar the things which are Caesar's; and unto God the things that are God's.

[22] When they had heard these words, they marvelled, and left him, and went their way.

14.8 The Afterlife

Then the Saduccees had a go on the problems of Resurrection.

Mark 12 18 - 34

[18] Then come unto him the Sadducees, which say there is no resurrection; and they asked him, saying,

[19] Master, Moses wrote unto us, If a man's brother die, and leave his wife behind him, and leave no children, that his brother should take his wife, and raise up seed unto his brother.

[20] Now there were seven brethren: and the first took a wife, and dying left no seed.

[21] And the second took her, and died, neither left he any seed: and the third likewise.

[22] And the seven had her, and left no seed: last of all the woman died also.

[23] In the resurrection therefore, when they shall rise, whose wife shall she be of them? for the seven had her to wife.

[24] And Jesus answering said unto them, Do ye not therefore err, because ye know not the scriptures, neither the power of God?

[25] For when they shall rise from the dead, they neither marry, nor are given in marriage; but are as the angels which are in heaven.

[26] And as touching the dead, that they rise: have ye not read in the book of Moses, how in the bush God spake unto him, saying, I am the God of Abraham, and the God of Isaac, and the God of Jacob?

[27] He is not the God of the dead, but the God of the living: ye therefore do greatly err.

[28] And one of the scribes came, and having heard them reasoning together, and perceiving that he had answered them well, asked him, Which is the first commandment of all?

[29] And Jesus answered him, The first of all the commandments is, Hear, O Israel; The Lord our God is one Lord:

[30] And thou shalt love the Lord thy God with all thy heart, and with all thy soul, and with all thy mind, and with all thy strength: this is the first commandment.

[31] And the second is like, namely this, Thou shalt love thy neighbour as thyself. There is none other commandment greater than these.

[32] And the scribe said unto him, Well, Master, thou hast said the truth: for there is one God; and there is none other but he:

[33] And to love him with all the heart, and with all the understanding, and with all the soul, and with all the strength, and to love his neighbour as himself, is more than all whole burnt offerings and sacrifices.

[34] And when Jesus saw that he answered discreetly, he said unto him, Thou art not far from the kingdom of God. And no man after that durst ask him any question.

Luke 20 27 - 38

[27] Then came to him certain of the Sadducees, which deny that there is any resurrection; and they asked him,

[28] Saying, Master, Moses wrote unto us, If any man's brother die, having a wife, and he die without children, that his brother should take his wife, and raise up seed unto his brother.

[29] There were therefore seven brethren: and the first took a wife, and died without children.

[30] And the second took her to wife, and he died childless.

[31] And the third took her; and in like manner the seven also: and they left no children, and died.

[32] Last of all the woman died also.

[33] Therefore in the resurrection whose wife of them is she? for seven had her to wife.

[34] And Jesus answering said unto them, The children of this world marry, and are given in marriage:

[35] But they which shall be accounted worthy to obtain that world, and the resurrection from the dead, neither marry, nor are given in marriage:

[36] Neither can they die any more: for they are equal unto the angels; and are the children of God, being the children of the resurrection.

[37] Now that the dead are raised, even Moses shewed at the bush, when he calleth the Lord the God of Abraham, and the God of Isaac, and the God of Jacob.

[38] For he is not a God of the dead, but of the living: for all live unto him.

Matthew 22 23 - 33

[23] The same day came to him the Sadducees, which say that there is no resurrection, and asked him,

[24] Saying, Master, Moses said, If a man die, having no children, his brother shall marry his wife, and raise up seed unto his brother.

[25] Now there were with us seven brethren: and the first, when he had married a wife, deceased, and, having no issue, left his wife unto his brother:

[26] Likewise the second also, and the third, unto the seventh.

[27] And last of all the woman died also.

[28] Therefore in the resurrection whose wife shall she be of the seven? for they all had her.

[29] Jesus answered and said unto them, Ye do err, not knowing the scriptures, nor the power of God.

[30] For in the resurrection they neither marry, nor are given in marriage, but are as the angels of God in heaven.

[31] But as touching the resurrection of the dead, have ye not read that which was spoken unto you by God, saying,

[32] I am the God of Abraham, and the God of Isaac, and the God of Jacob? God is not the God of the dead, but of the living.

[33] And when the multitude heard this, they were astonished at his doctrine.

14.9 The Greater Law

The Pharisees tried a different approach but again Jesus turns their arguments against them.

Matthew 22 34 - 46

[34] But when the Pharisees had heard that he had put the Sadducees to silence, they were gathered together.

[35] Then one of them, which was a lawyer, asked him a question, tempting him, and saying,

[36] Master, which is the great commandment in the law?

[37] Jesus said unto him, Thou shalt love the Lord thy God with all thy heart, and with all thy soul, and with all thy mind.

[38] This is the first and great commandment.

[39] And the second is like unto it, Thou shalt love thy neighbour as thyself.

[40] On these two commandments hang all the law and the prophets.

[41] While the Pharisees were gathered together, Jesus asked them,

[42] Saying, What think ye of Christ? whose son is he? They say unto him, The Son of David.

[43] He saith unto them, How then doth David in spirit call him Lord, saying,

[44] The LORD said unto my Lord, Sit thou on my right hand, till I make thine enemies thy footstool?

[45] If David then call him Lord, how is he his son?

[46] And no man was able to answer him a word, neither durst any man from that day forth ask him any more questions.

Jesus' answers had silenced his critics for a while and He warned the people about taking people at face value. His first example related to the lawyers.

Mark 12 35 - 40

[35] And Jesus answered and said, while he taught in the temple, How say the scribes that Christ is the Son of David?

[36] For David himself said by the Holy Ghost, The Lord said to my Lord, Sit thou on my right hand, till I make thine enemies thy footstool.

[37] David therefore himself calleth him Lord; and whence is he then his son? And the common people heard him gladly.

[38] And he said unto them in his doctrine, Beware of the scribes, which love to go in long clothing, and love salutations in the marketplaces,

[39] And the chief seats in the synagogues, and the uppermost rooms at feasts:

[40] Which devour widows' houses, and for a pretence make long prayers: these shall receive greater damnation.

Matthew gives a fuller answer.

Matthew 23 1 - 39
[1] Then spake Jesus to the multitude, and to his disciples,
[2] Saying, The scribes and the Pharisees sit in Moses' seat:
[3] All therefore whatsoever they bid you observe, that observe and do; but do not ye after their works: for they say, and do not.
[4] For they bind heavy burdens and grievous to be borne, and lay them on men's shoulders; but they themselves will not move them with one of their fingers.
[5] But all their works they do for to be seen of men: they make broad their phylacteries, and enlarge the borders of their garments,
[6] And love the uppermost rooms at feasts, and the chief seats in the synagogues,
[7] And greetings in the markets, and to be called of men, Rabbi, Rabbi.
[8] But be not ye called Rabbi: for one is your Master, even Christ; and all ye are brethren.
[9] And call no man your father upon the earth: for one is your Father, which is in heaven.
[10] Neither be ye called masters: for one is your Master, even Christ.
[11] But he that is greatest among you shall be your servant.
[12] And whosoever shall exalt himself shall be abased; and he that shall humble himself shall be exalted.
[13] But woe unto you, scribes and Pharisees, hypocrites! for ye shut up the kingdom of heaven against men: for ye neither go in yourselves, neither suffer ye them that are entering to go in.
[14] Woe unto you, scribes and Pharisees, hypocrites! for ye devour widows' houses, and for a pretence make long prayer: therefore ye shall receive the greater damnation.
[15] Woe unto you, scribes and Pharisees, hypocrites! for ye compass sea and land to make one proselyte, and when he is made, ye make him twofold more the child of hell than yourselves.
[16] Woe unto you, ye blind guides, which say, Whosoever shall swear by the temple, it is nothing; but whosoever shall swear by the gold of the temple, he is a debtor!
[17] Ye fools and blind: for whether is greater, the gold, or the temple that sanctifieth the gold?
[18] And, Whosoever shall swear by the altar, it is nothing; but whosoever sweareth by the gift that is upon it, he is guilty.
[19] Ye fools and blind: for whether is greater, the gift, or the altar that sanctifieth the gift?

[20] Whoso therefore shall swear by the altar, sweareth by it, and by all things thereon.

[21] And whoso shall swear by the temple, sweareth by it, and by him that dwelleth therein.

[22] And he that shall swear by heaven, sweareth by the throne of God, and by him that sitteth thereon.

[23] Woe unto you, scribes and Pharisees, hypocrites! for ye pay tithe of mint and anise and cummin, and have omitted the weightier matters of the law, judgment, mercy, and faith: these ought ye to have done, and not to leave the other undone.

[24] Ye blind guides, which strain at a gnat, and swallow a camel.

[25] Woe unto you, scribes and Pharisees, hypocrites! for ye make clean the outside of the cup and of the platter, but within they are full of extortion and excess.

[26] Thou blind Pharisee, cleanse first that which is within the cup and platter, that the outside of them may be clean also.

[27] Woe unto you, scribes and Pharisees, hypocrites! for ye are like unto whited sepulchres, which indeed appear beautiful outward, but are within full of dead men's bones, and of all uncleanness.

[28] Even so ye also outwardly appear righteous unto men, but within ye are full of hypocrisy and iniquity.

[29] Woe unto you, scribes and Pharisees, hypocrites! because ye build the tombs of the prophets, and garnish the sepulchres of the righteous,

[30] And say, If we had been in the days of our fathers, we would not have been partakers with them in the blood of the prophets.

[31] Wherefore ye be witnesses unto yourselves, that ye are the children of them which killed the prophets.

[32] Fill ye up then the measure of your fathers.

[33] Ye serpents, ye generation of vipers, how can ye escape the damnation of hell?

[34] Wherefore, behold, I send unto you prophets, and wise men, and scribes: and some of them ye shall kill and crucify; and some of them shall ye scourge in your synagogues, and persecute them from city to city:

[35] That upon you may come all the righteous blood shed upon the earth, from the blood of righteous Abel unto the blood of Zacharias son of Barachias, whom ye slew between the temple and the altar.

[36] Verily I say unto you, All these things shall come upon this generation.

[37] O Jerusalem, Jerusalem, thou that killest the prophets, and stonest them which are sent unto thee, how often would I have gathered thy children together, even as a hen gathereth her chickens under her wings, and ye would not!

[38] Behold, your house is left unto you desolate.

[39] For I say unto you, Ye shall not see me henceforth, till ye shall say, Blessed is he that cometh in the name of the Lord.

14.10 Is Jesus David's Son?

Jesus seems to have answered all the points raised by the Jewish authorities but they want to know which house he is from. Isaiah had forecast the Messiah would come from the house of David. The gospellers now mix up the very different concepts of a 'house' and a father-son relationship. (See section 2.8)

Luke 20 39 - 47
[39] Then certain of the scribes answering said, Master, thou hast well said.
[40] And after that they durst not ask him any question at all.
[41] And he said unto them, How say they that Christ is David's son?
[42] And David himself saith in the book of Psalms, The LORD said unto my Lord, Sit thou on my right hand,
[43] Till I make thine enemies thy footstool.
[44] David therefore calleth him Lord, how is he then his son?
[45] Then in the audience of all the people he said unto his disciples,
[46] Beware of the scribes, which desire to walk in long robes, and love greetings in the markets, and the highest seats in the synagogues, and the chief rooms at feasts;
[47] Which devour widows' houses, and for a shew make long prayers: the same shall receive greater damnation.

14.11 Rasing the Temple

Jesus appears to forecast the destruction of the Temple which took place in 70 AD.

Mark 13 1 - 2
1: And as he went out of the temple, one of his disciples saith unto him, Master, see what manner of stones and what buildings are here!
2: And Jesus answering said unto him, Seest thou these great buildings? there shall not be left one stone upon another, that shall not be thrown down.

Luke 21 5 - 6
[5] And as some spake of the temple, how it was adorned with goodly stones and gifts, he said,

[6] As for these things which ye behold, the days will come, in the which there shall not be left one stone upon another, that shall not be thrown down.

Matthew 24 1 - 2
[1] And Jesus went out, and departed from the temple: and his disciples came to him for to shew him the buildings of the temple.
[2] And Jesus said unto them, See ye not all these things? verily I say unto you, There shall not be left here one stone upon another, that shall not be thrown down.

E - MONDAY EVENING

We do not know how late Jesus was on Monday evening but we presume he returned to Bethany.

F – TUESDAY

We presume Jesus returned to Jerusalem and continued the debates.

Chapter 15 Conspiracy and Betrayal

15.1 What is the Truth?

By the start of Holy Week it had become clear that the Jewish authorities, particularly the Pharisees, saw Jesus not as the long prophesied Messiah; but as a serious threat to their power. They had tried several times to arrest him while he was addressing crowds but backed off at the last moment. However they had generally succeeded in disillusioning the Jerusalem crowds.

His followers had, for the most part deserted him. He was left with only his Disciples and a few intimate friends. Even among the Disciples, Judas was not to be trusted.

We have two principal sources to go on: first the accounts in the Gospels and second what has appeared recently in the Gospel of Judas which throws a very different light on events.

Over the centuries Judas has been portrayed as the archetypical bad guy who would betray his friends. That is the picture the gospellers are keen to portray but when you look at the family relationships around the house at Bethany (see section 13.3) it becomes obvious that Jesus was in fact Judas's brother-in-law.

The Gospel of Judas records conversations between Jesus and Judas and it can be inferred that Judas was party to knowledge about Jesus and his mission and was complicit with Jesus in ensuring that the final week went to plan to demonstrate finally the divinity of Jesus.

Let's start with what the gospellers say about the events leading to Jesus' arrest.

G - TUESDAY EVENING

15.2   Judas does a deal

Judas went to see the chief priests to see how much they would pay for him to betray Jesus.

Matthew 26 14 - 16

[14] Then one of the twelve, called Judas Iscariot, went unto the chief priests,

[15] And said unto them, What will ye give me, and I will deliver him unto you? And they covenanted with him for thirty pieces of silver.

[16] And from that time he sought opportunity to betray him.

Mark 14 10 - 11

[10] And Judas Iscariot, one of the twelve, went unto the chief priests, to betray him unto them.

[11] And when they heard it, they were glad, and promised to give him money. And he sought how he might conveniently betray him.

Luke 22 1 - 6

[1] Now the feast of unleavened bread drew nigh, which is called the Passover.

[2] And the chief priests and scribes sought how they might kill him; for they feared the people.

[3] Then entered Satan into Judas surnamed Iscariot, being of the number of the twelve.

[4] And he went his way, and communed with the chief priests and captains, how he might betray him unto them.

[5] And they were glad, and covenanted to give him money.

[6] And he promised, and sought opportunity to betray him unto them in the absence of the multitude.

15.3 Jesus realises his death is imminent

Jesus now knows that his time has come. This must be after supper on the Tuesday.

John 13 1 - 2

[1] Now before the feast of the passover, when Jesus knew that his hour was come that he should depart out of this world unto the Father, having loved his own which were in the world, he loved them unto the end.

[2] And supper being ended, the devil having now put into the heart of Judas Iscariot, Simon's son, to betray him;

15.4 Washing the Disciple's Feet

The ceremony John now describes involves Jesus ritually washing the feet of his disciples.

John 13 3 - 17

[3] Jesus knowing that the Father had given all things into his hands, and that he was come from God, and went to God;

[4] He riseth from supper, and laid aside his garments; and took a towel, and girded himself.

[5] After that he poureth water into a bason, and began to wash the disciples' feet, and to wipe them with the towel wherewith he was girded.

[6] Then cometh he to Simon Peter: and Peter saith unto him, Lord, dost thou wash my feet?

[7] Jesus answered and said unto him, What I do thou knowest not now; but thou shalt know hereafter.

[8] Peter saith unto him, Thou shalt never wash my feet. Jesus answered him, If I wash thee not, thou hast no part with me.

[9] Simon Peter saith unto him, Lord, not my feet only, but also my hands and my head.

[10] Jesus saith to him, He that is washed needeth not save to wash his feet, but is clean every whit: and ye are clean, but not all.

[11] For he knew who should betray him; therefore, said he, Ye are not all clean.

[12] So after he had washed their feet, and had taken his garments, and was set down again, he said unto them, Know ye what I have done to you?

[13] Ye call me Master and Lord: and ye say well; for so I am.

[14] If I then, your Lord and Master, have washed your feet; ye also ought to wash one another's feet.

[15] For I have given you an example, that ye should do as I have done to you.

[16] Verily, verily, I say unto you, The servant is not greater than his lord; neither he that is sent greater than he that sent him.

[17] If ye know these things, happy are ye if ye do them.

15.5 Jesus warns the disciples

John hints at scripture needing to be fulfilled as the reason Jesus now alerts the disciples to the betrayal.

John 13 18 - 22

[18] I speak not of you all: I know whom I have chosen: but that the scripture may be fulfilled, He that eateth bread with me hath lifted up his heel against me.

[19] Now I tell you before it come, that, when it is come to pass, ye may believe that I am he.

[20] Verily, verily, I say unto you, He that receiveth whomsoever I send receiveth me; and he that receiveth me receiveth him that sent me.

[21] When Jesus had thus said, he was troubled in spirit, and testified, and said, Verily, verily, I say unto you, that one of you shall betray me.

[22] Then the disciples looked one on another, doubting of whom he spake.

Simon Peter knows that it is John who is closest to Jesus and tries to get him to spill the beans.

John 13 23 - 27

[23] Now there was leaning on Jesus' bosom one of his disciples, whom Jesus loved.

[24] Simon Peter therefore beckoned to him, that he should ask who it should be of whom he spake.

[25] He then lying on Jesus' breast saith unto him, Lord, who is it?

[26] Jesus answered, He it is, to whom I shall give a sop, when I have dipped it. And when he had dipped the sop, he gave it to Judas Iscariot, the son of Simon.

[27] And after the sop Satan entered into him. Then said Jesus unto him, That thou doest, do quickly.

The other disciples saw Judas leave and assume that he left to make preparation for what was to be the last supper, as he was the person who looked after the group's money.

John 13 28 - 30

[28] Now no man at the table knew for what intent he spake this unto him.

[29] For some of them thought, because Judas had the bag, that Jesus had said unto him, Buy those things that we have need of against the feast; or, that he should give something to the poor.

[30] He then having received the sop went immediately out: and it was night.

Mark has a very much abbreviated version of the incident.

Mark 14 17 - 21
[17] And in the evening he cometh with the twelve.
[18] And as they sat and did eat, Jesus said, Verily I say unto you, One of you which eateth with me shall betray me.
[19] And they began to be sorrowful, and to say unto him one by one, Is it I? and another said, Is it I?
[20] And he answered and said unto them, It is one of the twelve, that dippeth with me in the dish.
[21] The Son of man indeed goeth, as it is written of him: but woe to that man by whom the Son of man is betrayed! good were it for that man if he had never been born.

Matthew notes that the incident did not occur in Jerusalem and gives confirmation to John's timetable although it is obvious that whoever wrote this was not present at the time.

Matthew 20 17 - 19
[17] And Jesus going up to Jerusalem took the twelve disciples apart in the way, and said unto them,
[18] Behold, we go up to Jerusalem; and the Son of man shall be betrayed unto the chief priests and unto the scribes, and they shall condemn him to death,
[19] And shall deliver him to the Gentiles to mock, and to scourge, and to crucify him: and the third day he shall rise again.

15.6 Peter is warned

Peter had tried to get the identity of the betrayer via John but had not succeeded so approaches Jesus directly. But he gets an answer he was not expecting.

John 13 36 - 38
[36] Simon Peter said unto him, Lord, whither goest thou? Jesus answered him, Whither I go, thou canst not follow me now; but thou shalt follow me afterwards.
[37] Peter said unto him, Lord, why cannot I follow thee now? I will lay down my life for thy sake.
[38] Jesus answered him, Wilt thou lay down thy life for my sake? Verily, verily, I say unto thee, The cock shall not crow, till thou hast denied me thrice.

Luke includes the warning to Peter in the middle of his farewell speech.

Luke 22 31 - 34
[31] And the Lord said, Simon, Simon, behold, Satan hath desired to have you, that he may sift you as wheat:
[32] But I have prayed for thee, that thy faith fail not: and when thou art converted, strengthen thy brethren.
[33] And he said unto him, Lord, I am ready to go with thee, both into prison, and to death.
[34] And he said, I tell thee, Peter, the cock shall not crow this day, before that thou shalt thrice deny that thou knowest me.

15.7 The Gospel of Judas

In recent years a gospel attributed to Judas has emerged It throws a completely different light on both the character of Judas and his relationship with Jesus. We can recall that Judas was probably Jesus' brother-in-law and therefore a close family member, closer than any of the other disciples. It would seem therefore quite possible that it was in Judas that Jesus confided and got him to ensure his arrest.

The Gospel of Judas consists of conversations between the Apostle Judas and Jesus It is believed to have been written by Gnostic followers of Jesus, rather than by Judas himself, and, since it contains late second century theology, probably dates from no earlier than the second century. In 180 AD, Irenaeus, the Bishop of Lyons, wrote a document in which he railed against this gospel, indicating the book was already in circulation. The only copy of the Gospel of Judas known to exist is a Coptic text that has been carbon dated to 280 AD, plus or minus 60 years. A translation of the text was first published in early 2006 by the National Geographical Society.

In contrast to the canonical gospels which paint Judas as a betrayer of Christ who delivered him up to the authorities for crucifixion in exchange for money, the Gospel of Judas portrays Judas' actions as done in obedience to instructions given by Christ. The document also suggests that Christ planned the course of events which led to his death. This portrayal seems to conform to a notion current in some forms of Gnosticism, that the human form is a spiritual prison, that Judas thus served Christ by helping to release Christ's soul from its physical constraints, and that two kinds of human beings exist: the men furnished with the immortal soul which is "from the eternal realms" and "will abide there always" ("the strong and holy generation. with no ruler over it", to whom Judas belongs), and the other ones, the majority of mankind, who are mortal and therefore unable to reach the salvation. The Gospel of Judas does not claim that the other disciples knew about Jesus's true teachings. On the contrary, it asserts that they had not learned the true Gospel, which Jesus taught only to Judas Iscariot, the sole follower belonging to the "holy generation" among the disciples.

We summarise some selected parts of the text to illustrate the history rather than the thoughts of Jesus.

The English translation of the text is available on the New York Times website. It records a somewhat different view of Jesus' mission and how it was conducted than appears in the canonical gospels. Also a conversation between Jesus and Judas about three days before the Passover.

Jesus had performed many miracles and other wonders to demonstrate the love of God and free humanity from its sins. He often appeared before his disciples as a child rather than an adult and was trying to get people to understand mysteries beyond this world. When he found his disciples praying piously, he was wont to laugh at their seriousness and told them they should be praising God.

He also makes the point that while the disciples think they know him, they really do not.

The disciples get angry at this but he challenges them to stand up and show what it is like to be a perfect human. Only Judas believed he could; but he was unable to stand up and look Jesus in the eye. Judas said he knew where Jesus came from, an immortal realm called Barbelo; but claimed he was unworthy to utter the name of the person who sent him. Jesus then invites Judas to step aside a moment while he tells him of the mysteries of the kingdom. He forecasts that this knowledge will cause him much grief and that the rest of the disciples will have to replace him. Judas wants to know what will become of him and Jesus tells him he will be reviled but hints that he will ascend to what he refers to as the 'Holy Generation'

While Jesus was praying the high priests approached Judas to ask what he was up to. He was somewhat perplexed because he did not understand why they were so angry with Jesus and why had the god within them so provoked them. Nevertheless, Judas told them what they wanted to know and received money in return.

PART 4
THE PASSION

The debates are over. The Jewish Authorities have concluded that Jesus is dangerous and must be taken out. They have conspired with Judas and turned the population against him.

First Jesus says farewell to his followers and goes to the Mount of Olives to pray. Here he is arrested and taken for trial to the Roman authorities. They want nothing to do with the affair but pressure from the mob forces them to take the easy option and condemn Jesus to death.

The crucifixion takes place and all his followers are heartbroken. He is buried in a tomb but when his wife and mother come to visit they are amazed that the tomb is empty.

Within a few days most of his followers are aware that Jesus is alive and a new force is created.

Chapter 16 The Farewell

H – WEDNESDAY

The Passion begins with the Last Supper. Traditionally Christians have viewed it as a celebration of the Passover and have made great play of the symbolism of The Lamb. It is evident however from John's account that it was nothing of the kind. It was a farewell meal and John hardly mentions it. Instead John dwells on the cycle of life, death and regeneration which is so obvious in the plant world and Jesus expounded it in human terms.

16.1 Preparing for the Last Supper

The descriptions of the Last Supper in the four Gospels are in sharp contrast and often contradictory. According to John it was a farewell meal held not on the eve of Passover (Thursday) as recorded by the other Gospel writers but on the Wednesday. By the time of the eve of Passover, Jesus would already be arrested. It is not surprising therefore that John does not describe the Passover rituals involving bread and wine and we can reasonably infer that the other Gospellers were simply seeking to establish the basis of the ceremonial meal which had become the focus of Christian Worship by the turn of the first century. This seems to have been a development of the Jewish Passover ceremonies which had been adapted to Christian use.

Matthew describes how the disciples made the arrangements.

Matthew 26 17 - 19
[17] Now the first day of the feast of unleavened bread the disciples came to Jesus, saying unto him, Where wilt thou that we prepare for thee to eat the passover?
[18] And he said, Go into the city to such a man, and say unto him, The Master saith, My time is at hand; I will keep the passover at thy house with my disciples.
[19] And the disciples did as Jesus had appointed them; and they made ready the passover.

Mark gives a few extra details.

Mark 14 12 - 16

[12] And the first day of unleavened bread, when they killed the passover, his disciples said unto him, Where wilt thou that we go and prepare that thou mayest eat the passover?

[13] And he sendeth forth two of his disciples, and saith unto them, Go ye into the city, and there shall meet you a man bearing a pitcher of water: follow him.

[14] And wheresoever he shall go in, say ye to the goodman of the house, The Master saith, Where is the guestchamber, where I shall eat the passover with my disciples?

15: And he will shew you a large upper room furnished and prepared: there make ready for us.

16: And his disciples went forth, and came into the city, and found as he had said unto them: and they made ready the passover.

And Luke gives some different details.

Luke 22 7 - 13

[7] Then came the day of unleavened bread, when the passover must be killed.

[8] And he sent Peter and John, saying, Go and prepare us the passover, that we may eat.

[9] And they said unto him, Where wilt thou that we prepare?

[10] And he said unto them, Behold, when ye are entered into the city, there shall a man meet you, bearing a pitcher of water; follow him into the house where he entereth in.

[11] And ye shall say unto the goodman of the house, The Master saith unto thee, Where is the guestchamber, where I shall eat the passover with my disciples?

[12] And he shall shew you a large upper room furnished: there make ready.

[13] And they went, and found as he had said unto them: and they made ready the passover.

J-WEDNESDAY EVENING

16.2 The Origins of Holy Communion

John does not mention the ritual sanctification of bread and wine; but the other three Gospellers do. It is a key question as to whether the meal was a celebration of Passover, ie the protection of the Jews from the plagues of Egypt as recounted in the book of Exodus, or a much older Jewish recreation of the eternal cycle of life and death and regeneration.

Matthew, Mark and Luke record much the same version of a typical Passover meal which has become the basis of the Eucharist.

Matthew 26 26 - 29

[26] And as they were eating, Jesus took bread, and blessed it, and brake it, and gave it to the disciples, and said, Take, eat; this is my body.
[27] And he took the cup, and gave thanks, and gave it to them, saying, Drink ye all of it;
[28] For this is my blood of the New Testament, which is shed for many for the remission of sins.
[29] But I say unto you, I will not drink henceforth of this fruit of the vine, until that day when I drink it new with you in my Father's kingdom.

Mark 14 22 - 25

[22] And as they did eat, Jesus took bread, and blessed, and brake it, and gave to them, and said, Take, eat: this is my body.
[23] And he took the cup, and when he had given thanks, he gave it to them: and they all drank of it.
[24] And he said unto them, This is my blood of the new testament, which is shed for many.
[25] Verily I say unto you, I will drink no more of the fruit of the vine, until that day that I drink it new in the kingdom of God.

Luke 22 17 - 20

[17] And he took the cup, and gave thanks, and said, Take this, and divide it among yourselves:
[18] For I say unto you, I will not drink of the fruit of the vine, until the kingdom of God shall come.

[19] And he took bread, and gave thanks, and brake it, and gave unto them, saying, This is my body which is given for you: this do in remembrance of me.

[20] Likewise also the cup after supper, saying, This cup is the new testament in my blood, which is shed for you.

16.3 Jesus Says Farewell to the Disciples

After the Last Supper Jesus turned to the disciples and made a speech of farewell which only John reports in full. He spoke of love and warned what was to come. He finished with a prayer Luke places the speech part before and part after the celebration.

Luke 22 14 - 16

[14] And when the hour was come, he sat down, and the twelve apostles with him.

[15] And he said unto them, With desire I have desired to eat this passover with you before I suffer:

[16] For I say unto you, I will not any more eat thereof, until it be fulfilled in the kingdom of God.

John 14 1 - 14

[1] Let not your heart be troubled: ye believe in God, believe also in me.

[2] In my Father's house are many mansions: if it were not so, I would have told you. I go to prepare a place for you.

[3] And if I go and prepare a place for you, I will come again, and receive you unto myself; that where I am, there ye may be also.

[4] And whither I go ye know, and the way ye know.

[5] Thomas saith unto him, Lord, we know not whither thou goest; and how can we know the way?

[6] Jesus saith unto him, I am the way, the truth, and the life: no man cometh unto the Father, but by me.

[7] If ye had known me, ye should have known my Father also: and from henceforth ye know him, and have seen him.

[8] Philip saith unto him, Lord, shew us the Father, and it sufficeth us.

[9] Jesus saith unto him, Have I been so long time with you, and yet hast thou not known me, Philip? he that hath seen me hath seen the Father; and how sayest thou then, Shew us the Father?

[10] Believest thou not that I am in the Father, and the Father in me? the words that I speak unto you I speak not of myself: but the Father that dwelleth in me, he doeth the works.

[11] Believe me that I am in the Father, and the Father in me: or else believe me for the very works' sake.

[12] Verily, verily, I say unto you, He that believeth on me, the works that I do shall he do also; and greater works than these shall he do; because I go unto my Father.

[13] And whatsoever ye shall ask in my name, that will I do, that the Father may be glorified in the Son.

[14] If ye shall ask any thing in my name, I will do it.

Jesus forecasts the coming of the Holy Spirit.

John 14 15 - 31

[15] If ye love me, keep my commandments.

[16] And I will pray the Father, and he shall give you another Comforter, that he may abide with you forever;

[17] Even the Spirit of truth; whom the world cannot receive, because it seeth him not, neither knoweth him: but ye know him; for he dwelleth with you, and shall be in you.

[18] I will not leave you comfortless: I will come to you.

[19] Yet a little while, and the world seeth me no more; but ye see me: because I live, ye shall live also.

[20] At that day ye shall know that I am in my Father, and ye in me, and I in you.

[21] He that hath my commandments, and keepeth them, he it is that loveth me: and he that loveth me shall be loved of my Father, and I will love him, and will manifest myself to him.

[22] Judas saith unto him, not Iscariot, Lord, how is it that thou wilt manifest thyself unto us, and not unto the world?

[23] Jesus answered and said unto him, If a man love me, he will keep my words: and my Father will love him, and we will come unto him, and make our abode with him.

[24] He that loveth me not keepeth not my sayings: and the word which ye hear is not mine, but the Father's which sent me.

[25] These things have I spoken unto you, being yet present with you.

[26] But the Comforter, which is the Holy Ghost, whom the Father will send in my name, he shall teach you all things, and bring all things to your remembrance, whatsoever I have said unto you.

[27] Peace I leave with you, my peace I give unto you: not as the world giveth, give I unto you. Let not your heart be troubled, neither let it be afraid.

[28] Ye have heard how I said unto you, I go away, and come again unto you. If ye loved me, ye would rejoice, because I said, I go unto the Father: for my Father is greater than I.

[29] And now I have told you before it come to pass, that, when it is come to pass, ye might believe.

[30] Hereafter I will not talk much with you: for the prince of this world cometh, and hath nothing in me.

[31] But that the world may know that I love the Father; and as the Father gave me commandment, even so I do. Arise, let us go hence.

He goes on to tell the parable of true vine and explains how life regenerates itself. This is the key to the real meaning of the Last Supper.

John 15 1 - 9

[1] I am the true vine, and my Father is the husbandman.

[2] Every branch in me that beareth not fruit he taketh away: and every branch that beareth fruit, he purgeth it, that it may bring forth more fruit.

[3] Now ye are clean through the word which I have spoken unto you.

[4] Abide in me, and I in you. As the branch cannot bear fruit of itself, except it abide in the vine; no more can ye, except ye abide in me.

[5] I am the vine, ye are the branches: He that abideth in me, and I in him, the same bringeth forth much fruit: for without me ye can do nothing.

[6] If a man abide not in me, he is cast forth as a branch, and is withered; and men gather them, and cast them into the fire, and they are burned.

[7] If ye abide in me, and my words abide in you, ye shall ask what ye will, and it shall be done unto you.

[8] Herein is my Father glorified, that ye bear much fruit; so shall ye be my disciples.

[9] As the Father hath loved me, so have I loved you: continue ye in my love.

And he repeats the main thrust of his ministry that God is love.

John 15 10 - 27

[10] If ye keep my commandments, ye shall abide in my love; even as I have kept my Father's commandments, and abide in his love.

[11] These things have I spoken unto you, that my joy might remain in you, and that your joy might be full.

[12] This is my commandment, That ye love one another, as I have loved you.

[13] Greater love hath no man than this, that a man lay down his life for his friends.

[14] Ye are my friends, if ye do whatsoever I command you.

[15] Henceforth I call you not servants; for the servant knoweth not what his lord doeth: but I have called you friends; for all things that I have heard of my Father I have made known unto you.

[16] Ye have not chosen me, but I have chosen you, and ordained you, that ye should go and bring forth fruit, and that your fruit should remain: that whatsoever ye shall ask of the Father in my name, he may give it you.

[17] These things I command you, that ye love one another.

[18] If the world hate you, ye know that it hated me before it hated you.

[19] If ye were of the world, the world would love his own: but because ye are not of the world, but I have chosen you out of the world, therefore the world hateth you.

[20] Remember the word that I said unto you, The servant is not greater than his lord. If they have persecuted me, they will also persecute you; if they have kept my saying, they will keep yours also.

[21] But all these things will they do unto you for my name's sake, because they know not him that sent me.

[22] If I had not come and spoken unto them, they had not had sin: but now they have no cloke for their sin.

[23] He that hateth me hateth my Father also.

[24] If I had not done among them the works which none other man did, they had not had sin: but now have they both seen and hated both me and my Father.

[25] But this cometh to pass, that the word might be fulfilled that is written in their law, They hated me without a cause.

[26] But when the Comforter is come, whom I will send unto you from the Father, even the Spirit of truth, which proceedeth from the Father, he shall testify of me:

[27] And ye also shall bear witness, because ye have been with me from the beginning

16.4 The Disciples are warned to be Armed

Jesus warns the Apostles that the way ahead will be hard and, in Luke's account, there is a bitter dispute among the disciples; but Jesus carries on his farewell speech and at the end suggests that they should arm themselves with swords.

Luke 22 21 - 30

[21] But, behold, the hand of him that betrayeth me is with me on the table.

[22] And truly the Son of man goeth, as it was determined: but woe unto that man by whom he is betrayed!

[23] And they began to inquire among themselves, which of them it was that should do this thing.

[24] And there was also a strife among them, which of them should be accounted the greatest.

[25] And he said unto them, The kings of the Gentiles exercise lordship over them; and they that exercise authority upon them are called benefactors.

[26] But ye shall not be so: but he that is greatest among you, let him be as the younger; and he that is chief, as he that doth serve.

[27] For whether is greater, he that sitteth at meat, or he that serveth? is not he that sitteth at meat? but I am among you as he that serveth.

[28] Ye are they which have continued with me in my temptations.

[29] And I appoint unto you a kingdom, as my Father hath appointed unto me;

[30] That ye may eat and drink at my table in my kingdom, and sit on thrones judging the twelve tribes of Israel. .

Luke 22 35 - 38

[36] Then said he unto them, But now, he that hath a purse, let him take it, and likewise his scrip: and he that hath no sword, let him sell his garment, and buy one.

[37] For I say unto you, that this that is written must yet be accomplished in me, And he was reckoned among the transgressors: for the things concerning me have an end.

[38] And they said, Lord, behold, here are two swords. And he said unto them, It is enough.

Chapter 17 The Mount of Olives

17.1 Going to the Mountain

According to Matthew and Mark, the first stop after the supper is the Mount of Olives. The Mount of Olives is separated from the main part of Jerusalem by a deep valley through which a small river, the Kedron, flows. You can either descend a steep slope, cross the river and then ascend another very steep slope or walk around the perimeter of the gorge. Bethany, now known as Eizanya, where we believe the last supper was held, is a few miles to the southeast of Jerusalem and to get from there to Jerusalem one passes close to the Mount of Olives.

Matthew 26 30 - 35

[30] And when they had sung an hymn, they went out into the mount of Olives.

[31] Then saith Jesus unto them, All ye shall be offended because of me this night: for it is written, I will smite the shepherd, and the sheep of the flock shall be scattered abroad.

[32] But after I am risen again, I will go before you into Galilee.

[33] Peter answered and said unto him, Though all men shall be offended because of thee, yet will I never be offended.

[34] Jesus said unto him, Verily I say unto thee, That this night, before the cock crow, thou shalt deny me thrice.

[35] Peter said unto him, Though I should die with thee, yet will I not deny thee. Likewise also said all the disciples.

Mark 14 26 - 31

[26] And when they had sung an hymn, they went out into the mount of Olives.

[27] And Jesus saith unto them, All ye shall be offended because of me this night: for it is written, I will smite the shepherd, and the sheep shall be scattered.

[28] But after that I am risen, I will go before you into Galilee.

[29] But Peter said unto him, Although all shall be offended, yet will not I.

[30] And Jesus saith unto him, Verily I say unto thee, That this day, even in this night, before the cock crow twice, thou shalt deny me thrice.

[31] But he spake the more vehemently, If I should die with thee, I will not deny thee in any wise. Likewise also said they all.

John 18 1
[1] When Jesus had spoken these words, he went forth with his disciples over the brook Cedron, where was a garden, into the which he entered, and his disciples.

17.2 Jesus Prays in the Garden

The garden was Gethsemane and Jesus takes his last opportunity for a period of prayer. His words are recorded - but who by? - All the disciples were asleep.

Matthew 26 36 - 46
[36] Then cometh Jesus with them unto a place called Gethsemane, and saith unto the disciples, Sit ye here, while I go and pray yonder.
[37] And he took with him Peter and the two sons of Zebedee, and began to be sorrowful and very heavy.
[38] Then saith he unto them, My soul is exceeding sorrowful, even unto death: tarry ye here, and watch with me.
[39] And he went a little further, and fell on his face, and prayed, saying, O my Father, if it be possible, let this cup pass from me: nevertheless not as I will, but as thou wilt.
[40] And he cometh unto the disciples, and findeth them asleep, and saith unto Peter, What, could ye not watch with me one hour?
[41] Watch and pray, that ye enter not into temptation: the spirit indeed is willing, but the flesh is weak.
[42] He went away again the second time, and prayed, saying, O my Father, if this cup may not pass away from me, except I drink it, thy will be done.
[43] And he came and found them asleep again: for their eyes were heavy.
[44] And he left them, and went away again, and prayed the third time, saying the same words.
[45] Then cometh he to his disciples, and saith unto them, Sleep on now, and take your rest: behold, the hour is at hand, and the Son of man is betrayed into the hands of sinners.
[46] Rise, let us be going: behold, he is at hand that doth betray me.

Mark 14 32 - 42
[32] And they came to a place which was named Gethsemane: and he saith to his disciples, Sit ye here, while I shall pray.

[33] And he taketh with him Peter and James and John, and began to be sore amazed, and to be very heavy;

[34] And saith unto them, My soul is exceeding sorrowful unto death: tarry ye here, and watch.

[35] And he went forward a little, and fell on the ground, and prayed that, if it were possible, the hour might pass from him.

[36] And he said, Abba, Father, all things are possible unto thee; take away this cup from me: nevertheless not what I will, but what thou wilt.

[37] And he cometh, and findeth them sleeping, and saith unto Peter, Simon, sleepest thou? couldest not thou watch one hour?

[38] Watch ye and pray, lest ye enter into temptation. The spirit truly is ready, but the flesh is weak.

[39] And again he went away, and prayed, and spake the same words.

[40] And when he returned, he found them asleep again, (for their eyes were heavy,) neither wist they what to answer him.

[41] And he cometh the third time, and saith unto them, Sleep on now, and take your rest: it is enough, the hour is come; behold, the Son of man is betrayed into the hands of sinners.

[42] Rise up, let us go; lo, he that betrayeth me is at hand.

Luke too places this episode on the Mount of Olives.

Luke 22 39 - 46

[39] And he came out, and went, as he was wont, to the mount of Olives; and his disciples also followed him.

[40] And when he was at the place, he said unto them, Pray that ye enter not into temptation.

[41] And he was withdrawn from them about a stone's cast, and kneeled down, and prayed,

[42] Saying, Father, if thou be willing, remove this cup from me: nevertheless not my will, but thine, be done.

[43] And there appeared an angel unto him from heaven, strengthening him.

[44] And being in an agony he prayed more earnestly: and his sweat was as it were great drops of blood falling down to the ground.

[45] And when he rose up from prayer, and was come to his disciples, he found them sleeping for sorrow,

[46] And said unto them, Why sleep ye? rise and pray, lest ye enter into temptation.

We now come to the crucial part of the story. The Last Supper has taken place and Jesus is about to be arrested. According to John, Jesus now delivers a long sermon but it really appears that John is recalling Jesus' words over a long period of time -

It is apparent that Jesus frequently came to the garden to pray and contemplate, sometimes being alone and sometimes with some of his disciples with him.

The four Gospellers all recall what happened but they all seem to have quite different memories. Matthew recalls lots of parables which are covered in Chapter 11.

Only John, Mark and Matthew would have been there and one gets the impression that, when they report on the event, they merely recall lots of things Jesus said to them in private over the years.

17.3 Judas identifies Jesus

Judas had been aware of where he would be and had taken a detachment of soldiers to intercept him. When Jesus saw them coming he asked then what they wanted and when they said it was for him he readily identified himself to them. John does not recount the praying and the sleeping disciples.

John 18 2 -
[2] And Judas also, which betrayed him, knew the place: for Jesus ofttimes resorted thither with his disciples.
[3] Judas then, having received a band of men and officers from the chief priests and Pharisees, cometh thither with lanterns and torches and weapons.
[4] Jesus therefore, knowing all things that should come upon him, went forth, and said unto them, Whom seek ye?
[5] They answered him, Jesus of Nazareth. Jesus saith unto them, I am he. And Judas also, which betrayed him, stood with them.
[6] As soon then as he had said unto them, I am he, they went backward, and fell to the ground.
[7] Then asked he them again, Whom seek ye? And they said, Jesus of Nazareth.
[8] Jesus answered, I have told you that I am he: if therefore ye seek me, let these go their way:

[9] That the saying might be fulfilled, which he spake, Of them which thou gavest me have I lost none.

Peter tries to defend Jesus and draws his sword.

John 18 10 - 11

[10] Then Simon Peter having a sword drew it, and smote the high priest's servant, and cut off his right ear. The servant's name was Malchus.

[11] Then said Jesus unto Peter, Put up thy sword into the sheath: the cup which my Father hath given me, shall I not drink it?

[12] Then the band and the captain and officers of the Jews took Jesus, and bound him,

Luke's account is similar; but he does not identify Peter.

Luke 22 47 - 51

[47] And while he yet spake, behold a multitude, and he that was called Judas, one of the twelve, went before them, and drew near unto Jesus to kiss him.

[48] But Jesus said unto him, Judas, betrayest thou the Son of man with a kiss?

[49] When they which were about him saw what would follow, they said unto him, Lord, shall we smite with the sword?

[50] And one of them smote the servant of the high priest, and cut off his right ear.

[51] And Jesus answered and said, Suffer ye thus far. And he touched his ear, and healed him..

Matthew's account is not too different although he does not recall Peter's actions.

Matthew 26 47 - 50

[47] And while he yet spake, lo, Judas, one of the twelve, came, and with him a great multitude with swords and staves, from the chief priests and elders of the people.

[48] Now he that betrayed him gave them a sign, saying, Whomsoever I shall kiss, that same is he: hold him fast.

[49] And forthwith he came to Jesus, and said, Hail, master; and kissed him.

[50] And Jesus said unto him, Friend, wherefore art thou come? Then came they, and laid hands on Jesus, and took him.

Mark's version agrees

Mark 14 43-45

[43] And immediately, while he yet spake, cometh Judas, one of the twelve, and with him a great multitude with swords and staves, from the chief priests and the scribes and the elders.

[44] And he that betrayed him had given them a token, saying, Whomsoever I shall kiss, that same is he; take him, and lead him away safely.

[45] And as soon as he was come, he goeth straightway to him, and saith, Master, master; and kissed him.

17.4 Jesus is arrested

John's account of the arrest is very simple:

John 18 12 - 13

[12] Then the band and the captain and officers of the Jews took Jesus, and bound him,

[13] And led him away to Annas first; for he was father in law to Caiaphas, which was the high priest that same year.

Mark's account goes into a lot more detail and he adds an intriguing footnote about a naked young man. Could this have been John Mark?

Mark 14 46 - 53

[46] And they laid their hands on him, and took him.

[47] And one of them that stood by drew a sword, and smote a servant of the high priest, and cut off his ear.

[48] And Jesus answered and said unto them, Are ye come out, as against a thief, with swords and with staves to take me?

[49] I was daily with you in the temple teaching, and ye took me not: but the scriptures must be fulfilled.

[50] And they all forsook him, and fled.

[51] And there followed him a certain young man, having a linen cloth cast about his naked body; and the young men laid hold on him:

[52] And he left the linen cloth, and fled from them naked.

[53] And they led Jesus away to the high priest: and with him were assembled all the chief priests and theelders and the scribes.

Luke omits several details.

Luke 22 52 - 54
[52] Then Jesus said unto the chief priests, and captains of the temple, and the elders, which were come to him, Be ye come out, as against a thief, with swords and staves?
[53] When I was daily with you in the temple, ye stretched forth no hands against me: but this is your hour, and the power of darkness.
[54] Then took they him, and led him, and brought him into the high priest's house. And Peter followed afar off.

Matthew sees a parallel in the Old Testament and the key number 'twelve' appears.

Matthew 26 50 - 56
[50] And Jesus said unto him, Friend, wherefore art thou come? Then came they, and laid hands on Jesus, and took him.
[51] And, behold, one of them which were with Jesus stretched out his hand, and drew his sword, and struck a servant of the high priest's, and smote off his ear.
[52] Then said Jesus unto him, Put up again thy sword into his place: for all they that take the sword shall perish with the sword.
[53] Thinkest thou that I cannot now pray to my Father, and he shall presently give me more than twelve legions of angels?
[54] But how then shall the scriptures be fulfilled, that thus it must be?
[55] In that same hour said Jesus to the multitudes, Are ye come out as against a thief with swords and staves for to take me? I sat daily with you teaching in the temple, and ye laid no hold on me.
[56] But all this was done, that the scriptures of the prophets might be fulfilled. Then all the disciples forsook him, and fled.

Chapter 18 Trial

18.1 The Conspiracy

Jesus' trial needs to be set against the background of the relationship between the Jews and the Romans. The Romans had occupied Palestine in 63 BC and Herod the Great had been appointed in 40 BC. Herod had been accepted as a client king and ruled until he died in 4 BC when the territory was split into three with Herod Antipas governing Galilee and his brother Archaelus governing Judea and Samaria. In 6 AD Archaelus was deemed incompetent and the whole of the kingdom went to Antipas.

However he was not allowed to call himself King, merely Tetrarch. He was quite bitter about this. So when people starting referring to Jesus as 'King' he saw this a terrible threat to his position.

The religious establishment had a very different view of Jesus. To them he was a heretic who ignored Jewish customs and practices and preached a philosophy quite alien to them.

The Tetrarch and the Priests therefore were quite clear that they wanted to see the back of Jesus and Pontius Pilate who was Roman Governor at the time was more concerned with maintaining order than the life of a single Jew. So proceedings against Jesus had to begin in religious courts.

18.2 Questioning by Annas

Jesus was taken to the High Priest's house where he was first questioned by Annas, who was Caiaphas' father-in-law.

John 18.14

[14] Now Caiaphas was he, which gave counsel to the Jews, that it was expedient that one man should die for the people. .

Annas tried to deal with the matter himself, but gave up and handed Jesus over to Caiaphas.

John 18 19 - 24

[19] The high priest then asked Jesus of his disciples, and of his doctrine.
[20] Jesus answered him, I spake openly to the world; I ever taught in the synagogue, and in the temple, whither the Jews always resort; and in secret have I said nothing.
[21] Why askest thou me? ask them which heard me, what I have said unto them: behold, they know what I said.
[22] And when he had thus spoken, one of the officers which stood by struck Jesus with the palm of his hand, saying, Answerest thou the high priest so?
[23] Jesus answered him, If I have spoken evil, bear witness of the evil: but if well, why smitest thou me?
[24] Now Annas had sent him bound unto Caiaphas the high priest.

18.3 Trial Before the Council

John gives no information at all about what went on between Caiaphas and Jesus, almost certainly because the conversation was in private. If anyone had known the details it would have been John. In his version Caiaphas is merely the agent of Annas who takes Jesus to the Roman Governor.

Matthew, Mark and Luke describe a trial before the Jewish Council, a somewhat unlikely event as the formality of convening the Council would have taken much longer than the few hours over the night of Thursday/Friday as most of the members would have been deeply involved in their Passover observances. All three versions hint at brutality on the part of the High Priest's men

Matthew 26 57 - 68

[57] And they that had laid hold on Jesus led him away to Caiaphas the high priest, where the scribes and the elders were assembled.
[58] But Peter followed him afar off unto the high priest's palace, and went in, and sat with the servants, to see the end.
[59] Now the chief priests, and elders, and all the council, sought false witness against Jesus, to put him to death;
[60] But found none: yea, though many false witnesses came, yet found they none. At the last came two false witnesses,
[61] And said, This fellow said, I am able to destroy the temple of God, and to build it in three days.

[62] And the high priest arose, and said unto him, Answerest thou nothing? what is it which these witness against thee?

[63] But Jesus held his peace. And the high priest answered and said unto him, I adjure thee by the living God, that thou tell us whether thou be the Christ, the Son of God.

[64] Jesus saith unto him, Thou hast said: nevertheless I say unto you, Hereafter shall ye see the Son of man sitting on the right hand of power, and coming in the clouds of heaven.

[65] Then the high priest rent his clothes, saying, He hath spoken blasphemy; what further need have we of witnesses? behold, now ye have heard his blasphemy.

[66] What think ye? They answered and said, He is guilty of death.

[67] Then did they spit in his face, and buffeted him; and others smote him with the palms of their hands,

[68] Saying, Prophesy unto us, thou Christ, Who is he that smote thee?

Mark 14 53 - 65

[53] And they led Jesus away to the high priest: and with him were assembled all the chief priests and the elders and the scribes.

[54] And Peter followed him afar off, even into the palace of the high priest: and he sat with the servants, and warmed himself at the fire.

[55] And the chief priests and all the council sought for witness against Jesus to put him to death; and found none.

[56] For many bare false witness against him, but their witness agreed not together.

[57] And there arose certain, and bare false witness against him, saying,

[58] We heard him say, I will destroy this temple that is made with hands, and within three days I will build another made without hands.

[59] But neither so did their witness agree together.

[60] And the high priest stood up in the midst, and asked Jesus, saying, Answerest thou nothing? what is it which these witness against thee?

[61] But he held his peace, and answered nothing. Again the high priest asked him, and said unto him, Art thou the Christ, the Son of the Blessed?

[62] And Jesus said, I am: and ye shall see the Son of man sitting on the right hand of power, and coming in the clouds of heaven.

[63] Then the high priest rent his clothes, and saith, What need we any further witnesses?

[64] Ye have heard the blasphemy: what think ye? And they all condemned him to be guilty of death.

[65] And some began to spit on him, and to cover his face, and to buffet him, and to say unto him, Prophesy: and the servants did strike him with the palms of their hands. .

Luke times the trial at day break the next morning. This makes for an almost impossible chronology. If one believes Luke's version between about 6 am and 9 am there was the trial before the Council, the trial before Pilate, An interview with King Herod, the offer to release Barrabas, the mocking and scourging by the Roman soldiers and the procession to Golgotha.

Luke 22.66 to 23.1

[66] And as soon as it was day, the elders of the people and the chief priests and the scribes came together, and led him into their council, saying,
[67] Art thou the Christ? tell us. And he said unto them, If I tell you, ye will not believe:
[68] And if I also ask you, ye will not answer me, nor let me go.
[69] Hereafter shall the Son of man sit on the right hand of the power of God.
[70] Then said they all, Art thou then the Son of God? And he said unto them, Ye say that I am.
[71] And they said, What need we any further witness? for we ourselves have heard of his own mouth.
[1] And the whole multitude of them arose, and led him unto Pilate. .

18.4 Peter's Denials

Jesus had been accompanied by one of his disciples who knew the High Priest well. Throughout his Gospel, John never mentions himself by name, he always refers to 'another disciple' or 'the one Jesus loved'. It is easy therefore to jump to the conclusion that it was John who was with Jesus, but it seems more likely that in this case the 'other disciple' was in fact Judas and it would explain why Peter was reluctant to accept the invitation to come into the courtyard. He had realised that Judas was the betrayer and was not willing to fall into a further trap. However, he came in and warmed himself at the brazier in the courtyard.

John 18 15 - 18

[15] And Simon Peter followed Jesus, and so did another disciple: that disciple was known unto the high priest, and went in with Jesus into the palace of the high priest.
[16] But Peter stood at the door without. Then went out that other disciple, which was known unto the high priest, and spake unto her that kept the door, and brought in Peter.
[17] Then saith the damsel that kept the door unto Peter, Art not thou also one of this man's disciples? He saith, I am not.

[18] And the servants and officers stood there, who had made a fire of coals; for it was cold: and they warmed themselves: and Peter stood with them, and warmed himself.

Mark 14 66 - 70
[66] And as Peter was beneath in the palace, there cometh one of the maids of the high priest:
[67] And when she saw Peter warming himself, she looked upon him, and said, And thou also wast with Jesus of Nazareth.
[68] But he denied, saying, I know not, neither understand I what thou sayest. And he went out into the porch; and the cock crew.
[69] And a maid saw him again, and began to say to them that stood by, This is one of them.
[70] And he denied it again. And a little after, they that stood by said again to Peter, Surely thou art one of them: for thou art a Galilaean, and thy speech agreeth thereto.

Luke on the other hand tells it slightly differently.

Luke 22 54 - 62
[54] Then took they him, and led him, and brought him into the high priest's house. And Peter followed afar off.
[55] And when they had kindled a fire in the midst of the hall, and were set down together, Peter sat down among them.
[56] But a certain maid beheld him as he sat by the fire, and earnestly looked upon him, and said, This man was also with him.
[57] And he denied him, saying, Woman, I know him not.
[58] And after a little while another saw him, and said, Thou art also of them. And Peter said, Man, I am not.
[59] And about the space of one hour after another confidently affirmed, saying, Of a truth this fellow also was with him: for he is a Galilaean.
[60] And Peter said, Man, I know not what thou sayest. And immediately, while he yet spake, the cock crew.
[61] And the Lord turned, and looked upon Peter. And Peter remembered the word of the Lord, how he had said unto him, Before the cock crow, thou shalt deny me thrice.
[62] And Peter went out, and wept bitterly.

K THURSDAY

When the dawn was about to break one of the others there, who had been part of the arresting party, thought they recognised Peter. He was emphatic that they had made a mistake.

John 18 25 - 27
[25] And Simon Peter stood and warmed himself. They said therefore unto him, Art not thou also one of his disciples? He denied it, and said, I am not.
[26] One of the servants of the high priest, being his kinsman whose ear Peter cut off, saith, Did not I see thee in the garden with him?
[27] Peter then denied again: and immediately the cock crew.

Matthew's tale is much the same as is Mark's.

Matthew 26 69 - 75
[69] Now Peter sat without in the palace: and a damsel came unto him, saying, Thou also wast with Jesus of Galilee.
[70] But he denied before them all, saying, I know not what thou sayest.
[71] And when he was gone out into the porch, another maid saw him, and said unto them that were there, This fellow was also with Jesus of Nazareth.
[72] And again he denied with an oath, I do not know the man.
[73] And after a while came unto him they that stood by, and said to Peter, Surely thou also art one of them; for thy speech bewrayeth thee.
[74] Then began he to curse and to swear, saying, I know not the man. And immediately the cock crew.
[75] And Peter remembered the word of Jesus, which said unto him, Before the cock crow, thou shalt deny me thrice. And he went out, and wept bitterly.

Mark 14 70 - 72
[70] And he denied it again. And a little after, they that stood by said again to Peter, Surely thou art one of them: for thou art a Galilaean, and thy speech agreeth thereto.
[71] But he began to curse and to swear, saying, I know not this man of whom ye speak.
[72] And the second time the cock crew. And Peter called to mind the word that Jesus said unto him, Before the cock crow twice, thou shalt deny me thrice. And when he thought thereon, he wept.

18.5 Jesus is taken to Pilate

Pontius Pilate was the Roman Governor of Judea. Only he could authorise the death penalty and he was none too anxious to get embroiled in what he saw as a purely internal Jewish matter.

Matthew 27 1 - 2

[1] When the morning was come, all the chief priests and elders of the people took counsel against Jesus to put him to death:

[2] And when they had bound him, they led him away, and delivered him to Pontius Pilate the governor.

John 18 28 - 32

[28] Then led they Jesus from Caiaphas unto the hall of judgment: and it was early; and they themselves went not into the judgment hall, lest they should be defiled; but that they might eat the passover.

[29] Pilate then went out unto them, and said, What accusation bring ye against this man?

[30] They answered and said unto him, If he were not a malefactor, we would not have delivered him up unto thee.

[31] Then said Pilate unto them, Take ye him, and judge him according to your law. The Jews therefore said unto him, It is not lawful for us to put any man to death:

[32] That the saying of Jesus might be fulfilled, which he spake, signifying what death he should die.

Pilate had Jesus brought before and questioned him, deciding that whatever he had done it was not a crime worthy of the death penalty.

John 18 33 - 38

[33] Then Pilate entered into the judgment hall again, and called Jesus, and said unto him, Art thou the King of the Jews?

[34] Jesus answered him, Sayest thou this thing of thyself, or did others tell it thee of me?

[35] Pilate answered, Am I a Jew? Thine own nation and the chief priests have delivered thee unto me: what hast thou done?

[36] Jesus answered, My kingdom is not of this world: if my kingdom were of this world, then would my servants fight, that I should not be delivered to the Jews: but now is my kingdom not from hence.

[37] Pilate therefore said unto him, Art thou a king then? Jesus answered, Thou sayest that I am a king. To this end was I born, and for this cause

came I into the world, that I should bear witness unto the truth. Every one that is of the truth heareth my voice.

[38] Pilate saith unto him, What is truth? And when he had said this, he went out again unto the Jews, and saith unto them, I find in him no fault at all.

Matthew 27 11 - 14

[11] And Jesus stood before the governor: and the governor asked him, saying, Art thou the King of the Jews? And Jesus said unto him, Thou sayest.

[12] And when he was accused of the chief priests and elders, he answered nothing.

[13] Then said Pilate unto him, Hearest thou not how many things they witness against thee?

[14] And he answered him to never a word; insomuch that the governor marvelled greatly.

Mark 15 1 - 5

[1] And straightway in the morning the chief priests held a consultation with the elders and scribes and the whole council, and bound Jesus, and carried him away, and delivered him to Pilate.

[2] And Pilate asked him, Art thou the King of the Jews? And he answering said unto him, Thou sayest it.

[3] And the chief priests accused him of many things: but he answered nothing.

[4] And Pilate asked him again, saying, Answerest thou nothing? behold how many things they witness against thee.

[5] But Jesus yet answered nothing; so that Pilate marvelled.

In Luke's version the first confrontation was between Pilate and the Jewish Assembly with Jesus there as evidence. Pilate at first decided that the matter should be dealt with by Herod Antipas who was the Tetrach of Galilee and Peraea.

Luke 23 1 - 7

[1] And the whole multitude of them arose, and led him unto Pilate.

[2] And they began to accuse him, saying, We found this fellow perverting the nation, and forbidding to give tribute to Caesar, saying that he himself is Christ a King.

[3] And Pilate asked him, saying, Art thou the King of the Jews? And he answered him and said, Thou sayest it.

[4] Then said Pilate to the chief priests and to the people, I find no fault in this man.

[5] And they were the more fierce, saying, He stirreth up the people, teaching throughout all Jewry, beginning from Galilee to this place.
[6] When Pilate heard of Galilee, he asked whether the man were a Galilaean.
[7] And as soon as he knew that he belonged unto Herod's jurisdiction, he sent him to Herod, who himself also was at Jerusalem at that time.

Herod welcomed the opportunity to talk to Jesus and spoke to him at some length. He had heard of Jesus and wanted to assess whether or not he really was a threat to his throne.

Luke 23 8 - 9
[8] And when Herod saw Jesus, he was exceeding glad: for he was desirous to see him of a long season, because he had heard many things of him; and he hoped to have seen some miracle done by him.
[9] Then he questioned with him in many words; but he answered him nothing.

But the Chief Priest and his followers appeared and demanded action. At this point Jesus was dressed up in the robe and ridiculed by Herod's soldiers, rather than the Roman ones. Luke hints at a secret pact between Herod and Pilate to settle an old feud.

Luke 23 10 - 12
[10] And the chief priests and scribes stood and vehemently accused him.
[11] And Herod with his men of war set him at nought, and mocked him, and arrayed him in a gorgeous robe, and sent him again to Pilate.
[12] And the same day Pilate and Herod were made friends together: for before they were at enmity between themselves.

18.6 Pilate offers to Release Jesus

Pilate tried first to simply release Jesus as a Passover amnesty; but the Jews were adamant.

John 18 39 - 40
[39] But ye have a custom, that I should release unto you one at the passover: will ye therefore that I release unto you the King of the Jews?
[40] Then cried they all again, saying, Not this man, but Barabbas. Now Barabbas was a robber. .

Matthew 27 15 - 18

[15] Now at that feast the governor was wont to release unto the people a prisoner, whom they would.

[16] And they had then a notable prisoner, called Barabbas.

[17] Therefore when they were gathered together, Pilate said unto them, Whom will ye that I release unto you? Barabbas, or Jesus which is called Christ?

[18] For he knew that for envy they had delivered him.

Mark and Luke treat it all as a single episode.

Mark 15 6 - 15

[6] Now at that feast he released unto them one prisoner, whomsoever they desired.

[7] And there was one named Barabbas, which lay bound with them that had made insurrection with him, who had committed murder in the insurrection.

[8] And the multitude crying aloud began to desire him to do as he had ever done unto them.

[9] But Pilate answered them, saying, Will ye that I release unto you the King of the Jews?

[10] For he knew that the chief priests had delivered him for envy.

[11] But the chief priests moved the people, that he should rather release Barabbas unto them.

[12] And Pilate answered and said again unto them, What will ye then that I shall do unto him whom ye call the King of the Jews?

[13] And they cried out again, Crucify him.

[14] Then Pilate said unto them, Why, what evil hath he done? And they cried out the more exceedingly, Crucify him.

[15: And so Pilate, willing to content the people, released Barabbas unto them, and delivered Jesus, when he had scourged him, to be crucified.

Luke 23 13 - 25

[13] And Pilate, when he had called together the chief priests and the rulers and the people,

[14] Said unto them, Ye have brought this man unto me, as one that perverteth the people: and, behold, I, having examined him before you, have found no fault in this man touching those things whereof ye accuse him:

[15] No, nor yet Herod: for I sent you to him; and, lo, nothing worthy of death is done unto him.

[16] I will therefore chastise him, and release him.

[17] (For of necessity he must release one unto them at the feast.)

[18] And they cried out all at once, saying, Away with this man, and release unto us Barabbas:

[19] (Who for a certain sedition made in the city, and for murder, was cast into prison.)

[20] Pilate therefore, willing to release Jesus, spake again to them.

[21] But they cried, saying, Crucify him, crucify him.

[22] And he said unto them the third time, Why, what evil hath he done? I have found no cause of death in him: I will therefore chastise him, and let him go.

[23] And they were instant with loud voices, requiring that he might be crucified. And the voices of them and of the chief priests prevailed.

[24] And Pilate gave sentence that it should be as they required.

[25] And he released unto them him that for sedition and murder was cast into prison, whom they had desired; but he delivered Jesus to their will. .

L THURSDAY EVENING

Jesus is still in the hands of the Romans and in one of their prisons. Pilate still is not sure what the best course of action would be so he hands him over to his soldiers to see if a good flogging will resolve the matter.

18.7 Jesus is Flogged

Pilate then decided to give Jesus a flogging and his soldiers made him an object of derision.

John 19 1 - 3

[1] Then Pilate therefore took Jesus, and scourged him.

[2] And the soldiers platted a crown of thorns, and put it on his head, and they put on him a purple robe,

[3] And said, Hail, King of the Jews! and they smote him with their hands.

In other versions this comes after the final condemnation.

Matthew 27 27 - 31

[27] Then the soldiers of the governor took Jesus into the common hall, and gathered unto him the whole band of soldiers.

[28] And they stripped him, and put on him a scarlet robe.

[29] And when they had platted a crown of thorns, they put it upon his head, and a reed in his right hand: and they bowed the knee before him, and mocked him, saying, Hail, King of the Jews!

[30] And they spit upon him, and took the reed, and smote him on the head.
[31] And after that they had mocked him, they took the robe off from him, and put his own raiment on him, and led him away to crucify him.

Mark 15 16 - 20

[16] And the soldiers led him away into the hall, called Praetorium; and they all together the whole band.
[17] And they clothed him with purple, and platted a crown of thorns, and put it about his head,
[18] And began to salute him, Hail, King of the Jews!
[19] And they smote him on the head with a reed, and did spit upon him, and bowing their knees worshipped him.
[20] And when they had mocked him, they took off the purple from him, and put his own clothes on him, and led him out to crucify him.

M FRIDAY

18.8 Pilate Washes his Hands of the Affair

Pilate's wife warned him about a dream she had had and pressed him to release Jesus.

Matthew 27.19

[19] When he was set down on the judgment seat, his wife sent unto him, saying, Have thou nothing to do with that just man: for I have suffered many things this day in a dream because of him.

So, Pilate tried again to release Jesus but the Jews would have none of it.

John 19 4 - 7

[4] Pilate therefore went forth again, and saith unto them, Behold, I bring him forth to you, that ye may know that I find no fault in him.
[5] Then came Jesus forth, wearing the crown of thorns, and the purple robe. And Pilate saith unto them, Behold the man!
[6] When the chief priests therefore and officers saw him, they cried out, saying, Crucify him, crucify him. Pilate saith unto them, Take ye him, and crucify him: for I find no fault in him.
[7] The Jews answered him, We have a law, and by our law he ought to die, because he made himself the Son of God.

Matthew 27 20 - 23

[20] But the chief priests and elders persuaded the multitude that they should ask Barabbas, and destroy Jesus.

[21] The governor answered and said unto them, Whether of the twain will ye that I release unto you? They said, Barabbas.

[22] Pilate saith unto them, What shall I do then with Jesus which is called Christ? They all say unto him, Let him be crucified.

[23] And the governor said, Why, what evil hath he done? But they cried out the more, saying, Let him be crucified.

By this time Pilate was getting pretty fed up with the Jews but afraid he was about to have a revolt on his hands. He questioned Jesus again but could get nothing out of him. He tried every means he had at his disposal to set Jesus free but the Jews threatened to make trouble if he did. One question - was Jesus flogged by the Jews or by Roman soldiers?

John 19 8 - 12

[8] When Pilate therefore heard that saying, he was the more afraid;

[9] And went again into the judgment hall, and saith unto Jesus, Whence art thou? But Jesus gave him no answer.

[10] Then saith Pilate unto him, Speakest thou not unto me? knowest thou not that I have power to crucify thee, and have power to release thee?

[11] Jesus answered, Thou couldest have no power at all against me, except it were given thee from above: therefore he that delivered me unto thee hath the greater sin.

[12] And from thenceforth Pilate sought to release him: but the Jews cried out, saying, If thou let this man go, thou art not Caesar's friend: whosoever maketh himself a king speaketh against Caesar.

Matthew 27 24 - 26

[24] When Pilate saw that he could prevail nothing, but that rather a tumult was made, he took water, and washed his hands before the multitude, saying, I am innocent of the blood of this just person: see ye to it.

[25] Then answered all the people, and said, His blood be on us, and on our children.

[26] Then released he Barabbas unto them: and when he had scourged Jesus, he delivered him to be crucified.

Finally, Pilate had little choice but to convene the formal tribunal and condemn Jesus to death by crucifixion. John gives the time as around 3 pm on Thursday when everyone was preparing for the Passover which would start on the Friday at sunset.

John 19 13 - 16
[13] When Pilate therefore heard that saying, he brought Jesus forth, and sat down in the judgment seat in a place that is called the Pavement, but in the Hebrew, Gabbatha.
[14] And it was the preparation of the passover, and about the sixth hour: and he saith unto the Jews, Behold your King!
[15] But they cried out, Away with him, away with him, crucify him. Pilate saith unto them, Shall I crucify your King? The chief priest answered, We have no king but Caesar.
[16] Then delivered he him therefore unto them to be crucified. And they took Jesus, and led him away.

18.9 Judas Realises his Error

When Judas realised that Jesus had been condemned to death he was full of remorse.

Matthew 27 3 - 10
[3] Then Judas, which had betrayed him, when he saw that he was condemned, repented himself, and brought again the thirty pieces of silver to the chief priests and elders,
[4] Saying, I have sinned in that I have betrayed the innocent blood. And they said, What is that to us? see thou to that.
[5] And he cast down the pieces of silver in the temple, and departed, and went and hanged himself.
[6] And the chief priests took the silver pieces, and said, It is not lawful for to put them into the treasury, because it is the price of blood.
[7] And they took counsel, and bought with them the potter's field, to bury strangers in.
[8] Wherefore that field was called, The field of blood, unto this day.
[9] Then was fulfilled that which was spoken by Jeremy the prophet, saying, And they took the thirty pieces of silver, the price of him that was valued, whom they of the children of Israel did value;
[10] And gave them for the potter's field, as the Lord appointed me.

Chapter 19 Crucifixion

The trial is over. The Romans have effectively washed their hands of the matter although they have to actually enforce the verdict. Herod Antipas is satisfied that a potential rival is being eliminated although he is not happy with the inscription that the Romans are insistent on. The Jews want the matter over and done with before sunset on Friday.

A question that has been debated for years was "exactly on what date did the crucifixion take place?" The Jewish calendar started with the new moon which heralded spring and the Passover was fourteen or fifteen days later to coincide with the full Moon. If it was likely to coincide with the Sabbath (Saturday) it could be brought forward a day. The generally agreed date for the crucifixion is now Friday Third April 33 AD.

19.1 The Way to Calvary

Jesus would have been made to carry his own cross to the place outside the city where executions took place. This would have been only the cross piece to which he was fastened. However, as he was weak from the flogging, Simon was made to carry it for him. Pilate finally exerted his authority by insisting upon his own wording of the charge to explain the execution.

Matthew 27.32
[32] And as they came out, they found a man of Cyrene, Simon by name: him they compelled to bear his cross.

John 19 17 - 22
[17] And he bearing his cross went forth into a place called the place of a skull, which is called in the Hebrew Golgotha:
[18] Where they crucified him, and two other with him, on either side one, and Jesus in the midst.
[19] And Pilate wrote a title, and put it on the cross. And the writing was, JESUS OF NAZARETH THE KING OF THE JEWS.
[20] This title then read many of the Jews: for the place where Jesus was crucified was nigh to the city: and it was written in Hebrew, and Greek, and Latin.

[21] Then said the chief priests of the Jews to Pilate, Write not, The King of the Jews; but that he said, I am King of the Jews.

[22] Pilate answered, What I have written I have written.

Mark 15 21 - 22

[21] And they compel one Simon a Cyrenian, who passed by, coming out of the country, the father of Alexander and Rufus, to bear his cross.

[22 And they bring him unto the place Golgotha, which is, being interpreted, The place of a skull.

Mark 15 25 - 27

25: And it was the third hour, and they crucified him.

26: And the superscription of his accusation was written over, THE KING OF THE JEWS.

27: And with him they crucify two thieves; the one on his right hand, and the other on his left.

Luke 23 26 to 34

[26] And as they led him away, they laid hold upon one Simon, a Cyrenian, coming out of the country, and on him they laid the cross, that he might bear it after Jesus.

[27] And there followed him a great company of people, and of women, which also bewailed and lamented him.

[28] But Jesus turning unto them said, Daughters of Jerusalem, weep not for me, but weep for yourselves, and for your children.

[29] For, behold, the days are coming, in the which they shall say, Blessed are the barren, and the wombs that never bare, and the paps which never gave suck.

[30] Then shall they begin to say to the mountains, Fall on us; and to the hills, Cover us.

[31] For if they do these things in a green tree, what shall be done in the dry?

[32] And there were also two other, malefactors, led with him to be put to death.

[33] And when they were come to the place, which is called Calvary, there they crucified him, and the malefactors, one on the right hand, and the other on the left.

[34] Then said Jesus, Father, forgive them; for they know not what they do.

19.2 Jesus is Offered a Pain Killer

Before being nailed to the cross Jesus is offered drugged wine. This has two effects, first to make the victim confused and suffer less pain; but second and more importantly to make it easier for the executioners to carry out their grisly task.

Matthew 27 33 - 34

[33] And when they were come unto a place called Golgotha, that is to say, a place of a skull,

[34] They gave him vinegar to drink mingled with gall: and when he had tasted thereof, he would not drink.

Mark 15 23

[23] And they gave him to drink wine mingled with myrrh: but he received it not.

19.3 The Soldiers Divide His Clothes

Jesus' clothing was divided into four parts which makes one wonder how many clothes he actually wore, especially as the tunic was treated separately.

John 19 23 - 24

[23] Then the soldiers, when they had crucified Jesus, took his garments, and made four parts, to every soldier a part; and also his coat: now the coat was without seam, woven from the top throughout.

[24] They said therefore among themselves, Let us not rend it, but cast lots for it, whose it shall be: that the scripture might be fulfilled, which saith, They parted my raiment among them, and for my vesture they did cast lots. These things therefore the soldiers did.

Matthew 27 35 - 38

[35] And they crucified him, and parted his garments, casting lots: that it might be fulfilled which was spoken by the prophet, They parted my garments among them, and upon my vesture did they cast lots.

[36] And sitting down they watched him there;

[37] And set up over his head his accusation written, THIS IS JESUS THE KING OF THE JEWS.

[38] Then were there two thieves crucified with him, one on the right hand, and another on the left.

Mark 15.24

[24] And when they had crucified him, they parted his garments, casting lots upon them, what every man should take.

Luke 23.34

[34] Then said Jesus, Father, forgive them; for they know not what they do. And they parted his raiment, and cast lots. And they parted his raiment, and cast lots.

19.4 Jesus takes Care of His Mother

His mother was with him to the end. She would need looking after. Jesus entrusted this to 'the disciple whom he loved', assumed to be John. Interestingly the other two women at the crucifixion were Mary's sister and Mary of Magdala. In view of the close association between Mary the sister of Martha, it is amazing that she was not listed as being there. One can only draw the conclusion that she and Mary of Magdala were one and the same person. Also where was Joseph of Arimathea? He will re-appear shortly; but is his absence the reason for charging John with looking after his mother?

John 19 25 - 27

[25] Now there stood by the cross of Jesus his mother, and his mother's sister, Mary the wife of Cleophas, and Mary Magdalene.
[26] When Jesus therefore saw his mother, and the disciple standing by, whom he loved, he saith unto his mother, Woman, behold thy son!
[27] Then saith he to the disciple, Behold thy mother! And from that hour that disciple took her unto his own home.

19.5 Jesus is Taunted on the Cross

Part of the punishment of crucifixion was the public humiliation it engendered. As usual the crowds were out in force.

Matthew 27 39 - 44

[39] And they that passed by reviled him, wagging their heads,
[40] And saying, Thou that destroyest the temple, and buildest it in three days, save thyself. If thou be the Son of God, come down from the cross.
[41] Likewise also the chief priests mocking him, with the scribes and elders, said,
[42] He saved others; himself he cannot save. If he be the King of Israel, let him now come down from the cross, and we will believe him.
[43] He trusted in God; let him deliver him now, if he will have him: for he said, I am the Son of God.

[44] The thieves also, which were crucified with him, cast the same in his teeth.

Mark 15 29 - 32

[29] And they that passed by railed on him, wagging their heads, and saying, Ah, thou that destroyest the temple, and buildest it in three days,

[30] Save thyself, and come down from the cross.

[31] Likewise also the chief priests mocking said among themselves with the scribes, He saved others; himself he cannot save.

[32] Let Christ the King of Israel descend now from the cross, that we may see and believe. And they that were crucified with him reviled him.

Luke 23 35 - 43

[35] And the people stood beholding. And the rulers also with them derided him, saying, He saved others; let him save himself, if he be Christ, the chosen of God.

[36] And the soldiers also mocked him, coming to him, and offering him vinegar,

[37] And saying, If thou be the king of the Jews, save thyself.

[38] And a superscription also was written over him in letters of Greek, and Latin, and Hebrew, THIS IS THE KING OF THE JEWS.

[39] And one of the malefactors which were hanged railed on him, saying, If thou be Christ, save thyself and us.

[40] But the other answering rebuked him, saying, Dost not thou fear God, seeing thou art in the same condemnation?

[41] And we indeed justly; for we receive the due reward of our deeds: but this man hath done nothing amiss.

[42] And he said unto Jesus, Lord, remember me when thou comest into thy kingdom.

[43] And Jesus said unto him, Verily I say unto thee, To day shalt thou be with me in paradise.

19.6 Jesus cries for Help

In Matthew's account Jesus almost gives up and the onlookers rush to give him the pain killing drink he has just refused.

Matthew 27 45 - 49

[45] Now from the sixth hour there was darkness over all the land unto the ninth hour.

[46] And about the ninth hour Jesus cried with a loud voice, saying, Eli, Eli, lama sabachthani? that is to say, My God, my God, why hast thou forsaken me?

[47] Some of them that stood there, when they heard that, said, This man calleth for Elias.

[48] And straightway one of them ran, and took a spunge, and filled it with vinegar, and put it on a reed, and gave him to drink.

[49] The rest said, Let be, let us see whether Elias will come to save him.

Mark 15 33 - 36

[33] And when the sixth hour was come, there was darkness over the whole land until the ninth hour.

[34] And at the ninth hour Jesus cried with a loud voice, saying, Eloi, Eloi, lama sabachthani? which is, being interpreted, My God, my God, why hast thou forsaken me?

[35] And some of them that stood by, when they heard it, said, Behold, he calleth Elias.

[36] And one ran and filled a spunge full of vinegar, and put it on a reed, and gave him to drink, saying, Let alone; let us see whether Elias will come to take him down.

19.7 Jesus Dies on the Cross

John's account of the last moments is simple. Jesus asks for a drink, receives one and dies.

John 19 28 - 30

[28] After this, Jesus knowing that all things were now accomplished, that the scripture might be fulfilled, saith, I thirst.

[29] Now there was set a vessel full of vinegar: and they filled a spunge with vinegar, and put it upon hyssop, and put it to his mouth.

[30] When Jesus therefore had received the vinegar, he said, It is finished: and he bowed his head, and gave up the ghost.

As usual Matthew's version is much more dramatic and apocalyptic.

Matthew 27 50 - 54

[50] Jesus, when he had cried again with a loud voice, yielded up the ghost.

[51] And, behold, the veil of the temple was rent in twain from the top to the bottom; and the earth did quake, and the rocks rent;

[52] And the graves were opened; and many bodies of the saints which slept arose,

[53] And came out of the graves after his resurrection, and went into the holy city, and appeared unto many.

[54] Now when the centurion, and they that were with him, watching Jesus, saw the earthquake, and those things that were done, they feared greatly, saying, Truly this was the Son of God.

Mark draws on Matthew's account but is somewhat less dramatic.

Mark 15 37 - 41

[37] And Jesus cried with a loud voice, and gave up the ghost.

[38] And the veil of the temple was rent in twain from the top to the bottom.

[39] And when the centurion, which stood over against him, saw that he so cried out, and gave up the ghost, he said, Truly this man was the Son of God.

[40] There were also women looking on afar off: among whom was Mary Magdalene, and Mary the mother of James the less and of Joses, and Salome;

[41] (Who also, when he was in Galilee, followed him, and ministered unto him;) and many other women which came up with him unto Jerusalem. .

Luke describes what seems very much like an eclipse of the sun to accompany Jesus's death. However, there was no eclipse at this time so we can take all the reports of earthquakes and so on as corresponding with Jesus' death as merely dramatic amplification.

Luke 23 44 - 49

[44] And it was about the sixth hour, and there was a darkness over all the earth until the ninth hour.

[45] And the sun was darkened, and the veil of the temple was rent in the midst.

[46] And when Jesus had cried with a loud voice, he said, Father, into thy hands I commend my spirit: and having said thus, he gave up the ghost.

[47] Now when the centurion saw what was done, he glorified God, saying, Certainly this was a righteous man.

[48] And all the people that came together to that sight, beholding the things which were done, smote their breasts, and returned.

[49] And all his acquaintance, and the women that followed him from Galilee,

Chapter 20 – Resurrection

N FRIDAY EVENING

20.1 Jesus is taken from the Cross

Ordinarily the Romans simply left victims of crucifixion to die a slow agonising death. They provided a small wooden support for the feet which enabled the victim to keep raising himself enough to let air into the lungs, otherwise death was fairly swift from suffocation. When they wanted to speed things up they simply broke the victim's legs to prevent this happening. In Jesus case this was not necessary.

John 19 31 - 37

[31] The Jews therefore, because it was the preparation, that the bodies should not remain upon the cross on the sabbath day, (for that sabbath day was an high day,) besought Pilate that their legs might be broken, and that they might be taken away.

[32] Then came the soldiers, and brake the legs of the first, and of the other which was crucified with him.

[33] But when they came to Jesus, and saw that he was dead already, they brake not his legs:

[34] But one of the soldiers with a spear pierced his side, and forthwith came there out blood and water.

[35] And he that saw it bare record, and his record is true: and he knoweth that he saith true, that ye might believe.

[36] For these things were done, that the scripture should be fulfilled, A bone of him shall not be broken.

[37] And again another scripture saith, They shall look on him whom they pierced.

20.2   Burial in the Tomb

One of the influential citizens who had kept quiet about their support for Jesus now came forward to claim the body. It had to be buried hurriedly before the Sabbath started, ie before nightfall on the Friday. It seems strange that Joseph should re-appear at this point to claim Jesus' body and provide a tomb but it makes perfect sense if indeed he was Jesus' earthly father and husband of Mary. It is also clear that the tomb was close to where the execution took place and not in the Church of the Holy Sepulchre.

John 19 38 - 42

[38] And after this Joseph of Arimathaea, being a disciple of Jesus, but secretly for fear of the Jews, besought Pilate that he might take away the body of Jesus: and Pilate gave him leave. He came therefore, and took the body of Jesus.

[39] And there came also Nicodemus, which at the first came to Jesus by night, and brought a mixture of myrrh and aloes, about an hundred pound weight.

[40] Then took they the body of Jesus, and wound it in linen clothes with the spices, as the manner of the Jews is to bury.

[41] Now in the place where he was crucified there was a garden; and in the garden a new sepulchre, wherein was never man yet laid.

[42] There laid they Jesus therefore because of the Jews' preparation day; for the sepulchre was nigh at hand.

Matthew also identifies the man as Joseph of Arimathea.

Matthew 27 55 - 61

[55] And many women were there beholding afar off, which followed Jesus from Galilee, ministering unto him:

[56] Among which was Mary Magdalene, and Mary the mother of James and Joses, and the mother of Zebedee's children.

[57] When the even was come, there came a rich man of Arimathaea, named Joseph, who also himself was Jesus' disciple:

[58] He went to Pilate, and begged the body of Jesus. Then Pilate commanded the body to be delivered.

[59] And when Joseph had taken the body, he wrapped it in a clean linen cloth,

[60] And laid it in his own new tomb, which he had hewn out in the rock: and he rolled a great stone to the door of the sepulchre, and departed.

[61] And there was Mary Magdalene, and the other Mary, sitting over against the sepulchre.

Mark's version is similar, but records Pilate's surprise that it was all dealt with so quickly.

Mark 15 42 - 47

42: And now when the even was come, because it was the preparation, that is, the day before the sabbath,

43: Joseph of Arimathaea, and honourable counseller, which also waited for the kingdom of God, came, and went in boldly unto Pilate, and craved the body of Jesus.

44: And Pilate marvelled if he were already dead: and calling unto him the centurion, he asked him whether he had been any while dead.

45: And when he knew it of the centurion, he gave the body to Joseph.

46: And he bought fine linen, and took him down, and wrapped him in the linen, and laid him in a sepulchre which was hewn out of a rock, and rolled a stone unto the door of the sepulchre.

47: And Mary Magdalene and Mary the mother of Joses beheld where he was laid.

20.3 The Pharisees make sure the Tomb is Guarded

The Pharisees had listened to Jesus and his claim that he would rise from the dead so they took steps to ensure it did not happen.

Matthew 27 62 - 66

[62] Now the next day, that followed the day of the preparation, the chief priests and Pharisees came together unto Pilate,

[63] Saying, Sir, we remember that that deceiver said, while he was yet alive, After three days I will rise again.

[64] Command therefore that the sepulchre be made sure until the third day, lest his disciples come by night, and steal him away, and say unto the people, He is risen from the dead: so the last error shall be worse than the first.

[65] Pilate said unto them, Ye have a watch: go your way, make it as sure as ye can.

[66] So they went, and made the sepulchre sure, sealing the stone, and setting a watch.

P SATURDAY

Nothing much is happening on the Saturday with Jesus lying in the tomb guarded by the Roman soldiers as requested by the Pharisees.

Q SUNDAY

20.4 Mary and Simon Peter find
the Empty Tomb

On the Sunday morning Mary and Simon Peter came down to the tomb to perform the burial rites. They had been prevented from coming down on the Sabbath (Saturday) as this was classified as work and hence forbidden. They were amazed at what they found, or rather didn't find. John's version of events is simple and sober.

> **John 20 1 - 8**
> [1] The first day of the week cometh Mary Magdalene early, when it was yet dark, unto the sepulchre, and seeth the stone taken away from the sepulchre.
> [2] Then she runneth, and cometh to Simon Peter, and to the other disciple, whom Jesus loved, and saith unto them, They have taken away the Lord out of the sepulchre, and we know not where they have laid him.
> [3] Peter therefore went forth, and that other disciple, and came to the sepulchre.
> [4] So they ran both together: and the other disciple did outrun Peter, and came first to the sepulchre.
> [5] And he stooping down, and looking in, saw the linen clothes lying; yet went he not in.
> [6] Then cometh Simon Peter following him, and went into the sepulchre, and seeth the linen clothes lie,
> [7] And the napkin, that was about his head, not lying with the linen clothes, but wrapped together in a place by itself.
> [8] Then went in also that other disciple, which came first to the sepulchre, and he saw, and believed.

Matthew tells it somewhat differently making the whole thing very dramatic. In his version it is two women, both called Mary who make the visit. Matthew uses an Angel to deal with the problem of the Roman guards and to convey the message of Jesus' resurrection.

Matthew 28 1 - 7

[1] In the end of the sabbath, as it began to dawn toward the first day of the week, came Mary Magdalene and the other Mary to see the sepulchre.

[2] And, behold, there was a great earthquake: for the angel of the Lord descended from heaven, and came and rolled back the stone from the door, and sat upon it.

[3] His countenance was like lightning, and his raiment white as snow:

[4] And for fear of him the keepers did shake, and became as dead men.

[5] And the angel answered and said unto the women, Fear not ye: for I know that ye seek Jesus, which was crucified.

[6] He is not here: for he is risen, as he said. Come, see the place where the Lord lay.

[7] And go quickly, and tell his disciples that he is risen from the dead; and, behold, he goeth before you into Galilee; there shall ye see him: lo, I have told you.

Mark's version is somewhere between the two, he has three women, the angel messenger and the message to go to Galilee.

Mark 16 1 - 8

[1] And when the sabbath was past, Mary Magdalene, and Mary the mother of James, and Salome, had bought sweet spices, that they might come and anoint him.

[2] And very early in the morning the first day of the week, they came unto the sepulchre at the rising of the sun.

[3] And they said among themselves, Who shall roll us away the stone from the door of the sepulchre?

[4] And when they looked, they saw that the stone was rolled away: for it was very great.

[5] And entering into the sepulchre, they saw a young man sitting on the right side, clothed in a long white garment; and they were affrighted.

[6] And he saith unto them, Be not affrighted: Ye seek Jesus of Nazareth, which was crucified: he is risen; he is not here: behold the place where they laid him.

[7] But go your way, tell his disciples and Peter that he goeth before you into Galilee: there shall ye see him, as he said unto you.

[8] And they went out quickly, and fled from the sepulchre; for they trembled and were amazed: neither said they anything to any man; for they were afraid.

20.5 Mary Magdalene sees the Risen Jesus

The disciples went back home and Mary Magdalene was left in tears.

John 20 10 - 18

[10] Then the disciples went away again unto their own home.

[11] But Mary stood without at the sepulchre weeping: and as she wept, she stooped down, and looked into the sepulchre,

[12] And seeth two angels in white sitting, the one at the head, and the other at the feet, where the body of Jesus had lain.

[13] And they say unto her, Woman, why weepest thou? She saith unto them, Because they have taken away my Lord, and I know not where they have laid him.

[14] And when she had thus said, she turned herself back, and saw Jesus standing, and knew not that it was Jesus.

[15] Jesus saith unto her, Woman, why weepest thou? whom seekest thou? She, supposing him to be the gardener, saith unto him, Sir, if thou have borne him hence, tell me where thou hast laid him, and I will take him away.

[16] Jesus saith unto her, Mary. She turned herself, and saith unto him, Rabboni; which is to say, Master.

[17] Jesus saith unto her, Touch me not; for I am not yet ascended to my Father: but go to my brethren, and say unto them, I ascend unto my Father, and your Father; and to my God, and your God.

[18] Mary Magdalene came and told the disciples that she had seen the Lord, and that he had spoken these things unto her.

Again, Matthew's story is quite different the women recognise Jesus immediately and the message to the disciples to 'return to Galilee' comes from Jesus himself.

Matthew 28 8 - 10

[8] And they departed quickly from the sepulchre with fear and great joy; and did run to bring his disciples word.

[9] And as they went to tell his disciples, behold, Jesus met them, saying, All hail. And they came and held him by the feet, and worshipped him.

[10] Then said Jesus unto them, Be not afraid: go tell my brethren that they go into Galilee, and there shall they see me.

Mark agrees with John that it was to Mary of Magdala that Jesus first appeared. But after the message of his resurrection had been given to the disciples.

Mark 16 8 - 11

[8] And they went out quickly, and fled from the sepulchre; for they trembled and were amazed: neither said they anything to any man; for they were afraid.

[9] Now when Jesus was risen early the first day of the week, he appeared first to Mary Magdalene, out of whom he had cast seven devils.

[10] And she went and told them that had been with him, as they mourned and wept.

[11]And they, when they had heard that he was alive, and had been seen of her, believed not.

20.6 The Guards are Sworn to Secrecy

In Matthew's version the guards went and told the chief priests what had happened. As the guard had been supplied by the Romans this was rather an odd thing for them to have done. Surely they would have reported first to the Roman authorities.

Matthew 28 11 - 15

[11] Now when they were going, behold, some of the watch came into the city, and shewed unto the chief priests all the things that were done.

[12] And when they were assembled with the elders, and had taken counsel, they gave large money unto the soldiers,

[13] Saying, Say ye, His disciples came by night, and stole him away while we slept.

[14] And if this come to the governor's ears, we will persuade him, and secure you.

[15] So they took the money, and did as they were taught: and this saying is commonly reported among the Jews until this day.

20.7 Jesus appears to the Rest of the Disciples

That same Sunday evening when the disciples were gathered together Jesus came and stood with them.

John 20 19 - 23

[19] Then the same day at evening, being the first day of the week, when the doors were shut where the disciples were assembled for fear of the Jews, came Jesus and stood in the midst, and saith unto them, Peace be unto you.

[20] And when he had so said, he shewed unto them his hands and his side. Then were the disciples glad, when they saw the Lord.

[21] Then said Jesus to them again, Peace be unto you: as my Father hath sent me, even so send I you.

[22] And when he had said this, he breathed on them, and saith unto them, Receive ye the Holy Ghost:

[23] Whose soever sins ye remit, they are remitted unto them; and whose soever sins ye retain, they are retained.

20.8 The Road to Emmaus

Two of Jesus's disciples set out for Galilee as instructed; but meet him on the road to Emmaus. Emmaus in modern times is the site of a warm spring to the west of Tiberius near the sea of Galilee but in biblical times there were two possible sites. Luke identifies it as 60 furlongs from Jerusalem but the two possibilities were 30 or 160 furlongs away. It seems most likely that Luke's copyist dropped a digit and that it was the modern Nicopolis ('Imwas) that was referred to, on the way from Jerusalem to Galilee.

Mark is very brief about the meeting

[Mark 16 12 - 13

12] After that he appeared in another form unto two of them, as they walked, and went into the country.

[13] And they went and told it unto the residue: neither believed they them.

Luke gives a much fuller account.

Luke 24 13 - 32

[13] And, behold, two of them went that same day to a village called Emmaus, which was from Jerusalem about threescore furlongs.

[14] And they talked together of all these things which had happened.

[15] And it came to pass, that, while they communed together and reasoned, Jesus himself drew near, and went with them.

[16] But their eyes were holden that they should not know him.

[17] And he said unto them, What manner of communications are these that ye have one to another, as ye walk, and are sad?

[18] And the one of them, whose name was Cleopas, answering said unto him, Art thou only a stranger in Jerusalem, and hast not known the things which are come to pass therein these days?

[19] And he said unto them, What things? And they said unto him, Concerning Jesus of Nazareth, which was a prophet mighty in deed and word before God and all the people:

[20] And how the chief priests and our rulers delivered him to be condemned to death, and have crucified him.

[21] But we trusted that it had been he which should have redeemed Israel: and beside all this, to day is the third day since these things were done.

[22] Yea, and certain women also of our company made us astonished, which were early at the sepulchre;

[23] And when they found not his body, they came, saying, that they had also seen a vision of angels, which said that he was alive.

[24] And certain of them which were with us went to the sepulchre, and found it even so as the women had said: but him they saw not.

[25] Then he said unto them, O fools, and slow of heart to believe all that the prophets have spoken:

[26] Ought not Christ to have suffered these things, and to enter into his glory?

[27] And beginning at Moses and all the prophets, he expounded unto them in all the scriptures the things concerning himself.

[28] And they drew nigh unto the village, whither they went: and he made as though he would have gone further.

[29] But they constrained him, saying, Abide with us: for it is toward evening, and the day is far spent. And he went in to tarry with them.

[30] And it came to pass, as he sat at meat with them, he took bread, and blessed it, and brake, and gave to them.

[31] And their eyes were opened, and they knew him; and he vanished out of their sight.

[32] And they said one to another, Did not our heart burn within us, while he talked with us by the way, and while he opened to us the scriptures?

20.9 Doubting Thomas

Thomas had missed out on the first appearances on Easter Sunday and was hard to be convinced.

John 20 24 - 25

[24] But Thomas, one of the twelve, called Didymus, was not with them when Jesus came.

[25] The other disciples therefore said unto him, We have seen the Lord. But he said unto them, Except I shall see in his hands the print of the nails, and put my finger into the print of the nails, and thrust my hand into his side, I will not believe.

A week later Thomas receives the proof he has been seeking

John 20 26 - 29

[26] And after eight days again his disciples were within, and Thomas with them: then came Jesus, the doors being shut, and stood in the midst, and said, Peace be unto you.

[27] Then saith he to Thomas, reach hither thy finger, and behold my hands; and reach hither thy hand, and thrust it into my side: and be not faithless, but believing.

[28] And Thomas answered and said unto him, My Lord and my God.

[29] Jesus saith unto him, Thomas, because thou hast seen me, thou hast believed: blessed are they that have not seen, and yet have believed.

Luke is obviously referring to the same incident when he recounts how the two disciples returned from Emmaus.

Luke 24 33-43

[33] And they rose up the same hour, and returned to Jerusalem, and found the eleven gathered together, and them that were with them,

[34] Saying, The Lord is risen indeed, and hath appeared to Simon.

[35] And they told what things were done in the way, and how he was known of them in breaking of bread.

[36] And as they thus spake, Jesus himself stood in the midst of them, and saith unto them, Peace be unto you.

[37] But they were terrified and affrighted, and supposed that they had seen a spirit.

[38] And he said unto them, Why are ye troubled? and why do thoughts arise in your hearts?

[39] Behold my hands and my feet, that it is I myself: handle me, and see; for a spirit hath not flesh and bones, as ye see me have.

[40] And when he had thus spoken, he shewed them his hands and his feet.

[41] And while they yet believed not for joy, and wondered, he said unto them, Have ye here any meat?

[42] And they gave him a piece of a broiled fish, and of an honeycomb.

[43] And he took it, and did eat before them.

20.10 The Final Commands

In Matthew, Mark and Luke we hear of the final commands that Jesus gave his disciples. Matthew sets this on a mountain in Galilee, Mark and Luke set it in Jerusalem.

In Mark's version it seems to come after the two disciples had returned from Emmaus.

Mark 16 14 - 18

[14] Afterward he appeared unto the eleven as they sat at meat, and upbraided them with their unbelief and hardness of heart, because they believed not them which had seen him after he was risen.

[15] And he said unto them, Go ye into all the world, and preach the gospel to every creature

[16] He that believeth and is baptized shall be saved; but he that believeth not shall be damned.

[17] And these signs shall follow them that believe; In my name shall they cast out devils; they shall speak with new tongues;

[18] They shall take up serpents; and if they drink any deadly thing, it shall not hurt them; they shall lay hands on the sick, and they shall recover.

Luke's version seems to tie the occasion to the point a week after Easter Sunday when Thomas's doubts were resolved.

20.11 Parting at Bethany

Luke takes Jerusalem as the starting point for the church, for in his version, Jesus's final commands are given in that city. He leads them in a walk to Bethany, the home of Mary and Martha and promptly vanishes. They return to Jerusalem to begin his work.

Luke 24 44 - 53

[44] And he said unto them, These are the words which I spake unto you, while I was yet with you, that all things must be fulfilled, which were written in the law of Moses, and in the prophets, and in the psalms, concerning me.

[45] Then opened he their understanding, that they might understand the scriptures,

[46] And said unto them, Thus it is written, and thus it behoved Christ to suffer, and to rise from the dead the third day:

[47] And that repentance and remission of sins should be preached in his name among all nations, beginning at Jerusalem.

[48] And ye are witnesses of these things.

[49] And, behold, I send the promise of my Father upon you: but tarry ye in the city of Jerusalem, until ye be endued with power from on high.

[50] And he led them out as far as to Bethany, and he lifted up his hands, and blessed them.

[51] And it came to pass, while he blessed them, he was parted from them, and carried up into heaven.

[52] And they worshipped him, and returned to Jerusalem with great joy:

[53] And were continually in the temple, praising and blessing God. Amen.

This is where Luke's gospel ends. Mark does not name the place.

Mark 16 19 - 20
[19] So then after the Lord had spoken unto them, he was received up into heaven, and sat on the right hand of God.
[20] And they went forth, and preached everywhere, the Lord working with them, and confirming the word with signs following. Amen.

Here Mark's Gospel ends.

20.12 Meeting on the Mountain

In Matthew's version the disciples go straight back to Galilee and meet Jesus on the mountain as arranged to receive their final commands.

Matthew 28 16 - 20
[16] Then the eleven disciples went away into Galilee, into a mountain where Jesus had appointed them.
[17] And when they saw him, they worshipped him: but some doubted.
[18] And Jesus came and spake unto them, saying, All power is given unto me in heaven and in earth.
[19] Go ye therefore, and teach all nations, baptizing them in the name of the Father, and of the Son, and of the Holy Ghost:
[20] Teaching them to observe all things whatsoever I have commanded you: and, lo, I am with you alway, even unto the end of the world. Amen.

Here Matthew's Gospel ends.

20.13 Meeting on the Beach

John does not record the final commands, but he agrees with Matthew that some at least of the disciples returned to Galilee where later a number of them were back at their former profession, fishing, when a stranger appeared.

John 21 1 - 23
[1] After these things Jesus shewed himself again to the disciples at the sea of Tiberias; and on this wise shewed he himself.
[2] There were together Simon Peter, and Thomas called Didymus, and Nathanael of Cana in Galilee, and the sons of Zebedee, and two other of his disciples.

[3] Simon Peter saith unto them, I go a fishing. They say unto him, We also go with thee. They went forth, and entered into a ship immediately; and that night they caught nothing.

[4] But when the morning was now come, Jesus stood on the shore: but the disciples knew not that it was Jesus.

[5] Then Jesus saith unto them, Children, have ye any meat? They answered him, No.

[6] And he said unto them, Cast the net on the right side of the ship, and ye shall find. They cast therefore, and now they were not able to draw it for the multitude of fishes.

[7] Therefore that disciple whom Jesus loved saith unto Peter, It is the Lord. Now when Simon Peter heard that it was the Lord, he girt his fisher's coat unto him, (for he was naked,) and did cast himself into the sea.

[8] And the other disciples came in a little ship; (for they were not far from land, but as it were two hundred cubits,) dragging the net with fishes.

[9] As soon then as they were come to land, they saw a fire of coals there, and fish laid thereon, and bread.

[10] Jesus saith unto them, Bring of the fish which ye have now caught.

[11] Simon Peter went up, and drew the net to land full of great fishes, and hundred and fifty and three: and for all there were so many, yet was not the net broken.

[12] Jesus saith unto them, Come and dine. And none of the disciples durst ask him, Who art thou? knowing that it was the Lord.

[13] Jesus then cometh, and taketh bread, and giveth them, and fish likewise.

[14] This is now the third time that Jesus shewed himself to his disciples, after that he was risen from the dead.

[15] So when they had dined, Jesus saith to Simon Peter, Simon, son of Jonas, lovest thou me more than these? He saith unto him, Yea, Lord; thou knowest that I love thee. He saith unto him, Feed my lambs.

[16] He saith to him again the second time, Simon, son of Jonas, lovest thou me? He saith unto him, Yea, Lord; thou knowest that I love thee. He saith unto him, Feed my sheep.

[17] He saith unto him the third time, Simon, son of Jonas, lovest thou me? Peter was grieved because he said unto him the third time, Lovest thou me? And he said unto him, Lord, thou knowest all things; thou knowest that I love thee. Jesus saith unto him, Feed my sheep.

[18] Verily, verily, I say unto thee, When thou wast young, thou girdedst thyself, and walkedst whither thou wouldest: but when thou shalt be old, thou shalt stretch forth thy hands, and another shall gird thee, and carry thee whither thou wouldest not.

[19] This spake he, signifying by what death he should glorify God. And when he had spoken this, he saith unto him, Follow me.

[20] Then Peter, turning about, seeth the disciple whom Jesus loved following; which also leaned on his breast at supper, and said, Lord, which is he that betrayeth thee?

[21] Peter seeing him saith to Jesus, Lord, and what shall this man do?

[22] Jesus saith unto him, If I will that he tarry till I come, what is that to thee? follow thou me.

[23] Then went this saying abroad among the brethren, that that disciple should not die: yet Jesus said not unto him, He shall not die; but, If I will that he tarry till I come, what is that to thee?

20.14 John makes his Assertions

At the end of his narrative John twice asserts the truth of what he had written and emphasised that he had not put it all down.

John 20 30 - 31

[30] And many other signs truly did Jesus in the presence of his disciples, which are not written in this book:

[31] But these are written, that ye might believe that Jesus is the Christ, the Son of God; and that believing ye might have life through his name.

John 21 24 - 25

[24] This is the disciple which testifieth of these things, and wrote these things: and we know that his testimony is true.

[25] And there are also many other things which Jesus did, the which, if they should be written every one, I suppose that even the world itself could not contain the books that should be written. Amen.

Here John's gospel ends.

20.15 Josephus notes the Resurrection

Josephus is writing about what appears to the Roman Authorities as sedition as they were protesting about his reticence to condemn Jesus and had mistakes about providing a new water supply. In order to determine what was going on, Pilate dressed some of his soldiers in civilian clothes with hidden daggers and sent them among the crowds, trapped part of the crowd and summarily executed those who would not do as they were told.

He then makes a comment about Jesus

Josephus Antiquities Book 8 Chapter 3 part 3

Now there was about this time, Jesus, a wise man, if it be lawful to call him a man, for he was a doer of wonderful works, a teacher of such men as receive the truth with pleasure. He drew over to him both many of the Jews and many of the Gentiles. He was the Christ; and when Pilate, at the suggestion of the principal men amongst us, had condemned him to the cross, those that loved him at the first did not forsake him, for he appeared to them alive again on the third day, as the divine prophets had foretold these and ten thousand other wonderful things concerning him; and the tribes of Christians, so named from him, are not extinct at this day.

PART 5
THE CHURCH

Jesus is alive and many people are encountering him; but then we get the story of the Ascension and the Apostles and Disciples are left to spread the word.

The Apostles divide the world between them and at set out on their task. A significant new player appears in the person of Paul and he travels around the eastern Mediterranean giving his interpretation of Jesus' message.

Individual Christians band together for worship and form groups of believers around the known world. They need patrons and priests and scriptures. Then as the Apostles die out they need bishops and organisation to keep the faith alive.

Peter and Paul come to Rome and are martyred, suffering the fate of many Christians who die for their faith amidst terrible persecution.

Eventually however Christianity becomes the official religion of the Roman Empire

Chapter 21 The Church in Judea

21.1 Where did the Church Begin?

A key question which was to become very important in the future. Did it start in Jerusalem or in Galilee? We have a clear discrepancy between Luke and Mark on the one hand and John and Matthew on the other. Luke and Mark were adamant that the disciples had been instructed to remain in Jerusalem:

> **Acts 1 1 - 5**
> [1] The former treatise have I made, O Theophilus, of all that Jesus began both to do and teach,
> [2] Until the day in which he was taken up, after that he through the Holy Ghost had given commandments unto the apostles whom he had chosen:
> [3] To whom also he shewed himself alive after his passion by many infallible proofs, being seen of them forty days, and speaking of the things pertaining to the kingdom of God:
> [4] And, being assembled together with them, commanded them that they should not depart from Jerusalem, but wait for the promise of the Father, which, saith he, ye have heard of me.
> [5] For John truly baptized with water; but ye shall be baptized with the Holy Ghost not many days hence.

John and Matthew recorded the message that the disciples must return to Galilee to meet Jesus there after his death. Both place the final appearances in Galilee. In John's case it is almost a re-construction of the feeding of the five thousand and the miracle of the fishes, in Matthew's case it is on the mountain, a very similar account as Luke's description of the Ascension (below) but set in Galilee, not on the Mount of Olives.

Unfortunately, for this critical period, we have only Luke's accounts of the early church to go on, as recorded in Acts, and we have seen how essentially unreliable Luke is as a historian, prone to develop stories full of imagery to get across his key messages. A few glimpses will come through Paul's letters, but only as asides.

Over the next two hundred years or so, three strands would develop within the church. The Hellenist strand of Paul which would eventually triumph and become the western church centred on Rome, the Jewish strand of James which would almost disappear from the scene and the Johannine or Gnostic strand which would be suppressed and dismissed as heresy, but which seems to have survived in many strange ways.

Crucial to this dispute is the personality of Paul. whom we will deal with in Chapter 22.

But first back to the main story.

21.2 The Ascension

Luke places the final appearance of Jesus on the Mount of Olives, near Jerusalem.

Acts 1 6 - 14

[6] When they therefore were come together, they asked of him, saying, Lord, wilt thou at this time restore again the kingdom to Israel?

[7] And he said unto them, It is not for you to know the times or the seasons, which the Father hath put in his own power.

[8] But ye shall receive power, after that the Holy Ghost is come upon you: and ye shall be witnesses unto me both in Jerusalem, and in all Judaea, and in Samaria, and unto the uttermost part of the earth.

[9] And when he had spoken these things, while they beheld, he was taken up; and a cloud received him out of their sight.

[10] And while they looked stedfastly toward heaven as he went up, behold, two men stood by them in white apparel;

[11] Which also said, Ye men of Galilee, why stand ye gazing up into heaven? this same Jesus, which is taken up from you into heaven, shall so come in like manner as ye have seen him go into heaven.

[12] Then returned they unto Jerusalem from the mount called Olivet, which is from Jerusalem a sabbath day's journey.

[13] And when they were come in, they went up into an upper room, where abode both Peter, and James, and John, and Andrew, Philip, and Thomas, Bartholomew, and Matthew, James the son of Alphaeus, and Simon Zelotes, and Judas the brother of James.

[14] These all continued with one accord in prayer and supplication, with the women, and Mary the mother of Jesus, and with his brethren.

21.3 The Replacement of Judas

There was obviously some special significance in the number twelve as the apostles were anxious to bring their number back to that figure after the death of Judas Iscariot There was some debate as between Joseph and Matthias with the latter being appointed to make up the twelve..

Acts 1 15 - 26

[15] And in those days Peter stood up in the midst of the disciples, and said, (the number of names together were about an hundred and twenty,)

[16] Men and brethren, this scripture must needs have been fulfilled, which the Holy Ghost by the mouth of David spake before concerning Judas, which was guide to them that took Jesus.

[17] For he was numbered with us, and had obtained part of this ministry.

[18] Now this man purchased a field with the reward of iniquity; and falling headlong, he burst asunder in the midst, and all his bowels gushed out.

[19] And it was known unto all the dwellers at Jerusalem; insomuch as that field is called in their proper tongue, Aceldama, that is to say, The field of blood.

[20] For it is written in the book of Psalms, Let his habitation be desolate, and let no man dwell therein: and his bishoprick let another take.

[21] Wherefore of these men which have companied with us all the time that the Lord Jesus went in and out among us,

[22] Beginning from the baptism of John, unto that same day that he was taken up from us, must one be ordained to be a witness with us of his resurrection.

[23] And they appointed two, Joseph called Barsabas, who was surnamed Justus, and Matthias.

[24] And they prayed, and said, Thou, Lord, which knowest the hearts of all men, shew whether of these two thou hast chosen,

[25] That he may take part of this ministry and apostleship, from which Judas by transgression fell, that he might go to his own place.

[26] And they gave forth their lots; and the lot fell upon Matthias; and he was numbered with the eleven apostles.

21.4 The Birth of the Church

We usually date the birth of the church to the events at Pentecost, rather than from the time when Jesus issued his final commands to the apostles or from when he referred to Peter as the rock upon which the church would be founded.

Acts 2 1 - 13

[1] And when the day of Pentecost was fully come, they were all with one accord in one place.

[2] And suddenly there came a sound from heaven as of a rushing mighty wind, and it filled all the house where they were sitting.

[3] And there appeared unto them cloven tongues like as of fire, and it sat upon each of them.

[4] And they were all filled with the Holy Ghost, and began to speak with other tongues, as the Spirit gave them utterance.

[5] And there were dwelling at Jerusalem Jews, devout men, out of every nation under heaven.

[6] Now when this was noised abroad, the multitude came together, and were confounded, because that every man heard them speak in his own language.

[7] And they were all amazed and marvelled, saying one to another, Behold, are not all these which speak Galilaeans?

[8] And how hear we every man in our own tongue, wherein we were born?

[9] Parthians, and Medes, and Elamites, and the dwellers in Mesopotamia, and in Judaea, and Cappadocia, in Pontus, and Asia,

[10] Phrygia, and Pamphylia, in Egypt, and in the parts of Libya about Cyrene, and strangers of Rome, Jews and proselytes,

[11] Cretes and Arabians, we do hear them speak in our tongues the wonderful works of God.

[12] And they were all amazed, and were in doubt, saying one to another, What meaneth this?

[13] Others mocking said, these men are full of new wine.

Peter had by now become the acknowledged leader of the church and he stood up to make a speech in defense of the rest of the disciples:

Acts 2 14 - 36

[14] But Peter, standing up with the eleven, lifted up his voice, and said unto them, Ye men of Judaea, and all ye that dwell at Jerusalem, be this known unto you, and hearken to my words:

[15] For these are not drunken, as ye suppose, seeing it is but the third hour of the day.

[16] But this is that which was spoken by the prophet Joel;

[17] And it shall come to pass in the last days, saith God, I will pour out of my Spirit upon all flesh: and your sons and your daughters shall prophesy, and your young men shall see visions, and your old men shall dream dreams:

[18] And on my servants and on my handmaidens, I will pour out in those days of my Spirit; and they shall prophesy:

[19] And I will shew wonders in heaven above, and signs in the earth beneath; blood, and fire, and vapour of smoke:

[20] The sun shall be turned into darkness, and the moon into blood, before that great and notable day of the Lord come:

[21] And it shall come to pass, that whosoever shall call on the name of the Lord shall be saved.

[22] Ye men of Israel, hear these words; Jesus of Nazareth, a man approved of God among you by miracles and wonders and signs, which God did by him in the midst of you, as ye yourselves also know:

[23] Him, being delivered by the determinate counsel and foreknowledge of God, ye have taken, and by wicked hands have crucified and slain:

[24] Whom God hath raised up, having loosed the pains of death: because it was not possible that he should be holden of it.

[25] For David speaketh concerning him, I foresaw the Lord always before my face, for he is on my right hand, that I should not be moved:

[26] Therefore did my heart rejoice, and my tongue was glad; moreover also my flesh shall rest in hope:

[27] Because thou wilt not leave my soul in hell, neither wilt thou suffer thine Holy One to see corruption.

[28] Thou hast made known to me the ways of life; thou shalt make me full of joy with thy countenance.

[29] Men and brethren, let me freely speak unto you of the patriarch David, that he is both dead and buried, and his sepulchre is with us unto this day.

[30] Therefore being a prophet, and knowing that God had sworn with an oath to him, that of the fruit of his loins, according to the flesh, he would raise up Christ to sit on his throne;

[31] He seeing this before spake of the resurrection of Christ, that his soul was not left in hell, neither his flesh did see corruption.

[32] This Jesus hath God raised up, whereof we all are witnesses.

[33] Therefore being by the right hand of God exalted, and having received of the Father the promise of the Holy Ghost, he hath shed forth this, which ye now see and hear.

[34] For David is not ascended into the heavens: but he saith himself, The LORD said unto my Lord, Sit thou on my right hand,

[35] Until I make thy foes thy footstool.

[36] Therefore let all the house of Israel know assuredly, that God hath made that same Jesus, whom ye have crucified, both Lord and Christ.

It had an immediate effect and he increased the size of the church from 120 to over 3000 in one day.

Acts 2 37 - 41

[37] Now when they heard this, they were pricked in their heart, and said unto Peter and to the rest of the apostles, Men and brethren, what shall we do?

[38] Then Peter said unto them, Repent, and be baptized every one of you in the name of Jesus Christ for the remission of sins, and ye shall receive the gift of the Holy Ghost.

[39] For the promise is unto you, and to your children, and to all that are afar off, even as many as the Lord our God shall call.

[40] And with many other words did he testify and exhort, saying, Save yourselves from this untoward generation.

[41] Then they that gladly received his word were baptized: and the same day there were added unto them about three thousand souls.

They continued to meet and pray together and their numbers increased steadily.

Acts 2 42 – 47

[42] And they continued stedfastly in the apostles' doctrine and fellowship, and in breaking of bread, and in prayers.

[43] And fear came upon every soul: and many wonders and signs were done by the apostles.

[44] And all that believed were together, and had all things common;

[45] And sold their possessions and goods, and parted them to all men, as every man had need.

[46] And they, continuing daily with one accord in the temple, and breaking bread from house to house, did eat their meat with gladness and singleness of heart,

[47] Praising God, and having favour with all the people. And the Lord added to the church daily such as should be saved.

21.5 James

James, reputed to have been the brother of Jesus, was a very pious man steeped in the Jewish traditions and seeing Christianity more as a branch of traditional Judaism than a new religion.

A second century writer named Heggisippus is quoted by Eusebius (Chapter 23) how James became the dominant figure among Christians in Palestine.

Heggesippus Book 5

Control of the Church passed to the apostles, together with the Lord's brother James, whom everyone from the Lord's time till our own has called The Righteous, for there were many Jamess, but this one was holy from his birth; he drank no wine or intoxicating liquor and ate no animal food; no razor came near his head, he did not smear himself with oil and took no baths. He alone was permitted to enter the Holy Place for his garments were not of wool but of linen. He used to enter the Sanctuary alone and was often found on his knees beseeching forgiveness for the people so that his knees grew hard like a camel's.

There were several leading Christians named James and it is often difficult to know which one was being referred to. The key one was James the Righteous otherwise known as the brother of the Lord. He had been seen as the leader of the Church in Judea, Eusebius refers to him as the first Bishop of Jerusalem but it is doubtful if that concept was in fact developed at the time.

Eusebius Book 2 Chapter 23

When Paul appealed to Caesar and was sent to Rome by Festus, the Jews were disappointed of the hope in which they had devised their plot against him and turned their attention to James the Lord's brother, who had been elected by the apostles to the episcopal throne at Jerusalem. This is the crime that they committed against him. They brought him into their midst and in the presence of the whole populace demanded a denial of his belief in Christ. But when, contrary to all expectation, he spoke as he liked and showed undreamt-of fearlessness in the face of the enormous throng, declaring that our Saviour and Lord, Jesus, was the Son of God, they could not endure his testimony any longer, since he was universally regarded as the most righteous of men because of the heights of philosophy and religion which he scaled in his life. So they killed him, seizing the opportunity for getting their own way provided by the absence of a government, for at that very time Festus had died in Judaea, leaving the province without governor or procurator.

21.6 Peter Performs a Miracle

Acts 3 1 - 10

[1] Now Peter and John went up together into the temple at the hour of prayer, being the ninth hour.

[2] And a certain man lame from his mother's womb was carried, whom they laid daily at the gate of the temple which is called Beautiful, to ask alms of them that entered into the temple;

[3] Who seeing Peter and John about to go into the temple asked an alms.

[4] And Peter, fastening his eyes upon him with John, said, Look on us.

[5] And he gave heed unto them, expecting to receive something of them.

[6] Then Peter said, Silver and gold have I none; but such as I have give I thee: In the name of Jesus Christ of Nazareth rise up and walk.

[7] And he took him by the right hand, and lifted him up: and immediately his feet and ancle bones received strength.

[8] And he leaping up stood, and walked, and entered with them into the temple, walking, and leaping, and praising God.

[9] And all the people saw him walking and praising God:

[10] And they knew that it was he which sat for alms at the Beautiful gate of the temple: and they were filled with wonder and amazement at that which had happened unto him.

This immediately aroused the interest of the crowd and Peter uses the opportunity to preach a sermon.

Acts 3 11 - 16

[11] And as the lame man which was healed held Peter and John, all the people ran together unto them in the porch that is called Solomon's, greatly wondering.

[12] And when Peter saw it, he answered unto the people, Ye men of Israel, why marvel ye at this? or why look ye so earnestly on us, as though by our own power or holiness we had made this man to walk?

[13] The God of Abraham, and of Isaac, and of Jacob, the God of our fathers, hath glorified his Son Jesus; whom ye delivered up, and denied him in the presence of Pilate, when he was determined to let him go.

[14] But ye denied the Holy One and the Just, and desired a murderer to be granted unto you;

[15] And killed the Prince of life, whom God hath raised from the dead; whereof we are witnesses.

[16] And his name through faith in his name hath made this man strong, whom ye see and know: yea, the faith which is by him hath given him this perfect soundness in the presence of you all.

21.7 The Apostles are put in Prison

One can almost see the Jewish Authorities reaction to this new phenomenon 'Oh not again!' They round up the apostles and put them in prison.

Acts 4 1 - 4

[1] And as they spake unto the people, the priests, and the captain of the temple, and the Sadducees, came upon them,

[2] Being grieved that they taught the people, and preached through Jesus the resurrection from the dead.

[3] And they laid hands on them, and put them in hold unto the next day: for it was now eventide.

[4] Howbeit many of them which heard the word believed; and the number of the men was about five thousand.

And then put them on trial before the Council.

Acts 4 5 - 20

[5] And it came to pass on the morrow, that their rulers, and elders, and scribes,

[6] And Annas the high priest, and Caiaphas, and John, and Alexander, and as many as were of the kindred of the high priest, were gathered together at Jerusalem.

[7] And when they had set them in the midst, they asked, By what power, or by what name, have ye done this?

[8] Then Peter, filled with the Holy Ghost, said unto them, Ye rulers of the people, and elders of Israel,

[9] If we this day be examined of the good deed done to the impotent man, by what means he is made whole;

[10] Be it known unto you all, and to all the people of Israel, that by the name of Jesus Christ of Nazareth, whom ye crucified, whom God raised from the dead, even by him doth this man stand here before you whole.

[11] This is the stone which was set at nought of you builders, which is become the head of the corner.

[12] Neither is there salvation in any other: for there is none other name under heaven given among men, whereby we must be saved.

[13] Now when they saw the boldness of Peter and John, and perceived that they were unlearned and ignorant men, they marvelled; and they took knowledge of them, that they had been with Jesus.

[14] And beholding the man which was healed standing with them, they could say nothing against it.

[15] But when they had commanded them to go aside out of the council, they conferred among themselves,

[16] Saying, What shall we do to these men? for that indeed a notable miracle hath been done by them is manifest to all them that dwell in Jerusalem; and we cannot deny it.

[17] But that it spread no further among the people, let us straitly threaten them, that they speak henceforth to no man in this name.

[18] And they called them, and commanded them not to speak at all nor teach in the name of Jesus.

[19] But Peter and John answered and said unto them, Whether it be right in the sight of God to hearken unto you more than unto God, judge ye.

[20] For we cannot but speak the things which we have seen and heard.

The Council were left in a severe dilemma, not wishing to repeat the events of Passover when they clearly now did not have the support of the crowd.

Acts 4 21 - 22

[21] So when they had further threatened them, they let them go, finding nothing how they might punish them, because of the people: for all men glorified God for that which was done.

[22] For the man was above forty years old, on whom this miracle of healing was shewed.

The Christians saw this as a moral victory and uttered a prayer of thanksgiving.

Acts 4 23 - 31

[23] And being let go, they went to their own company, and reported all that the chief priests and elders had said unto them.

[24] And when they heard that, they lifted up their voice to God with one accord, and said, Lord, thou art God, which hast made heaven, and earth, and the sea, and all that in them is:

[25] Who by the mouth of thy servant David hast said, Why did the heathen rage, and the people imagine vain things?

[26] The kings of the earth stood up, and the rulers were gathered together against the Lord, and against his Christ.

[27] For of a truth against thy holy child Jesus, whom thou hast anointed, both Herod, and Pontius Pilate, with the Gentiles, and the people of Israel, were gathered together,

[28] For to do whatsoever thy hand and thy counsel determined before to be done.

[29] And now, Lord, behold their threatenings: and grant unto thy servants, that with all boldness they may speak thy word,

[30] By stretching forth thine hand to heal; and that signs and wonders may be done by the name of thy holy child Jesus.

[31] And when they had prayed, the place was shaken where they were assembled together; and they were all filled with the Holy Ghost, and they spake the word of God with boldness.

21.8 Further Conflict with Authority

Luke tells another similar tale of conflict with the Jewish authorities but it seems to be just another version of the same incidents.

Acts 5 17 - 26

[17] Then the high priest rose up, and all they that were with him, (which is the sect of the Sadducees,) and were filled with indignation,

[18] And laid their hands on the apostles, and put them in the common prison.

[19] But the angel of the Lord by night opened the prison doors, and brought them forth, and said,

[20] Go, stand and speak in the temple to the people all the words of this life.

[21] And when they heard that, they entered into the temple early in the morning, and taught. But the high priest came, and they that were with him, and called the council together, and all the senate of the children of Israel and sent to the prison to have them brought.

[22] But when the officers came, and found them not in the prison, they returned, and told,

[23] Saying, The prison truly found we shut with all safety, and the keepers standing without before the doors: but when we had opened, we found no man within.

[24] Now when the high priest and the captain of the temple and the chief priests heard these things, they doubted of them whereunto this would grow.

[25] Then came one and told them, saying, Behold, the men whom ye put in prison are standing in the temple, and teaching the people.

[26] Then went the captain with the officers, and brought them without violence: for they feared the people, lest they should have been stoned.

Acts 5 27 - 32

[27] And when they had brought them, they set them before the council: and the high priest asked them,

[28] Saying, Did not we straitly command you that ye should not teach in this name? and, behold, ye have filled Jerusalem with your doctrine, and intend to bring this man's blood upon us.

[29] Then Peter and the other apostles answered and said, We ought to obey God rather than men.

[30] The God of our fathers raised up Jesus, whom ye slew and hanged on a tree.

[31] Him hath God exalted with his right hand to be a Prince and a Saviour, for to give repentance to Israel, and forgiveness of sins.

[32] And we are his witnesses of these things; and so is also the Holy Ghost, whom God hath given to them that obey him.

Gamaliel offered his advice which was taken:

Acts 5 33 - 39

[33] When they heard that, they were cut to the heart, and took counsel to slay them.

[34] Then stood there up one in the council, a Pharisee, named Gamaliel, a doctor of the law, had in reputation among all the people, and commanded to put the apostles forth a little space;

[35] And said unto them, Ye men of Israel, take heed to yourselves what ye intend to do as touching these men.

[36] For before these days rose up Theudas, boasting himself to be somebody; to whom a number of men, about four hundred, joined themselves: who was slain; and all, as many as obeyed him, were scattered, and brought to nought.

[37] After this man rose up Judas of Galilee in the days of the taxing, and drew away much people after him: he also perished; and all, even as many as obeyed him, were dispersed.

[38] And now I say unto you, Refrain from these men, and let them alone: for if this counsel or this work be of men, it will come to nought:

[39] But if it be of God, ye cannot overthrow it; lest haply ye be found even to fight against God.

And the Apostles were flogged and let go.

Acts 5 40 - 42

[40] And to him they agreed: and when they had called the apostles, and beaten them, they commanded that they should not speak in the name of Jesus, and let them go.

[41] And they departed from the presence of the council, rejoicing that they were counted worthy to suffer shame for his name.

[42] And daily in the temple, and in every house, they ceased not to teach and preach Jesus Christ.

21.9 The First Priests are Ordained

By now numbers were getting too large for the apostles to do all the ministering themselves and so they ordained six men to assist them.

Acts 6 1 - 7

[1] And in those days, when the number of the disciples was multiplied, there arose a murmuring of the Grecians against the Hebrews, because their widows were neglected in the daily ministration.

[2] Then the twelve called the multitude of the disciples unto them, and said, It is not reason that we should leave the word of God, and serve tables.

[3] Wherefore, brethren, look ye out among you seven men of honest report, full of the Holy Ghost and wisdom, whom we may appoint over this business.

[4] But we will give ourselves continually to prayer, and to the ministry of the word.

[5] And the saying pleased the whole multitude: and they chose Stephen, a man full of faith and of the Holy Ghost, and Philip, and Prochorus, and Nicanor, and Timon, and Parmenas, and Nicolas a proselyte of Antioch:

[6] Whom they set before the apostles: and when they had prayed, they laid their hands on them.

[7] And the word of God increased; and the number of the disciples multiplied in Jerusalem greatly; and a great company of the priests were obedient to the faith.

21.10 Stephen's Martyrdom

Among the new priests was Stephen

Acts 6 8 - 15

[8] And Stephen, full of faith and power, did great wonders and miracles among the people.

[9] Then there arose certain of the synagogue, which is called the synagogue of the Libertines, and Cyrenians, and Alexandrians, and of them of Cilicia and of Asia, disputing with Stephen.

[10] And they were not able to resist the wisdom and the spirit by which he spake.

[11] Then they suborned men, which said, We have heard him speak blasphemous words against Moses, and against God.

[12] And they stirred up the people, and the elders, and the scribes, and came upon him, and caught him, and brought him to the council,

[13] And set up false witnesses, which said, This man ceaseth not to speak blasphemous words against this holy place, and the law:

[14] For we have heard him say, that this Jesus of Nazareth shall destroy this place, and shall change the customs which Moses delivered us.

[15] And all that sat in the council, looking stedfastly on him, saw his face as it had been the face of an angel.

And when the Authorities began to harass the Christians he gave them a detailed history lesson This was enough to enrage them even more and Stephen was put to death.

Acts 7 1 - 53
[1] Then said the high priest, Are these things so?

Abraham
[2] And he said, Men, brethren, and fathers, hearken; The God of glory appeared unto our father Abraham, when he was in Mesopotamia, before he dwelt in Charran,

[3] And said unto him, Get thee out of thy country, and from thy kindred, and come into the land which I shall shew thee.

[4] Then came he out of the land of the Chaldaeans, and dwelt in Charran: and from thence, when his father was dead, he removed him into this land, wherein ye now dwell.

[5] And he gave him none inheritance in it, no, not so much as to set his foot on: yet he promised that he would give it to him for a possession, and to his seed after him, when as yet he had no child.

[6] And God spake on this wise, That his seed should sojourn in a strange land; and that they should bring them into bondage, and entreat them evil four hundred years.

[7] And the nation to whom they shall be in bondage will I judge, said God: and after that shall they come forth, and serve me in this place. .

[8] And he gave him the covenant of circumcision: and so Abraham begat Isaac, and circumcised him the eighth day; and Isaac begat Jacob; and Jacob begat the twelve patriarchs.

Egypt

[9] And the patriarchs, moved with envy, sold Joseph into Egypt: but God was with him,

[10] And delivered him out of all his afflictions, and gave him favour and wisdom in the sight of Pharaoh king of Egypt; and he made him governor over Egypt and all his house.

[11] Now there came a dearth over all the land of Egypt and Chanaan, and great affliction: and our fathers found no sustenance.

[12] But when Jacob heard that there was corn in Egypt, he sent out our fathers first.

[13] And at the second time Joseph was made known to his brethren; and Joseph's kindred was made known unto Pharaoh.

[14] Then sent Joseph, and called his father Jacob to him, and all his kindred, threescore and fifteen souls.

[15] So Jacob went down into Egypt, and died, he, and our fathers,

[16] And were carried over into Sychem, and laid in the sepulchre that Abraham bought for a sum of money of the sons of Emmor the father of Sychem.

Moses

[17] But when the time of the promise drew nigh, which God had sworn to Abraham, the people grew and multiplied in Egypt,

[18] Till another king arose, which knew not Joseph.

[19] The same dealt subtilly with our kindred, and evil entreated our fathers, so that they cast out their young children, to the end they might not live.

[20] In which time Moses was born, and was exceeding fair, and nourished up in his father's house three months:

[21] And when he was cast out, Pharaoh's daughter took him up, and nourished him for her own son.

[22] And Moses was learned in all the wisdom of the Egyptians, and was mighty in words and in deeds.

[23] And when he was full forty years old, it came into his heart to visit his brethren the children of Israel.

[24] And seeing one of them suffer wrong, he defended him, and avenged him that was oppressed, and smote the Egyptian:

[25] For he supposed his brethren would have understood how that God by his hand would deliver them: but they understood not.

[26] And the next day he shewed himself unto them as they strove, and would have set them at one again, saying, Sirs, ye are brethren; why do ye wrong one to another?

[27] But he that did his neighbour wrong thrust him away, saying, Who made thee a ruler and a judge over us?

[28] Wilt thou kill me, as thou diddest the Egyptian yesterday?

[29] Then fled Moses at this saying, and was a stranger in the land of Madian, where he begat two sons.

[30] And when forty years were expired, there appeared to him in the wilderness of mount Sina an angel of the Lord in a flame of fire in a bush.

[31] When Moses saw it, he wondered at the sight: and as he drew near to behold it, the voice of the Lord came unto him,

[32] Saying, I am the God of thy fathers, the God of Abrham, and the God of Isaac, and the God of Jacob. Then Moses trembled, and durst not behold.

[33] Then said the Lord to him, Put off thy shoes from thy feet: for the place where thou standest is holy ground.

[34] I have seen, I have seen the affliction of my people which is in Egypt, and I have heard their groaning, and am come down to deliver them. And now come, I will send thee into Egypt.

Exodus

[35] This Moses whom they refused, saying, Who made thee a ruler and a judge? the same did God send to be a ruler and a deliverer by the hand of the angel which appeared to him in the bush.

[36] He brought them out, after that he had shewed wonders and signs in the land of Egypt, and in the Red sea, and in the wilderness forty years.

[37] This is that Moses, which said unto the children of Israel, A prophet shall the Lord your God raise up unto you of your brethren, like unto me; him shall ye hear.

[38] This is he, that was in the church in the wilderness with the angel which spake to him in the mount Sina, and with our fathers: who received the lively oracles to give unto us:

[39] To whom our fathers would not obey, but thrust him from them, and in their hearts turned back again into Egypt,

[40] Saying unto Aaron, Make us gods to go before us: for as for this Moses, which brought us out of the land of Egypt, we wot not what is become of him.

[41] And they made a calf in those days, and offered sacrifice unto the idol, and rejoiced in the works of their own hands.

[42] Then God turned, and gave them up to worship the host of heaven; as it is written in the book of the prophets, O ye house of Israel, have ye offered

to me slain beasts and sacrifices by the space of forty years in the wilderness?

[43] Yea, ye took up the tabernacle of Moloch, and the star of your god Remphan, figures which ye made to worship them: and I will carry you away beyond Babylon.

[44] Our fathers had the tabernacle of witness in the wilderness, as he had appointed, speaking unto Moses, that he should make it according to the fashion that he had seen.

[45] Which also our fathers that came after brought in with Jesus into the possession of the Gentiles, whom God drave out before the face of our fathers, unto the days of David;

[46] Who found favour before God, and desired to find a tabernacle for the God of Jacob.

[47] But Solomon built him an house.

[48] Howbeit the most High dwelleth not in temples made with hands; as saith the prophet,

[49] Heaven is my throne, and earth is my footstool: what house will ye build me? saith the Lord: or what is the place of my rest?

[50] Hath not my hand made all these things?

[51] Ye stiffnecked and uncircumcised in heart and ears, ye do always resist the Holy Ghost: as your fathers did, so do ye.

[52] Which of the prophets have not your fathers persecuted? and they have slain them which shewed before of the coming of the Just One; of whom ye have been now the betrayers and murderers:

[53] Who have received the law by the disposition of angels, and have not kept it.

Stephen is stoned to death.

Acts 7 54 - 60

[54] When they heard these things, they were cut to the heart, and they gnashed on him with their teeth.

[55] But he, being full of the Holy Ghost, looked up stedfastly into heaven, and saw the glory of God, and Jesus standing on the right hand of God,

[56] And said, Behold, I see the heavens opened, and the Son of man standing on the right hand of God.

[57] Then they cried out with a loud voice, and stopped their ears, and ran upon him with one accord,

[58] And cast him out of the city, and stoned him: and the witnesses laid down their clothes at a young man's feet, whose name was Saul.

[59] And they stoned Stephen, calling upon God, and saying, Lord Jesus, receive my spirit.

[60] And he kneeled down, and cried with a loud voice, Lord, lay not this sin to their charge. And when he had said this, he fell asleep.

21.11 Life in the Early Church

Luke now gives us a few glimpses into the life of the early church - sharing goods: -

Acts 4 32 - 35

[32] And the multitude of them that believed were of one heart and of one soul: neither said any of them that ought of the things which he possessed was his own; but they had all things common.
[33] And with great power gave the apostles witness of the resurrection of the Lord Jesus: and great grace was upon them all.
[34] Neither was there any among them that lacked: for as many as were possessors of lands or houses sold them, and brought the prices of the things that were sold,
[35] And laid them down at the apostles' feet: and distribution was made unto every man according as he had need.

The example of Joses.

Acts 4 36 - 37

[36] And Joses, who by the apostles was surnamed Barnabas, (which is, being interpreted, The son of consolation,) a Levite, and of the country of Cyprus,
[37] Having land, sold it, and brought the money, and laid it at the apostles' feet. Interpreted, Son of Encouragement), a Levite, a man of Cyprus by race, having a field, sold it, and brought the money and laid it at the apostles' feet.

And the example of Ananias.

Acts 5 1 - 12

[1] But a certain man named Ananias, with Sapphira his wife, sold a possession,
[2] And kept back part of the price, his wife also being privy to it, and brought a certain part, and laid it at the apostles' feet.
[3] But Peter said, Ananias, why hath Satan filled thine heart to lie to the Holy Ghost, and to keep back part of the price of the land?

[4] Whiles it remained, was it not thine own? and after it was sold, was it not in thine own power? why hast thou conceived this thing in thine heart? thou hast not lied unto men, but unto God.

[5] And Ananias hearing these words fell down, and gave up the ghost: and great fear came on all them that heard these things.

[6] And the young men arose, wound him up, and carried him out, and buried him.

[7] And it was about the space of three hours after, when his wife, not knowing what was done, came in.

[8] And Peter answered unto her, Tell me whether ye sold the land for so much? And she said, Yea, for so much.

[9] Then Peter said unto her, How is it that ye have agreed together to tempt the Spirit of the Lord? behold, the feet of them which have buried thy husband are at the door, and shall carry thee out.

[10] Then fell she down straightway at his feet, and yielded up the ghost: and the young men came in, and found her dead, and, carrying her forth, buried her by her husband.

[11] And great fear came upon all the church, and upon as many as heard these things.

[12] And by the hands of the apostles were many signs and wonders wrought among the people; (and they were all with one accord in Solomon's porch.

Finally, the meeting by Solomon's Gate.

Acts 5 13 - 16

[13] And of the rest durst no man join himself to them: but the people magnified them.

[14] And believers were the more added to the Lord, multitudes both of men and women.

[15] Insomuch that they brought forth the sick into the streets, and laid them on beds and couches, that at the least the shadow of Peter passing by might overshadow some of them.

[16] There came also a multitude out of the cities round about unto Jerusalem, bringing sick folks, and them which were vexed with unclean spirits: and they were healed everyone.

21.12 John Mark

We now come to one of the great mysteries of the early Church. Who was John Mark and why was it so important he escaped from Jerusalem?

Acts 12 11 - 12
[11] And when Peter was come to himself, he said, Now I know of a surety, that the Lord hath sent his angel, and hath delivered me out of the hand of Herod, and from all the expectation of the people of the Jews.
[12] And when he had considered the thing, he came to the house of Mary the mother of John, whose surname was Mark; where many were gathered together praying.

The most straightforward interpretation is that Mary Magdalene, the wife of Jesus, had a son by him named John Mark. In Jewish eyes Jesus' crime was that he had claimed to be 'King of the Jews' So another question is - which Herod are we talking about. The most likely is Herod Agrippa I who became king in 39 AD. With Jesus dead, Herod could feel safe and continue his rule over Palestine as a Roman puppet unchallenged. However, if it became known that Jesus had a son, then indeed Herod would have a rival to claim the kingship, and one who was unlikely to be as subservient to Roman rule as Herod had been. This would have been a much more cogent reason for this different Herod to have indulged in the slaughter of the innocents, placed by Matthew after Jesus' birth.

We now need to look at the story of the Magi in a different light.

21.13 The Magi

After Herod Agrippa had also taken in Judea, three men from the east turn up at Herod's court. They were probably Zoroastrians from Persia who had heard about the Jesus phenomenon and had come to Palestine to see for themselves. They ask Herod where they can make contact with members of Jesus' sect and especially with his son.

Matthew 2 1 - 5
[1] Now when Jesus was born in Bethlehem of Judaea in the days of Herod the king, behold, there came wise men from the east to Jerusalem,
[2] Saying, Where is he that is born King of the Jews? for we have seen his star in the east, and are come to worship him.
[3] When Herod the king had heard these things, he was troubled, and all Jerusalem with him.

[4] And when he had gathered all the chief priests and scribes of the people together, he demanded of them where Christ should be born.
[5] And they said unto him, In Bethlehem of Judaea: for thus it is written by the prophet,

This is what Matthew recounts, but did he make a slight change to protect John Mark by referring to Bethlehem rather than Bethany and was the question really about where the new 'king' was to be found. As Jesus' heir and successor he too would have been referred to as 'the anointed one' which is what the original text in Greek said. This news would have come as a terrible shock to Herod who thought he had dealt with the threat with the deaths of John the Baptist and Jesus. Someone at Herod's court would almost certainly have known the town where John Mark was born but probably not the exact house. Herod sees an opportunity and calls the Magi back:-

Matthew 2 7 - 15
[7] Then Herod, when he had privily called the wise men, inquired of them diligently what time the star appeared.
[8] And he sent them to Bethlehem, and said, Go and search diligently for the young child; and when ye have found him, bring me word again, that I may come and worship him also.
[9] When they had heard the king, they departed; and, lo, the star, which they saw in the east, went before them, till it came and stood over where the young child was.
[10] When they saw the star, they rejoiced with exceeding great joy.
[11] And when they were come into the house, they saw the young child with Mary his mother, and fell down, and worshipped him: and when they had opened their treasures, they presented unto him gifts; gold, and frankincense, and myrrh.
[12] And being warned of God in a dream that they should not return to Herod, they departed into their own country another way.
[13] And when they were departed, behold, the angel of the Lord appeareth to Joseph in a dream, saying, Arise, and take the young child and his mother, and flee into Egypt, and be thou there until I bring thee word: for Herod will seek the young child to destroy him.
[14] When he arose, he took the young child and his mother by night, and departed into Egypt:
[15] And was there until the death of Herod: that it might be fulfilled which was spoken of the Lord by the prophet, saying, Out of Egypt have I called my son.

Thus, the episode of the three wise men can be interpreted quite differently and one can see how the early gospel writers distorted the story for security reasons. The three wise men could have been Peter, Paul and Barnabus rather than men from the east and the interrogation been that of Peter while in prison, Herod having heard rumours of a son and wanting better intelligence. This version of events can explain the tradition of Mary Magdalene moving from Jerusalem to live in southern France and the genesis of the 'Sang Real' legend.

A key question however is how old would the child have been. In the normal course of Jewish life Jesus and Mary would have married in their late teens, say around 15 AD and had their first child fairly soon afterwards, say 16 AD. Jesus' death occurred Iin 33 AD when he would have been in his late thirties and Paul's conversion say a year later in 34 AD. Herod Agrippa I became tetrarch of Galillee in 39 AD and king of Judea about two years later so the visit of the wise men would have come around 42 AD. By this time John Mark would have been around twenty six and therefore would have been seen as a very obvious threat to Herod, hence the need to pretend he was but still a baby.

21.14 Herod's Persecution

Herod decided that the best way to deal with the problem was to attack the leadership of the new church. James was the first to go and Peter too fell into his hands.

Acts 12 1 - 5
[1] Now about that time Herod the king stretched forth his hands to vex certain of the church.
[2] And he killed James the brother of John with the sword.
[3] And because he saw it pleased the Jews, he proceeded further to take Peter also. (Then were the days of unleavened bread.)
[4] And when he had apprehended him, he put him in prison, and delivered him to four quaternions of soldiers to keep him; intending after Easter to bring him forth to the people.
[5] Peter therefore was kept in prison: but prayer was made without ceasing of the church unto God for him.

However, Peter managed to escape, thanks, as Luke tells, to the intervention of an Angel.

Acts 12 6 - 11

[6] And when Herod would have brought him forth, the same night Peter was sleeping between two soldiers, bound with two chains: and the keepers before the door kept the prison.

[7] And, behold, the angel of the Lord came upon him, and a light shined in the prison: and he smote Peter on the side, and raised him up, saying, Arise up quickly. And his chains fell off from his hands.

[8] And the angel said unto him, Gird thyself, and bind on thy sandals. And so, he did. And he saith unto him, Cast thy garment about thee, and follow me.

[9] And he went out, and followed him; and wist not that it was true which was done by the angel; but thought he saw a vision.

[10] When they were past the first and the second ward, they came unto the iron gate that leadeth unto the city; which opened to them of his own accord: and they went out, and passed on through one street; and forthwith the angel departed from him.

[11] And when Peter was come to himself, he said, Now I know of a surety, that the Lord hath sent his angel, and hath delivered me out of the hand of Herod, and from all the expectation of the people of the Jews.

The guards suffer as a result.

Acts 12 18 - 19

[18] Now as soon as it was day, there was no small stir among the soldiers, what was become of Peter.

[19] And when Herod had sought for him, and found him not, he examined the keepers, and commanded that they should be put to death. And he went down from Judaea to Caesarea, and there abode.

Peter then goes to see other Christians to warn them.

21.15 The House at Bethany

It was to the house of John Mark's mother that Peter went after he escaped from prison, no doubt to warn her that the secret had been forced out of him.

Acts 12 12 - 17

[12] And when he had considered the thing, he came to the house of Mary the mother of John, whose surname was Mark; where many were gathered together praying.

[13] And as Peter knocked at the door of the gate, a damsel came to hearken, named Rhoda.

[14] And when she knew Peter's voice, she opened not the gate for gladness, but ran in, and told how Peter stood before the gate.

[15] And they said unto her, Thou art mad. But she constantly affirmed that it was even so. Then said they, It is his angel.

[16] But Peter continued knocking: and when they had opened the door, and saw him, they were astonished.

[17] But he, beckoning unto them with the hand to hold their peace, declared unto them how the Lord had brought him out of the prison. And he said, Go shew these things unto James, and to the brethren. And he departed, and went into another place.

So, we learn that Mary's house was a place where Christians gathered and that she had a servant named Rhoda - coincidentally based on the Greek for 'gold'.

Herod Agrippa I then takes off for Caesarea should read where he is die in 44 AD.

Acts 12 20 - 25

[20] And Herod was highly displeased with them of Tyre and Sidon: but they came with one accord to him, and, having made Blastus the king's chamberlain their friend, desired peace; because their country was nourished by the king's country.

[21] And upon a set day Herod, arrayed in royal apparel, sat upon his throne, and made an oration unto them.

[22] And the people gave a shout, saying, It is the voice of a god, and not of a man.

[23] And immediately the angel of the Lord smote him, because he gave not God the glory: and he was eaten of worms, and gave up the ghost.

Our next reference to John Mark is when Paul and Barnabus take him with them when they leave Jerusalem. This is after Paul's conversion (see Section 22.8)

Acts 12 24 - 25

[24] But the word of God grew and multiplied.

[25] And Barnabas and Saul returned from Jerusalem, when they had fulfilled their ministry, and took with them John, whose surname was Mark.

This would then indicate that Mary's house was in the Jerusalem area rather than Galilee and one can assume that it was the house at Bethany. For Paul it was a famous victory - he now had control over Jesus' family and could set about creating a new religion centred not on Jerusalem but on Rome. But did he?

The 'star' can be interpreted as the son of Jesus and the news of his existence. It was this visit that alerted the Christians to the threat so they persuaded the Magi to go straight home and not to inform Herod. They realised the need to smuggle John Mark out of the country as quickly as possible. Matthew describes the warnings as 'dreams'.

Matthew 2 v 12
[12] And being warned of God in a dream that they should not return to Herod, they departed into their own country another way.

It was not just John Mark who was in danger, it was Mary as well, so her relative (father-in-law) Joseph of Arimathea was asked to get her to Alexandria.

Matthew 2 13-14
[13] And when they were departed, behold, the angel of the Lord appeareth to Joseph in a dream, saying, Arise, and take the young child and his mother, and flee into Egypt, and be thou there until I bring thee word: for Herod will seek the young child to destroy him.
[14] When he arose, he took the young child and his mother by night, and departed into Egypt:

Matthew has continued with the subterfuge. John Mark has escaped with Paul, Mary has escaped to Egypt and a false age and location was given. Herod was furious.

Matthew 2 15 - 16
[15] And was there until the death of Herod: that it might be fulfilled which was spoken of the Lord by the prophet, saying, Out of Egypt have I called my son.
[16] Then Herod, when he saw that he was mocked of the wise men, was exceeding wroth, and sent forth, and slew all the children that were in Bethlehem, and in all the coasts thereof, from two years old and under, according to the time which he had diligently inquired of the wise men. .

This is a much more believable scenario than the version recorded by Matthew in his Gospel and Luke (in Acts), Two slight changes: 'Bethany instead of 'Bethlehem' and 'just after Jesus death' rather than 'just after his birth'. Again if one remembers the relationship between Luke and Paul and Paul's need to establish the primacy of Rome, he would not have liked it known that Paul did not control Jesus' family.

It also ties in neatly with the numerous myths and legends associating Mary Magdalene with Provence in Southern France. The legend recalls a long and dangerous sea voyage which finally brings the party to what is now the town of Saintes Maries de la Mer in the Camargue region.

21.16 The Start of Persecution

What had been merely harassment now turned to outright persecution, lead by Saul of Tarsus.

> ### Acts 8 1 - 3
> [1] And Saul was consenting unto his death. And at that time there was a great persecution against the church which was at Jerusalem; and they were all scattered abroad throughout the regions of Judaea and Samaria, except the apostles.
> [2] And devout men carried Stephen to his burial, and made great lamentation over him.
> [3] As for Saul, he made havock of the church, entering into every house, and haling men and women committed them to prison.

However, the word continued to spread, not just in Palestine, but over all the Middle East.

> ### Acts 8 4 - 8
> [4] Therefore they that were scattered abroad went every where preaching the word.
> [5] Then Philip went down to the city of Samaria, and preached Christ unto them.
> [6] And the people with one accord gave heed unto those things which Philip spake, hearing and seeing the miracles which he did.
> [7] For unclean spirits, crying with loud voice, came out of many that were possessed with them: and many taken with palsies, and that were lame, were healed.
> [8] And there was great joy in that city.

Acts 8 9 - 13

[9] But there was a certain man, called Simon, which beforetime in the same city used sorcery, and bewitched the people of Samaria, giving out that himself was some great one:

[10] To whom they all gave heed, from the least to the greatest, saying, This man is the great power of God.

[11] And to him they had regard, because that of long time he had bewitched them with sorceries.

[12] But when they believed Philip preaching the things concerning the kingdom of God, and the name of Jesus Christ, they were baptized, both men and women.

[13] Then Simon himself believed also: and when he was baptized, he continued with Philip, and wondered, beholding the miracles and signs which were done.

21.17 Simon Tries to Buy Power

By now the Apostles were performing miracles regularly and were wielding obvious power over the crowds. Simon wanted to get in on the act as he saw it as a great opportunity to make money.

Acts 8 14 - 25

[14] Now when the apostles which were at Jerusalem heard that Samaria had received the word of God, they sent unto them Peter and John:

[15] Who, when they were come down, prayed for them, that they might receive the Holy Ghost:

[16] (For as yet he was fallen upon none of them: only they were baptized in the name of the Lord Jesus.)

[17] Then laid they their hands on them, and they received the Holy Ghost.

[18] And when Simon saw that through laying on of the apostles' hands the Holy Ghost was given, he offered them money,

[19] Saying, Give me also this power, that on whomsoever I lay hands, he may receive the Holy Ghost.

[20] But Peter said unto him, Thy money perish with thee, because thou hast thought that the gift of God may be purchased with money.

[21] Thou hast neither part nor lot in this matter: for thy heart is not right in the sight of God.

[22] Repent therefore of this thy wickedness, and pray God, if perhaps the thought of thine heart may be forgiven thee.

[23] For I perceive that thou art in the gall of bitterness, and in the bond of iniquity.

[24] Then answered Simon, and said, Pray ye to the Lord for me, that none of these things which ye have spoken come upon me.

[25] And they, when they had testified and preached the word of the Lord, returned to Jerusalem, and preached the gospel in many villages of the Samaritans.

[26] And the angel of the Lord spake unto Philip, saying, Arise, and go toward the south unto the way that goeth down from Jerusalem unto Gaza, which is desert.

21.18 Philip and the Eunuch

Acts 8 26 - 40

[27] And he arose and went: and, behold, a man of Ethiopia, an eunuch of great authority under Candace queen of the Ethiopians, who had the charge of all her treasure, and had come to Jerusalem for to worship,

[28] Was returning, and sitting in his chariot read Esaias the prophet.

[29] Then the Spirit said unto Philip, Go near, and join thyself to this chariot.

[30] And Philip ran thither to him, and heard him read the prophet Esaias, and said, Understandest thou what thou readest?

[31] And he said, How can I, except some man should guide me? And he desired Philip that he would come up and sit with him.

[32] The place of the scripture which he read was this, He was led as a sheep to the slaughter; and like a lamb dumb before his shearer, so opened he not his mouth:

[33] In his humiliation his judgment was taken away: and who shall declare his generation? for his life is taken from the earth.

[34] And the eunuch answered Philip, and said, I pray thee, of whom speaketh the prophet this? of himself, or of some other man?

[35] Then Philip opened his mouth, and began at the same scripture, and preached unto him Jesus.

[36] And as they went on their way, they came unto a certain water: and the eunuch said, See, here is water; what doth hinder me to be baptized?

[37] And Philip said, If thou believest with all thine heart, thou mayest. And he answered and said, I believe that Jesus Christ is the Son of God.

[38] And he commanded the chariot to stand still: and they went down both into the water, both Philip and the eunuch; and he baptized him.

[39] And when they were come up out of the water, the Spirit of the Lord caught away Philip, that the eunuch saw him no more: and he went on his way rejoicing.

[40] But Philip was found at Azotus: and passing through he preached in all the cities, till he came to Caesarea.

21.19 Herod Agrippa's Death

At this point it is worth looking at what happens in the future. Herod Agrippa I came to a very untimely end in 44 AD when he was at Caesaria presiding over games in honour of the Emperor Claudius. Josephus merely mentions Agrippa's death in passing and hints at a Roman conspiracy:

Josephus Wars of the Jews Book II-chapter XI para 6
So now riches flowed in to Agrippa by his enjoyment of so large a dominion; nor did he abuse the money he had on small mattters, but he began to encompass Jerusalem with such a wall, had it been brought to perfection, had made it impracticable for the Romans to take it by siege; but his death which happened at Caesarea before he had raised the walls to their due height, prevented him. He had then reigned three years, he had governed his tetrarchies three other years.

Luke gives a bit more information on how he died but it seems more likely Herod has a stroke..

Acts 12 21 - 23
[21] And upon a set day Herod, arrayed in royal apparel, sat upon his throne, and made an oration unto them.
[22] And the people gave a shout, saying, It is the voice of a god, and not of a man.
[23] And immediately the angel of the Lord smote him, because he gave not God the glory: and he was eaten of worms, and gave up the ghost.

While all this had been going on we have the conversion of persecutor Saul into Apostle Paul. (See chapter 22) The news of Agrippa's death would have spread quite quickly and reached Pamphylia (see section 23.3) where Paul was on his first missionary journey and among his companions was John Mark who realised the immediate danger had gone with the death of Agrippa and decided to return to Jerusalem, believing his mother would have returned as well.

Acts 13 13
[13] Now when Paul and his company loosed from Paphos, they came to Perga in Pamphylia: and John departing from them returned to Jerusalem.

One can imagine Paul's fury at this. In protecting John Mark from persecution Paul believed he had Jesus' family under his control. But John Mark would have been brought up as a strict Jew and would have been on his uncle James' side in the disputes over whether or not Christians had first to become Jews. The fury comes to a head when Paul is about to set out on his second journey. He is not willing to have with him someone who is the opposing camp. (see Section 24.1)

Acts 15 36 - 41

[36] And some days after Paul said unto Barnabas, Let us go again and visit our brethren in every city where we have preached the word of the Lord, and see how they do.

[37] And Barnabas determined to take with them John, whose surname was Mark.

[38] But Paul thought not good to take him with them, who departed from them from Pamphylia, and went not with them to the work.

[39] And the contention was so sharp between them, that they departed asunder one from the other: and so Barnabas took Mark, and sailed unto Cyprus;

[40] And Paul chose Silas, and departed, being recommended by the brethren unto the grace of God.

[41] And he went through Syria and Cilicia, confirming the churches.

This is the last we hear of John Mark, however it does raise the question as to whether John Mark was the same person as Mark, the Evangelist. What perhaps seems more likely was that John Mark, as the person most likely to know about Jesus' life and the most concerned about his own safety, wrote what is often seen as the proto-gospel from which the three synoptic gospels, Matthew, Mark, and Luke were derived. It is also worthy of note that the Gnostic gospel 'secret Mark' had a lot more information than the other three.

Chapter 22 The Conversion of Paul

It was the conversion of Paul on the road to Damascus which set in train the sequence of events which culminated in Christianity becoming the official religion of the Roman Empire. Hitherto Paul, or Saul of Tarsus, as he was then known, was one of the chief persecutors of the Christians. Many of his letters have been preserved and incorporated into the New Testament. In them he developed the basic theology which was to guide the church for the next two thousand years. He amplified and extended many of Jesus' sayings but added a whole lot more. He can be considered the archetype of the misogyny which has dominated the church's approach to women and settled once and for all the question as to whether gentiles could become Christian. The two questions are related in that Jewishness descends through the mother, not the father which is the norm for most other ethnic groups.

22.1 The Vision

Acts 9 1 - 9

[1] And Saul, yet breathing out threatenings and slaughter against the disciples of the Lord, went unto the high priest,

[2] And desired of him letters to Damascus to the synagogues, that if he found any of this way, whether they were men or women, he might bring them bound unto Jerusalem.

[3] And as he journeyed, he came near Damascus: and suddenly there shined round about him a light from heaven:

[4] And he fell to the earth, and heard a voice saying unto him, Saul, Saul, why persecutest thou me?

[5] And he said, Who art thou, Lord? And the Lord said, I am Jesus whom thou persecutest: it is hard for thee to kick against the pricks.

[6] And he trembling and astonished said, Lord, what wilt thou have me to do? And the Lord said unto him, Arise, and go into the city, and it shall be told thee what thou must do.

[7] And the men which journeyed with him stood speechless, hearing a voice, but seeing no man.

[8] And Saul arose from the earth; and when his eyes were opened, he saw no man: but they led him by the hand, and brought him into Damascus.
[9] And he was three days without sight, and neither did eat nor drink.

Paul later recalls his conversion and records that he actually spent the next few days in 'Arabia' - probably the land of the Nabatean Arabs to the south of Damascus. He also recalled that he was not in touch with the majority of Christians in Judea; only Peter and James.

Galations 1 13 - 17

[13] For ye have heard of my conversation in time past in the Jews' religion, how that beyond measure I persecuted the church of God, and wasted it:
[14] And profited in the Jews' religion above many my equals in mine own nation, being more exceedingly zealous of the traditions of my fathers.
[15] But when it pleased God, who separated me from my mother's womb, and called me by his grace,
[16] To reveal his Son in me, that I might preach him among the heathen; immediately I conferred not with flesh and blood:
[17] Neither went I up to Jerusalem to them which were apostles before me; but I went into Arabia, and returned again unto Damascus..

Luke seemingly did not know about the time in Arabia and moves Paul next to the house of Ananias in Damascus, after Ananias had restored Paul's sight.

Acts 9 10 - 19

[10] And there was a certain disciple at Damascus, named Ananias; and to him said the Lord in a vision, Ananias. And he said, Behold, I am here, Lord.
[11] And the Lord said unto him, Arise, and go into the street which is called Straight, and inquire in the house of Judas for one called Saul, of Tarsus: for, behold, he prayeth,
[12] And hath seen in a vision a man named Ananias coming in, and putting his hand on him, that he might receive his sight.
[13] Then Ananias answered, Lord, I have heard by many of this man, how much evil he hath done to thy saints at Jerusalem:
[14] And here he hath authority from the chief priests to bind all that call on thy name.
[15] But the Lord said unto him, Go thy way: for he is a chosen vessel unto me, to bear my name before the Gentiles, and kings, and the children of Israel:
[16] For I will shew him how great things he must suffer for my name's sake.

[17] And Ananias went his way, and entered into the house; and putting his hands on him said, Brother Saul, the Lord, even Jesus, that appeared unto thee in the way as thou camest, hath sent me, that thou mightest receive thy sight, and be filled with the Holy Ghost.

[18] And immediately there fell from his eyes as it had been scales: and he received sight forthwith, and arose, and was baptized.

[19] And when he had received meat, he was strengthened. Then was Saul certain days with the disciples which were at Damascus.

Paul almost immediately changes his stance and begins to preach Jesus as the son of God.

Acts 9 20 - 22

[20] And straightway he preached Christ in the synagogues, that he is the Son of God.

[21] But all that heard him were amazed, and said; Is not this he that destroyed them which called on this name in Jerusalem, and came hither for that intent, that he might bring them bound unto the chief priests?

[22] But Saul increased the more in strength, and confounded the Jews which dwelt at Damascus, proving that this is very Christ.

22.2 Paul's Escape

Paul was evidently antagonising the Jewish community in Damascus and they conspired to catch him and kill him.

Acts 9 23 - 30

[23] And after that many days were fulfilled, the Jews took counsel to kill him:

[24] But their laying await was known of Saul. And they watched the gates day and night to kill him.

[25] Then the disciples took him by night, and let him down by the wall in a basket.

[26] And when Saul was come to Jerusalem, he assayed to join himself to the disciples: but they were all afraid of him, and believed not that he was a disciple.

[27] But Barnabas took him, and brought him to the apostles, and declared unto them how he had seen the Lord in the way, and that he had spoken to him, and how he had preached boldly at Damascus in the name of Jesus.

[28] And he was with them coming in and going out at Jerusalem.

[29] And he spake boldly in the name of the Lord Jesus, and disputed against the Grecians: but they went about to slay him.

[30] Which when the brethren knew, they brought him down to Caesarea, and sent him forth to Tarsus.

Paul's later recollections were quite different to those of Luke, he recalled that his trip up to Jerusalem was just to see Peter and James. And that it was much later, after he came back from his first journey and before his third journey.

Galations 1 18 - 24

[18] Then after three years I went up to Jerusalem to see Peter, and abode with him fifteen days.

[19] But other of the apostles saw I none, save James the Lord's brother.

[20] Now the things which I write unto you, behold, before God, I lie not.

[21] Afterwards I came into the regions of Syria and Cilicia;

[22] And was unknown by face unto the churches of Judaea which were in Christ:

[23] But they had heard only, That he which persecuted us in times past now preacheth the faith which once he destroyed.

[24] And they glorified God in me.

22.3 The Church grows

Paul and Luke now seem to agree that it was Peter and James based in Jerusalem who were leading the Christians there and causing a steady growth in numbers. Luke documents a number of specific cases of conversion. First Aeneas.

Acts 9 31 - 35

[31] Then had the churches rest throughout all Judaea and Galilee and Samaria, and were edified; and walking in the fear of the Lord, and in the comfort of the Holy Ghost, were multiplied.

[32] And it came to pass, as Peter passed throughout all quarters, he came down also to the saints which dwelt at Lydda.

[33] And there he found a certain man named Aeneas, which had kept his bed eight years, and was sick of the palsy.

[34] And Peter said unto him, Aeneas, Jesus Christ maketh thee whole: arise, and make thy bed. And he arose immediately.

[35] And all that dwelt at Lydda and Saron saw him, and turned to the Lord.

And then Tabitha

Acts 9 36 -43

[36] Now there was at Joppa a certain disciple named Tabitha, which by interpretation is called Dorcas: this woman was full of good works and almsdeeds which she did.

[37] And it came to pass in those days, that she was sick, and died: whom when they had washed, they laid her in an upper chamber.

[38] And forasmuch as Lydda was nigh to Joppa, and the disciples had heard that Peter was there, they sent unto him two men, desiring him that he would not delay to come to them.

[39] Then Peter arose and went with them. When he was come, they brought him into the upper chamber: and all the widows stood by him weeping, and shewing the coats and garments which Dorcas made, while she was with them.

[40] But Peter put them all forth, and kneeled down, and prayed; and turning him to the body said, Tabitha, arise. And she opened her eyes: and when she saw Peter, she sat up.

[41] And he gave her his hand, and lifted her up, and when he had called the saints and widows, presented her alive.

[42] And it was known throughout all Joppa; and many believed in the Lord.

[43] And it came to pass, that he tarried many days in Joppa with one Simon a tanner.

22.4 Cornelius

Acts 10 1 - 8

[1] There was a certain man in Caesarea called Cornelius, a centurion of the band called the Italian band,

[2] A devout man, and one that feared God with all his house, which gave much alms to the people, and prayed to God alway.

[3] He saw in a vision evidently about the ninth hour of the day an angel of God coming in to him, and saying unto him, Cornelius.

[4] And when he looked on him, he was afraid, and said, What is it, Lord? And he said unto him, Thy prayers and thine alms are come up for a memorial before God.

[5] And now send men to Joppa, and call for one Simon, whose surname is Peter:

[6] He lodgeth with one Simon a tanner, whose house is by the sea side: he shall tell thee what thou oughtest to do.

[7] And when the angel which spake unto Cornelius was departed, he called two of his household servants, and a devout soldier of them that waited on him continually;

[8] And when he had declared all these things unto them, he sent them to Joppa.

Peter is challenged on dietary laws.

Acts 10 9 - 16

[9] On the morrow, as they went on their journey, and drew nigh unto the city, Peter went up upon the housetop to pray about the sixth hour:

[10] And he became very hungry, and would have eaten: but while they made ready, he fell into a trance,

[11] And saw heaven opened, and a certain vessel descending unto him, as it had been a great sheet knit at the four corners, and let down to the earth:

[12] Wherein were all manner of fourfooted beasts of the earth, and wild beasts, and creeping things, and fowls of the air.

[13] And there came a voice to him, Rise, Peter; kill, and eat.

[14] But Peter said, Not so, Lord; for I have never eaten any thing that is common or unclean.

[15] And the voice spake unto him again the second time, What God hath cleansed, that call not thou common.

[16] This was done thrice: and the vessel was received up again into heaven.

Peter is taken back to Cornelius.

Acts 10 17 - 43

[17] Now while Peter doubted in himself what this vision which he had seen should mean, behold, the men which were sent from Cornelius had made inquiry for Simon's house, and stood before the gate,

[18] And called, and asked whether Simon, which was surnamed Peter, were lodged there.

[19] While Peter thought on the vision, the Spirit said unto him, Behold, three men seek thee.

[20] Arise therefore, and get thee down, and go with them, doubting nothing: for I have sent them.

[21] Then Peter went down to the men which were sent unto him from Cornelius; and said, Behold, I am he whom ye seek: what is the cause wherefore ye are come?

[22] And they said, Cornelius the centurion, a just man, and one that feareth God, and of good report among all the nation of the Jews, was warned from God by an holy angel to send for thee into his house, and to hear words of thee.

[23] Then called he them in, and lodged them. And on the morrow Peter went away with them, and certain brethren from Joppa accompanied him.

[24] And the morrow after they entered into Caesarea. And Cornelius waited for them, and had called together his kinsmen and near friends.

[25] And as Peter was coming in, Cornelius met him, and fell down at his feet, and worshipped him.

[26] But Peter took him up, saying, Stand up; I myself also am a man.

[27] And as he talked with him, he went in, and found many that were come together.

[28] And he said unto them, Ye know how that it is an unlawful thing for a man that is a Jew to keep company, or come unto one of another nation; but God hath shewed me that I should not call any man common or unclean.

[29] Therefore came I unto you without gainsaying, as soon as I was sent for: I ask therefore for what intent ye have sent for me?

[30] And Cornelius said, Four days ago I was fasting until this hour; and at the ninth hour I prayed in my house, and, behold, a man stood before me in bright clothing,

[31] And said, Cornelius, thy prayer is heard, and thine alms are had in remembrance in the sight of God.

[32] Send therefore to Joppa, and call hither Simon, whose surname is Peter; he is lodged in the house of one Simon a tanner by the sea side: who, when he cometh, shall speak unto thee.

[33] Immediately therefore I sent to thee; and thou hast well done that thou art come. Now therefore are we all here present before God, to hear all things that are commanded thee of God.

[34] Then Peter opened his mouth, and said, Of a truth I perceive that God is no respecter of persons:

[35] But in every nation he that feareth him, and worketh righteousness, is accepted with him.

[36] The word which God sent unto the children of Israel, preaching peace by Jesus Christ: (he is Lord of all:)

[37] That word, I say, ye know, which was published throughout all Judaea, and began from Galilee, after the baptism which John preached;

[38] How God anointed Jesus of Nazareth with the Holy Ghost and with power: who went about doing good, and healing all that were oppressed of the devil; for God was with him.

[39] And we are witnesses of all things which he did both in the land of the Jews, and in Jerusalem; whom they slew and hanged on a tree:

[40] Him God raised up the third day, and shewed him openly;

[41] Not to all the people, but unto witnesses chosen before of God, even to us, who did eat and drink with him after he rose from the dead.

[42] And he commanded us to preach unto the people, and to testify that it is he which was ordained of God to be the Judge of quick and dead.
[43] To him give all the prophets witness, that through his name whosoever believeth in him shall receive remission of sins.

22.5 Jews and Gentiles

The question as to who was eligible to become a Christian soon emerged. The Hellenist tradition which Paul espoused was quite clear on the matter. Jesus had come to save all mankind and Christianity was for Jews and Gentiles alike. The remaining original apostles in Jerusalem however believed that in order to become a Christian one must first become a Jew. This argument was to dominate church affairs for a long time. There was another problem with this. Technically to be a Jew one had to have been born of a Jewish mother. It was a racial or cultural affair, not a religious one. For Paul the matter was simple; to become a Christian one had to believe and a cosmetic change to a man's genitals to make him look like a Jew, said absolutely nothing about what the man believed. This also partly explains why Paul seems to exhibit a degree of misogyny and steers clear of mentioning either Mary in his epistles.

Acts 10 44 - 48
[44] While Peter yet spake these words, the Holy Ghost fell on all them which heard the word.
[45] And they of the circumcision which believed were astonished, as many as came with Peter, because that on the Gentiles also was poured out the gift of the Holy Ghost.
[46] For they heard them speak with tongues, and magnify God. Then answered Peter,
[47] Can any man forbid water, that these should not be baptized, which have received the Holy Ghost as well as we?
[48] And he commanded them to be baptized in the name of the Lord. Then prayed they him to tarry certain days.

The strict Jews in Jerusalem were not happy about gentiles being baptised.

Acts 11 1 - 3
[1] And the apostles and brethren that were in Judaea heard that the Gentiles had also received the word of God.
[2] And when Peter was come up to Jerusalem, they that were of the circumcision contended with him,
[3] Saying, Thou wentest in to men uncircumcised, and didst eat with them.

Another issue was eating certain meats, especially pork. Then Peter explained his dream.

Acts 11 4 - 17

[4] But Peter rehearsed the matter from the beginning, and expounded it by order unto them, saying,

[5] I was in the city of Joppa praying: and in a trance I saw a vision, A certain vessel descend, as it had been a great sheet, let down from heaven by four corners; and it came even to me:

[6] Upon the which when I had fastened mine eyes, I considered, and saw fourfooted beasts of the earth, and wild beasts, and creeping things, and fowls of the air.

[7] And I heard a voice saying unto me, Arise, Peter; slay and eat.

[8] But I said, Not so, Lord: for nothing common or unclean hath at any time entered into my mouth.

[9] But the voice answered me again from heaven, What God hath cleansed, that call not thou common.

[10] And this was done three times: and all were drawn up again into heaven.

[11] And, behold, immediately there were three men already come unto the house where I was, sent from Caesarea unto me.

[12] And the spirit bade me go with them, nothing doubting. Moreover these six brethren accompanied me, and we entered into the man's house:

[13] And he shewed us how he had seen an angel in his house, which stood and said unto him, Send men to Joppa, and call for Simon, whose surname is Peter;

[14] Who shall tell thee words, whereby thou and all thy house shall be saved.

[15] And as I began to speak, the Holy Ghost fell on them, as on us at the beginning.

[16] Then remembered I the word of the Lord, how that he said, John indeed baptized with water; but ye shall be baptized with the Holy Ghost.

[17] Forasmuch then as God gave them the like gift as he did unto us, who believed on the Lord Jesus Christ; what was I, that I could withstand God?

At last the Jewish Christians accept that Jesus came for everyone. That circumcision was not a requirement and neither was obedience to dietary laws.

Acts 11 18

When they heard these things, they held their peace, and glorified God, saying, "Then God has also granted to the Gentiles repentance to life!"

Paul later writes to the Christians at Ephesus to assure them that the matter was settled and that Christians need not follow Jewish law.

Ephesians 2 11 - 19

[11] In whom also we have obtained an inheritance, being predestinated according to the purpose of him who worketh all things after the counsel of his own will:

[12] That we should be to the praise of his glory, who first trusted in Christ.

[13] In whom ye also trusted, after that ye heard the word of truth, the gospel of your salvation: in whom also after that ye believed, ye were sealed with that holy Spirit of promise,

[14] Which is the earnest of our inheritance until the redemption of the purchased possession, unto the praise of his glory.

[15] Wherefore I also, after I heard of your faith in the Lord Jesus, and love unto all the saints,

[16] Cease not to give thanks for you, making mention of you in my prayers;

[17 That the God of our Lord Jesus Christ, the Father of glory, may give unto you the spirit of wisdom and revelation in the knowledge of him:

[18] The eyes of your understanding being enlightened; that ye may know what is the hope of his calling, and what the riches of the glory of his inheritance in the saints,

[19] And what is the exceeding greatness of his power to us-ward who believe, according to the working of his mighty power,

22.6 Famine Relief

An opportunity to demonstrate the universality of the church in a very practical way arose when famine loomed.

Acts 11 19 - 30

[19] Now they which were scattered abroad upon the persecution that arose about Stephen travelled as far as Phenice, and Cyprus, and Antioch, preaching the word to none but unto the Jews only.

[20] And some of them were men of Cyprus and Cyrene, which, when they were come to Antioch, spake unto the Grecians, preaching the Lord Jesus.

[21] And the hand of the Lord was with them: and a great number believed, and turned unto the Lord.

[22] Then tidings of these things came unto the ears of the church which was in Jerusalem: and they sent forth Barnabas, that he should go as far as Antioch.

[23] Who, when he came, and had seen the grace of God, was glad, and exhorted them all, that with purpose of heart they would cleave unto the Lord.

[24] For he was a good man, and full of the Holy Ghost and of faith: and much people was added unto the Lord.

[25] Then departed Barnabas to Tarsus, for to seek Saul:

[26] And when he had found him, he brought him unto Antioch. And it came to pass, that a whole year they assembled themselves with the church, and taught much people. And the disciples were called Christians first in Antioch.

[27] And in these days came prophets from Jerusalem unto Antioch.

[28] And there stood up one of them named Agabus, and signified by the spirit that there should be great dearth throughout all the world: which came to pass in the days of Claudius Caesar.

[29] Then the disciples, every man according to his ability, determined to send relief unto the brethren which dwelt in Judaea:

[30] Which also they did, and sent it to the elders by the hands of Barnabas and Saul. .

It seems that at this point Paul sees his mission as preaching to the Gentiles as he recalls in his letter to the Romans - see section 30.4. He makes visits to many places and preaches to Christian congregations, but his main aim is to convert the Gentiles.

When Barnabas and Saul return from their famine relief expedition they take John Mark with them because they sense the danger he is in.

Acts 12 24 - 25
[24] But the word of God grew and multiplied.

[25] And Barnabas and Saul returned from Jerusalem, when they had fulfilled their ministry, and took with them John, whose surname was Mark

Chapter 23 Paul's First Journeys

Paul made three missionary journeys before his final one to Rome. What we know of them was mainly recorded by Luke in his Acts of the Apostles chapters 13 to 28, but Paul himself makes a few comments in his Epistles and Eusebius fills in some later details.

We start the story at Antioch in what is now Syria. Paul and Barnabus had been sent to Jerusalem on a famine relief mission (see section 22.8) and when they returned to Antioch, they were told to make their way around the Aegean to visit the Christian communities and help them understand the message.

It was these journeys around the Roman Empire which set in train the events which eventually led to Christianity becoming the dominant religion in Europe centred in Rome.

The itineraries of his journeys are recorded in Acts, however there is plenty of room for confusion. First there were two places called Antioch, one in Syria (now Antakya in southern Turkey) and one in Galatia. It was the Syrian one which was Paul's main base and where he received his Commission. The other one is sometimes referred to as Pisidian Antioch (now near Yalvac) so we will use the convention of referring to them as Antioch S and Antioch P where the text is otherwise unclear. A second reason for confusion is that Acts was written by Luke and he too did a fair bit of travelling, often with Barnabus so occasionally it is not clear whether a part of a journey is being made by Luke or Paul. Thirdly many of the place names have changed and need careful identification with modern names.

We will use the name Paul, rather than Saul from now on as this is what he is more usually known as.

23.1 The Commission

The story begins at Antioch S when Paul and Barnabus were given their commission.

> **Acts 13 1 - 3**
> [1] Now there were in the church that was at Antioch certain prophets and teachers; as Barnabas, and Simeon that was called Niger, and Lucius of Cyrene, and Manaen, which had been brought up with Herod the tetrarch, and Saul.
> [2] As they ministered to the Lord, and fasted, the Holy Ghost said, separate me Barnabas and Saul for the work whereunto I have called them.
> [3] And when they had fasted and prayed, and laid their hands on them, they sent them away. .

Their first journey was undertaken in 46 to 48 AD. Their journey began at Antioch S where the church was strong and had many followers. They travelled to the nearest port, Seleucia, now Samandag and sailed first to Cyprus. They traversed the island from Salanus (Salamis) to Paphos and then sailed to Perga (Murtana) on the south coast of what is now Turkey. They continued northwards to the other Antioch (P).

After being expelled for causing a riot they went eastwards to Iconium visiting Lystra and Derbe almost reaching Paul's birthplace. Then they retrace their steps back to Antioch P and then Antioch S.

Another journey was taken to Jerusalem in a vain attempt to resolve the 'Gentile or Jew?' question. As we read of these journeys there is no hint as to how Paul supported himself or paid his boat fares.

23.2 Cyprus

> **Acts 13 4 - 12**
> [4] So they, being sent forth by the Holy Ghost, departed unto Seleucia; and from thence they sailed to Cyprus.
> [5] And when they were at Salamis, they preached the word of God in the synagogues of the Jews: and they had also John to their minister.
> [6] And when they had gone through the isle unto Paphos, they found a certain sorcerer, a false prophet, a Jew, whose name was Bar-jesus:
> [7] Which was with the deputy of the country, Sergius Paulus, a prudent man; who called for Barnabas and Saul, and desired to hear the word of God.

[8] But Elymas the sorcerer (for so is his name by interpretation) withstood them, seeking to turn away the deputy from the faith.

[9] Then Saul, (who also is called Paul,) filled with the Holy Ghost, set his eyes on him,

[10] And said, O full of all subtilty and all mischief, thou child of the devil, thou enemy of all righteousness, wilt thou not cease to pervert the right ways of the Lord?

[11] And now, behold, the hand of the Lord is upon thee, and thou shalt be blind, not seeing the sun for a season. And immediately there fell on him a mist and a darkness; and he went about seeking some to lead him by the hand.

[12] Then the deputy, when he saw what was done, believed, being astonished at the doctrine of the Lord.

23.3 Antioch P

Antioch P was a Greek speaking enclave within Phrygia on the slopes of the Sultan Daglari range of mountains. It sat astride a main trading route and had a very mixed population with many Jews.

Acts 13 13 - 16

[13] Now when Paul and his company loosed from Paphos, they came to Perga in Pamphylia: and John departing from them returned to Jerusalem.

[14] But when they departed from Perga, they came to Antioch in Pisidia, and went into the synagogue on the sabbath day, and sat down.

[15] And after the reading of the law and the prophets the rulers of the synagogue sent unto them, saying, Ye men and brethren, if ye have any word of exhortation for the people, say on.

[16] Then Paul stood up, and beckoning with his hand said, Men of Israel, and ye that fear God, give audience. ...

Paul speaks to the Jews and recounts key parts of their history and quoting Psalm 2. He tries to relate Jesus with the promised 'King of the Jews'

Acts 13 17 - 41

[17] The God of this people of Israel chose our fathers, and exalted the people when they dwelt as strangers in the land of Egypt, and with an high arm brought he them out of it.

[18] And about the time of forty years suffered he their manners in the wilderness.

[19] And when he had destroyed seven nations in the land of Chanaan, he divided their land to them by lot.

[20] And after that he gave unto them judges about the space of four hundred and fifty years, until Samuel the prophet.

[21] And afterward they desired a king: and God gave unto them Saul the son of Cis, a man of the tribe of Benjamin, by the space of forty years.

[22] And when he had removed him, he raised up unto them David to be their king; to whom also he gave testimony, and said, I have found David the son of Jesse, a man after mine own heart, which shall fulfil all my will.

[23] Of this man's seed hath God according to his promise raised unto Israel a Saviour, Jesus:

[24] When John had first preached before his coming the baptism of repentance to all the people of Israel.

[25] And as John fulfilled his course, he said, Whom think ye that I am? I am not he. But, behold, there cometh one after me, whose shoes of his feet I am not worthy to loose.

[26] Men and brethren, children of the stock of Abraham, and whosoever among you feareth God, to you is the word of this salvation sent.

[27] For they that dwell at Jerusalem, and their rulers, because they knew him not, nor yet the voices of the prophets which are read every sabbath day, they have fulfilled them in condemning him.

[28] And though they found no cause of death in him, yet desired they Pilate that he should be slain.

[29] And when they had fulfilled all that was written of him, they took him down from the tree, and laid him in a sepulchre.

[30] But God raised him from the dead:

[31] And he was seen many days of them which came up with him from Galilee to Jerusalem, who are his witnesses unto the people.

[32] And we declare unto you glad tidings, how that the promise which was made unto the fathers,

[33] God hath fulfilled the same unto us their children, in that he hath raised up Jesus again; as it is also written in the second psalm, Thou art my Son, this day have I begotten thee.

[34] And as concerning that he raised him up from the dead, now no more to return to corruption, he said on this wise, I will give you the sure mercies of David.

[35] Wherefore he saith also in another psalm, Thou shalt not suffer thine Holy One to see corruption.

[36] For David, after he had served his own generation by the will of God, fell on sleep, and was laid unto his fathers, and saw corruption:

[37] But he, whom God raised again, saw no corruption.

[38] Be it known unto you therefore, men and brethren, that through this man is preached unto you the forgiveness of sins:

[39] And by him all that believe are justified from all things, from which ye could not be justified by the law of Moses.

[40] Beware therefore, lest that come upon you, which is spoken of in the prophets;

[41] Behold, ye despisers, and wonder, and perish: for I work a work in your days, a work which ye shall in no wise believe, though a man declare it unto you.

There were Gentiles around who were interested in what they had to say'

Acts 13 42 - 43

[42] And when the Jews were gone out of the synagogue, the Gentiles besought that these words might be preached to them the next sabbath.

[43] Now when the congregation was broken up, many of the Jews and religious proselytes followed Paul and Barnabas: who, speaking to them, persuaded them to continue in the grace of God.

The next Sabbath Paul's words sparked a riot and they were expelled.

Acts 13 44 - 52

[44] And the next sabbath day came almost the whole city together to hear the word of God.

[45] But when the Jews saw the multitudes, they were filled with envy, and spake against those things which were spoken by Paul, contradicting and blaspheming.

[46] Then Paul and Barnabas waxed bold, and said, It was necessary that the word of God should first have been spoken to you: but seeing ye put it from you, and judge yourselves unworthy of everlasting life, lo, we turn to the Gentiles.

[47] For so hath the Lord commanded us, saying, I have set thee to be a light of the Gentiles, that thou shouldest be for salvation unto the ends of the earth.

[48] And when the Gentiles heard this, they were glad, and glorified the word of the Lord: and as many as were ordained to eternal life believed.

[49] And the word of the Lord was published throughout all the region.

[50] But the Jews stirred up the devout and honourable women, and the chief men of the city, and raised persecution against Paul and Barnabas, and expelled them out of their coasts.

[51] But they shook off the dust of their feet against them, and came unto Iconium.

[52] And the disciples were filled with joy, and with the Holy Ghost.

23.4 Iconium

Iconium (modern Konia) stood on the edge of a desert plateau with the Pisidian mountains to the west. While it was mainly Phrygian in language and culture it was gradually becoming Hellenised and had a large Jewish population.

Acts 14 1 - 7

[1] And it came to pass in Iconium, that they went both together into the synagogue of the Jews, and so spake, that a great multitude both of the Jews and also of the Greeks believed.

[2] But the unbelieving Jews stirred up the Gentiles, and made their minds evil affected against the brethren.

[3] Long time therefore abode they speaking boldly in the Lord, which gave testimony unto the word of his grace, and granted signs and wonders to be done by their hands.

[4] But the multitude of the city was divided: and part held with the Jews, and part with the apostles.

[5] And when there was an assault made both of the Gentiles, and also of the Jews with their rulers, to use them despitefully, and to stone them,

[6] They were ware of it, and fled unto Lystra and Derbe, cities of Lycaonia, and unto the region that lieth round about:

[7] And there they preached the gospel.

23.5 Lystra

Lystra is a city just to the south of Iconium. Paul performs a miracle to heal a cripple and they preach the gospel. At first they were confused with Jupiter and Mercury, but when they had preached the local Jewish establishment from Antioch P arrived and tried to kill them.

Acts 14 8 - 20

[8] And there sat a certain man at Lystra, impotent in his feet, being a cripple from his mother's womb, who never had walked:

[9] The same heard Paul speak: who stedfastly beholding him, and perceiving that he had faith to be healed,

[10] Said with a loud voice, Stand upright on thy feet. And he leaped and walked.

[11] And when the people saw what Paul had done, they lifted up their voices, saying in the speech of Lycaonia, The gods are come down to us in the likeness of men.

[12] And they called Barnabas, Jupiter; and Paul, Mercurius, because he was the chief speaker.

[13] Then the priest of Jupiter, which was before their city, brought oxen and garlands unto the gates, and would have done sacrifice with the people.

[14] Which when the apostles, Barnabas and Paul, heard of, they rent their clothes, and ran in among the people, crying out,

[15] And saying, Sirs, why do ye these things? We also are men of like passions with you, and preach unto you that ye should turn from these vanities unto the living God, which made heaven, and earth, and the sea, and all things that are therein:

[16] Who in times past suffered all nations to walk in their own ways.

[17] Nevertheless he left not himself without witness, in that he did good, and gave us rain from heaven, and fruitful seasons, filling our hearts with food and gladness.

[18] And with these sayings scarce restrained they the people, that they had not done sacrifice unto them.

[19] And there came thither certain Jews from Antioch and Iconium, who persuaded the people, and, having stoned Paul, drew him out of the city, supposing he had been dead.

[20] Howbeit, as the disciples stood round about him, he rose up, and came into the city: and the next day he departed with Barnabas to Derbe.

23.6 Derbe

Derbe lies to the south east of Lystra on the road to Tarsus, Paul's birthplace. This was the farthest point on his first journey and he now retraces his steps back to Antioch.

Acts 14 21 - 23

[21] And when they had preached the gospel to that city, and had taught many, they returned again to Lystra, and to Iconium, and Antioch,

[22] Confirming the souls of the disciples, and exhorting them to continue in the faith, and that we must through much tribulation enter into the kingdom of God.

[23] And when they had ordained them elders in every church, and had prayed with fasting, they commended them to the Lord, on whom they believed.

23.7 Return to Antioch S

They retrace their steps back to Attalia where they sail for Selucia and back to Antioch S.

Acts 14 24 - 28

[24] And after they had passed throughout Pisidia, they came to Pamphylia.

[25] And when they had preached the word in Perga, they went down into Attalia:

[26] And thence sailed to Antioch, from whence they had been recommended to the grace of God for the work which they fulfilled.

[27] And when they were come, and had gathered the church together, they rehearsed all that God had done with them, and how he had opened the door of faith unto the Gentiles.

[28] And there they abode long time with the disciples.

23.8 Antioch

At Antioch Paul found himself in the midst of a theological dispute. It was a key question for Christianity, was it for the Jews or for the whole of mankind? Did one have first to become a Jew before one could become a Christian? The issue was symbolised by the Jewish requirement for circumcision. The Judaean Church under James saw themselves merely a sect of Judaism whereas Paul had much more global aspirations.

Acts 15 1 - 2

[1] And certain men which came down from Judaea taught the brethren, and said, Except ye be circumcised after the manner of Moses, ye cannot be saved.

[2] When therefore Paul and Barnabas had no small dissension and disputation with them, they determined that Paul and Barnabas, and certain other of them, should go up to Jerusalem unto the apostles and elders about this question.

23.9 Jerusalem

Paul then set out for Jerusalem to try to resolve the matter.

Acts 15 3 - 29

[3] And being brought on their way by the church, they passed through Phenice and Samaria, declaring the conversion of the Gentiles: and they caused great joy unto all the brethren.

[4] And when they were come to Jerusalem, they were received of the church, and of the apostles and elders, and they declared all things that God had done with them.

[5] But there rose up certain of the sect of the Pharisees which believed, saying, That it was needful to circumcise them, and to command them to keep the law of Moses.

[6] And the apostles and elders came together for to consider of this matter.

[7] And when there had been much disputing, Peter rose up, and said unto them, Men and brethren, ye know how that a good while ago God made choice among us, that the Gentiles by my mouth should hear the word of the gospel, and believe.

[8] And God, which knoweth the hearts, bare them witness, giving them the Holy Ghost, even as he did unto us;

[9] And put no difference between us and them, purifying their hearts by faith.

[10] Now therefore why tempt ye God, to put a yoke upon the neck of the disciples, which neither our fathers nor we were able to bear?

[11] But we believe that through the grace of the Lord Jesus Christ we shall be saved, even as they.

[12] Then all the multitude kept silence, and gave audience to Barnabas and Paul, declaring what miracles and wonders God had wrought among the Gentiles by them.

[13] And after they had held their peace, James answered, saying, Men and brethren, hearken unto me:

[14] Simeon hath declared how God at the first did visit the Gentiles, to take out of them a people for his name.

[15] And to this agree the words of the prophets; as it is written,

[16] After this I will return, and will build again the tabernacle of David, which is fallen down; and I will build again the ruins thereof, and I will set it up:

[17] That the residue of men might seek after the Lord, and all the Gentiles, upon whom my name is called, saith the Lord, who doeth all these things.

[18] Known unto God are all his works from the beginning of the world.

[19] Wherefore my sentence is, that we trouble not them, which from among the Gentiles are turned to God:

[20] But that we write unto them, that they abstain from pollutions of idols, and from fornication, and from things strangled, and from blood.

[21] For Moses of old time hath in every city them that preach him, being read in the synagogues every sabbath day.

[22] Then pleased it the apostles and elders, with the whole church, to send chosen men of their own company to Antioch with Paul and Barnabas; namely, Judas surnamed Barsabas, and Silas, chief men among the brethren:

[23] And they wrote letters by them after this manner; The apostles and elders and brethren send greeting unto the brethren which are of the Gentiles in Antioch and Syria and Cilicia:

[24] Forasmuch as we have heard, that certain which went out from us have troubled you with words, subverting your souls, saying, Ye must be circumcised, and keep the law: to whom we gave no such commandment:

[25] It seemed good unto us, being assembled with one accord, to send chosen men unto you with our beloved Barnabas and Paul,

[26] Men that have hazarded their lives for the name of our Lord Jesus Christ.

[27] We have sent therefore Judas and Silas, who shall also tell you the same things by mouth.

[28] For it seemed good to the Holy Ghost, and to us, to lay upon you no greater burden than these necessary things;

[29] That ye abstain from meats offered to idols, and from blood, and from things strangled, and from fornication: from which if ye keep yourselves, ye shall do well. Fare ye well.

23.10 Antioch

Acts 15 30 - 35

[30] So when they were dismissed, they came to Antioch: and when they had gathered the multitude together, they delivered the epistle:

[31] Which when they had read, they rejoiced for the consolation.

[32] And Judas and Silas, being prophets also themselves, exhorted the brethren with many words, and confirmed them.

[33] And after they had tarried there a space, they were let go in peace from the brethren unto the apostles.

[34] Notwithstanding it pleased Silas to abide there still.

[35] Paul also and Barnabas continued in Antioch, teaching and preaching the word of the Lord, with many others also.

Chapter 24 Paul's Second Journey

24.1 Retracing Steps

Paul's second journey dates from 49-52 AD. He and Barnabus had returned from Jerusalem in 48 AD where they had resumed their life of ministry and evangelism. They decided to retrace their earlier journey to see how the Christians were getting on, however this time Barnabus did the Cyprus part with John Mark and Paul the Phrygian part with Silas. Paul and Silas travelled by land this time going first to Derbe and then Lystra.

Acts 15.36 to 16.5

[36] And some days after Paul said unto Barnabas, Let us go again and visit our brethren in every city where we have preached the word of the Lord, and see how they do.

[37] And Barnabas determined to take with them John, whose surname was Mark.

[38] But Paul thought not good to take him with them, who departed from them from Pamphylia, and went not with them to the work.

[39] And the contention was so sharp between them, that they departed asunder one from the other: and so Barnabas took Mark, and sailed unto Cyprus;

[40] And Paul chose Silas, and departed, being recommended by the brethren unto the grace of God.

[41] And he went through Syria and Cilicia, confirming the churches.

[1] Then came he to Derbe and Lystra: and, behold, a certain disciple was there, named Timotheus, the son of a certain woman, which was a Jewess, and believed; but his father was a Greek:

[2] Which was well reported of by the brethren that were at Lystra and Iconium.

[3] Him would Paul have to go forth with him; and took and circumcised him because of the Jews which were in those quarters: for they knew all that his father was a Greek.

[4] And as they went through the cities, they delivered them the decrees for to keep, that were ordained of the apostles and elders which were at Jerusalem.

[5] And so were the churches established in the faith, and increased in number daily.

24.2 Barred from Asia

Presumably they also visited Iconium and Antioch P but instead of turning north and travelling through Mysia (which adjoins the Hellespont) and Bithnya (adjoining the south western coast of the Black Sea) Paul senses his mission should take him rather to Macedonia and Greece so they headed for the port of Troas near the entrance to the Dardanelles.

Acts 16 6 - 10

[6] Now when they had gone throughout Phrygia and the region of Galatia, and were forbidden of the Holy Ghost to preach the word in Asia,

[7] After they were come to Mysia, they assayed to go into Bithynia: but the Spirit suffered them not.

[8] And they passing by Mysia came down to Troas.

[9] And a vision appeared to Paul in the night; There stood a man of Macedonia, and prayed him, saying, Come over into Macedonia, and help us.

[10] And after he had seen the vision, immediately we endeavored to go into Macedonia, assuredly gathering that the Lord had called us for to preach the gospel unto them.

24.3 Macedonia

From Troas their ship took them first to the island of Samothrace then via Neapolis to Phillipi, a city which is now uninhabited near the river Angista on the coast of Macedonia. Luke now starts using 'we' instead of 'he' indicating that he was now part of the contingent. When they arrived in Phillipi they baptised Lydia and stayed with her.

Acts 16 11 - 15

[11] Therefore loosing from Troas, we came with a straight course to Samothracia, and the next day to Neapolis;

[12] And from thence to Philippi, which is the chief city of that part of Macedonia, and a colony: and we were in that city abiding certain days.

[13] And on the sabbath we went out of the city by a river side, where prayer was wont to be made; and we sat down, and spake unto the women which resorted thither.

[14] And a certain woman named Lydia, a seller of purple, of the city of Thyatira, which worshipped God, heard us: whose heart the Lord opened, that she attended unto the things which were spoken of Paul.

[15] And when she was baptized, and her household, she besought us, saying, If ye have judged me to be faithful to the Lord, come into my house, and abide there. And she constrained us.

On another occasion they came across a slave girl who seems to have been being sold as a prostitute. Paul takes action to release her and is promptly arrested and put in the stocks.

Acts 16 16 - 24

[16] And it came to pass, as we went to prayer, a certain damsel possessed with a spirit of divination met us, which brought her masters much gain by soothsaying:

[17] The same followed Paul and us, and cried, saying, These men are the servants of the most high God, which shew unto us the way of salvation.

[18] And this did she many days. But Paul, being grieved, turned and said to the spirit, I command thee in the name of Jesus Christ to come out of her. And he came out the same hour.

[19] And when her masters saw that the hope of their gains was gone, they caught Paul and Silas, and drew them into the marketplace unto the rulers,

[20] And brought them to the magistrates, saying, These men, being Jews, do exceedingly trouble our city,

[21] And teach customs, which are not lawful for us to receive, neither to observe, being Romans.

[22] And the multitude rose up together against them: and the magistrates rent off their clothes, and commanded to beat them.

[23] And when they had laid many stripes upon them, they cast them into prison, charging the jailor to keep them safely:

[24] Who, having received such a charge, thrust them into the inner prison, and made their feet fast in the stocks.

Then in the middle of the night an earthquake opened the prison but the group did not try to escape, much to the relief of the Jailer.

Acts 16 25 - 34

[25] And at midnight Paul and Silas prayed, and sang praises unto God: and the prisoners heard them.

[26] And suddenly there was a great earthquake, so that the foundations of the prison were shaken: and immediately all the doors were opened, and every one's bands were loosed.

[27] And the keeper of the prison awaking out of his sleep, and seeing the prison doors open, he drew out his sword, and would have killed himself, supposing that the prisoners had been fled.

[28] But Paul cried with a loud voice, saying, Do thyself no harm: for we are all here.

[29] Then he called for a light, and sprang in, and came trembling, and fell down before Paul and Silas,

[30] And brought them out, and said, Sirs, what must I do to be saved?

[31] And they said, Believe on the Lord Jesus Christ, and thou shalt be saved, and thy house.

[32] And they spake unto him the word of the Lord, and to all that were in his house.

[33] And he took them the same hour of the night, and washed their stripes; and was baptized, he and all his, straightway.

[34] And when he had brought them into his house, he set meat before them, and rejoiced, believing in God with all his house.

Next day they were released and the magistrates realised they had made a serious mistake in flogging and imprisoning Roman citizens.

Acts 16 35 - 40

[35] And when it was day, the magistrates sent the serjeants, saying, Let those men go.

[36] And the keeper of the prison told this saying to Paul, The magistrates have sent to let you go: now therefore depart, and go in peace.

[37] But Paul said unto them, They have beaten us openly uncondemned, being Romans, and have cast us into prison; and now do they thrust us out privily? nay verily; but let them come themselves and fetch us out.

[38] And the serjeants told these words unto the magistrates: and they feared, when they heard that they were Romans.

[39] And they came and besought them, and brought them out, and desired them to depart out of the city.

[40] And they went out of the prison, and entered into the house of Lydia and when they had seen the brethren, they comforted them, and departed.

It would appear that here he met a man named Epaphroditus who perhaps acted as his guide for the rest of his journey. He is referred to later in Paul's letter to the Philippians which was written in Rome by Epaphroditis:-

Philippians 2 25 - 28

[25] t I supposed it necessary to send to you Epaphroditus, my brother, and companion in labour, and fellow soldier, but your messenger, and he that ministered to my wants.

[26] For he longed after you all, and was full of heaviness, because that ye had heard that he had been sick.

[27] For indeed he was sick nigh unto death: but God had mercy on him; and not on him only, but on me also, lest I should have sorrow upon sorrow. [28] I sent him therefore the more carefully, that, when ye see him again, ye may rejoice, and that I may be the less sorrowful.

And in his letter to the Corinthians he recalls the visit of Titus

2 Corinthians 7 5 - 8
[5] For when we were come into Macedonia, our flesh had no rest, but we were troubled on every side; without were fighting's, within were fears.
[6] Nevertheless God, that comforted those that are cast down, comforted us by the coming of Titus;
[7] And not by his coming only, but* by the consolation wherewith he was comforted in you, when he told us your earnest desire, your mourning, your fervent mind toward me; so that I rejoiced the more.
[8] For though I made you sorry with a letter, I do not repent, though I did repent: for I perceive that the same epistle hath made you sorry, though it were but for a season.

24.4 Thessalonika

From Phillipi they journeyed south west along the coast. They passed Amphipolis which guarded the bridge over the river Strimon and then via Appolonia to Thessalonika which was very much the cross roads between Greece and Macedonia as well as a major seaport.

Acts 17 1 - 9
[1] Now when they had passed through Amphipolis and Apollonia, they came to Thessalonica, where was a synagogue of the Jews:
[2] And Paul, as his manner was, went in unto them, and three sabbath days reasoned with them out of the scriptures,
[3] Opening and alleging, that Christ must needs have suffered, and risen again from the dead; and that this Jesus, whom I preach unto you, is Christ.
[4] And some of them believed, and consorted with Paul and Silas; and of the devout Greeks a great multitude, and of the chief women not a few.
[5] But the Jews which believed not, moved with envy, took unto them certain lewd fellows of the baser sort, and gathered a company, and set all the city on an uproar, and assaulted the house of Jason, and sought to bring them out to the people.
[6] And when they found them not, they drew Jason and certain brethren unto the rulers of the city, crying, These that have turned the world upside down are come hither also;

[7] Whom Jason hath received: and these all do contrary to the decrees of Caesar, saying that there is another king, one Jesus.

[8] And they troubled the people and the rulers of the city, when they heard these things.

[9] And when they had taken security of Jason, and of the other, they let them go.

24.5 Beroea

Beroea (now Veroia) lies many miles inland

Acts 17 10 - 14

[10] And the brethren immediately sent away Paul and Silas by night unto Berea: who coming thither went into the synagogue of the Jews.

[11] These were more noble than those in Thessalonica, in that they received the word with all readiness of mind, and searched the scriptures daily, whether those things were so.

[12] Therefore many of them believed; also of honourable women which were Greeks, and of men, not a few.

[13] But when the Jews of Thessalonica had knowledge that the word of God was preached of Paul at Berea, they came thither also, and stirred up the people.

[14] And then immediately the brethren sent away Paul to go as it were to the sea: but Silas and Timotheus abode there still.

24.6 Athens

From Beroea Paul came back down to the coast and followed it until he reached Athens. Here he argued with Greek pagans who seemed to think he was trying to import some foreign gods.

Acts 17 15 - 21

[15] And they that conducted Paul brought him unto Athens: and receiving a commandment unto Silas and Timotheus for to come to him with all speed, they departed.

[16] Now while Paul waited for them at Athens, his spirit was stirred in him, when he saw the city wholly given to idolatry.

[17] Therefore disputed he in the synagogue with the Jews, and with the devout persons, and in the market daily with them that met with him.

[18] Then certain philosophers of the Epicureans, and of the Stoicks, encountered him. And some said, What will this babbler say? other some, He seemeth to be a setter forth of strange gods: because he preached unto them Jesus, and the resurrection.

[19] And they took him, and brought him unto Areopagus, saying, May we know what this new doctrine, whereof thou speakest, is?

[20] For thou bringest certain strange things to our ears: we would know therefore what these things mean.

[21] (For all the Athenians and strangers which were there spent their time in nothing else, but either to tell, or to hear some new thing.)

Paul had noticed an altar to an 'unknown god' and took advantage.

Acts 17 22 - 34

[22] Then Paul stood in the midst of Mars' hill, and said, Ye men of Athens, I perceive that in all things ye are too superstitious.

[23] For as I passed by, and beheld your devotions, I found an altar with this inscription, TO THE UNKNOWN GOD. Whom therefore ye ignorantly worship, him declare I unto you.

[24] God that made the world and all things therein, seeing that he is Lord of heaven and earth, dwelleth not in temples made with hands;

[25] Neither is worshipped with men's hands, as though he needed any thing, seeing he giveth to all life, and breath, and all things;

[26] And hath made of one blood all nations of men for to dwell on all the face of the earth, and hath determined the times before appointed, and the bounds of their habitation;

[27] That they should seek the Lord, if haply they might feel after him, and find him, though he be not far from every one of us:

[28] For in him we live, and move, and have our being; as certain also of your own poets have said, For we are also his offspring.

[29] Forasmuch then as we are the offspring of God, we ought not to think that the Godhead is like unto gold, or silver, or stone, graven by art and man's device.

[30] And the times of this ignorance God winked at; but now commanded all men every where to repent:

[31] Because he hath appointed a day, in the which he will judge the world in righteousness by that man whom he hath ordained; whereof he hath given assurance unto all men, in that he hath raised him from the dead.

[32] And when they heard of the resurrection of the dead, some mocked: and others said, We will hear thee again of this matter.

[33] So Paul departed from among them.

[34] Howbeit certain men clave unto him, and believed: among the which was Dionysius the Areopagite, and a woman named Damaris, and others with them.

24.7 Corinth

His next stop was at Corinth, due west of Athens. He meets up with Jews who have been expelled from Rome by the Emperor Claudius.

Acts 18 1 - 4

[1] After these things Paul departed from Athens, and came to Corinth;

[2] And found a certain Jew named Aquila, born in Pontus, lately come from Italy, with his wife Priscilla; (because that Claudius had commanded all Jews to depart from Rome:) and came unto them.

[3] And because he was of the same craft, he abode with them, and wrought: for by their occupation they were tentmakers.

[4] And he reasoned in the synagogue every sabbath, and persuaded the Jews and the Greeks.

After Silas and Timothy had joined them from Macedonia the party found themselves at odds with the Jews.

Acts 18 5 - 11

[5] And when Silas and Timotheus were come from Macedonia, Paul was pressed in the spirit, and testified to the Jews that Jesus was Christ.

[6] And when they opposed themselves, and blasphemed, he shook his raiment, and said unto them, Your blood be upon your own heads; I am clean: from henceforth I will go unto the Gentiles.

[7] And he departed thence, and entered into a certain man's house, named Justus, one that worshipped God, whose house joined hard to the synagogue.

[8] And Crispus, the chief ruler of the synagogue, believed on the Lord with all his house; and many of the Corinthians hearing believed, and were baptized.

[9] Then spake the Lord to Paul in the night by a vision, Be not afraid, but speak, and hold not thy peace:

[10] For I am with thee, and no man shall set on thee to hurt thee: for I have much people in this city.

[11] And he continued there a year and six months, teaching the word of God among them.

Achaia was the Roman province which included Athens and Corinth and when the Jews tried to have Paul convicted of contravening Jewish laws the Proconsul Galilo effectively told them to get lost.

Acts 18 12 - 17

[12] And when Gallio was the deputy of Achaia, the Jews made insurrection with one accord against Paul, and brought him to the judgment seat,

[13] Saying, This fellow persuaded men to worship God contrary to the law.

[14] And when Paul was now about to open his mouth, Gallio said unto the Jews, If it were a matter of wrong or wicked lewdness, O ye Jews, reason would that I should bear with you:

[15] But if it be a question of words and names, and of your law, look ye to it; for I will be no judge of such matters.

[16] And he drave them from the judgment seat.

[17] Then all the Greeks took Sosthenes, the chief ruler of the synagogue, and beat him before the judgment seat. And Gallio cared for none of those things.

Paul seems to have wanted to visit Macedonia a second time but got diverted as he noted in one of his Epistles.

2 Corinthians 1 15 - 17

[15] And in this confidence I was minded to come unto you before, that ye might have a second benefit;

[16] And to pass by you into Macedonia, and to come again out of Macedonia unto you, and of you to be brought on my way toward Judaea.

[17] When I therefore was thus minded, did I use lightness? or the things that I purpose, do I purpose according to the flesh, that with me there should be yea yea, and nay nay?

He later tells them he will be sending Titus and asks them to help him in his work.

2 Corinthians 8 10 - 21

[10] And herein I give my advice: for this is expedient for you, who have begun before, not only to do, but also to be forward a year ago.

[11] Now therefore perform the doing of it; that as there was a readiness to will, so there may be a performance also out of that which ye have.

[12] For if there be first a willing mind, it is accepted according to that a man hath, and not according to that he hath not.

[13] For I mean not that other men be eased, and ye burdened:

[14] But by an equality, that now at this time your abundance may be a supply for their want, that their abundance also may be a supply for your want: that there may be equality:

[15] As it is written, He that had gathered much had nothing over; and he that had gathered little had no lack.

311

[16] But thanks be to God, which put the same earnest care into the heart of Titus for you.

[17] For indeed he accepted the exhortation; but being more forward, of his own accord he went unto you.

[18] And we have sent with him the brother, whose praise is in the gospel throughout all the churches;

[19] And not that only, but who was also chosen of the churches to travel with us with this grace, which is administered by us to the glory of the same Lord, and declaration of your ready mind:

[20] Avoiding this, that no man should blame us in this abundance which is administered by us:

[21] Providing for honest things, not only in the sight of the Lord, but also in the sight of men.

24.8 Ephesus

After his stay in Corinth they set off back to Antioch P by sea, calling in on Ephesus.

Acts 18 18 - 19

[18] And Paul after this tarried there yet a good while, and then took his leave of the brethren, and sailed thence into Syria, and with him Priscilla and Aquila; having shorn his head in Cenchrea: for he had a vow.

[19] And he came to Ephesus, and left them there: but he himself entered into the synagogue, and reasoned with the Jews.

24.9 Antioch S

The story now becomes somewhat confusing. It would seem he spent just enough time in Ephesus to meet with the Christians there and then set sail again for Caesarea and back to Antioch S staying only briefly before he again visited Galatia and Phrygia and back overland to Ephesus.

Acts 18 20 - 23

[20] When they desired him to tarry longer time with them, he consented not;

[21] But bade them farewell, saying, I must by all means keep this feast that cometh in Jerusalem: but I will return again unto you, if God will. And he sailed from Ephesus.

[22] And when he had landed at Caesarea, and gone up, and saluted the church, he went down to Antioch.

[23] And after he had spent some time there, he departed, and went over all the country of Galatia and Phrygia in order, strengthening all the disciples. .

24.10 Apollos at Corinth

Meanwhile a man named Apollus had gone from Ephesus to Corinth to preach the word

Acts 18 24 - 28

[24] And a certain Jew named Apollos, born at Alexandria, an eloquent man, and mighty in the scriptures, came to Ephesus.

[25] This man was instructed in the way of the Lord; and being fervent in the spirit, he spake and taught diligently the things of the Lord, knowing only the baptism of John.

[26] And he began to speak boldly in the synagogue: whom when Aquila and Priscilla had heard, they took him unto them, and expounded unto him the way of God more perfectly.

[27] And when he was disposed to pass into Achaia, the brethren wrote, exhorting the disciples to receive him: who, when he was come, helped them much which had believed through grace:

[28] For he mightily convinced the Jews, and that publicly, shewing by the scriptures that Jesus was Christ.

24.11 Paul in Galatia and Phrygia

After he had returned to Antioch S Paul decided to return to Ephesus overland going back through Galatia and Phrygia visiting Tarsus, Derbe, Lystra and Iconium and pausing at Antioch P. Over the next two years Paul was working with the people of Asia Minor.

Acts 19 1 - 12

[1] And it came to pass, that, while Apollos was at Corinth, Paul having passed through the upper coasts came to Ephesus: and finding certain disciples,

[2] He said unto them, Have ye received the Holy Ghost since ye believed? And they said unto him, We have not so much as heard whether there be any Holy Ghost.

[3] And he said unto them, Unto what then were ye baptized? And they said, Unto John's baptism.

[4] Then said Paul, John verily baptized with the baptism of repentance, saying unto the people, that they should believe on him which should come after him, that is, on Christ Jesus.

[5] When they heard this, they were baptized in the name of the Lord Jesus.

[6] And when Paul had laid his hands upon them, the Holy Ghost came on them; and they spake with tongues, and prophesied.

[7] And all the men were about twelve.

[8] And he went into the synagogue, and spake boldly for the space of three months, disputing and persuading the things concerning the kingdom of God.

[9] But when divers were hardened, and believed not, but spake evil of that way before the multitude, he departed from them, and separated the disciples, disputing daily in the school of one Tyrannus.

[10] And this continued by the space of two years; so that all they which dwelt in Asia heard the word of the Lord Jesus, both Jews and Greeks.

[11] And God wrought special miracles by the hands of Paul:

[12] So that from his body were brought unto the sick handkerchiefs or aprons, and the diseases departed from them, and the evil spirits went out of them.

24.12 Conflict with Jewish Exorcists

During this period Paul was still having problems with strict Jews.

Acts 19 13 - 20

[13] Then certain of the vagabond Jews, exorcists, took upon them to call over them which had evil spirits the name of the Lord Jesus, saying, We adjure you by Jesus whom Paul preached.

[14] And there were seven sons of one Sceva, a Jew, and chief of the priests, which did so.

[15] And the evil spirit answered and said, Jesus I know, and Paul I know; but who are ye?

[16] And the man in whom the evil spirit was leaped on them, and overcame them, and prevailed against them, so that they fled out of that house naked and wounded.

[17] And this was known to all the Jews and Greeks also dwelling at Ephesus; and fear fell on them all, and the name of the Lord Jesus was magnified.

[18] And many that believed came, and confessed, and shewed their deeds.

[19] Many of them also which used curious arts brought their books together, and burned them before all men: and they counted the price of them, and found it fifty thousand pieces of silver.

[20] So mightily grew the word of God and prevailed.

24.13 Paul makes plans for his next visit

Paul decides he needs to visit Greece and Macedonia again and sends Timothy and Erastus to make preparations.

Acts 19 21 - 22

[21] After these things were ended, Paul purposed in the spirit, when he had passed through Macedonia and Achaia, to go to Jerusalem, saying, After I have been there, I must also see Rome.

[22] So he sent into Macedonia two of them that ministered unto him, Timotheus and Erastus; but he himself stayed in Asia for a season. .

24.14 Conflict with Diana Worshippers

It is not only the strict Jews which threaten the Christian communities - Pagans see them as spoiling their trade.

Acts 19 23 - 41

[23] And the same time there arose no small stir about that way.

[24] For a certain man named Demetrius, a silversmith, which made silver shrines for Diana, brought no small gain unto the craftsmen;

[25] Whom he called together with the workmen of like occupation, and said, Sirs, ye know that by this craft we have our wealth.

[26] Moreover ye see and hear, that not alone at Ephesus, but almost throughout all Asia, this Paul hath persuaded and turned away much people, saying that they be no gods, which are made with hands:

[27] So that not only this our craft is in danger to be set at nought; but also that the temple of the great goddess Diana should be despised, and her magnificence should be destroyed, whom all Asia and the world worshipped.

[28] And when they heard these sayings, they were full of wrath, and cried out, saying, Great is Diana of the Ephesians.

[29] And the whole city was filled with confusion: and having caught Gaius and Aristarchus, men of Macedonia, Paul's companions in travel, they rushed with one accord into the theatre.

[30] And when Paul would have entered in unto the people, the disciples suffered him not.

[31] And certain of the chief of Asia, which were his friends, sent unto him, desiring him that he would not adventure himself into the theatre.

[32] Some therefore cried one thing, and some another: for the assembly was confused; and the more part knew not wherefore they were come together.

[33] And they drew Alexander out of the multitude, the Jews putting him forward. And Alexander beckoned with the hand, and would have made his defense unto the people.

[34] But when they knew that he was a Jew, all with one voice about the space of two hours cried out, Great is Diana of the Ephesians.

[35] And when the town clerk had appeased the people, he said, Ye men of Ephesus, what man is there that know not how that the city of the Ephesians is a worshipper of the great goddess Diana, and of the image which fell down from Jupiter?

[36] Seeing then that these things cannot be spoken against, ye ought to be quiet, and to do nothing rashly.

[37] For ye have brought hither these men, which are neither robbers of churches, nor yet blasphemers of your goddess.

[38] Wherefore if Demetrius, and the craftsmen which are with him, have a matter against any man, the law is open, and there are deputies: let them implead one another.

[39] But if ye inquire anything concerning other matters, it shall be determined in a lawful assembly.

[40] For we are in danger to be called in question for this day's uproar, there being no cause whereby we may give an account of this concourse.

[41] And when he had thus spoken, he dismissed the assembly.

Chapter 25 Paul's Third Journey

Paul's third journey is often thought of as starting in Antioch S; but we have taken the first two years when he was working in Asia Minor as the tail end of his second journey as he appears to make his plans for this journey while at Ephesus (see section 24.13) He travelled by land from Ephesus to Troas and re-visited the coast of Macedonia before Athens and Corinth. Then he retraced his steps back to Neapolis before a long sea voyage, calling in at many points of Asia to Tyre and finished up in Jerusalem. Luke tells us nothing about Paul's time in Macedonia and Greece

25.1 Macedonia and Greece

Luke says nothing about Paul's journey across Asia Minor and very little about his time on the European side. Rather than return by sea he comes back overland from Greece to Neapolis and then by sea to Troas.

Acts 20 1 - 6

[1] And after the uproar was ceased, Paul called unto him the disciples, and embraced them, and departed for to go into Macedonia.

[2] And when he had gone over those parts, and had given them much exhortation, he came into Greece,

[3] And there abode three months. And when the Jews laid wait for him, as he was about to sail into Syria, he purposed to return through Macedonia.

[4] And there accompanied him into Asia Sopater of Berea; and of the Thessalonians, Aristarchus and Secundus; and Gaius of Derbe, and Timotheus; and of Asia, Tychicus and Trophimus.

[5] These going before tarried for us at Troas.

[6] And we sailed away from Philippi after the days of unleavened bread, and came unto them to Troas in five days; where we abode seven days.

At Troas Paul heals Eutychus.

Acts 20 7 - 12

[7] And upon the first day of the week, when the disciples came together to break bread, Paul preached unto them, ready to depart on the morrow; and continued his speech until midnight.

[8] And there were many lights in the upper chamber, where they were gathered together.

[9] And there sat in a window a certain young man named Eutychus, being fallen into a deep sleep: and as Paul was long preaching, he sunk down with sleep, and fell down from the third loft, and was taken up dead.

[10] And Paul went down, and fell on him, and embracing him said, Trouble not yourselves; for his life is in him.

[11] When he therefore was come up again, and had broken bread, and eaten, and talked a long while, even till break of day, so he departed.

[12] And they brought the young man alive, and were not a little comforted.

Paul comments on his visit in his second letter to the Corinthians.

2 Corinthians 2 12 - 13

12 Furthermore, when I came to Troas to preach Christ's gospel, and a door was opened unto me of the Lord,

13 I had no rest in my spirit, because I found not Titus my brother: but taking my leave of them, I went from thence into Macedonia.

25.2 Miletus

Luke joined Paul at Assos to take him back to Jerusalem.

Acts 20 13 - 30

[13] And we went before to ship, and sailed unto Assos, there intending to take in Paul: for so had he appointed, minding himself to go afoot.

[14] And when he met with us at Assos, we took him in, and came to Mitylene.

[15] And we sailed thence, and came the next day over against Chios; and the next day we arrived at Samos, and tarried at Trogyllium; and the next day we came to Miletus.

[16] For Paul had determined to sail by Ephesus, because he would not spend the time in Asia: for he hasted, if it were possible for him, to be at Jerusalem the day of Pentecost.

[17] And from Miletus he sent to Ephesus, and called the elders of the church.

[18] And when they were come to him, he said unto them, Ye know, from the first day that I came into Asia, after what manner I have been with you at all seasons,

[19] Serving the Lord with all humility of mind, and with many tears, and temptations, which befell me by the lying in wait of the Jews:

[20] And how I kept back nothing that was profitable unto you, but have shewed you, and have taught you publickly, and from house to house,

[21] Testifying both to the Jews, and also to the Greeks, repentance toward God, and faith toward our Lord Jesus Christ.

[22] And now, behold, I go bound in the spirit unto Jerusalem, not knowing the things that shall befall me there:

[23] Save that the Holy Ghost witnesseth in every city, saying that bonds and afflictions abide me.

[24] But none of these things move me, neither count I my life dear unto myself, so that I might finish my course with joy, and the ministry, which I have received of the Lord Jesus, to testify the gospel of the grace of God.

[25] And now, behold, I know that ye all, among whom I have gone preaching the kingdom of God, shall see my face no more.

[26] Wherefore I take you to record this day, that I am pure from the blood of all men.

[27] For I have not shunned to declare unto you all the counsel of God.

[28] Take heed therefore unto yourselves, and to all the flock, over the which the Holy Ghost hath made you overseers, to feed the church of God, which he hath purchased with his own blood.

[29] For I know this, that after my departing shall grievous wolves enter in among you, not sparing the flock.

[30] Also of your own selves shall men arise, speaking perverse things, to draw away disciples after them.

25.3 Sailing the Aegean

Acts 21 1 - 6

[1] And it came to pass, that after we were gotten from them, and had launched, we came with a straight course unto Coos, and the day following unto Rhodes, and from thence unto Patara:

[2] And finding a ship sailing over unto Phenicia, we went aboard, and set forth.

[3] Now when we had discovered Cyprus, we left it on the left hand, and sailed into Syria, and landed at Tyre: for there the ship was to unlade her burden.

[4] And finding disciples, we tarried there seven days: who said to Paul through the Spirit, that he should not go up to Jerusalem.

[5] And when we had accomplished those days, we departed and went our way; and they all brought us on our way, with wives and children, till we were out of the city: and we kneeled down on the shore, and prayed.

[6] And when we had taken our leave one of another, we took ship; and they returned home again.

25.4 Ptolemaia and Judea

Acts 21 7 - 14

[7] And when we had finished our course from Tyre, we came to Ptolemais, and saluted the brethren, and abode with them one day.

[8] And the next day we that were of Paul's company departed, and came unto Caesarea: and we entered into the house of Philip the evangelist, which was one of the seven; and abode with him.

[9] And the same man had four daughters, virgins, which did prophesy.

[10] And as we tarried there many days, there came down from Judaea a certain prophet, named Agabus.

[11] And when he was come unto us, he took Paul's girdle, and bound his own hands and feet, and said, Thus saith the Holy Ghost, So shall the Jews at Jerusalem bind the man that owneth this girdle, and shall deliver him into the hands of the Gentiles.

[12] And when we heard these things, both we, and they of that place, besought him not to go up to Jerusalem.

[13] Then Paul answered, What mean ye to weep and to break mine heart? for I am ready not to be bound only, but also to die at Jerusalem for the name of the Lord Jesus.

[14] And when he would not be persuaded, we ceased, saying, The will of the Lord be done.

Chapter 26 Paul in Trouble

Paul had arrived back in Caesaria and was staying with Philip, but despite the prophecy of Agabus he was determined to make his first visit to Jerusalem for fourteen years and address again the problem of Jew versus Gentile.

26.1 Jerusalem

Acts 21 15 - 17

[15] And after those days we took up our carriages, and went up to Jerusalem.

[16] There went with us also certain of the disciples of Caesarea, and brought with them one Mnason of Cyprus, an old disciple, with whom we should lodge.

[17] And when we were come to Jerusalem, the brethren received us gladly.

At Jerusalem he had to pay a courtesy visit to James who was after all the recognised head of the earthly church. The old controversy was about to erupt again. James had been converting Gentiles to Judaism before they could become Christians and assuring the priests that they were all part of Judaism and not a separate religion.

Acts 21 18 - 26

[18] And the day following Paul went in with us unto James; and all the elders were present.

[19] And when he had saluted them, he declared particularly what things God had wrought among the Gentiles by his ministry.

[20] And when they heard it, they glorified the Lord, and said unto him, Thou seest, brother, how many thousands of Jews there are which believe; and they are all zealous of the law:

[21] And they are informed of thee, that thou teachest all the Jews which are among the Gentiles to forsake Moses, saying that they ought not to circumcise their children, neither to walk after the customs.

[22] What is it therefore? the multitude must needs come together: for they will hear that thou art come.

[23] Do therefore this that we say to thee: We have four men which have a vow on them;

[24] Them take, and purify thyself with them, and be at charges with them, that they may shave their heads: and all may know that those things, whereof they were informed concerning thee, are nothing; but that thou thyself also walkest orderly, and keepest the law.

[25] As touching the Gentiles which believe, we have written and concluded that they observe no such thing, save only that they keep themselves from things offered to idols, and from blood, and from strangled, and from fornication.

[26] Then Paul took the men, and the next day purifying himself with them entered into the temple, to signify the accomplishment of the days of purifcation, until that an offering should be offered for every one of them.

Later, when Paul was in Rome and writing to the Galations he recalls this visit to Jerusalem and his disagreements with Jewish Christians, particularly over the question of circumcision

Galations 2 1 - 10

[1] Then fourteen years after I went up again to Jerusalem with Barnabas, and took Titus with me also.

[2] And I went up by revelation, and communicated unto them that gospel which I preach among the Gentiles, but privately to them which were of reputation, lest by any means I should run, or had run, in vain.

[3] But neither Titus, who was with me, being a Greek, was compelled to be circumcised:

[4] And that because of false brethren unawares brought in, who came in privily to spy out our liberty which we have in Christ Jesus, that they might bring us into bondage:

[5] To whom we gave place by subjection, no, not for an hour; that the truth of the gospel might continue with you.

[6] But of these who seemed to be somewhat, (whatsoever they were, it maketh no matter to me: God accepteth no man's person:) for they who seemed to be somewhat in conference added nothing to me:

[7] But contrariwise, when they saw that the gospel of the uncircumcision was committed unto me, as the gospel of the circumcision was unto Peter;

[8] (For he that wrought effectually in Peter to the apostleship of the circumcision, the same was mighty in me toward the Gentiles:)

[9] And when James, Cephas, and John, who seemed to be pillars, perceived the grace that was given unto me, they gave to me and Barnabas the right hands of fellowship; that we should go unto the heathen, and they unto the circumcision.

[10] Only they would that we should remember the poor; the same which I also was forward to do.

Paul evidently thought the matter had been settled and that he was free to establish his own sect among the pagans while remaining friends with the church in Judea which was to be seen as a sect of Judaism and therefore subject to Jewish laws and customs. He was wrong!

26.2 Non-Jews in the Temple

Jews visiting Jerusalem from Asia had recognised some of Paul's companions as Greeks and had assumed he had taken them into the Temple. This started a riot.

Acts 21 27 - 32

[27] And when the seven days were almost ended, the Jews which were of Asia, when they saw him in the temple, stirred up all the people, and laid hands on him,
[28] Crying out, Men of Israel, help: This is the man, that teacheth all men everywhere against the people, and the law, and this place: and further brought Greeks also into the temple, and hath polluted this holy place.
[29] (For they had seen before with him in the city Trophimus an Ephesian, whom they supposed that Paul had brought into the temple.)
[30] And all the city was moved, and the people ran together: and they took Paul, and drew him out of the temple: and forthwith the doors were shut.
[31] And as they went about to kill him, tidings came unto the chief captain of the band, that all Jerusalem was in an uproar.
[32] Who immediately took soldiers and centurions, and ran down unto them: and when they saw the chief captain and the soldiers, they left beating of Paul.

The Romans immediately arrested Paul, assuming he had committed some crime and took him to the barracks to be questioned. The Commandant stepped forward, arrested him and ordered him to be chained.

Acts 21 33 - 36

[33] Then the chief captain came near, and took him, and commanded him to be bound with two chains; and demanded who he was, and what he had done.
[34] And some cried one thing, some another, among the multitude: and when he could not know the certainty for the tumult, he commanded him to be carried into the castle.
[35] And when he came upon the stairs, so it was, that he was borne of the soldiers for the violence of the people.
[36] For the multitude of the people followed after, crying, Away with him.

Finally, the commandant was able to make some sense of the situation, realising he was not the man who had caused trouble before.

Acts 21 37 - 39
[37] And as Paul was to be led into the castle, he said unto the chief captain, May I speak unto thee? Who said, Canst thou speak Greek?
[38] Art not thou that Egyptian, which before these days madest an uproar, and leddest out into the wilderness four thousand men that were murderers?
[39] But Paul said, I am a man which am a Jew of Tarsus, a city in Cilicia, a citizen of no mean city: and, I beseech thee, suffer me to speak unto the people.

26.3 Recounting the Conversion

Paul offered to speak to the crowd to try to allay their hostility He tells them of his conversion.

Acts 21.40 to 22.21
[40] And when he had given him licence, Paul stood on the stairs, and beckoned with the hand unto the people. And when there was made a great silence, he spake unto them in the Hebrew tongue, saying,
[1] Men, brethren, and fathers, hear ye my defence which I make now unto you.
[2] (And when they heard that he spake in the Hebrew tongue to them, they kept the more silence: and he saith,)
[3] I am verily a man which am a Jew, born in Tarsus, a city in Cilicia, yet brought up in this city at the feet of Gamaliel, and taught according to the perfect manner of the law of the fathers, and was zealous toward God, as ye all are this day.
[4] And I persecuted this way unto the death, binding and delivering into prisons both men and women.
[5] As also the high priest doth bear me witness, and all the estate of the elders: from whom also I received letters unto the brethren, and went to Damascus, to bring them which were there bound unto Jerusalem, for to be punished.
[6] And it came to pass, that, as I made my journey, and was come nigh unto Damascus about noon, suddenly there shone from heaven a great light round about me.
[7] And I fell unto the ground, and heard a voice saying unto me, Saul, Saul, why persecutest thou me?

[8] And I answered, Who art thou, Lord? And he said unto me, I am Jesus of Nazareth, whom thou persecutest.

[9] And they that were with me saw indeed the light, and were afraid; but they heard not the voice of him that spake to me.

[10] And I said, What shall I do, Lord? And the Lord said unto me, Arise, and go into Damascus; and there it shall be told thee of all things which are appointed for thee to do.

[11] And when I could not see for the glory of that light, being led by the hand of them that were with me, I came into Damascus.

[12] And one Ananias, a devout man according to the law, having a good report of all the Jews which dwelt there,

[13] Came unto me, and stood, and said unto me, Brother Saul, receive thy sight. And the same hour I looked up upon him.

[14] And he said, The God of our fathers hath chosen thee, that thou shouldest know his will, and see that Just One, and shouldest hear the voice of his mouth.

[15] For thou shalt be his witness unto all men of what thou hast seen and heard.

[16] And now why tarriest thou? arise, and be baptized, and wash away thy sins, calling on the name of the Lord.

[17] And it came to pass, that, when I was come again to Jerusalem, even while I prayed in the temple, I was in a trance;

[18] And saw him saying unto me, Make haste, and get thee quickly out of Jerusalem: for they will not receive thy testimony concerning me.

[19] And I said, Lord, they know that I imprisoned and beat in every synagogue them that believed on thee:

[20] And when the blood of thy martyr Stephen was shed, I also was standing by, and consenting unto his death, and kept the raiment of them that slew him.

[21] And he said unto me, Depart: for I will send thee far hence unto the Gentiles.

It was to no avail. The crowd were not interested in Paul's explanation. The Romans were about to flog Paul until they realised he was a Roman citizen by birth.

Acts 22 22 - 29

[22] And they gave him audience unto this word, and then lifted up their voices, and said, Away with such a fellow from the earth: for it is not fit that he should live.

[23] And as they cried out, and cast off their clothes, and threw dust into the air,

[24] The chief captain commanded him to be brought into the castle, and bade that he should be examined by scourging; that he might know wherefore they cried so against him.

[25] And as they bound him with thongs, Paul said unto the centurion that stood by, Is it lawful for you to scourge a man that is a Roman, and uncondemned?

[26] When the centurion heard that, he went and told the chief captain, saying, Take heed what thou doest: for this man is a Roman.

[27] Then the chief captain came, and said unto him, Tell me, art thou a Roman? He said, Yea.

[28] And the chief captain answered, With a great sum obtained I this freedom. And Paul said, But I was free born.

[29] Then straightway they departed from him which should have examined him: and the chief captain also was afraid, after he knew that he was a Roman, and because he had bound him.

26.4 Paul addresses the Council

The Commandant still could not understand what all the fuss was about so he called the Jewish Council together and got Paul to address them.

Acts 22.30 to 23.5

[30] On the morrow, because he would have known the certainty wherefore he was accused of the Jews, he loosed him from his bands, and commanded the chief priests and all their council to appear, and brought Paul down, and set him before them.

[1] And Paul, earnestly beholding the council, said, Men and brethren, I have lived in all good conscience before God until this day.

[2] And the high priest Ananias commanded them that stood by him to smite him on the mouth.

[3] Then said Paul unto him, God shall smite thee, thou whited wall: for sittest thou to judge me after the law, and commandest me to be smitten contrary to the law?

[4] And they that stood by said, Revilest thou God's high priest?

[5] Then said Paul, I wist not, brethren, that he was the high priest: for it is written, Thou shalt not speak evil of the ruler of thy people.

Paul now began to try to sow seeds of dissent between the Pharisees and the Saducees.

Acts 23 6 - 11

[6] But when Paul perceived that the one part were Sadducees, and the other Pharisees, he cried out in the council, Men and brethren, I am a Pharisee, the son of a Pharisee: of the hope and resurrection of the dead I am called in question.

[7] And when he had so said, there arose a dissension between the Pharisees and the Sadducees: and the multitude was divided.

[8] For the Sadducees say that there is no resurrection, neither angel, nor spirit: but the Pharisees confess both.

[9] And there arose a great cry: and the scribes that were of the Pharisees' part arose, and strove, saying, We find no evil in this man: but if a spirit or an angel hath spoken to him, let us not fight against God.

[10] And when there arose a great dissension, the chief captain, fearing lest Paul should have been pulled in pieces of them, commanded the soldiers to go down, and to take him by force from among them, and to bring him into the castle.

[11] And the night following the Lord stood by him, and said, Be of good cheer, Paul: for as thou hast testified of me in Jerusalem, so must thou bear witness also at Rome.

26.5 The Plot to kill Paul

The Pharisees and Saducees got together and plotted to persuade the Commandant to hand Paul over to them so they could settle the matter. But their idea of settling it was to kill Paul.

Acts 23 12 - 15

[12] And when it was day, certain of the Jews banded together, and bound themselves under a curse, saying that they would neither eat nor drink till they had killed Paul.

[13] And they were more than forty which had made this conspiracy.

[14] And they came to the chief priests and elders, and said, We have bound ourselves under a great curse, that we will eat nothing until we have slain Paul.

[15] Now therefore ye with the council signify to the chief captain that he bring him down unto you tomorrow, as though ye would inquire something more perfectly concerning him: and we, or ever he come near, are ready to kill him.

Paul's nephew got to hear of the plot and got word to the Commandant who immediately decided the matter was beyond his competence and dispatched Paul to the Governor in Caesaria.

Acts 23 16 - 35

[16] And when Paul's sister's son heard of their lying in wait, he went and entered into the castle, and told Paul.

[17] Then Paul called one of the centurions unto him, and said, Bring this young man unto the chief captain: for he hath a certain thing to tell him.

[18] So he took him, and brought him to the chief captain, and said, Paul the prisoner called me unto him, and prayed me to bring this young man unto thee, who hath something to say unto thee.

[19] Then the chief captain took him by the hand, and went with him aside privately, and asked him, What is that thou hast to tell me?

[20] And he said, The Jews have agreed to desire thee that thou wouldest bring down Paul tomorrow into the council, as though they would inquire somewhat of him more perfectly.

[21] But do not thou yield unto them: for there lie in wait for him of them more than forty men, which have bound themselves with an oath, that they will neither eat nor drink till they have killed him: and now are they ready, looking for a promise from thee.

[22] So the chief captain then let the young man depart, and charged him, See thou tell no man that thou hast shewed these things to me.

[23] And he called unto him two centurions, saying, Make ready two hundred soldiers to go to Caesarea, and horsemen threescore and ten, and spearmen two hundred, at the third hour of the night;

[24] And provide them beasts, that they may set Paul on, and bring him safe unto Felix the governor.

[25] And he wrote a letter after this manner:

[26] Claudius Lysias unto the most excellent governor Felix sendeth greeting.

[27] This man was taken of the Jews, and should have been killed of them: then came I with an army, and rescued him, having understood that he was a Roman.

[28] And when I would have known the cause wherefore they accused him, I brought him forth into their council:

[29] Whom I perceived to be accused of questions of their law, but to have nothing laid to his charge worthy of death or of bonds.

[30] And when it was told me how that the Jews laid wait for the man, I sent straightway to thee, and gave commandment to his accusers also to say before thee what they had against him. Farewell.

[31] Then the soldiers, as it was commanded them, took Paul, and brought him by night to Antipatris.

[32] On the morrow they left the horsemen to go with him, and returned to the castle:

[33] Who, when they came to Caesarea, and delivered the epistle to the governor, presented Paul also before him.

[34] And when the governor had read the letter, he asked of what province he was. And when he understood that he was of Cilicia;

[35] I will hear thee, said he, when thine accusers are also come. And he commanded him to be kept in Herod's judgment hall. .

26.6 Paul on Trial

The representatives of the Council duly arrived together with their lawyer who put the case for the Council

Acts 24 1 - 9

[1] And after five days Ananias the high priest descended with the elders, and with a certain orator named Tertullus, who informed the governor against Paul.

[2] And when he was called forth, Tertullus began to accuse him, saying, Seeing that by thee we enjoy great quietness, and that very worthy deeds are done unto this nation by thy providence,

[3] We accept it always, and in all places, most noble Felix, with all thankfulness.

[4] Notwithstanding, that I be not further tedious unto thee, I pray thee that thou wouldest hear us of thy clemency a few words.

[5] For we have found this man a pestilent fellow, and a mover of sedition among all the Jews throughout the world, and a ringleader of the sect of the Nazarenes:

[6] Who also hath gone about to profane the temple: whom we took, and would have judged according to our law.

[7] But the chief captain Lysias came upon us, and with great violence took him away out of our hands,

[8] Commanding his accusers to come unto thee: by examining of whom thyself mayest take knowledge of all these things, whereof we accuse him.

[9] And the Jews also assented, saying that these things were so.

Paul denied the charges

Acts 24 10 - 21

[10] Then Paul, after that the governor had beckoned unto him to speak, answered, Forasmuch as I know that thou hast been of many years a judge unto this nation, I do the more cheerfully answer for myself:

[11] Because that thou mayest understand, that there are yet but twelve days since I went up to Jerusalem for to worship.

[12] And they neither found me in the temple disputing with any man, neither raising up the people, neither in the synagogues, nor in the city:

[13] Neither can they prove the things whereof they now accuse me.

[14] But this I confess unto thee, that after the way which they call heresy, so worship I the God of my fathers, believing all things which are written in the law and in the prophets:

[15] And have hope toward God, which they themselves also allow, that there shall be a resurrection of the dead, both of the just and unjust.

[16] And herein do I exercise myself, to have always a conscience void of offence toward God, and toward men.

[17] Now after many years I came to bring alms to my nation, and offerings.

[18] Whereupon certain Jews from Asia found me purified in the temple, neither with multitude, nor with tumult.

[19] Who ought to have been here before thee, and object, if they had ought against me.

[20] Or else let these same here say, if they have found any evil doing in me, while I stood before the council,

[21] Except it be for this one voice, that I cried standing among them, Touching the resurrection of the dead I am called in question by you this day.

Felix was well aware of the Christians and the religious sensibilities of the Jews. He decided to keep Paul under open arrest and in the weeks that followed engaged him in conversation hoping to get a bribe from him.

Acts 24 22 - 26

[22] And when Felix heard these things, having more perfect knowledge of that way, he deferred them, and said, When Lysias the chief captain shall come down, I will know the uttermost of your matter.

[23] And he commanded a centurion to keep Paul, and to let him have liberty, and that he should forbid none of his acquaintance to minister or come unto him.

[24] And after certain days, when Felix came with his wife Drusilla, which was a Jewess, he sent for Paul, and heard him concerning the faith in Christ.

[25] And as he reasoned of righteousness, temperance, and judgment to come Felix trembled, and answered, Go thy way for this time; when I have a convenient season, I will call for thee.

[26] He hoped also that money should have been given him of Paul, that he might loose him: wherefore he sent for him the oftener, and communed with him.

26.7 A New Governor

Eventually Felix's term as Governor came to an end and he was succeeded by Festus who was not about to make any quick decisions and went off to Jerusalem to acquaint himself with his new responsibilities.

Acts 24.27 to 25.5

[27] But after two years Porcius Festus came into Felix' room: and Felix, willing to shew the Jews a pleasure, left Paul bound.

[1] Now when Festus was come into the province, after three days he ascended from Caesarea to Jerusalem.

[2] Then the high priest and the chief of the Jews informed him against Paul, and besought him,

[3] And desired favour against him, that he would send for him to Jerusalem, laying wait in the way to kill him.

[4] But Festus answered, that Paul should be kept at Caesarea, and that he himself would depart shortly thither.

[5] Let them therefore, said he, which among you are able, go down with me, and accuse this man, if there be any wickedness in him.

When he got back to Caesaria Paul was brought before him and insisted that he be tried in Rome under Roman law, not Jerusalem under Jewish law.

Acts 25 6 - 12

[6] And when he had tarried among them more than ten days, he went down unto Caesarea; and the next day sitting on the judgment seat commanded Paul to be brought.

[7] And when he was come, the Jews which came down from Jerusalem stood round about, and laid many and grievous complaints against Paul, which they could not prove.

[8] While he answered for himself, Neither against the law of the Jews, neither against the temple, nor yet against Caesar, have I offended any thing at all.

[9] But Festus, willing to do the Jews a pleasure, answered Paul, and said, Wilt thou go up to Jerusalem, and there be judged of these things before me?

[10] Then said Paul, I stand at Caesar's judgment seat, where I ought to be judged: to the Jews have I done no wrong, as thou very well knowest.

[11] For if I be an offender, or have committed any thing worthy of death, I refuse not to die: but if there be none of these things whereof these accuse me, no man may deliver me unto them. I appeal unto Caesar.

[12] Then Festus, when he had conferred with the council, answered, Hast thou appealed unto Caesar? unto Caesar shalt thou go.

26.8 Agrippa's Intervention

Herod Agrippa II was the son of Herod Agrippa I who had persecuted the Christians and arrested Peter. The son however was more tolerant. He had become Tetrarch of Batanaea and Trachinitis as well as king of Chalcis in southern Lebanon when his father died in 44 AD and the Emperor Nero had added Tiberius to his kingdom. It was he who supplied Josephus with much of the material for his history.

He paid a courtesy call on the new Roman Governor who sought his advice. He was travelling with his sister Bernice with whom he was having an incestuous relationship.

Acts 25 13 - 21
[13] And after certain days king Agrippa and Bernice came unto Caesarea to salute Festus.
[14] And when they had been there many days, Festus declared Paul's cause unto the king, saying, There is a certain man left in bonds by Felix:
[15] About whom, when I was at Jerusalem, the chief priests and the elders of the Jews informed me, desiring to have judgment against him.
[16] To whom I answered, It is not the manner of the Romans to deliver any man to die, before that he which is accused have the accusers face to face, and have licence to answer for himself concerning the crime laid against him.
[17] Therefore, when they were come hither, without any delay on the morrow I sat on the judgment seat, and commanded the man to be brought forth.
[18] Against whom when the accusers stood up, they brought none accusation of such things as I supposed:
[19] But had certain questions against him of their own superstition, and of one Jesus, which was dead, whom Paul affirmed to be alive.
[20] And because I doubted of such manner of questions, I asked him whether he would go to Jerusalem, and there be judged of these matters.
[21] But when Paul had appealed to be reserved unto the hearing of Augustus, I commanded him to be kept till I might send him to Caesar.

Agrippa was intrigued and wanted to speak directly with Paul.

Acts 25.22 to 26.8

[22] Then Agrippa said unto Festus, I would also hear the man myself. To morrow, said he, thou shalt hear him.

[23] And on the morrow, when Agrippa was come, and Bernice, with great pomp, and was entered into the place of hearing, with the chief captains, and principal men of the city, at Festus' commandment Paul was brought forth.

[24] And Festus said, King Agrippa, and all men which are here present with us, ye see this man, about whom all the multitude of the Jews have dealt with me, both at Jerusalem, and also here, crying that he ought not to live any longer.

[25] But when I found that he had committed nothing worthy of death, and that he himself hath appealed to Augustus, I have determined to send him.

[26] Of whom I have no certain thing to write unto my lord. Wherefore I have brought him forth before you, and specially before thee, O king Agrippa, that, after examination had, I might have somewhat to write.

[27] For it seemeth to me unreasonable to send a prisoner, and not withal to signify the crimes laid against him.

[1] Then Agrippa said unto Paul, Thou art permitted to speak for thyself. Then Paul stretched forth the hand, and answered for himself:

[2] I think myself happy, king Agrippa, because I shall answer for myself this day before thee touching all the things whereof I am accused of the Jews:

[3] Especially because I know thee to be expert in all customs and questions which are among the Jews: wherefore I beseech thee to hear me patiently.

[4] My manner of life from my youth, which was at the first among mine own nation at Jerusalem, know all the Jews;

[5] Which knew me from the beginning, if they would testify, that after the most straitest sect of our religion I lived a Pharisee.

[6] And now I stand and am judged for the hope of the promise made of God unto our fathers:

[7] Unto which promise our twelve tribes, instantly serving God day and night, hope to come. For which hope's sake, king Agrippa, I am accused of the Jews.

[8] Why should it be thought a thing incredible with you, that God should raise the dead?

Paul recalls his persecution of the Christians and his conversion.

Acts 26 9 - 18

[9] I verily thought with myself, that I ought to do many things contrary to the name of Jesus of Nazareth.

[10] Which thing I also did in Jerusalem: and many of the saints did I shut up in prison, having received authority from the chief priests; and when they were put to death, I gave my voice against them.

[11] And I punished them oft in every synagogue, and compelled them to blaspheme; and being exceedingly mad against them, I persecuted them even unto strange cities.

[12] Whereupon as I went to Damascus with authority and commission from the chief priests,

[13] At midday, O king, I saw in the way a light from heaven, above the brightness of the sun, shining round about me and them which journeyed with me.

[14] And when we were all fallen to the earth, I heard a voice speaking unto me, and saying in the Hebrew tongue, Saul, Saul, why persecutest thou me? it is hard for thee to kick against the pricks.

[15] And I said, Who art thou, Lord? And he said, I am Jesus whom thou persecutest.

[16] But rise, and stand upon thy feet: for I have appeared unto thee for this purpose, to make thee a minister and a witness both of these things which thou hast seen, and of those things in the which I will appear unto thee;

[17] Delivering thee from the people, and from the Gentiles, unto whom now I send thee,

[18] To open their eyes, and to turn them from darkness to light, and from the power of Satan unto God, that they may receive forgiveness of sins, and inheritance among them which are sanctified by faith that is in me.

Paul's explanations sounded like madness to Felix, especially as Agrippa was recognised as the leading Jew. However, Paul had confidence that Agrippa was a reasonable man, and so it turned out.

[19] Whereupon, O king Agrippa, I was not disobedient unto the heavenly vision:

[20] But shewed first unto them of Damascus, and at Jerusalem, and throughout all the coasts of Judaea, and then to the Gentiles, that they should repent and turn to God, and do works meet for repentance.

[21] For these causes the Jews caught me in the temple, and went about to kill me.

[22] Having therefore obtained help of God, I continue unto this day, witnessing both to small and great, saying none other things than those which the prophets and Moses did say should come:

[23] That Christ should suffer, and that he should be the first that should rise from the dead, and should shew light unto the people, and to the Gentiles.

[24] And as he thus spake for himself, Festus said with a loud voice, Paul, thou art beside thyself; much learning doth make thee mad.

[25] But he said, I am not mad, most noble Festus; but speak forth the words of truth and soberness.

[26] For the king knoweth of these things, before whom also I speak freely: for I am persuaded that none of these things are hidden from him; for this thing was not done in a corner.

[27] King Agrippa, believest thou the prophets? I know that thou believest.

[28] Then Agrippa said unto Paul, Almost thou persuadest me to be a Christian.

[29] And Paul said, I would to God, that not only thou, but also all that hear me this day, were both almost, and altogether such as I am, except these bonds.

[30] And when he had thus spoken, the king rose up, and the governor, and Bernice, and they that sat with them:

[31] And when they were gone aside, they talked between themselves, saying, This man doeth nothing worthy of death or of bonds.

[32] Then said Agrippa unto Festus, This man might have been set at liberty, if he had not appealed unto Caesar.

Chapter 27 - Paul's Final Journey – Rome

27.1 Voyage to Crete

The die was cast. Paul had got his wish to be tried before the emperor in Rome. They were put aboard a ship sailing for Asia with the intention of changing ships there for Italy, but things were not going to turn out as planned. Luke's description of the voyage is both informative and graphic, giving a lot of detail about seaborne trade at the time.

Acts 27 1 - 8

[1] And when it was determined that we should sail into Italy, they delivered Paul and certain other prisoners unto one named Julius, a centurion of Augustus' band.

[2] And entering into a ship of Adramyttium, we launched, meaning to sail by the coasts of Asia; one Aristarchus, a Macedonian of Thessalonica, being with us.

[3] And the next day we touched at Sidon. And Julius courteously entreated Paul, and gave him liberty to go unto his friends to refresh himself.

[4] And when we had launched from thence, we sailed under Cyprus, because the winds were contrary.

[5] And when we had sailed over the sea of Cilicia and Pamphylia, we came to Myra, a city of Lycia.

[6] And there the centurion found a ship of Alexandria sailing into Italy; and he put us therein.

[7] And when we had sailed slowly many days, and scarce were come over against Cnidus, the wind not suffering us, we sailed under Crete, over against Salmone;

[8] And, hardly passing it, came unto a place which is called The fair havens; nigh whereunto was the city of Lasea.

27.2 Weathering the Storm

The delays due to bad weather had put them well behind schedule and now with the weather worsening there were real dangers ahead. Paul advised caution.

Acts 27 9 - 10

[9] Now when much time was spent, and when sailing was now dangerous, because the fast was now already past, Paul admonished them,

[10] And said unto them, Sirs, I perceive that this voyage will be with hurt and much damage, not only of the lading and ship, but also of our lives.

Quite reasonably the centurion, who was under pressure to deliver his prisoners to Rome, was more inclined to heed the shipowner than the prisoner.

Acts 27 11 - 12

[11] Nevertheless the centurion believed the master and the owner of the ship, more than those things which were spoken by Paul.
[12] And because the haven was not commodious to winter in, the more part advised to depart thence also, if by any means they might attain to Phenice, and there to winter; which is an haven of Crete, and lieth toward the south west and north west.

It did not take long for them to run into trouble as they ran past Crete.

Acts 27 13 - 20

[13] And when the south wind blew softly, supposing that they had obtained their purpose, loosing thence, they sailed close by Crete.
[14] But not long after there arose against it a tempestuous wind, called Euroclydon.
[15] And when the ship was caught, and could not bear up into the wind, we let her drive.
[16] And running under a certain island which is called Clauda, we had much work to come by the boat:
[17] Which when they had taken up, they used helps, undergirding the ship; and, fearing lest they should fall into the quicksands, strake sail, and so were driven.
[18] And we being exceedingly tossed with a tempest, the next day they lightened the ship;
[19] And the third day we cast out with our own hands the tackling of the ship.
[20] And when neither sun nor stars in many days appeared, and no small tempest lay on us, all hope that we should be saved was then taken away.

Paul was now in a position to say 'I told you so' but still they were not inclined to listen:

Acts 27 21 - 26

[21] But after long abstinence Paul stood forth in the midst of them, and said, Sirs, ye should have hearkened unto me, and not have loosed from Crete, and to have gained this harm and loss.

[22] And now I exhort you to be of good cheer: for there shall be no loss of any man's life among you, but of the ship.

[23] For there stood by me this night the angel of God, whose I am, and whom I serve,

[24] Saying, Fear not, Paul; thou must be brought before Caesar: and, lo, God hath given thee all them that sail with thee.

[25] Wherefore, sirs, be of good cheer: for I believe God, that it shall be even as it was told me.

[26] Howbeit we must be cast upon a certain island.

Eventually they sensed they were approaching land and took soundings. At long last the centurion began to take notice of what Paul was saying.

Acts 27 27 - 38

[27] But when the fourteenth night was come, as we were driven up and down in Adria, about midnight the shipmen deemed that they drew near to some country;

[28] And sounded, and found it twenty fathoms: and when they had gone a little further, they sounded again, and found it fifteen fathoms.

[29] Then fearing lest we should have fallen upon rocks, they cast four anchors out of the stern, and wished for the day.

[30] And as the shipmen were about to flee out of the ship, when they had let down the boat into the sea, under colour as though they would have cast anchors out of the foreship,

[31] Paul said to the centurion and to the soldiers, Except these abide in the ship, ye cannot be saved.

[32] Then the soldiers cut off the ropes of the boat, and let her fall off.

[33] And while the day was coming on, Paul besought them all to take meat, saying, This day is the fourteenth day that ye have tarried and continued fasting, having taken nothing.

[34] Wherefore I pray you to take some meat: for this is for your health: for there shall not an hair fall from the head of any of you.

[35] And when he had thus spoken, he took bread, and gave thanks to God in presence of them all: and when he had broken it, he began to eat.

[36] Then were they all of good cheer, and they also took some meat.

[37] And we were in all in the ship two hundred threescore and sixteen souls.

[38] And when they had eaten enough, they lightened the ship, and cast out the wheat into the sea. .

27.3 Malta

Daybreak revealed the land to them. They were off Gozo, a small island which was part of Malta. The soldiers by now were fed up with the whole business but the centurion was clear that it was his duty to get Paul and his party to Rome.

Acts 27 39 - 44

[39] And when it was day, they knew not the land: but they discovered a certain creek with a shore, into the which they were minded, if it were possible, to thrust in the ship.

[40] And when they had taken up the anchors, they committed themselves unto the sea, and loosed the rudder bands, and hoised up the mainsail to the wind, and made toward shore.

[41] And falling into a place where two seas met, they ran the ship aground; and the forepart stuck fast, and remained unmoveable, but the hinder part was broken with the violence of the waves.

[42] And the soldiers' counsel was to kill the prisoners, lest any of them should swim out, and escape.

[43] But the centurion, willing to save Paul, kept them from their purpose; and commanded that they which could swim should cast themselves first into the sea, and get to land:

[44] And the rest, some on boards, and some on broken pieces of the ship. And so it came to pass, that they escaped all safe to land.

Paul's prophecy had come true. The ship and all its cargo were lost, but no lives had been lost. On Gozo they were well received and Paul's status as a Roman citizen earned him the hospitality of the Chief Magistrate, something that would never have been granted to a mere prisoner.

Acts 28 1 - 10

[1] And when they were escaped, then they knew that the island was called Melita.

[2] And the barbarous people shewed us no little kindness: for they kindled a fire, and received us every one, because of the present rain, and because of the cold.

[3] And when Paul had gathered a bundle of sticks, and laid them on the fire, there came a viper out of the heat, and fastened on his hand.

[4] And when the barbarians saw the venomous beast hang on his hand, they said among themselves, No doubt this man is a murderer, whom, though he hath escaped the sea, yet vengeance suffereth not to live.

[5] And he shook off the beast into the fire, and felt no harm.

[6] Howbeit they looked when he should have swollen, or fallen down dead suddenly: but after they had looked a great while, and saw no harm come to him, they changed their minds, and said that he was a god.

[7] In the same quarters were possessions of the chief man of the island, whose name was Publius; who received us, and lodged us three days courteously.

[8] And it came to pass, that the father of Publius lay sick of a fever and of a bloody flux: to whom Paul entered in, and prayed, and laid his hands on him, and healed him.

[9] So when this was done, others also, which had diseases in the island, came, and were healed:

[10] Who also honoured us with many honours; and when we departed, they laded us with such things as were necessary.

27.4 The Last Lap

They stayed out the rest of the winter on Gozo but had to wait for another ship before they could continue their journey. The last lap of the voyage was comparatively uneventful and at last they reached Rome.

Acts 28 11 - 15

[11] And after three months we departed in a ship of Alexandria, which had wintered in the isle, whose sign was Castor and Pollux.

[12] And landing at Syracuse, we tarried there three days.

[13] And from thence we fetched a compass, and came to Rhegium: and after one day the south wind blew, and we came the next day to Puteoli:

[14] Where we found brethren, and were desired to tarry with them seven days: and so we went toward Rome.

[15] And from thence, when the brethren heard of us, they came to meet us as far as Appiiforum, and The three taverns: whom when Paul saw, he thanked God, and took courage.

27.5 Paul's Arrival

Paul arrived in Rome around 58 AD after his voyage in captivity from Jerusalem. It is difficult to determine whether or not he was really still under arrest when he arrived but he seemed to get a good reception although he retained a Roman guard.

Acts 28 16 - 31

[16] And when we came to Rome, the centurion delivered the prisoners to the captain of the guard: but Paul was suffered to dwell by himself with a soldier that kept him.

[17] And it came to pass, that after three days Paul called the chief of the Jews together: and when they were come together, he said unto them, Men and brethren, though I have committed nothing against the people, or customs of our fathers, yet was I delivered prisoner from Jerusalem into the hands of the Romans.

[18] Who, when they had examined me, would have let me go, because there was no cause of death in me.

[19] But when the Jews spake against it, I was constrained to appeal unto Caesar; not that I had ought to accuse my nation of.

[20] For this cause therefore have I called for you, to see you, and to speak with you: because that for the hope of Israel I am bound with this chain.

[21] And they said unto him, We neither received letters out of Judaea concerning thee, neither any of the brethren that came shewed or spake any harm of thee.

[22] But we desire to hear of thee what thou thinkest: for as concerning this sect, we know that everywhere it is spoken against.

[23] And when they had appointed him a day, there came many to him into his lodging; to whom he expounded and testified the kingdom of God, persuading them concerning Jesus, both out of the law of Moses, and out of the prophets, from morning till evening.

[24] And some believed the things which were spoken, and some believed not.

[25] And when they agreed not among themselves, they departed, after that Paul had spoken one word, Well spake the Holy Ghost by Esaias the prophet unto our fathers,

[26] Saying, Go unto this people, and say, Hearing ye shall hear, and shall not understand; and seeing ye shall see, and not perceive:

[27] For the heart of this people is waxed gross, and their ears are dull of hearing, and their eyes have they closed; lest they should see with their eyes, and hear with their ears, and understand with their heart, and should be converted, and I should heal them.

[28] Be it known therefore unto you, that the salvation of God is sent unto the Gentiles, and that they will hear it.

[29] And when he had said these words, the Jews departed, and had great reasoning among themselves.

[30] And Paul dwelt two whole years in his own hired house, and received all that came in unto him,

[31] Preaching the kingdom of God, and teaching those things which concern the Lord Jesus Christ, with all confidence, no man forbidding him.

27.6 The Result of the Trial

For a reason known only to himself Luke ends the Acts of the Apostles here with Paul's arrival in Rome. It is left to Eusebius to fill in the next steps. The first acquittal is assumed on the basis of Paul's two years of unfettered preaching. He then goes on another undocumented missionary journey and returns to Rome a second time to await his fate.

Eusebius Book 2 Chapter 22

As successor to Felix, Nero sent Festus, It was in his time that Paul was put on trial, and then conveyed in fetters to Rome. With him went Aristarchus, to whom somewhere in the epistles he naturally refers as a fellow-prisoner. And Luke, who committed to writing the Acts of the Apostles, ended his story at this point, after informing us that Paul spent two complete years at Rome under no restraint and preached the word of God without hindrance.

There is evidence that, having then been brought to trial, the apostle again set out on the ministry of preaching, and having appeared a second time in the same city found fulfilment in his martyrdom.

In the course of this imprisonment he composed the second Epistle to Timothy, referring both to his earlier trial and to his impending fulfilment. Listen to his testimony on this point.

At my first trial nobody supported me: they all left me to my fate-' may God forgive them! But the Lord stood by me and gave me strength, that through me the message might be fully proclaimed in the hearing of the whole pagan world. Thus I was rescued out of the lion's mouth!

This passage proves beyond question that on the first occasion, in order that the message proclaimed through him might be fully preached, he was rescued out of the lion's mouth, the reference being apparently to Nero, because of his bestial cruelty. He does not go on to add anything like 'he will rescue me out of the lion's mouth', for he saw by the Spirit that his death was imminent. And so after the words 'and I was rescued out of the lion's mouth' he goes on to say.

'The Lord will rescue me from every evil attempt and keep me safe for His heavenly kingdom ', indicating his forthcoming martyrdom. This he foretells more clearly still in the same letter, when he says:

'For I am already being offered as a sacrifice, and the time for my departure has come.' In this second Epistle to Timothy he remarks that only Luke is with him as he writes, and at his first trial not even he: presumably that is why Luke concluded the Acts of the Apostles at that point, having traced the course of events throughout the time he was with Paul. I have said this to show that it was not during the stay in Rome described by Luke that Paul's martyrdom was accomplished. The probability is that since at first Nero's disposition was milder, it was easier for Paul's defence of the Faith to be received, but that when he had gone on to commit abominable crimes, above all else he launched his attack on the apostles.

27.7 Peter and Paul die in Rome

The tradition is that St Peter came to live in Rome in his old age and was eventually crucified upside down in the persecutions of Nero. However, about the only evidence for this comes from the writings of Irenaeus In 180 AD he wrote his "Refutation and Overthrow of Gnosis" and he mentions St Peter in book 3 chapter 1 section 1. Eusebius writing around 330 AD reports:

Eusebius book 2 chapter 25

When Nero's power was now firmly established he gave himself up to unholy practices and took up arms against the God of the universe. To describe the monster of depravity that he became lies outside the scope of the present work. Many writers have recorded the facts about him in minute detail, enabling anyone who wishes to get a complete picture of his perverse and extraordinary madness, which led him to the senseless destruction of innumerable lives, and drove him in the end to such a lust for blood that he did not spare even his nearest and dearest but employed a variety of methods to do away with mother, brothers, and wife alike, to say nothing of countless other members of his family, as if they were personal and public enemies. All this left one crime still to be added to his account - he was the first of the emperors be the declared enemy of the worship of Almighty God. To this the Roman Tertullian refers in the following terms:

Study your records: there you will find that Nero was the first to persecute this teaching when, after subjugating the entire East, in Rome especially he treated everyone with savagery. That such a man was author of our chastisement fills us with pride. For anyone who knows him can understand that anything not supremely good would never have been condemned by Nero.

So, it came about that this man, the first to be heralded as a conspicuous fighter against God, was led on to murder the apostles. It is recorded that in his reign Paul was beheaded in Rome itself; and that Peter likewise was crucified, and the record is confirmed by the fact that the cemeteries there are still called by the names of Peter and Paul, and equally so by a churchman named Gaius, who was living while Zephyrinus as Bishop of Rome.

In his published Dialogue with Proclus, the leader of the Phrygian heretics, Gaius has this to say about the places where the mortal remains of the two apostles have been reverently laid:

I can point out the monuments of the victorious apostles. If you will go as far as the Vatican or the Ostian Way, you will find the monuments of those who founded this church. That they were both martyred at the same time Bishop Dionysius of Corinth informs us in a letter written to the Romans:

In this way by your impressive admonition you have bound together all that has grown from the seed which Peter and Paul sowed in Romans and Corinthians alike.

For both of them sowed in our Corinth and taught us jointly: in Italy too they taught jointly in the same city, and were martyred at the same time.

These evidences make the truth of my account still more certain.

27.8 Peter's Wife

Peter seems to have been married and his wife was executed before him. Clement recalls the scene.

Clement Miscellanies VII

We are told that when blessed Peter saw his wife led away to death, he was glad that her call had come and that she was returning home, and spoke to her in the most encouraging and comforting tones, addressing her by name: "My dear, remember the Lord" Such was the marriage of the blessed, and their consummate feeling towards their dearest.

Actually, both Peter and Paul must have been married at some time else they would never have been allowed to preach in synagogues.

27.9 The Apostles and their Territories

In the aftermath of the execution of Peter and Paul, Eusebius reminds us of how the several apostles had allocated the Roman world between them.

Eusebius Book 3 Chaps 1 and 2

Meanwhile the holy apostles and disciples of our Saviour were scattered over the whole world. Thomas, tradition tells us, was chosen for Parthia, Andrew for Scythia, John for Asia, where he remained till his death at Ephesus. Peter seems to have preached in Pontus, Galatia and Bithynia, Cappadocia and Asia, to the Jews of the Dispersion. Finally, he came to Rome where he was crucified, head downwards at his own request. What need be said of Paul, who from Jerusalem as far as Illyricum preached in all its fullness the gospel of Christ, and later was martyred in Rome under Nero? This is exactly what Origen tells us in Volume III of his Commentary on Genesis. After the martyrdom of Paul and Peter the first man to be appointed Bishop of Rome was Linus.

PART 6
THE MESSAGE

In this final part we look at some of the factors which turned Christianity from a minority and persecuted sect of Judaism to be the official religion of the Roman Empire. We look at how the message came to be set down in writing, how the diaspora helped to spread it around the empire, what happened in key areas and who some of the key players were.

At first the message is passed on by word of mouth. Converts to Christianity can hear it from people who were around to hear Jesus speak. But as time goes by the need to write it down for posterity becomes apparent.

Few people are literate, so the work is left to a few of whom Paul seems the most prolific as he writes his Epistles to send to the various churches.

Some of the story cannot be told explicitly as this would endanger key players, so when it comes to recording Jesus' life, the circumstances around some events have to be disguised.

Furthermore, many of the key events are now so far back in time that there is no one around who actually recalls them, so the gospellers have to resort to the prophets. What was prophesied? So that is what must have happened. What did Jesus say when he was alone? - We have to guess.

In 70 AD the Romans tire of Jewish obstructiveness and rebellion and disperse them around the Empire. The groups of Christians amongst them join with Gentile Christians and new scholars arise who interpret the message in terms which make sense to their specific circumstances.

Gradually there comes agreement as to which of the many manuscripts available will be accepted by everyone as the New Testament and the Emperor Constantine sees Christianity as a means of uniting his Empire. Then his mother Helena tours the eastern Empire selecting sites which best fit the events recorded, tourism is born through pilgrimage. But that's another story.

Chapter 28 Writing it Down

In this chapter we will consider how and when the early Christians set down their recollections of Jesus and his teachings and how we came to the body of literature we now know as the New Testament. One thing we can be pretty sure of is that Jesus himself did not write any of it.

28.1 Who was Literate?

Peter and Paul were dead, James had been beheaded and the Apostles had divided the world so that each could evangelise a particular part of it.

We can reasonably assume that most of the Apostles, were illiterate and the messages had to be passed on orally. However there was a realisation that the story needed to be preserved in a written form. Paul seems to have been a prolific writer but he was interested in interpreting what he saw as Jesus's message so his Epistles contain relatively little history.

Someone at some time between around 40 and 100 AD did start to write things down. The Gospels seem to indicate that there were two main strands of the history. First what we regard as the proto-gospel which formed the basis for Matthew, Mark and Luke's versions and second the Gospel of John whose version seems to be much more aware of the context and although he is trying to focus on the message, the history he recounts is more realistic than the fanciful reconstructions of Luke, Scholars have been arguing about authorship, authenticity and dates for most of the last two millennia and I would not like to enter those controversies but merely put forward my own thesis.

28.2 Security

The first thing we have to remember is that Christianity was seen by both Roman and Jewish rulers as essentially subversive. Herod Agrippa I was obsessed by the idea that a putative king was at large who could usurp him. He had dealt with John the Baptist and James the brother of Jesus and he appreciated that the Romans had disposed of Jesus, although the rumours of his resurrection were quite disturbing. But the visit of the magi and the thought that Jesus had a son meant that, in Gallilee at least, detailed knowledge was a dangerous commodity.

So precious is the secret of a blood descendant of Jesus that great efforts are made to remove all direct references from the account of Jesus life which forms the basis for the Gospels of both Mark and Matthew. They do not want to remove the references completely and so they leave them in, but delete all the key words which establish the direct links and make a few minor changes to places and times to disguise the real truth. The early Christians would know the real facts and would understand the cryptic references. Later of course when the people who were alive at the time were all dead and gone, the secret was still necessary to keep as Roman persecution had taken over from that of the Jewish Authorities, but the only documentation was in code and no-one understood the code. Thus, when Luke came to write his account, he knew the bare facts and, like Uncle Remus, developed fantastic stories to explain them.

28.3 The New Testament Canon

The collection of writings that were deemed authoritative developed slowly over the first three centuries and it was at Nicaea that the final list was generally approved although a few additional manuscripts were collected to form a New Testament Apocrypha although this has had little acceptance since.

In the period 50-150 AD four Gospels, The Acts and a number of Epistles were widely circulated and Irenaeus around 180 AD published his list. It was some time before Revelation was included. It was the list agreed at Nicaea and published by Athanasius in 367 AD that was finally accepted as the canonical list and when Pope Damascus commissioned the Latin version, called the Vulgate, in 383 AD, that list was used and has stood the test of time.

28.4 The New Testament Apocrypha

We are fairly familiar with the Old Testament Apocrypha as a set of 15 books which are retained in the Roman Catholic canon, but excluded from the Jewish and Protestant canons. There are however a large number of books, of which only a fragment survives in some cases, of books which were excluded from the New Testament canon, first drawn up by Irenaeus in 186 AD and finally agreed as late as 692 AD at the second Trullan Council, although it is not much different from that of Athanasius in 367 AD.

In the early church a manuscript was a precious item. Most congregations would have a copy of only one or two books and often only a part of a book at that. There were many more books in circulation than eventually formed part of the canon and over the years there have been many disputes and questions as to why a particular book was or was not included.

The essential question for us however is do any of these alternative books throw any light on the history of the early church. The answer sadly, is not much.

Some of these books were accepted as part of the New Testament by various churches around the world. However, most churches dropped them after Irenaus issued his list and the assumption was that all the non-canonical books would be destroyed as they were deemed heretical. However, many churches and especially monasteries hung on to them and hid them away.

28.5 The Dead Sea Scrolls

Another intriguing source of material is the collection of fragments found in and around Qumran and popularly known as the Dead Sea Scrolls. Unfortunately, there has been an inordinate delay in publishing this material in a form that can be understood by anyone, least of all a layman. Rumours abound and dark intrigues are hinted of but very little tangible evidence has emerged. What is of particular interest is that in most cases the texts discovered are the oldest known versions, generally of books of the Old Testament and for many of these Old Testament books we also have commentaries which throw a new light on their interpretation.

There is very little of New Testament relevance save a series of texts which demonstrate fairly clearly that many of Jesus' reported sayings were not new but had formed part of the philosophy of at least one Jewish sect for a hundred years or more before the Incarnation.

28.6 The Gnostic Tradition

Gnosticism is based upon its adherents possessing secret knowledge and of course if everyone had the knowledge it would no longer be a secret. The greatest source of information comes from the documents found during excavations in upper Egypt in the 1940s and reveal philosophy rather than history.

The origins seem to be basically in the early second century with a definite Christian flavour, although many of the ideas are at odds with orthodox Christianity. However one can sense that in many cases Christian theology was developed as a counter to Gnosticism and men such as Valentinus, Cerdo and Marcion were excommunicated around 150 AD for holding Gnostic views.

Similar views surfaced again in France with the Cathars, closely allied to the Templars, and it was as a by product of the suppression of the Albigensian heresy, which was essentially Gnostic, in the early 1200s that the Templars were later suppressed in 1307.

The tradition has been linked both with the Essenes and with John and one may speculate that it was to the Essene centre whence he had come that John took Mary for safety after the crucifixion. Thus, many of the secrets could relate to the knowledge as to what really happened in those crucial years after the crucifixion.

28.7 The Secret Gospel of Mark

The discovery in 1958 of references to a fuller version of the Gospel of Mark in a letter ascribed to St Clement, brought out once more the idea that early Christianity was not all that it seemed. The picture, beloved of present day evangelicals of a church made up of small groups or pious potential martyrs, worshipping together and studying an early version of the King James Bible which had been produced for them almost immediately after the resurrection, is far from reality.

There is however, good evidence for an early Aramaic text of the Gospel, written perhaps around 60-70 AD which formed the basis of St Mark's Gospel. But when this was translated into Greek, perhaps around 80-90 AD it contained much more material than our canonical version of Mark. This Aramaic version was used first by John as the basis of his very theological Gospel and later by Matthew and Luke who embellished it with stories of the 'Just-so' type to fill in the gaps, and especially to cover Jesus' early life.

Of this 'original' Aramaic text no trace remains, but St Clement's comments and quotations, written about 180-200 AD, gives us a hint that the full version of Mark was very carefully edited into a number of different versions with the canonical Mark being the popular version for the poor, the slaves and the ill-educated. Further versions were available for the rich and better educated and for those who were privy to the innermost secrets of the church.

We have then at least three levels:

- The canonical Mark - available to all

- The secret Mark - available to those specially baptised at the Easter vigil.

- The unwritten tradition - so secret that it could no longer be written down and was passed on only to very carefully selected initiates.

28.8 Tradition

When the gospellers were writing, details of Jesus' birth were lost in the mists of time, but the events of Jesus' ministry and passion would still be vivid in many people's memory. Assuming that writing begins around 40 AD this would be ten years or so after Jesus' ministry; but his childhood would have been thirty years previously and his birth forty or more ago and who would have known Joseph, Mary and Jesus then anyway. Equally the visit of the Magi to Herod Agrippa I would have been only five or so years ago and the terrible consequences still fresh in the memory. The four gospellers treat these traditions in very different ways. John ignores them, Luke is primarily concerned with what happened after the Passion in his 'Acts of the Apostles' but he is aware that there are huge gaps in his story. He turns to Isaiah to construct what one can only described as a wholly fictional account of the birth and the events leading up to it. He was not trying to write history; but rather to explain how marvelous the birth of Jesus was, but in retrospect, knowing how Jesus developed.

He gave particular status to Bethlehem and Nazareth which those two towns saw as important commercial opportunities, particularly after the visit of Helena. It would not be long before the places Helena identified would surround themselves with myths and traditions which would all be good for business. A second Bethlehem, this time in Galilee, has attempted to lay claims to being the birthplace and there is some archaeological evidence to support this view but the Judean city has established the pre-eminence.

One thing that was probably well known was Jesus' connection to Egypt. Christians at the time of writing would not know most of the details but would be aware that Jesus spent his childhood there. They would also be aware of the later flight to Egypt by Mary Magdalene and the persecutions by Herod so the story of the flight by Mary and Joseph and the child Jesus in the Temple would fit in nicely.

Equally the Diaspora which saw the Jews expelled from Palestine and the pre-eminence of Rome as the leading city of the Empire, and the later occupation of the eastern and southern Mediterranean countries by Islam ensured that traditions based upon Rome would prevail and anything that detracted from this would be seen as subversive and to be suppressed as when the Cathars and other French sects which had maintained the traditions of St Mary Magdalene were suppressed in the thirteenth and fourteenth centuries.

We need also to look at the motives of Constantine, as he was using Christianity as a way of unifying and consolidating his empire. It was important to him to downgrade non-Roman traditions and when it came to select the canon of the New Testament he would be content to see other sources destroyed and liberties taken with the sequence of events.

Finally, we must look also at the events in Palestine between 33 AD when we suppose the Crucifixion took place and 70 AD when the Temple was destroyed. For much of this period Christians were regarded as a subversive threat to Jewish society and persecuted by Herod and his family.

This alone would have caused early writers and preachers to use code to disguise the real facts for security reasons. But when the gospellers and epistle writers came to write things down they would have had great difficulty is differentiating between coded imagery and historic fact, and as the coded imagery better elucidated what was seen as the Good News this would have been given preference anyway.

We have then a situation in which there were many powerful vested interests with a stake in suppressing and disguising the real facts. As in the stories to be found in the Old Testament where folk memory of ancient events and myths along the lines of the 'Just So' stories were woven together using different contexts to construct a claim for the Jews to the land of Israel, so with the New Testament were events taken out of sequence and context and woven with imagery to form a story which conveyed an essential message but lacking consistency and historical accuracy.

28.9 The Later Discoveries

It was not until the Vulgate, compiled by St Jerome in the late fourth century, that we have what we can see as a complete New Testament. Prior to that, each church had its own collection of manuscripts from which readings could be made to congregations although even then it was only short extracts that were read.

These manuscripts were regarded as very precious and it is quite clear that when the order went out that only material within the approved canon could be retained, many churches and monasteries ignored the call to destroy everything else.

Traces of the versions of these writings have appeared from time to time since the early 1800s but it is not until recently that almost complete works have emerged, mainly from sites in Sinai.

Most of these texts are now available on the internet and they throw some very different lights on the conventional account of Jesus' life. Eight documents are entitled Gospels; those of Thomas, Peter, The Egyptians, The Hebrews, The Saviour, Mary, Judas and Philip. As usual scholars are questioning authenticity and theologians are arguing that the reason they were not included in the canon is that they were incorrect.

Some of these have been mentioned in earlier chapters where their content clarifies the story, but there are so many of them known nowadays that it is far beyond the scope of this work to analyse their content. They will keep scholars busy for the next hundred years at least and even then there will be very little agreement.

Chapter 29 - The Diaspora

29.1 Background to the Diaspora

The Jews had always been a trading nation. Situated as they were near the cross roads of the great transcontinental trading routes linking China, India and Africa to Europe they had plenty of opportunity to meet traders from afar. They were close to Phoenicia, the ancient world's great maritime centre, and as a result there were Jewish settlements all around the Mediterranean.

Paul visited many of these settlements on his journeys and they were open house for the spread of Christianity. However, they always looked back to Jerusalem and Galilee as the centre of the new religion and James as Jesus' successor.

James, reputed to have been the brother of Jesus, was a very pious man steeped in the Jewish traditions and seeing Christianity more as a branch of traditional Judaism than a new religion. Over the next few years the Roman grip on Palestine was to tighten. Client kings such as Herod Antipas II who were supportive of Rome were left in post; but sects such as the Essenes were to be suppressed. The revolt of the Maccabees would be cruelly crushed culminating in the last stand at Masada and the Temple would be pulled down. Judaism as a religion in Palestine would be virtually eliminated and the surviving Jews spread around the Roman world. The Jesus movement in Palestine would disappear with Judaism leaving it all to the Church which Paul would create.

The New Testament makes almost no mention of this period as Acts focuses upon Paul's work. However, as background to what was to happen to the Christian church, we need to see what actually happened in Palestine between the crucifixion and the destruction of the Temple in 70 AD.

29.2 The Maccabbees

We need to go back a couple of centuries to 167 BC when Mattathias Maccabbeus led the revolt against king Antiochus I of Syria which resulted in an independent Jewish state being created in Palestine. The family ruled this state until overthrown by Herod the Great in 37 BC.

His two sons Judas and Simon developed followings which produced the two sects of Pharisees and Sadducees respectively. The rivalry between these two sects and the Herodians caused most of the ferment in Jewish Society which was apparent at the time and provided the background to Jesus' ministry.

This revolt is covered in the first and second books of Maccabbees.

29.3 The Roman Occupation

Palestine had become an insignificant corner of the Roman Empire when Pompey conquered the Selucids in 63 BC. Herod the Great was installed as a local king in 40 BC and, although not a Jew, he was not antipathetic towards them and around 20 BC began reconstructing David's Temple.

Roman attitudes to society and the economy were in sharp contract to those of the Jews. The Romans saw incorporation into the Empire as a way of controlling and increasing trade and commerce and thereby increasing the tax revenues that could be gleaned from the territory. So long as people were peaceful and paid their taxes the Romans could not care less about how the society was organised or what religion they practised.

The Jews saw things very differently. To them land was a sacred commodity given to them by God. They resented having to pay taxes which mostly went to support Roman military ventures elsewhere. Equally they saw the practice of pagan religions as blasphemous and not to be tolerated on Jewish soil. All of the groups and sects which made up Jewish society were fervent nationalists, eager to see the Romans and their puppet kings out of Palestine. All were looking for a Messiah who would be a leader in the mould of Judas Maccabbeus. They had been disappointed in Jesus and were still looking.

29.4 The Samaritan Demonstration

In 36 AD another would-be Messiah proclaimed that he knew where Moses had hidden the sacred Temple vessels, in a village named Tirathaba in Samaria. He called for people to gather there at the foot of Mount Gerizzim so he could unveil the relics. Pontius Pilate, the Roman governor got to hear of it and feared and uprising so he sent in the troops disperse the crowds who were either slaughtered in battle or executed.

The community was outraged and the Samaritan senate appealed to Vitellus, the President of Syria who was the chief Roman in the Province. Josephus recorded:

Josephus Antiquities book 18-chapter 4 part 2

But when the tumult was appeased, the Samaritan senate sent an embassy to Vitellus, a man that had been made Consul and who was now president of Syria, and accused Pilate of the murder of those that were killed; for that they did not go to Tirathaba in order to revolt from the Romans but to escape the violence of Pilate. So Vitellus sent Marcellus, a friend of his, to take care of the affairs of Judea, and ordered Pilate to go to Rome, to answer before the Emperor to the accusations of the Jews. So Pilate, when he had tarried ten years in Judea, made haste to Rome and this in obedience to the orders of Vitellus, which he durst not contradict, but before he could get to Rome Tiberius was dead.

29.5 The Destruction of Jerusalem

Jerusalem had been occupied by the Zealots in 66 AD who had built strong defences to keep the Romans at bay. Vespasian's son Titus led the Roman army that stormed and took the city in 70 AD. He saw the Temple as the central problem and set about demolishing it. It had been started by Herod the Great in around 40 BC and had only recently been completed.

Josephus has his version of the siege of Jerusalem which began in April AD 70 and culminated in the destruction of the temple and slaughter of the remaining inhabitants who had survived the famine.

Josephus Wars of the Jews Book 6 Chapter VIII

So, the Romans being now masters of the walls, they both placed their ensigns upon the tower they had gained as having found the end of this war much lighter than its beginning; for when they had gotten upon the last wall, without any bloodshed, they could hardly believe what they found to be true, but seeing nobody to oppose them they stood in doubt what such an unusual solitude could mean.

But when they went in numbers into the lanes of the city, with their swords drawn, they slew those whom they overtook without mercy and set fire to the houses whither the Jews were fled and burnt every soul in them and laid waste a great many of the rest; and when they were come to the houses to plunder them, they found entire families of dead men and the upper rooms full of dead corpses, that is of such as died by the famine; they stood in a horror at this sight and went out without touching anything.

But although they had this commiseration for such as were destroyed in that manner, yet had they not the same for those that were still alive, but they ran everyone through whom they met with and obstructed the lanes with their dead bodies and made the whole city run down with blood to such a degree indeed that the fire of many of the houses was quenched with these men's blood.

And truly so it happened, that though the slayers left off at the evening, yet did the fire greatly prevail in the night, and as all was burning came that eighth day of the month Gorpieus upon Jerusalem; a city that had been liable to so many miseries during this siege, that, had it always enjoyed as much happiness from its first foundation, it would certainly have been the envy of the world. Nor did it on any other account so much deserve these sore misfortunes as by producing such a generation of men as were the occasions of this its overthrow.

According to Josephus, the Roman soldiers grew furious with Jewish attacks and tactics and, against Titus' orders, set fire to an apartment adjacent to the Temple, which soon spread all throughout. Titus was furious as he had been looking for rich plunder but there was nothing, he could do about it. He set about destroying the rest of the city and slaying all the inhabitants; but the slaughter was too much even for the Romans and so Titus ordered that only those actually taking up arms against them should be slain.

Josephus Wars of the Jews Book 4 Chapter VIII

Now as soon as the army had no more people to slay or to plunder, because there remained none to be the objects of their fury (for they would not have spared any, had there remained any other work to be done), [Titus] Caesar gave orders that they should now demolish the entire city and Temple, but should leave as many of the towers standing as were of the greatest eminence; that is, Phasaelus, and

Hippicus, and Mariamne; and so much of the wall as enclosed the city on the west side.

Thus, take care of the affairs of Judea and ordered Pilate to go to Rome to answer before the Emperor to the accusations of the Jews. So Pilate made haste to Rome, but before he could get to Rome Tiberius was dead.

As a consequence Vitellus was well received when he visited Jerusalem but the accession of Caligula and the appointment of Herod Agrippa I changed everything. Caligula saw himself as a god and decreed he should be worshipped. The foreign minority in the city of Jamnia therefore set up an altar to Caligula. This outraged the Jewish majority who smashed the altar. The emperor retaliated by ordering a huge golden statue of Zeus erected in the Temple at Jerusalem and ordered that people worship it. The procurator Petronius, realising the impact this would have stalled and was fortunate in that Caligula was murdered and the order was quietly forgotten.

29.6 The Zealots

The Zealots were the fourth main sect in Palestine after the Pharisees, Saducees and Essenes, but whereas the others were merely unco-operative the zealots were active in trying to rid the country of the Romans. There were two main branches, the Sicarii, named for the short dagger they carried and the Stifos, for being the deceivers who led people into the desert.

The Sicarii were regarded as brigands and terrorists by the Romans and accused of all sorts of heinous crimes to which the Romans responded with their accustomed brutality. They were credited with having poisoned Herod Agrippa in 44 AD

When Paul was on trial a group of Jews, identified with the Zealots vowed to assassinate him.

Acts 23 12 - 22

[12] And when it was day, certain of the Jews banded together, and bound themselves under a curse, saying that they would neither eat nor drink till they had killed Paul.

[13] And they were more than forty which had made this conspiracy.

[14] And they came to the chief priests and elders, and said, We have bound ourselves under a great curse, that we will eat nothing until we have slain Paul.

[15] Now therefore ye with the council signify to the chief captain that he bring him down unto you tomorrow, as though ye would inquire something more perfectly concerning him: and we, or ever he come near, are ready to kill him.

[16] And when Paul's sister's son heard of their lying in wait, he went and entered into the castle, and told Paul.

[17] Then Paul called one of the centurions unto him, and said, Bring this young man unto the chief captain: for he hath a certain thing to tell him.

[18] So he took him, and brought him to the chief captain, and said, Paul the prisoner called me unto him, and prayed me to bring this young man unto thee, who hath something to say unto thee.

[19] Then the chief captain took him by the hand, and went with him aside privately, and asked him, What is that thou hast to tell me?

[20] And he said, The Jews have agreed to desire thee that thou wouldest bring down Paul tomorrow into the council, as though they would inquire somewhat of him more perfectly.

[21] But do not thou yield unto them: for there lie in wait for him of them more than forty men, which have bound themselves with an oath, that they will neither eat nor drink till they have killed him: and now are they ready, looking for a promise from thee.

[22] So the chief captain then let the young man depart, and charged him, See thou tell no man that thou hast shewed these things to me.

Over the next thirty or so years the activities of the Zealots turned pretty well to outright guerilla war with heavy casualties on both sides.

29.7 Masada

The Roman governor Gessius Florus was held responsible by Josephus for the final provocation of the Jews to rebel. In 66 AD Zealots seized Masada under Menachem but Eleazer murdered him in the Jerusalem Temple while he was praying with his bodyguard.

In the same year Cestius Gallus legate of Syria was defeated by the Zealots and retreated from Jerusalem losing 6,000 men in the rout and all his heavy catapults and rams and baggage. This defeat was seen by many as a positive omen that God was on their side.

In 67 AD Vespasian a veteran of wars in Britain was sent to Judea to crush the revolt. In 68 AD the monastery and community at Qumran was wiped out, with their library preserved in caves to become the Dead Sea Scrolls. On the 29th August 70 AD the city of Jerusalem was captured by Vespasian's son Titus.

Then in 73 AD Masada was captured. This was now a Zealot stronghold having been Herod's summer palace. The taking of Masada and the consequent suicide of the inhabitants is a story in itself; but it effectively saw the end of the Zealots as a major force.

Jerusalem had been totally destroyed: the Jewish state abolished and the Zealots eliminated. Palestine was now completely under the control of the Romans. The remaining Jews now fled to settlements all around the Roman Empire with large communities in Alexandria and Corinth which had previously been large Jewish centres. On the whole the Romans left them alone, preferring to focus their attentions on Christians and they generally prospered as traders and merchants. However they retained their religion and maintained the dream that some day they would return to Jerusalem.

Chapter 30 The Roman Empire

It is useful to look at the Roman World in the years leading up to Constantine and the Council of Nicea which made Christianity the official religion of the Empire. Christianity spread both from within the Jewish communities which had been dispersed around the Empire and from the evangelisation of pagan societies by the Apostles and their followers.

30.1 The Roman World

The Roman Empire reached its zenith around 117 AD under the Emperor Diocletian. It had spread from the Atlantic to the fringes of modern Iraq and from the Sahara desert to half way up Scotland. After this Rome was under pressure from all quarters and the Empire gradually retracted until the time of Constantine when it was found necessary to split into a western and an eastern empire, the latter focused on Constantinople.

Jews had established themselves in all parts of the Roman World, there were sizeable populations in almost all the major cities and centres of commerce. After the events of 70 AD and the destruction of the Temple it was these colonies which kept the Jewish faith alive.

They had already been recognised by Paul as fertile ground for the spread of Christianity and he personally visited many groups in his journeys. However, in most cases the word had reached these colonies before Paul's visit; but he established himself as their key link to the rest of Christendom, wrote epistles to many of them and essentially ensured that it was his version of Christianity which dominated the world in future. The church in Judea virtually disappeared, The Church in Alexandria developed into the Coptic church and the Gnostic tradition in Asia was so secretive and regarded as heretic that it too virtually disappeared.

The next two hundred years saw the church that Paul led suffer extreme persecution; but yet managing to spread throughout the Roman world to become the state religion of the Roman Empire. Building upon this position the church became the foundation of society in Europe which was generally known not as Europe but as Christendom until the Reformations of the sixteenth Century and thereafter becoming a major world religion as European trade and culture spread around the globe.

The key question is 'Why the persecution?' The Roman Empire was remarkably tolerant towards religions of all kinds and the reasons generally offered that it was because Christians refused to worship the Emperor begin to look pretty thin when one notes that Jews had also refused without incurring the same fate.

30.2 The Roman Empire

By the end of the first century the Roman Empire stretched from Britain in the northwest to Mesopotamia in the east and encompassed all the lands surrounding the Mediterranean. For the next few hundred years the Roman world would be characterised by three quite different but interacting features: the rule of law, trade and communications.

The rule of law tied the Empire together with both clear leadership and an army to enforce the leaders' rule. There would be many disputes and rival claimants for the positions of authority. The laws were often harsh and despotic; but there was a general acceptance that laws, whether imperial or local were there to be obeyed.

Apart from politics, trade was the keystone for the existence of the wealthier classes. They used their political influence to gain trade advantages, used the trade to build a fortune and then the fortune could be expended on enhancing one's political influence. Goods and services flowed along well established trade routes balancing supply and demand in a reasonably well regulated and well taxed economy.

The key to this all was communication. There were fleets of ships plying between ports in the Mediterranean and along the western shores. There were good roads with staging posts where horses could be changed, to bring messages and instructions to and from all corners of the Empire. A letter could reach Rome from almost anywhere within a matter of a week or two, there were many literates who could read and process the correspondence and keep records and troops could be moved readily over considerable distances in relatively short time.

Thus, the infrastructure was in place which enabled the church to spread the Gospel, to develop its theology and exert a considerable influence over the life of the Empire.

For the details of how this happened we have little more than the account by Eusebius written in the early fourth century and numerous local traditions. The names of many bishops, martyrs and saints have survived, many of the deeds ascribed to them are apocryphal; but we have enough to give at least a glimpse into the development of the church.

We have divided the Roman world into eight broad regions, not all of which would have been recognised in these times.

30.3 Italy

We will define this as roughly the modern country which of course included Rome. Paul wrote one epistle to the Romans. It grew to be the centre of the Christian world after the destruction of Jerusalem. As well as Peter and Paul there were many other 'fathers' of the Church, including Hippolytus.

30.4 Iberia

Iberia now consists of Spain and Portugal; but in the first and second centuries it referred to parts of the Balkans.

It would seem that Paul wanted to visit Spain after a visit to Rome. He identifies himself as the Apostle to the Gentiles who is intent on visiting Spain; but he writes to the Romans saying he will visit them on the way.

Romans 15 14 - 28
[14] And I myself also am persuaded of you, my brethren, that ye also are full of goodness, filled with all knowledge, able also to admonish one another.
[15] Nevertheless, brethren, I have written the more boldly unto you in some sort, as putting you in mind, because of the grace that is given to me of God,
[16]That I should be* the minister of Jesus Christ to the Gentiles, ministering the gospel of God, that the offering up of the Gentiles might be acceptable, being sanctified by the Holy Ghost.
[17] I have therefore whereof I may glory through Jesus Christ in those things which pertain to God.
[18] For I will not dare to speak of any of those things which Christ hath not wrought by me, to make the Gentiles obedient, by word and deed,

[19] Through mighty signs and wonders, by the power of the Spirit of God; so that from Jerusalem, and round about unto Illyricum, I have fully preached the gospel of Christ.

[20] Yea, so have I strived to preach the gospel, not where Christ was named, lest I should build upon another man's foundation:

[21] But as it is written, To whom he was not spoken of, they shall see: and they that have not heard shall understand.

[22] For which cause also I have been much hindered from coming to you.

[23] But now having no more place in these* parts, and having a great desire these many years to come unto you;

[24] Whensoever I take my journey into Spain, I will come to you: for I trust to see you in my journey, and to be brought on my way thitherward by you, if first I be somewhat filled with your company.

[25] But now I go unto Jerusalem to minister unto the saints.

[26] For it hath pleased them of Macedonia and Achaia to make a certain contribution for the poor saints which are at Jerusalem.

[27] It hath pleased them verily; and their debtors they are. For if the Gentiles have been made partakers of their spiritual things, their duty is also to minister unto them in carnal things.

[28] When therefore I have performed this, and have sealed to them this fruit, I will come by you into Spain.

It would seem from this that he intended the visit after he and Barnabus had visited Jerusalem for famine relief; (see section 22.8) but Luke makes no mention of the visit to Spain in Acts.

Spain seems to have been quite late in accepting Christianity and in 305 AD the report of the Synod of Elvira indicates that 'The church was greatly isolated from the general population'

30.5 Gaul

Gaul we will take as modern France but including the Netherlands and the parts of Germany and Switzerland running south of the Rhine.

There are many legends recording Mary Magdalene in Provence in the south of Gaul.

The first reference we have to Christianity in Gaul is the martyrdom of forty-eight in Lyon and reported by Eusebius. Lyon appears to have been the centre of Christianity but it spread throughout most of Gaul as recorded by Gregory of Tours.

30.6 Asia

Asia means all of Asia minor and the eastern Mediterranean including the Holy Land and reaching as far as the Euphrates Valley. Paul wrote one epistle to the Ephesians and one to each of the Hebrews, Colossians and Galatians.

Ignatius was bishop of Antioch in Syria at the beginning of the second Century and was taken to Rome to be martyred in 115 AD.

On the way he wrote letters to five other churches in Asia - Ephesus, Magnesia, Traites, Philadelphia and Smyrna. He also wrote to Polycarp, bishop of Smyrna, and to the church in Rome. Polycarp collected his letters and added one of his own. He is notable for presenting and arguing for the threefold ministry of bishops, priests and deacons indicating that this pattern was not as yet firmly established.

Justin was born in Palestine early in the second Century of Greek pagan parents. He is noted for a long debate with Trypho between 132 and 136 AD at Ephesus. In his Apologia addressed to the Emperor Antoninus Pius he sets out the basis for the Christian faith.

30.7 Africa

Africa runs from Egypt in the east to Morocco in the west and encompasses all the southern seaboard of the Mediterranean. Egypt and Alexandria in particular had been the base from which the Apostle Mark had conducted his evangelism. But there was another major centre of Christianity around Cyrene in present day Libya. In Egypt the Christians managed to distance themselves from the dominance of Rome to form the Coptic Church.

It is thought that Mark and John Mark are actually the same person and tradition is that he was born in Libya. This would tie in with the thought that Jesus was brought up in Alexandria with his earthly father Joseph and would return there with his new wife Mary Magdalene after his time with the Essene community at Qumran.

They would then go to live in the other Essene community in Libya where John Mark would be born. The family would return to Palestine when Jesus was ready to begin his mission, basing themselves in Nazareth and keeping close relations with Mary's family in Bethany.

John Mark returned to Alexandria after Peter and Paul were executed and became the leading figure in the Egyptian Church.

30.8 Britain

Britain includes the Celtic countries as well as the areas under Roman domination. As the place where Constantine was declared Emperor and the location for his conversion, Britain unwittingly played a crucial role in the development of the Church. There is no evidence of any sizeable Jewish colony in Britain so it must have been trade and social movement which brought Christianity to these shores.

In section 4.3 we have heard of the legend of Glastonbury which clearly, would have been a consequence of a trade link, but the more likely origins are to do with social movement particularly from members of the households of Roman officials who were posted to Britain and eventually settled there.

The earliest references are from Tertullian, writing around 200 AD and Origen writing around 240 AD. They indicate the Christianity had spread well beyond the parts of Britain accessible to Roman governance.
When Septimus Severus, the Roman Governor, was in Scotland in 208-9 AD, he left administration to Geta who tried and martyred St Alban at Verulanium. A short while later around 209 AD we hear of Julius and Aaron being martyred at Caerleon.

Places of Christian worship were destroyed during the reigns of emperors Diocletian and Galerius but there are no other traditions of martyrdom pre-Constantine.

In 314 AD three British Bishops attended the Council of Arles and it may be assumed that each of the twenty eight Roman cities had its bishop.

30.9 Greece

Greece will include modern Greece and the lands to its north as far as the Danube and Black Sea, including Constantinople and the Balkans. It will also include Cyprus, Crete and all the other islands of the eastern Mediterranean. Paul wrote two epistles to the Corinthians, two to the Thessalonians and one to the Phillipians.

The two key centres of Christianity were Corinth and Thessaloniki where Paul had visited; but the congregations had been established well beforehand. Their missionary work had extended to Albania and Bulgaria

30.10 Beyond the Roman Empire

It is reputed that Matthew took as his evangelistic area the territory of Parthia, modern Iran and he was supplemented by Thaddeus.

Thomas is reputed to have gone as far as India. Tradition has it that he visited in 52 AD and established seven congregations and that c189 AD Pantaenus arrived as a missionary from Alexandria.

Christianity also spread across the Rhine/Danube line to the countries of Central and Eastern Europe.

Chapter 31 - The Early Divines

I must acknowledge that the majority of this chapter is copied straight from the internet but I felt it worth adding as it gives a view of some of the key figures of the early church.

31.1 The Great Fathers

For the next 200 plus years the church expanded until Christianity became the official religion of the Roman Empire in 315 AD.

Where it expanded and how the church developed its theology and influence would fill several more books. However, that is mainly well recorded history. There were many quite different interpretations of the events of the first century mostly promulgated by scholars who were also leaders of the Church and not all beholden to Rome. In this chapter we mention a few of the more notable ones and recall some of their views on the developing theology.

We draw a line at around 350 AD just after Christianity became the official religion of the Roman Empire, thus we will not include most of what were regarded subsequently by the Church as the Great Fathers; but it is worthwhile to note them.

> Ambrose (340–397),
> Jerome (347–420),
> Augustine (354–430)
> Saint Gregory the Great (540–604)
> Basil the Great (c. 329–379)
> Athanasius (c. 296–373)
> Gregory of Nazianzus (329 – c. 389) and
> John Chrysostom (347–407)

31.2 Apostolic Fathers

The earliest Church Fathers, (within two generations of the Twelve Apostles of Christ) are usually called the Apostolic Fathers since tradition describes them as having been taught by the twelve. Important Apostolic Fathers include Clement of Rome, Ignatius of Antioch, Polycarp of Smyrna, and Papias of Hierapolis. In addition, the Didache and Shepherd of Hermas are usually placed among the writings of the Apostolic Fathers although their authors are unknown; like the works of Clement, Ignatius and Polycarp, they were first written in Koine Greek.

Clement of Rome

His epistle, 1 Clement (c. 96 AD), was copied and widely read in the early Church. Clement calls on the Christians of Corinth to maintain harmony and order. It is the earliest Christian text aside from the New Testament.

Ignatius of Antioch

Ignatius of Antioch (also known as Theophorus) (c. 35-110 AD) was the third bishop or Patriarch of Antioch and a student of the Apostle John. En route to his martyrdom in Rome, Ignatius wrote a series of letters which have been preserved. Important topics addressed in these letters include ecclesiology, the sacraments, the role of bishops, and the Incarnation of Christ. He is the second after Clement to mention Paul's epistles.

Polycarp of Smyrna

Polycarp of Smyrna (c. 69 – c.155 AD) was a Christian bishop of Smyrna (now İzmir in Turkey). It is recorded that he had been a disciple of "John." The options for this John are John, the son of Zebedee, traditionally viewed as the author of the Gospel of John, or John the Presbyter. Traditional advocates follow Eusebius in insisting that the apostolic connection of Polycarp was with John the Evangelist, and that he was the author of the Gospel of John, and thus the Apostle John.

Polycarp tried and failed to persuade Pope Anicetus to have the West celebrate Passover on fourteen Nisan, as in the East. Around 155 AD, the Smyrnans demanded Polycarp's execution as a Christian, and he died a martyr. The story of his martyrdom describes how the fire built around him would not burn him, and that when he was stabbed to death, so much blood issued from his body that it quenched the flames around him. Polycarp is recognized as a saint in both the Roman Catholic and Eastern Orthodox churches.

Papias of Hierapolis

Very little is known of Papias apart from what can be inferred from his own writings. He is described as "an ancient man who was a hearer of John and a companion of Polycarp" by Polycarp's disciple Irenaeus (c. 180 AD). Eusebius adds that Papias was Bishop of Hierapolis around the time of Ignatius of Antioch. In this office Papias was presumably succeeded by Abercius of Hierapolis. The name Papias was very common in the region, suggesting that he was probably a native of the area. The work of Papias is dated by most modern scholars to about 95–120 AD.

Despite indications that the work of Papias was still extant in the late Middle Ages, the full text is now lost. Extracts, however, appear in a number of other writings, some of which cite a book number

31.3 Greek Fathers

Those who wrote in Greek are called the Greek Fathers. In addition to the Apostolic Fathers, famous Greek Fathers include: Justin Martyr, Irenaeus of Lyons, Clement of Alexandria, Athanasius of Alexandria, John Chrysostom, Cyril of Alexandria, the Cappadocian Fathers (Basil of Caesarea, Gregory Nazianzus, Peter of Sebaste, Gregory of Nyssa), Maximus the Confessor, and John of Damascus.

Justin Martyr

Justin Martyr is regarded as the foremost interpreter of the theory of the Logos in the second century.

Irenaeus of Lyons

Irenaeus was bishop of Lugdunum in Gaul, which is now Lyon(s), France. His writings were formative in the early development of Christian theology, and he is recognized as a saint by both the Eastern Orthodox Church and the Roman Catholic Church. He was a notable early Christian apologist. He was also a disciple of Polycarp.

His best-known book, Against Heresies (c.180 AD) he enumerated heresies and attacked them. Irenaeus wrote that the only way for Christians to retain unity was to humbly accept one doctrinal authority - episcopal councils. Irenaeus proposed that the Gospels of Matthew, Mark, Luke and John all be accepted as canonical.

Clement of Alexandria

Clement of Alexandria was the first member of the church of Alexandria to be more than a name, and one of its most distinguished teachers. He united Greek philosophical traditions with Christian doctrine and valued Gnosis that with communion for all people could be held by common Christians. He developed a Christian Platonism. Like Origen, he arose from Catechetical School of Alexandria and was well versed in pagan literature.

Origen

Origen, or Origen Adamantius (c.185–c.254 AD) was a scholar and theologian. According to tradition, he was an Egyptian who taught in Alexandria, reviving the Catechetical School where Clement had taught. The patriarch of Alexandria at first supported Origen but later expelled him for being ordained without the patriarch's permission. He relocated to Caesarea Maritima and died there after being tortured during a persecution.

Using his knowledge of Hebrew, he produced a corrected Septuagint. He wrote commentaries on all the books of the Bible. In Peri Archon (First Principles), he articulated the first philosophical exposition of Christian doctrine. He interpreted scripture allegorically and showed himself to be a stoic, a Neo-Pythagorean, and a Platonist. Like Plotinus, he wrote that the soul passes through successive stages before incarnation as a human and after death, eventually reaching God. He imagined even demons being reunited with God.

For Origen, God was not Yahweh but the First Principle, and Christ, the Logos, was subordinate to him. His views of a hierarchical structure in the Trinity, the temporality of matter, "the fabulous preexistence of souls", and "the monstrous restoration which follows from it" were declared anathema in the sixth century. Because of his heretical views, Origen is technically not a Church Father by many definitions of that term but instead may simply be referred to as an ecclesiastical writer.

Athanasius of Alexandria

Athanasius is usually depicted with a book, an iconographic symbol of the importance of his writings. His Creed still appears in prayer books.

Athanasius of Alexandria (c.293 to 2 May 373 AD) was a theologian, Pope of Alexandria, and a noted Egyptian leader of the fourth century. He is remembered for his role in the conflict with Arianism and for his affirmation of the Trinity. At the First Council of Nicaea (325 AD), Athanasius argued against the Arian doctrine that Christ is of a distinct substance from the Father.

31.4 Cappadocian Fathers

The Cappadocian Fathers are Basil the Great (330–379 AD), who was bishop of Caesarea; Basil's younger brother Gregory of Nyssa (c.332–395 AD), who was bishop of Nyssa; and a close friend, Gregory of Nazianzus (329–389 AD), who became Patriarch of Constantinople. The Cappadocians promoted early Christian theology and are highly respected in both Western and Eastern churches as saints. They were a fourth-century monastic family, led by Saint Macrina the Younger (324–379 AD) to provide a central place for her brothers to study and meditate, and also to provide a peaceful shelter for their mother. Abbess Macrina fostered the education and development of her three brothers Basil the Great, Gregory of Nyssa and Peter of Sebaste (c.340 – 391 AD) who became bishop of Sebaste.

These scholars set out to demonstrate that Christians could hold their own in conversations with learned Greek-speaking intellectuals. They argued that Christian faith, while it was against many of the ideas of Plato and Aristotle (and other Greek Philosophers), it was an almost scientific and distinctive movement with the healing of the soul of man and his union with God at its centre. They made major contributions to the definition of the Trinity finalized at the First Council of Constantinople in 381 AD and the final version of the Nicene Creed.

Subsequent to the First Council of Nicea, Arianism did not simply disappear. The semi-Arians taught that the Son is of like substance with the Father (homoiousios), as against the outright Arians who taught that the Son was unlike the Father (heterousian). So the Son was held to be like the Father but not of the same essence as the Father. The Cappadocians worked to bring these semi-Arians back to the Orthodox cause. In their writings they made extensive use of the formula "three substances (hypostases) in one essence (homoousia)", and thus explicitly acknowledged a distinction between the Father and the Son (a distinction that Nicea had been accused of blurring) but at the same time insisting on their essential unity.

John Chrysostom

John Chrysostom (c.347 - c.407 AD), archbishop of Constantinople, is known for his eloquence in preaching and public speaking; his denunciation of abuse of authority by both ecclesiastical and political leaders, recorded sermons and writings making him the most prolific of the eastern fathers, and his ascetic sensibilities. After his death (or according to some sources, during his life) he was given the Greek epithet chrysostomos, meaning "golden mouthed", rendered in English as Chrysostom. Chrysostom is known within Christianity chiefly as a preacher and theologian, particularly in the Eastern Orthodox Church; he is the patron saint of orators in the Roman Catholic Church. Chrysostom is also noted for eight of his sermons that played a considerable part in the history of Christian antisemitism, diatribes against Judaizers composed while a presbyter in Antioch, which were extensively cited by the Nazis in their ideological campaign against the Jews.

31.5 Latin Fathers

Those fathers who wrote in Latin are called the Latin Fathers.

Tertullian

Quintus Septimius Florens Tertullianus (c.155–c.222 AD), who was converted to Christianity before 197 AD, was a prolific writer of apologetic, theological, controversial and ascetic works. He was born in Carthage, the son of a Roman centurion.

Tertullian denounced Christian doctrines he considered heretical, but later in life adopted Montanism, regarded as heretical by the mainstream Church, which prevented his canonization. He wrote three books in Greek and was the first great writer of Latin Christianity, thus sometimes known as the "Father of the Latin Church". He was evidently a lawyer in Rome. He is said to have introduced the Latin term trinitas with regard to the Divine (Trinity) to the Christian vocabulary.

In his Apologeticus, he was the first Latin author who qualified Christianity as the true religion, and systematically relegated the classical Roman Empire religion and other accepted cults to the position of mere "superstitions".

Later in life, Tertullian joined the Montanists, a heretical sect that appealed to his rigorism. He used the early church's symbol for fish - the Greek word for "fish" being Ictheos which is an acronym for Ιησοῦς Χριστός,

Θεοῦ Υἱός, Σωτήρ (Jesus Christ, God's Son, Saviour) - to explain the meaning of baptism since fish are born in water. He wrote that human beings are like little fish.

Cyprian of Carthage

Saint Cyprian (Thascius Caecilius Cyprianus) (died September 14, 258 AD) was bishop of Carthage and an important early Christian writer. He was born in North Africa, probably at the beginning of the third century, perhaps at Carthage, where he received an excellent classical (pagan) education. After converting to Christianity, he became a bishop and eventually died a martyr at Carthage. He emphasized the necessity of the unity of Christians with their bishops, and also the authority of the Roman See, which he claimed was the source of "priestly unity'".

Hilary of Poitiers

Hilary of Poitiers (c.300 – c.368 AD) was Bishop of Poitiers and is a Doctor of the Church. He was sometimes referred to as the "Hammer of the Arians" (Latin: Malleus Arianorum) and the "Athanasius of the West." His name comes from the Greek word for happy or cheerful. His optional memorial in the Roman Catholic calendar of saints is thirteenth January. In the past, when this date was occupied by the Octave Day of the Epiphany, his feast day was moved to the fourteenth January.

Ambrose of Milan

Saint Ambrose was an archbishop of Milan who became one of the most influential ecclesiastical figures of the fourth century. He is counted as one of the four original doctors of the Church. He offered a new perspective on the theory of atonement.

Pope Damasus I

Pope Damasus I (305 – 384 AD) was active in defending the Catholic Church against the threat of schisms. In two Roman synods (368 and 369 AD) he condemned the heresies of Apollinarianism and Macedonianism, and sent legates (papal representatives) to the First Council of Constantinople that was convoked in 381 AD to address these heresies. He also wrote in defence of the Roman See's authority, and inaugurated use of Latin in the Mass, instead of the Koine Greek that was still being used throughout the Church in the west in the liturgy.

Jerome of Stridonium

Jerome (c.347 - September 30, 420 AD) is best known as the translator of the Bible from Greek and Hebrew into Latin. He also was a Christian apologist. Jerome's edition of the Bible, the Vulgate, is still an important text of Catholicism. He is recognised by the Roman Catholic Church as a Doctor of the Church.

31.6 Syriac Fathers

A few Church Fathers wrote in Syriac; many of their works were also widely translated into Latin and Greek.

Aphrahat

Aphrahat (c. 270–c. 345 AD) was a Syriac-Christian author of the third century from the Adiabene region of Northern Mesopotamia, which was within the Persian Empire, who composed a series of twenty-three expositions or homilies on points of Christian doctrine and practice. He was born in Persia around 270 AD, but all his known works, the Demonstrations, come from later on in his life. He was an ascetic and celibate, and was almost definitely a son of the covenant (an early Syriac form of communal monasticism). He may have been a bishop, and later Syriac tradition places him at the head of Mar Matti monastery near Mosul, in what is now northern Iraq. He was a near contemporary to the slightly younger Ephrem the Syrian, but the latter lived within the sphere of the Roman Empire. Called the Persian Sage Aphrahat witnesses to the concerns of the early church beyond the eastern boundaries of the Roman Empire.

Ephrem the Syrian

Ephrem the Syrian (ca. 306 – 373 AD) was a Syriac deacon and a prolific Syriac-language hymnographer and theologian of the fourth century from the region of Syria. His works are hailed by Christians throughout the world, and many denominations venerate him as a saint. He has been declared a Doctor of the Church in Roman Catholicism. He is especially beloved in the Syriac Orthodox Church.

Ephrem wrote a wide variety of hymns, poems, and sermons in verse, as well as prose biblical exegesis. These were works of practical theology for the edification of the church in troubled times. So popular were his works, that, for centuries after his death, Christian authors wrote hundreds of pseudepigraphal works in his name. He has been called the most significant of all of the fathers of the Syriac-speaking church tradition.

Isaac of Antioch

The author of many homilies and poems. It is difficult to identify him specifically as he was writing about happenings for most of the 5th century. He wrote about games in 404, and earthquake in 459 and is believed to be a priest who travelled widely.

31.7 Desert Fathers

The Desert Fathers were early monastics living in the Egyptian desert; although they did not write as much, their influence was also great. Among them are Anthony the Great and Pachomius. Many of their, usually short, sayings are collected in the Apophthegmata Patrum *("Sayings of the Desert Fathers").*

32 Constantine and Nicea

The conversion of Emperor Constantine marks a radical change in the position of Christianity in the Roman world. He made it the official religion of the Roman Empire and established Rome as the geographical focal point of Christianity.

It was also around this time that many controversies were resolved including the determination of Easter and the Canon of the New Testament.

He called two great Councils of the Church to discuss many of these issues and these are dealt with in this chapter. However, there were still many dissenting voices and these alternative traditions will be dealt with in Chapter 33

32.1 Constantine

Flavius Valerius Aurelius Constantinus was born in Naissus around 272 AD. He is more generally known as Constantine the Great and was Roman Emperor from 306 to 337 AD. He was the first Roman Emperor to embrace Christianity, reportedly after seeing a cross of light in the sky during the battle of Milvian Ridge, but more likely under the influence of his mother Helena.

The great persecution of Christians had been ended in 311 AD with an edict of toleration which granted the right of Christians to practice their religion. Two years later in the Edict of Milan he restored property which had been confiscated from the church.

32.2 The First Council of Nicea

The First Council of the Church was convened by Emperor Constantine the Great upon the recommendations of a synod led by Hosius of Córdoba in the Eastertide of 325 AD. This synod had been charged with investigation of the trouble brought about by the Arian controversy in the Greek-speaking east. To most bishops, the teachings of Arius were heretical and dangerous to the salvation of souls. In the summer of 325 AD, the bishops of all provinces were summoned to Nicaea, a place reasonably accessible to many delegates, particularly those of Asia Minor, Georgia, Armenia, Syria, Palestine, Egypt, Greece, and Thrace.

Constantine had invited all 1,800 bishops of the Christian church within the Roman Empire (about 1,000 in the east and 800 in the west), but a smaller and unknown number attended. Eusebius of Caesarea counted more than 250, Athanasius of Alexandria counted 318, and Eustathius of Antioch estimated "about 270" (all three were present at the council). Later, Socrates Scholasticus recorded more than 300, and Evagrius, Hilary of Poitiers, Jerome, Dionysius Exiguus, and Rufinus recorded 318. This number 318 is preserved in the liturgies of the Eastern Orthodox Church and the Coptic Orthodox Church of Alexandria.

Delegates came from every region of the Roman Empire, including Britain. The participating bishops were given free travel to and from their episcopal sees to the council, as well as lodging. These bishops did not travel alone; each one had permission to bring with him two priests and three deacons, so the total number of attendees could have been above 1,800. Eusebius speaks of an almost innumerable host of accompanying priests, deacons, and acolytes.

The Eastern bishops formed the great majority. Of these, the first rank was held by the patriarchs: Alexander of Alexandria and Eustathius of Antioch. Many of the assembled fathers - for instance, Paphnutius of Thebes, Potamon of Heraclea, and Paul of Neocaesarea - had stood forth as confessors of the faith and came to the council with the marks of persecution on their faces. Historically, the influence of these marred confessors has been seen as substantial, but recent scholarship has called this into question.

32.3 The Arian Controversy

The Arian controversy arose in Alexandria when the newly reinstated presbyter Arius began to spread doctrinal views that were contrary to those of his bishop, St. Alexander of Alexandria. The disputed issues centred on the natures and relationship of God (the Father) and the Son of God (Jesus). The disagreements sprang from different ideas about the Godhead and what it meant for Jesus to be God's Son. Alexander maintained that the Son was divine in just the same sense that the Father is, coeternal with the Father, else he could not be a true Son.

Arius emphasized the supremacy and uniqueness of God the Father, meaning that the Father alone is almighty and infinite, and that therefore the Father's divinity must be greater than the Son's. Arius taught that the Son had a beginning, and that he possessed neither the eternity nor the true divinity of the Father, but was rather made "God" only by the Father's permission and power, and that the Son was rather the very first and the most perfect of God's creatures.

The Arian discussions and debates at the council extended from about May 20, 325 AD, through to about June 19. According to legendary accounts, debate became so heated that at one point, Arius was struck in the face by Nicholas of Myra, who would later be canonized. This account is almost certainly apocryphal, as Arius himself would not have been present in the council chamber due to the fact that he was not a bishop.

Much of the debate hinged on the difference between being "born" or "created" and being "begotten". Arians saw these as essentially the same; followers of Alexander did not. The exact meaning of many of the words used in the debates at Nicaea were still unclear to speakers of other languages. Greek words like "essence" (ousia), "substance" (hypostasis), "nature" (physis), "person" (prosopon) bore a variety of meanings drawn from pre-Christian philosophers, which could not but entail misunderstandings until they were cleared up. The word homoousia, in particular, was initially disliked by many bishops because of its associations with Gnostic heretics (who used it in their theology), and because their heresies had been condemned at the 264–268 AD Synods of Antioch.

32.4 The Nicene Creed

Thus, instead of a baptismal creed acceptable to both the Arians and their opponents the council promulgated one which was clearly opposed to Arianism and incompatible with the distinctive core of their beliefs. The text of this profession of faith is preserved in a letter of Eusebius to his congregation, in Athanasius, and elsewhere. Although the most vocal of anti-Arians, the Homoousians (from the Koine Greek word translated as "of same substance" which was condemned at the Council of Antioch in 264–268 AD) were in the minority, the Creed was accepted by the council as an expression of the bishops' common faith and the ancient faith of the whole Church.

Bishop Hosius of Cordova, one of the firm Homoousians, may well have helped bring the council to consensus. At the time of the council, he was the confidant of the emperor in all Church matters. Hosius stands at the head of the lists of bishops, and Athanasius ascribes to him the actual formulation of the creed. Great leaders such as Eustathius of Antioch, Alexander of Alexandria, Athanasius, and Marcellus of Ancyra all adhered to the Homoousian position.

In spite of his sympathy for Arius, Eusebius of Caesarea adhered to the decisions of the council, accepting the entire creed. The initial number of bishops supporting Arius was small. After a month of discussion, on June 19, there were only two left: Theonas of Marmarica in Libya, and Secundus of Ptolemais. Maris of Chalcedon, who initially supported Arianism, agreed to the whole creed. Similarly, Eusebius of Nicomedia and Theognis of Nice also agreed, except for certain statements.

The Emperor carried out his earlier statement: everybody who refused to endorse the Creed would be exiled. Arius, Theonas, and Secundus refused to adhere to the creed, and were thus exiled to Illyria, in addition to being excommunicated. The works of Arius were ordered to be confiscated and consigned to the flames, while his supporters considered as "enemies of Christianity." Nevertheless, the controversy continued in various parts of the empire.

The Creed was amended to a new version by the First Council of Constantinople in 381 AD.

32.5 The Dating of Easter

The feast of Easter is linked to the Jewish Passover and Feast of Unleavened Bread, as Christians believe that the crucifixion and resurrection of Jesus occurred at the time of those observances.

As early as Pope Sixtus I, some Christians had set Easter to a Sunday in the lunar month of Nisan. To determine which lunar month was to be designated as Nisan, Christians relied on the Jewish community. By the later third century some Christians began to express dissatisfaction with what they took to be the disorderly state of the Jewish calendar. They argued that contemporary Jews were identifying the wrong lunar month as the month of Nisan, choosing a month whose fourteenth day fell before the spring equinox.

Christians, these thinkers argued, should abandon the custom of relying on Jewish informants and instead do their own computations to determine which month should be styled Nisan, setting Easter within this independently computed, Christian Nisan, which would always locate the festival after the equinox. They justified this break with tradition by arguing that it was in fact the contemporary Jewish calendar that had broken with tradition by ignoring the equinox, and that in former times the fourteenth of Nisan had never preceded the equinox. Others felt that the customary practice of reliance on the Jewish calendar should continue, even if the Jewish computations were in error from a Christian point of view.

The controversy between those who argued for independent computations and those who argued for continued reliance on the Jewish calendar was formally resolved by the Council, which endorsed the independent procedure that had been in use for some time at Rome and Alexandria. Easter was henceforward to be a Sunday in a lunar month chosen according to Christian criteria - in effect, a Christian Nisan - not in the month of Nisan as defined by Jews. Those who argued for continued reliance on the Jewish calendar (called "protopaschites" by later historians) were urged to come around to the majority position. That they did not all immediately do so is revealed by the existence of sermons, canons, and tracts written against the protopaschite practice in the later fourth century.

These two rules, independence of the Jewish calendar and worldwide uniformity, were the only rules for Easter explicitly laid down by the Council. No details for the computation were specified; these were worked out in practice, a process that took centuries and generated a number of controversies. In particular, the Council did not seem to decree that Easter must fall on Sunday.

Nor did the Council decree that Easter must never coincide with Nisan fourteen (the first Day of Unleavened Bread, now commonly called "Passover") in the Hebrew calendar. By endorsing the move to independent computations, the Council had separated the Easter computation from all dependence, positive or negative, on the Jewish calendar. The "Zonaras proviso", the claim that Easter must always follow Nisan fourteen in the Hebrew calendar, was not formulated until after some centuries. By that time, the accumulation of errors in the Julian solar and lunar calendars had made it the de facto state of affairs that Julian Easter always followed Hebrew Nisan fourteen.

32.6 Canon Law

The council promulgated twenty new church laws, called canons, (though the exact number is subject to debate), that is, unchanging rules of discipline. The twenty as listed in the Nicene and Post-Nicene Fathers are as follows:

1. Prohibition of self-castration

2. Establishment of a minimum term for catechumens (persons studying for baptism)

3. Prohibition of the presence in the house of a cleric of a younger woman who might bring him under suspicion

4. Ordination of a bishop in the presence of at least three provincial bishops and confirmation by the metropolitan bishop

5. Provision for two provincial synods to be held annually

6. Confirmation of ancient customs giving jurisdiction over large regions to the bishops of Alexandria, Rome, and Antioch

7. Recognition of the honorary rights of the see of Jerusalem

8. Provision for agreement with the Novatianists, an early sect

9–14. Provision for mild procedure against the lapsed during the persecution under Licinius

15–16. Prohibition of the removal of priests

17. Prohibition of usury among the clergy

18. Precedence of bishops and presbyters before deacons in receiving the Eucharist (Holy Communion)

19. Declaration of the invalidity of baptism by Paulian heretics

20. Prohibition of kneeling on Sundays and during the Pentecost (the fifty days commencing on Easter). Standing was the normative posture for prayer at this time, as it still is among the Eastern Christians. Kneeling was considered most appropriate to penitential prayer, as distinct from the festive nature of Eastertide and its remembrance every Sunday. The canon itself was designed only to ensure uniformity of practise at the designated times.

Chapter 33 - Other Traditions

The previous chapter has charted what became the Catholic Church, based in Rome and taking over many of the roles of the former Western Roman Empire to form a supra- national state which we refer to as Christendom. However in the period we are covering, i.e. the first two centuries after Jesus' birth, there were many other movements, some of which like the Coptic Church survived the takeover of the Eastern Empire by Islam and remain in existence today, and some which were not content with the doctrines emanating from Rome and were developing their own doctrines and theology.

33.1 Religion

To understand these movements, we need to go back to the core of the concept of religion. We can define a *religion as a response of man to the wonders of the world around him allied to a real sense that there is something more to life than mere biological existence*. Most religions recognise a spiritual dimension to life and, in one way or another, the concept of a 'soul' which leaves the body at death.

Virtually all religions follow the same pattern:

> Someone, the founder, has an idea and turns it into a mission, occasionally writing down his idea

> The founder gathers around him a body of supporters and followers

> Someone organises the group in some way with a hierarchy of responsibilities and authority.

> The founder dies and his supporters write down what they can remember of the founder's ideas.

> In order to preserve the group, the founder's successors elaborate on the initial idea and set rules of conduct for followers to adhere to.

Failure to follow the rules is to be punished in the afterlife and adhering to them becomes a guarantee of success in the afterlife.

Mankind is divided into three categories, 'Adherents' who are guaranteed the success in the afterlife, 'Potential Converts' who might be brought into the fold and 'The Damned'

Usually, these movements develop from a precursor movement and accept some of the previous rules and doctrines but diverge on a number of key points. Thus one can see mainstream Christianity developing from Judaism and Protestant churches developing from the Roman Catholic Church

The divergences tend to develop from three main sources:

New philosophical thought

Adaptation to suit local circumstances

Rejection of Authority

It is the reaction of the central authority that is critical. The usual reaction to a new philosophical idea is to denounce it as heresy and then gradually allow it to decay or come to a compromise and accept some of the new ideas. With local adaptation a compromise is almost forced, as the central authority usually can either force a separation or accept the situation as a fact of life. When authority is rejected however, this almost always results in a complete breakdown of relations. We will use these three headings to follow some of the major alternative traditions.

33.2 New Philosophical Thought

The first and second centuries were filled with people who had been made to think more deeply about theological matters after Christianity had impinged upon them. These usually came from one or other of two backgrounds; Judaism and Greek Platonism.

One key group of beliefs is termed Gnosticism. This is very difficult to define in simple terms, but at the heart of it is the concept of a God who communicates to the world through various divine intermediaries, sometimes called 'angels' who guide men to reject creation as the work of the devil and purify their minds so as to attain eternal bliss.

33.3 Adaptation to suit Local Circumstances

In the very early years of the church the Apostles were sent to various countries to evangelize. The Church in Palestine under James was virtually wiped out by the diaspora, whereas the church In Egypt developed many unique features which generated the Coptic and Ethiopic traditions. In Syria and other parts of Asia Minor groups of Christians formed churches such as the Armenian or kept within a language group, developing their own traditions and practices.

The Gnostics were another group who had quite different philosophical approaches to the nature of religion and became almost a secret society.

Perhaps the most intriguing alternative tradition is the one that developed in southern France (Gaul as it was then) which was based on the legend that Mary Magdalene escaped persecution and fled to the area with Jesus' son, John Mark, to establish a dynasty which ruled Gaul for many centuries. The Albigensian heresy still sits at the heart of all the speculations relating to Rennes les Chateaux and the Templars.

A further adaptation relates to the distinction between 'culture' and 'religion'. Many evangelists tried to establish a religion based upon their practices and habits, or those of the community they were evangelising. Often the matter of diet or dress would appear. These are essentially cultural matters and relate very much to local climate conditions, but the religious zealots tried to make them religious matters and searched their scriptures for rulings on the matter which they then interpreted for their adherents as outward and visible signs of belonging.

We see examples such as eating fish on Fridays which was a Roman Catholic rule until fairly recently or making women wear veils which was imposed upon Iran after the return of the Ayatollas who found that the majority of women had changed their culture due to western influences.

Further examples can be found in the USA as various sects invented scriptoral reasons for not giving blood transfusions or not using iron.

33.4 Rejection of Authority

The second source of alternative tradition comes from churches which would not accept the Roman Catholic supremacy of the Vatican and the successors of Peter and Paul. The big split took place in the tenth century when the Eastern Orthodox churches were formed and another in the sixteenth century when Martin Luther listed his Articles.

There were great debates in Britain in the fourth to sixth centuries as vestiges of early Celtic Christianity vied with bishops such as Augustine and Birinus over such matters as the dating of Easter which were not resolved until the Synod of Whitby in 664 AD.

33.5 Finale

Well! We have come to the end. This has not been an academic treatise neither has it been an accurate historical tale. Rather it has been an attempt to get you to read the Bible in perspective, comparing different accounts and thinking about the realities of life in the first centuries. Few of the writers were concerned with history, what counted was the message and the same can be said for pretty well all of the sacred texts of the many religions of the world.

During my lifetime I have been fortunate and privileged to visit places well outside he Christian world and to meet with people with a very different faith to my own. Among them have been people who are so committed to their faith that they are ready to destroy people of other faiths, or even minor variations of their own and we have seen these intolerances result in persecution and worse over the centuries.

I must confess to having refused sacraments from people I regarded as unqualified and to be refused by those who thought me unqualified. I have seen of late, people move away from organised religion; but yet when a crisis comes they are in the forefront of helping their fellows. As I write we are in the throes of the covid19 pandemic and the reaction of almost everyone shows how Jesus' message has been understood. There is hope for the world.

When one looks back in history to see the wars and persecutions occasioned by attempts to impose faith upon religion and religion upon culture, the words of Jesus *'Love God and your neighbour as yourself'* should have been taken more notice of.

Appendices

Appendix 1 - Bibliography

This is not a comprehensive bibliography that one might find in a scholarly work. Rather it is a list of books that have have influenced me and to which I have referred.

Appendix 2 - Index to quotations

This tells you where to find quotations from the four Gospels and the Acts and also lists those quotations from other books of the New Testament and early historians.

Appendix 3 - General Index

This will guide you to text about people, places, events and other topics; but is not an index to the quotations.

Bibliography

Before I list some of the books that have influenced me or to which I have referred, I must first pay tribute to the internet and all those people who have written articles and placed copies of texts where everyone can access them. I have been particularly grateful to those who have placed copies of texts on the internet which I have copied. I apologize if I have infringed anyone's copyright but having played around with this project for some 15 years I simply cannot recall where I got the majority of the material from.

Over the years my book list has been depleted as I pass most of my theological books to Douai Abbey library - the best such library in Britain.

One of the problems of books about the Bible and early Christianity is to understand where the writer is coming from. Some are dedicated atheists determined to discredit it. At the other extreme are fundamentalists who will use the most devious arguments to explain away inconsistencies.

First of all, Bible Versions

> King James Bible
>> *I am still using the copy presented to me at school in 1946*
>
> The Jerusalem Bible
>> *Dating from 1966 very well set out and packed with notes and a chronological table*
>
> The New English Bible
>> *Dating from 1962 and the best English version I have come across*
>
> The Good News Bible
>> *An attempt to present the bible in everyday language.*
>
> The Amplified New Testament -
>> *Lockman Foundation 1958*
>
> The Qur'an - English translation ed by A B al-Mehri 2010
>> *It was a delight to be presented with this and be able to read it for myself*

The Gospel according to St John
> *I include this small pocket-sized booklet which was issued to soldiers engaged in the First World War and gave great comfort to many men.*

Uncover - See for yourself
> *The Gospel of Luke asking questions which are answered from a Christian Union website www.uncover.org.uk*

Reference books

Halley's Bible Handbook 1927
> *A most useful reference book*

Strong's Exhaustive Concordance 1894
> *An incredible index to the King James Version, even to indexing 'and'*

The World's Religions by Ninian Smart 1989
> *A summary of the religions that have been followed by man*

The Concise Oxford Dictionary of the Christian Church 1977
> *Ed E A Livingstone - very useful for getting some additional information.*

William Neil's One volume Bible Commentary 1962
> *Full of useful background information*

Nelson's Bible Concordance Bible Mapbook 1985
> *By Simon Jenkins - very useful for seeing relationships between places.*

Other Books

The Early History of the Christian Church by Louis Duchesne in three volumes 1905

The Works of Flavius Josephus tr William Whiston 1906

The Four Gospels in one story by Freeman Wills Croft 1949

Verdict on Jesus by Leslie Badham 1950

Eusebius - The History of the Church ed G A Williamson 1965

The Early Church by Henry Chadwick 1967

A History of Christianity by Paul Johnson 1976

The writings of the New Testament by Luke T Johnson 1986

Science and Religion by John Hedley Brooke 1991

The unauthorized version by Robin Lane-Fox 1991

The Oxford History of Christianity ed John McManners 1993

The Jesus Papyrus by Carsten Peter Thiede & Matthew D'Ancona 1996

The Jesus Mysteries by Timothy Freke and Peter Gandy 1999

The Bible in History by Thomas L Thompson 1999
A History of Christianity by Diarmaid MacCulloch 2009
The Greatest Show on Earth by Richard Dawkins 2009

Appendix 2 - Index to quotations

This index will indicate where in the text you can find a particular quotation from the bible or from another source. It is arranged by book and then chapter. To the right of the range of verses you will find a code which indicates Chapter - Section and sequence within section.

Note that not all the text of the Acts and the four Gospels have been quoted. In particular the preaching of Jesus is omitted.

MATTHEW

Chapter 20

17-19	15.5a

Chapter 21

5-Jan	14.1c
11-Jun	14.2b
13-Dec	7.2c
18 - 22	14.4b
23 - 27	14.6c
28 - 43	11.1c

Chapter 22

14-Jan	11.2a
15 - 22	14.7c
15 - 22	10.12a
23 - 28	10.3a
23 -33	14.8c
29 - 33	10.3b
34 - 46	14.9a

Chapter 23

Jan-39	14.9c

Chapter 24

2-Jan	14.11c
43 - 51	11.5a

Chapter 25

13-Jan	11.6a
14 - 30	11.4a
31 - 46	11.7a

Chapter 26

13-Jun	13.3c
14 - 16	15.2a
17 - 19	16.1a
26 - 29	16.2a
30 - 35	17.1a
36 - 46	17.2a
47 - 50	17.4d
50 - 56	17.5d
57 - 68	18.3a
69 - 75	18.4e

Chapter 27

2-Jan	18.5a
10-Mar	18.9a
14-Nov	18.5d
15 - 18	18.6b
19	18.8a
20 - 23	18.8c
24 - 26	18.8e
27 - 31	18.7b
32	19.1a
33 - 34	19.2a
35 - 38	19.1b
39 - 44	19.5a
45 - 49	19.6a
50 - 54	19.7b
57 - 61	20.2b
62 - 66	20.3a

Chapter 28

7-Jan	20.4b
10-Aug	20.5b
15-Nov	20.6a
16 - 20	20.12a

MARK

Luke

Chapter 1

25-May	3.1b
26 - 56	2.4d
57 - 80	3.1c

Chapter 2

1 – 7	2.5a
8 – 20	2.6a
21 - 24	2.7a
25 - 38	2.7b
41 - 52	4.1a

Chapter 3

20-Jan	3.2c
21 - 22	3.3b
23 - 38	2.9b

Chapter 4

13-Jan	4.6c

Chapter 6

5-Jan	10.5d
11-Jun	10.5g
13 - 16	6.5c

Chapter 7

35 - 39	13.3d
36 - 50	5.5b
39 - 50	13.3e

Chapter 8

3-Jan	5.3a
22 - 25	9.4a

Chapter 9

17-Oct	9.2d
28 - 36	9.6a

Chapter 10

38 - 42	5.5a

Chapter 18

35 - 43	8.10g

Chapter 19

28 - 35	14.1b
36 - 44	14.2c
45 - 46	7.2d

Chapter 20

8-Jan	14.6d
18-Sep	11.1b
21 - 26	14.7b
27 - 38	14.8b
39 - 47	14.10a

Chapter 21

4-Jan	11.3b
6-May	14.11b

Chapter 22

6-Jan	15.2c
13-Jul	16.1c
14 - 16	16.3a
17 - 20	16.2c
21 - 30	16.4a
31 - 34	15.6b

35 - 38	16.4b
39 - 46	17.2c
47 - 51	17.4c
52 - 54	17.5c
54 - 62	18.4c
66 - 71	18.3c

Chapter 23

1	18.3c
7-Jan	18.5f
9-Aug	18.5g
12-Oct	18.5h
13 - 25	18.6d
26 - 34	19.1e
34	19.3d
35 - 43	19.5c
44 - 49	19.7d

Chapter 24

13 - 32	20.8b
33 - 43	20.9c
44- 53	20.11a

Chapter 29

21-25	14.7b

JOHN

Chapter 1

4-Jan	10.8a
5-Jan	2.9c
9-Jun	3.3d
15	3.3e
19 - 28	3.4a
29 - 31	3.4b
32 - 34	3.3f
35 - 39	3.4c
40 - 42	6.5d
43 - 44	6.5j
45 - 51	6.5k

Chapter 2

11-Jan	5.4a
12-Nov	7.1a
13 - 16	7.2a
17 - 25	7.3a

Chapter 3

21-Jan	7.4a
22 - 24	3.5a
22 - 36	7.5a
25 - 36	3.5b

Chapter 4

3-Jan	7.5a
4-Jan	3.5c
26-Apr	7.6a
27 - 38	7.6b
39 - 44	7.6c
45 - 46	7.7a
46 - 54	8.3a

Chapter 5

15-Jan	8.4a
15 - 47	10.5a
39 - 47	10.9a

Chapter 6

15-Jan	9.2b
14 - 15	7.10a
16 - 24	9.3a
22 - 23	9.3d
22 - 26	7.13a
27 - 40	7.14a
41 - 59	7.14b
60 - 66	7.14c
67 - 71	7.14d

Chapter 7

9-Jan	12.1a
31-Oct	12.1b
32 - 36	12.1c
37 - 39	12.1d
40 - 44	12.1e
45 - 52	12.1f
53	12.2a

Chapter 8

11-Jan	12.2a
20-Dec	14.6a
30-Dec	12.3a
31 - 47	12.3b
48 - 59	12.3c

Chapter 9

7-Jan	8.10b
17-Aug	8.10c
18 - 23	8.10d
24 - 34	8.10e
35 - 41	8.10f

Chapter 10

18-Jan	11.8a
19 - 21	12.3d
22 - 39	12.4a
40 - 42	12.5a

Chapter 11

5-Jan	9.7a
16-Jun	9.7b
17-28	9.7c
27 - 37	9.7d
38 - 44	9.7e
45 - 54	12.6a
55 - 57	12.7a

Chapter 12

1	13.2a
8-Feb	13.3a
8-Jan	5.5d
11-Sep	13.2b
15-Dec	14.2a
20-36	14.5a

Chapter 13

17-Jan	17.2a
2-Jan	15.3a

17-Mar	15.4a	12-Aug	18.8d
18 - 22	15.5a	13 - 16	18.8f
23 - 27	15.5b	17 - 22	19.1b
28 - 30	15.5c	23 - 24	19.3a
36 - 38	15.6a	25 - 27	19.4a
		28 - 30	19.7a

Chapter 14

		31 - 37	20.1a
14-Jan	16.3b	38 - 42	20.2a
15 - 31	16.3c		

Chapter 20

Chapter 15

		8-Jan	20.4a
9-Jan	16.3d	18-Oct	20.5a
27-Oct	16.3e	19 - 23	20.7a
		24 - 25	20.9a

Chapter 17

		26 - 29	20.9b
3-Jan	10.8b	30 - 31	20.14a

Chapter 18

Chapter 21

		23-Jan	20.13a
1	17.3a	24 - 25	20.14b
9-Feb	17.4a		
11-Oct	17.4b		
13-Dec	17.5a		
14	18.2a		
15 - 18	18.4a		
19 - 24	18.2b		
25 - 27	18.4d		
28 - 32	18.5b		
33 - 38	18.5c		
39 - 40	18.6a		

Chapter 19

3-Jan	18.7a
7-Apr	18.8b

ACTS

Chapter 1

5-Jan	21.1a
14-Jun	21.2a
15 - 26	21.3a

Chapter 2

13-Jan	21.4a
14 - 36	21.4b
37 - 41	21.4c
42 - 47	21.4d

Chapter 3

10-Jan	21.6a
16-Nov	21.6b

Chapter 4

4-Jan	21.7a
20-May	21.7b
21 - 22	21.7c
23 - 31	21.7d
32 - 35	21.11a
36 - 37	21.11b

Chapter 5

12-Jan	21.11b
13 - 16	21.11c
17 - 26	21.8a
27 - 32	21.8b
33 - 39	21.8c
40 - 42	21.8d

Chapter 6

7-Jan	21.9a
15-Aug	21.10a

Chapter 7

Jan-53	21.10b
54 - 60	21.10c

Chapter 8

3-Jan	21.16a
8-Apr	21.16b
13-Sep	21.16c
14 - 25	21.17a
20 - 22	22.1d
26 - 40	21.18a

Chapter 9

9-Jan	22.1a
19-Oct	22.1c
20 - 22	22.1d
23 - 30	22.2a
31 - 35	22.3a
36 - 43	22.3b

Chapter 10

8-Jan	22.4a
16-Sep	22.4b
17 - 43	22,4c
44 - 48	22.5a

Chapter 11

3-Jan	22.5b
17-Apr	22.5c
18	22.5d
19 - 30	22.6a

Chapter 12

5-Jan	21.14a
11-Jun	21.14b
17-Nov	05.6a
12-Nov	21.12a
17-Dec	21.15a
18 - 19	21.14c
20 - 25	21.15b
21 - 23	21.19b
24 - 25	21.15c
24 - 25	22.6b

Chapter 13

3-Jan	23.1a
12-Apr	23.2a
13	21.19c
13 - 16	23.3a
17 - 41	23.3b
42 - 43	23.3c
44 - 52	23.3d

Chapter 14

7-Jan	23.4a
20-Aug	23.5a

21 - 23	23.6a				
24 - 28	23.7a				

Chapter 19

12-Jan	24.11a
13 - 20	24.12a
21 - 22	24.13a
23 - 41	24.14a

Chapter 24

9-Jan	26.6a
21-Oct	26.6b
22 - 26	26.6c
27	26.7a

Chapter 15

2-Jan	23.8a
29-Mar	23.9a
30 - 35	23.10a
36 - 41	21.19d
36 - 41	24.1a

Chapter 20

6-Jan	25.1a
12-Jul	25.1b
13 - 30	25.2a

Chapter 25

5-Jan	26.7a
12-Jun	26.7b
13 - 21	26.8a
22 - 27	26.8b

Chapter 16

5-Jan	24.1a
10-Jun	24.2a
15-Nov	24.3a
16 - 24	24.3b
25 - 34	24.3c
35 - 40	24.3d

Chapter 21

6-Jan	25.3a
14-Jul	25.4a
15 - 17	26.1a
18 - 26	26.1b
27 - 32	26.2a
32 - 36	26.2b
37 - 39	26.2c
40	26.3a

Chapter 26

8-Jan	26.8b
18-Sep	26.8c
19 - 32	26.8d

Chapter 17

9-Jan	24.4a
14-Oct	24.5a
15 - 21	24.6a
22 - 34	24.6b

Chapter 22

21-Jan	26.3a
22 - 29	26.3b
30	26.4a

Chapter 27

8-Jan	27.1a
10-Sep	27.2a
12-Nov	27.2b
13 - 20	27.2c
21 - 26	27.2d
27 - 38	27.2e
39 - 44	27.3a

Chapter 18

4-Jan	24.7a
11-May	24.7b
17-Dec	24.7c
18 - 19	24.8a
20 - 23	24.9a
24 - 28	24.10a

Chapter 23

5-Jan	26.4a
11-Jun	26.4b
22-Dec	29.6a
15-Dec	26.5a
16 - 35	26.5b

Chapter 28

10-Jan	27.3b
15-Nov	27.4a
16 - 31	27.5a

Other Sources

This part of the cross reference shows only where quotations from the name sources can be found

CLEMENT

27.8a

2ⁿᵈCORINTHIANS

24.3c

24.7c

24.7d

25.1c

EPHESIANS

22.5e

EUSEBIUS

4.5b

4.5c

21.5

22.9b

27.6a

27.7a

27.9a

GALATIONS

22.1b

22.2b

HEGGIESIPIUS

21.5a

JOSEPHUS

2.1a

4.5d

4.5e

20.15a

21.19a

29.4a

29.5a

29.5b

QUR'AN

2.2b

2.3a

2.3b

2.4a

2.4c

3.1c

PHILLIPIANS

24.3b

PLINY

4.5a

ROMANS

30.4

Appendix 3 - General Index

The index includes only the text of the book, not the quotations. The references are to sections. We do not index Jesus, God, angels or the gospellers.

A

F

G

H

N

T

ABOUT THE AUTHOR

John Chapman was born in Birmingham, England in 1935 and grew up mainly in Gloucestershire. He attended Southampton University and gained an honours degree in mathematics with aeronautics; but was seduced by the emerging computer technology. After a spell in Northern Ireland, he moved to Toronto where he worked for Ferranti-Packard with some of the brightest brains of the period and developed techniques for digitising oil-well logs to release fifty-year-old data to computer technology. After spells in Australia, Scotland and Sweden he returned to England in 1970 to work for ICL, having married Ann in 1966 and having three children. Here he continued to travel the world advising many institutions on how best to exploit the new technologies before retiring in 1992. He became a school inspector, served for nearly fifty years as a local councillor and became deeply immersed in local and military history being either the author or co-author of many books. He was also a leader in helping others, being the chairman of his local voluntary society for many years.

www.ingramcontent.com/pod-product-compliance
Lightning Source LLC
Chambersburg PA
CBHW020916140626
46545CB00015B/59